RIBBIN', JIVIN', AND
PLAYIN' THE DOZENS

DATE DUE

NOV 9 1998			

RIBBIN', JIVIN', AND PLAYIN' THE DOZENS
The Persistent Dilemma in Our Schools

SECOND EDITION

HERBERT L. FOSTER

To my wife Anita
and my daughters Donna and Andrea
And to my parents

CONTENTS

ACKNOWLEDGMENTS

I am indebted to many people for helping with this second edition. The help consisted of anything from suggestions, advice, library research assistance, the reporting of an incident that lead to a Reality, to a critical analysis of portions of the second edition. These people are: Nancy A. Biernat, Mrs. Rosá Bowles, Frank Corbett, Ron Crayton, Sylvia Crespo, Izzy DeJesus, Dr. Robert J. Gamble, Tom Gill, Professor Bruce Jackson, Denise LaRusch, Professor Murray Levine, Rosa E. Leon, Dr. Richard A. Marotta, Mary Pautler, Karen Perone, George Singfield, Phyllis Susser, Sylvia Valentine, Joyce V. Wheeler, Professor William L. Wilbanks, and the staff of Lockwood Library.

Thanks must also be remembered for those many friends and students from the "600" schools, other friends, colleagues, former SUNY at Buffalo undergraduate and graduate students, and others who helped in many ways with the first edition. They were: Frank C. Aquila, Jud Axelbank, Ray K. Bartoo, Harold Bass, Donald Brown, Jerry and Claudia Collins, Coy L. Cox, Professor Mary A. Davis, Leo DiMarco, Stephen J. DeGarmo, Denise Esposito, Philip Fanone, Jeanne Ferry, Harriet Ferrer Goldberg, Professor Robert J. Grantham, Emory Hightower. James K. Holder, Dr. Robert L. Infantino, Professor Murray Levine, Sid MacArthur, Aurie F. McCabe, Dr. Domenic J. Mettica, Joseph E. Moreus, Dr. Geraldine S. Mycio, Naomi Ploshnick, David A. Pratt, Judson T. Price, Jr., Michael R. Romance, Joseph Shanahan, Ameilia Sherrets, George Singfield, Jonathan Treible, Kathleen Voigt, Leonard Wells, Dr. Maggie Wright, and the staff of the New York City Fire Library.

Thanks also must go to my friends at Ballinger Publishing Company: Carol Franco, President; Gerald M. Galvin, Production Manager; and Dave Barber, Editorial Coordinator.

Finally, but not the least, my family who supported me continually with advice, ideas, and related newspaper clippings: my wife Anita, and daughters Donna and Andrea; my brothers, sister-in-laws, and brother-in law, Jerry and Joan, Jack and Zita, and George and Lenore. And, my mother-in-law, Harriet M. Greenberg.

FOREWORD

Adam Urbanski, Ph.D.
President, Rochester Teachers Association
(NYSUT/AFT)
Vice President, American Federation of
Teachers (AFL–CIO)

It was the day after report cards were received by my 11th-grade American Studies students. "Why did you flunk me?" one of them asked me. "I didn't do nothin!"

At first, I was surprised that he was surprised. "I didn't flunk you," I responded. "You failed—and probably because you didn't do nothin."

It didn't take us long to realize that we both functioned on different assumptions and with different perspectives. My surprised student assumed that he would receive a passing grade even without doing any classwork or homework. All he had to do, he thought, was stay out of trouble and not disrupt the class. After all, that's how he reached the 11th grade and he showed anger that anyone would "change the rules" on him this late in the game. Ultimately, however, we achieved an understanding that he would try to complete all the assignments, study for tests, participate in class and, if necessary, receive extra help and tutoring from me after school. He did—and he earned a passing final grade.

That incident made a deep impression on me. Ever since then, I have made it a point to ensure that all my students—especially the quiet one in the back of the room—understand the requirements for successful completion of the course. I no longer take it for granted that each student comes to my class with that realization.

Improved communication spells a better teaching-learning environment. Students should know what is expected of them. Similarly, teachers should learn the "language" of their students. Unfortunately, this information for teachers in inner-city schools is neither readily available in teacher-training colleges nor at numerous inservice sessions. In fact, the relative unavailability of this critical information makes this book all the more valuable and unique.

Herbert Foster's *Ribbin', Jivin', and Playin' the Dozens* is a helpful, informative text written by a sensitive and experienced teacher and teacher-trainer. He wrote the book because he feels that all teachers should know "what is really happening from the black youngster's point of view" so that school personnel do not "allow black children to get away with behavior that white children are not allowed to get away with." He deplores the fact that some educators " . . . generally unfamiliar with and often fearful of black school children, allow these children to create a violent and fearful school atmosphere in which learning is impossible."

Tragically, a disruptive atmosphere in our inner-city classrooms hurts all students—including those who do the disrupting. There can be no learning in an environment of fear or chaos. All teachers should insist that all students adhere to reasonable and fair rules. Overt or subconscious lowering of behavioral or academic standards for any students or group of students would, in itself, constitute the most insidious form of racism.

Foster understands that. And he has some specific suggestions for improving the communication in the inner-city schools so that effective teaching and learning could occur. For many years he taught in the "600" schools in New York City—special facilities designated as schools for the education of socially maladjusted and emotionally disturbed children. In fact, his first public school teaching assignment was at Haaren High School in New York City's "Hell Kitchen." His experiences there taught him many of the 99 Realities that he shares in his book. And Foster learned the hard way; he tells of the extreme fear and the thoughts of suicide. He confesses to moments of severe depression, feelings of dejection, failure, and despair. Eventually, he learned that the only way to be effective was to learn the language and the "games" that his students played. Love, good intentions and good will would not suffice. The teaching-learning process requires good teacher-student communication. And that communication, Foster insists, "depends upon the student's and the teacher's ability to understand what each is saying to the other."

Foster does not suggest that black urban students not be taught Standard English. He does suggest, however, that it is imperative to recognize that schools are verbal institutions and that educators must learn to read their students' words and action accurately. Otherwise, Foster argues, the teaching-learning process can be severely impaired. "Problems can be caused from double word meanings and unknown words either unknowingly or purposely. In some cases, the teacher may innocently use a word for which his students have another meaning . . ." Also, Foster points out, the students may use such words to test the teacher or to cause disruption of the teaching-learning process. The best protection against such dysfunctions in teacher-student communication is to better understand these words and their uses.

The author's advice is simple: Learn the words and become aware of the games that some students sometimes play. You can then "ameliorate rather than exacerbate simple situations that would otherwise interfere with the teaching and learning process." And he proceeds to usher his readers into the world of ribbin', chopping, sounding, medlin', ranking, chuckin', woofin', signifying, joaning, and playin' the dozens. Most teachers are not likely to learn about these street corner games in teacher-training colleges. The book offers a valuable service and very good advice for those who don't want to learn the hard way—as the author did.

Foster's second edition has been updated and expanded. In the second edition, he points out that the streetcorner behavior he first described and explained over ten years ago can now be observed in many aspects of American and international life. Streetcorner behavior is now observable on television, in sandlot, collegiate, and professional sports, in movies, in books—just about everywhere.

He accurately reveals that the behavior has now spread to almost all innercity, suburban, and rural schools, too. Therefore, many teachers with 10 to 25 years of experience who are accustomed to working primarily with middle-class youngsters are now being confounded, and sometimes frightened by black and white working-class youngsters using this behavior.

Foster also discusses and argues, as no one else has before, about the impact of teacher dress and grooming as important aspects of communication, and about the negative role that conscious and unconscious teacher attitudes and behavior have historically played. It must be noted that Foster has argued these points all along; he has not recently converted or joined someone else's bandwagon. In the second edition, however, he does an excellent job of presenting and expanding his scholarship.

His discussion of male secondary teacher dress and grooming should generate a much needed discussion of the controversy. His analysis of the reasons for disproportionate numbers of black, poor, and minority school-children being disciplined, suspended, or placed in special education will add a perspective that, for the first time, gets beyond the statistics.

Since the first edition of *Ribbin'*, Foster has received hundreds of letters thanking him for providing the readers with the insight that either kept them in teaching or helped them better understand, relate to, and teach their inner-city students. In one case, a teacher actually thanked him for saving her life. She experienced an incident that was almost a replication of a Reality described in *Ribbin'*. It was reading that Reality just prior to the incident that she felt saved her life.

Finally, it's very significant that Dr. Foster's book is an attempt to further mutual understanding and to equip teachers to be more effective in providing their students with the salable skills required for upward mobility in America. But to understand the games that students play does not mean that teachers should tolerate or condone such behavior. Indeed, Foster's book will help to avoid and overcome problems. This book is a service not only to urban teachers and students, but to all teachers and students.

1 WHY RIBBIN' IS EVEN MORE IMPORTANT TODAY

In a truly democratic society, every citizen should have "the right to a decent home, the right to an education, the right to adequate medical care, the right to a worthwhile job, . . . and the right to a fair trial in a fair court."

— Harry S. Truman, June 19, 1947[1]

Lower class behavior in general, and lower class black streetcorner behavior in particular, is still present in inner-city schools and has spread to most school and nonschool settings. Indeed, the language and behavior of the black streetcorner has spread visibly throughout the United States, if not the world.[2] The influence of lower class black streetcorner behavior can be observed in almost all aspects of everyday urban, suburban, and rural U.S. school and nonschool life. This cultural spread has been transmitted through the media, the literature, and the physical movement of blacks into areas from which they were previously excluded, such as certain sports, professions, and neighborhoods. As a result, many Americans are being exposed to unfamiliar language and behavior.

For example, in 1981, at half time of the NBC television broadcast of the Philadelphia-San Diego play-off game, Mike Adamle talked about a linebacker who had been around all week "selling wolf tickets."[3] Dave Anderson, writing in the *New York Times*, about John Thomas—the first to do a seven-foot indoor high jump—mentioned that, according to Thomas, "some of the kids I coach were woofing the old master last summer, so I did 6-6. That kept them quiet for a while."[4]

Almost any "Hill Street Blues" television episode will have comments such as, "I'm gonna drop a dime down town"; "That you fellas short out there?";

"You had Ditwiller pegged from the get go"; "chump change"; "Oreo pig"; "I wasn't runnin' out on ya, square biz"; and Hudson's tight with a cadre of Viet Nam Vets."[5]

Michael Herr in his book *Dispatches* about Viet Nam wrote:

> "Are guys sleeping in their flak jackets?"
> "Some do. I don'. Mayhew, crazy fucker, he sleep bare-ass. He so tough, man, li'l fucker, the hawk is out, an' he's in here bare-ass."
> "What's that? About the hawk?"
> "That means it's co-o-old Mother Fucker."[6]

Baseball fans may recall the seventh game of the 1982 World Series, when umpire Lee Weyer interceded suddenly in the spat between Joaquin Andujar, the St. Louis pitcher, and Jim Gantner, the Milwaukee second baseman. When interviewed later, Andujar said that Gantner "knows I have a hot temper. But when somebody's in the batter's box against me, he is my enemy. You call me a hot dog, it's OK. People have called me that before. But you start talking about my mother, we're going to fight, baby. You're in big trouble then."[7]

On the streetcorner, talking about someone's mother or other member of the family may be referred to as, among other names, "playing the dozens." Few whites have either been exposed to the dozens or understand the unwritten necessity to fight when someone talks about your "momma."

The high five slap of the hands has become universal.[8] Also, traditionally, white athletes wore low-cut crew socks and black teams such as the Harlem Globe Trotters wore knee socks. Today, you will see as many whites as blacks wearing knee socks.

Basketball from the 1940s up to the 1960s was a deliberate two-handed set shot and team sport game. The sport began to change and speed up somewhat when Hank Luisetti, from Stanford, popularized the one-handed shot.[9] However, as more and more streetcorner black athletes moved from high school to college, and then to professional basketball, the style of the game changed. The game became something of a microcosm of the streetcorner. It became faster, rougher, more competitive, more individualized, and more one on one. What had already happened in inner city schools and on many college basketball courts has been taking place in professional basketball. In his book *The Breaks of the Game*, David Halberstam wrote about this change in professional basketball. It is also descriptive of what had happened earlier in inner city schools and was beginning to happen in most suburban and rural schools.

> In the sixties the league . . . changed quickly. More and more blacks arrived. . . . What was happening in St. Louis was typical of what was happening around the league: as the game became more exciting, faster, blacker, it was moving ahead of the fans' capacity to accept it, to accept both the new level of play and the blackness of the players who exemplified it.[10]

Consciously or unconsciously, many whites, exposed to the above experiences, began to react in different ways to this streetcorner behavior: some were fearful, some were turned off, and some began to emulate the behavior. Numbers of white schoolchildren in integrated and nonintegrated schools began to try to walk, talk, and behave in a black streetcorner way. This phenomenon has now spread to almost all urban, suburban, and rural schools across the United States.

This movement of lower class behavior in general and lower class black streetcorner behavior in particular into school and nonschool settings has generated, in many cases, problems for everyone involved. The problems have occurred in school and nonschool settings and many of the incidents, regardless of the setting, have been similar.

Three examples of serious problems arising from the misunderstanding of the word "punk" took place in professional baseball, in a public school classroom, and in an institution of higher learning.

Baseball fans may remember the incident between Frank Lucchesi and Lenny Randle in 1977, when Frank Lucchesi was managing the Texas Rangers, and Lenny Randle was playing second base. According to the *New York Times:*

> The trouble began to brew last week when Lucchesi publicly referred to Randle as a punk in answer to Randle's demands that he be given a chance to play regularly or be traded to another team.
>   Randle said he approached Lucchesi today along the third-base line to talk to him and Lucchesi told him: "What do you got to say, punk."[11]

Reacting to being called a punk, Randle punched Lucchesi three times or more, which resulted in Lucchesi's being hospitalized.[12]

The second incident took place at a public school in a bedroom-and-farm community close to a large city. My colleague, George Singfield, and I were running a workshop when I described the above incident, and the one that follows about the use of the word punk on a college campus.

Suddenly, in the middle of our presentation, a young white male teacher jumped up and yelled, "That's what that was all about!" Later, he told us this story.

Without thinking much about it, he had called one of his black male students a punk. A day or so later, the principal, who happened to be black, and the youngster's parents entered his room. A heated discussion ensued about his calling their son a punk. The teacher could not understand why his student's parents were so bothered, and he showed the parents the dictionary definition for punk. Unimpressed with the Standard English definition for punk, they insisted that he not call their son a punk again; the principal sided with the parents. After some more discussion, the parents and principal left. However, neither the parents nor the principal explained to the teacher why they resented his use of the word punk.

The third incident went as follows:

A white student in a letter to the editor of Wesleyan University's *Argus*, referred to a black student as a punk. Because the white student was unaware that the black student's definition of punk was "homosexual" and that the black student came from a social class background that settled problems with fists, the white student was taken by surprise when "that night about a dozen Blacks went to [his] room and threatened him with physical harm if he did not retract his statement. The next night Walker paid another call on Berg, found him taking a shower and beat him up."[13]

About twenty-one months after the above professional baseball incident, Lucchesi and Randle, in an emotional scene, shook hands after their out-of-court settlement. Lucchesi[14]

> admitted in testimony this week that he had said four days before the fight that he was "tired of $80,000-a-year punks complaining 'play me or trade me.'" He said he learned later that among blacks, the term "punk" means "sissy" or "gay." Lucchesi is white and Randle is black. Lucchesi said he didn't intend to apply those terms to Randle.[15]

What is interesting about the second incident described above is that the principal, who was black, for some reason never explained to the teacher what punk meant to the student and his parents.[16] The teacher had to learn the meaning of the word from outside consultants.

In the same vein, when former President Jimmy Carter made his farewell speech to the largely Spanish-speaking members of the Organization of American States, he said that he was a "lame duck" chief executive. The translation drew laughter from the delegates because, in many Latin countries, *pato cojo*, the translation for lame duck, is slang either for someone who has no sex life or for someone who is a homosexual.[17]

In order to succeed in teaching more of their minority and poor students the requisite middle class salable and survival skills necessary for upward mobility in the United States, educators must (1) gain a greater awareness and understanding of lower class behavior in general and lower class black male streetcorner behavior in particular and (2) develop strategies that will allow them to cope positively with students exhibiting such behavior.

Educators must learn to overcome their historical ethnocentric behavior in order to educate the poor, the minority, and the new immigrant children who are beginning to make up a greater proportion of our school population. More creative efforts at the school level to accomplish this objective would cost our society far less than the eventual costs of chronic unemployment, welfare, drug addiction, crime, and incarceration.

Ernest L. Boyer, in his recent report on secondary education in the United States, emphasized the importance of working with and educating the so-called high-risk student.

Serving disadvantaged students is the urgent unfinished agenda for American education. Unless we find ways to overcome the problem of failure in the schools, generations of students will continue to be doomed to frustrating, unproductive lives. This nation cannot afford to pay the price of wasted youth.[18]

It is imperative, therefore, that all urban, suburban, and rural educators, and certainly professors of education, begin to understand those students exhibiting lower class behavior and, particularly, the black streetcorner behavior with which they are unfamiliar.

The urgency for this understanding is indicated because 44 percent of our high schools are now located in urban and suburban areas and serve 9.2 million students. Though 56 percent of our high schools are in rural areas, they educate only 4.1 million students. Furthermore, about one-half of our high schools have fewer than 600 students. Most students attend large urban high schools, "often with troubling effects."[19]

The problem is exacerbated in suburban and rural school districts with traditionally middle class children where there are now larger numbers of students from blue-collar, minority, and immigrant backgrounds. An analysis of 1980 census data indicated that blacks have increased as a percentage of the total population and in their numbers in the suburbs of most large cities during the 1970–1980 period. "Many of these suburbs were declining economically and in population growth, even though they may have represented a step up from life in the decaying core cities."[20]

As a consequence of this movement, many experienced teachers in these urban, suburban, or rural districts with ten to twenty-five years of experience are at a loss as to how to work with these new and "different" students. Suddenly, after many years of successfully teaching and becoming used to non-physical, verbal, and sexually restrained middle class students, these teachers are facing very real problems centered around discipline, respect, student self-direction, and academic ability.

Two examples of such teacher complaints are reported by Boyer in his study of high schools.

I'm not receiving the same positive response from my students. In the past, I felt more like a coach to my students, helping them achieve the highest level of skills they're capable of. But I've felt more in an adversarial position recently and I don't know why. It's almost as if they say, "I defy you to teach me." I had one class of students last year with a dozen chronic behavior problems. I dreaded dealing with that class every day. It affected my whole life.[21]

Being around young people is a reward in itself. But those rewards are getting fewer. . . . My major problem is how to motivate students who don't care about themselves. And my biggest frustration is their "what's the difference" attitude. Those who do care seem to be dwindling every year. You know, how many kids ever come back to say "thanks"?[22]

These newer students are most often minority, poor, or working class. And, in too many cases, the teachers receive very little, if any, real administrative support, effective in-service education, or relevant graduate course help.

As a result, some educators retire early. In the main, however, class lines are drawn more openly; the poor and minority students are suspended or placed in special education programs, and ethnocentric behavior, with all its consequences, takes over. Some of the problems resulting from this situation that have been identified and reported by numerous government and child advocacy agencies include: [23]

1. Minority, male, and poor children are assigned disproportionately to special education classes or, in some cases, are not assigned when such assignments would be appropriate.
2. Minority and poor children are being suspended with greater frequency and for longer periods than are their white counterparts.
3. Minority and poor children are assigned more often to classes for the retarded and emotionally disturbed while white children are assigned more often to classes for the brain injured or learning disabled.

Additional problems have also come about because in many of the more affluent suburban districts many children of professional parents are being sent to private secondary schools. Hence, the proportionate numbers of poor, minority, and immigrant children increases in the public schools.

With the advent of Public Law (PL) 94–142, the so-called mainstreaming law that mandated handicapped children be educated in the least restrictive environment, more minority and poor children have come into contact with a greater number of teachers.[24] Prior to the passage of PL 94–142, many of these handicapped children in the district were segregated in special classrooms with special teachers.

A related problem is found in some suburban districts that place a high priority on developing winning athletic teams. In many of these districts, coaches will import black inner city youngsters to play for them. In some of these schools, these athletes are allowed to participate in their sport while not adhering to the school's academic and behavioral standards and rules. This goes beyond what a white "jock" can usually get away with.

Moreover, an imported inner city athlete who is suspended from school may in some cases be allowed to practice, in violation of the district's rules. When such a suspension does take place, it can be assumed, for most districts, that it is for a very major and public infraction of a school or district rule.

In these schools, because the coaches are usually entrenched in the school's power structure, the most teachers will do is complain quietly to their trusted friends about the unmanageable and disrespectful imported black students. And because these teachers are angry and upset, they may vent their anger, frustration, and feelings of powerlessness on those students who are poor or minority. There are some indications, however, that secondary and higher education coaches and educators are beginning to make greater academic demands on their athletes.[25]

Despite all of these problems, in many schools with large numbers of poor and minority children, one can find exceptional principals, many effective teachers, and children who are learning.[26] Even in the most chaotic schools one can find teachers maintaining order and teaching.

SUMMARY

It is interesting to speculate about the number of Americans who have heard, observed, or participated in some of the behaviors or language just described. It is also interesting to wonder whether they understood or even heard some of the words used. For example, what did the football fan think of when Mike Adamle talked about selling wolf tickets? Do the "Hill Street Blues" viewers and listeners understand the jive lexicon used on the program?

Because educators are the adults and the professionals, the burden is on them to (1) understand the streetcorner behavior of their students; (2) investigate and understand why *they* are having so many problems with these students, rather than just wanting the students suspended or dumped into special education classes; (3) learn to modify their behavior, much of which is ethnocentric, in order to be better able to help their students modify their behavior; and (4) provide their students with the middle class salable skills that would enable them, if they so chose, to become economically as well or better off than their teachers.

If we could succeed in achieving this goal, perhaps our welfare roles would decrease and our jails and mental institutions would be wanting for inmates and patients. And maybe, just maybe, we would "play at war no more."

If you keep reading *Ribbin'*, you will be provided with the insight, the understanding, and the knowledge to achieve the objectives outlined and discussed in this chapter. You will also encounter 99 Realities: narratives of actual incidents involving streetcorner behavior drawn from my own experience and the accounts provided by colleagues. Each Reality will appear within the context of a particular behavioral or cultural theme to dramatize how teachers have responded to classroom conflict arising from social factors. These slices of life are meant to illuminate the variety of challenges a contemporary teacher may face and describe measures that can be adopted to restore order, gain greater pupil respect, and cultivate better learning.

NOTES TO CHAPTER 1

1. Diane Ravitch, *The Troubled Crusade: American Education, 1945–1980* (New York: Basic Books, 1983), p. 24.
2. "World Championship of Track & Field: Athletic Competition From Helsinki, Finland," NBC, August 8, 1983. A Polish athlete gave one of his countrymen a "high five" slap when he won his event. Richard A. Marotto, " 'Posin' to Be Chosen': An Ethnographic Study of Ten Lower Class Black Male Adolescents in an Urban High School," Dissertation Abstracts International (DAI) 39 (1978): 1234-A (State University of New York at Buffalo).
3. "Super Bowl XV," NBC, January 25, 1981.
4. Dave Anderson, "The Olympic Secret of John Thomas," *New York Times*, February 9, 1982, p. B18.
5. "Hill Street Blues," NBC, 1981, 1982, and 1983.
6. Michael Herr, *Dispatches* (New York: Knopf, 1978), p. 129.
7. Mark Wicker, "Andujar: Mr. Cardinal, *Buffalo News*, October 21, 1982, p. C3. See Chapter 6 for a discussion of the dozens.
8. Curry Kirkpatrick, "Whole Lot of Shakin' Going On," *Sports Illustrated*, February 16, 1981, pp. 62–66, 68–70, 72, 73–74; "World Championships of Track & Field: Athletic Competition From Helsinki, Finland," NBC, August 7, 1983.
9. Marty Glickman, "When Garden Was the Place for Basketball-Wise," *New York Times*, November 25, 1984, p. 2S.
10. David Halberstam, *The Breaks of the Game* (New York: Knopf, 1981), p. 148.
11. "Manager Hospitalized by Player's Punches," *New York Times*, March 29, 1977, pp. 21, 23.
12. Roy Blount, Jr., "The Fighting Side of Baseball," *Esquire*, July 1977, pp. 30, 32; Kent Hannon, "One Mindless Moment," *Sports Illustrated*, June 6, 1977, pp. 44, 49; "The Talk of the Town: Friend," *New Yorker*, April 3, 1978, pp. 28–29.
13. Herbert L. Foster, *Ribbin', Jivin', and Playin' the Dozens* (Cambridge, Mass.: Ballinger Publishing Company, 1974), p. 133; Richard J. Morgolis, "The Two Nations of Wesleyan University," *New York Times Magazine*, January 18, 1970, pp. 9, 49, 54, 60–62, 64.
14. "Suit by Lucchesi Ends Amicably," *New York Times*, December 9, 1978, p. 20.
15. Lucchesi Settles Amicably," *New York Post*, December 9, 1978, p. 39.
16. It is interesting that the black principal did not discuss with the teacher the other meaning of "punk." It may be that the principal, though he was black, did not know the other meaning, or he may simply have felt it inappropriate to discuss the definition.
    Related to this, many white educators assume that all black educators can relate to and understand all black children. Such an assumption on the

part of white educators has caused innumerable problems for black educators. Indeed, some black educators have more problems working with black children than do some white educators.

17. "Playboy After Hours," *Playboy*, April 1981, p. 27.

18. Ernest L. Boyer, *High School: A Report on Secondary Education in America*, (New York: Harper & Row, 1983), pp. 245–46.

19. Boyer, pp. 20, 233.

20. John Herbers, *New York Times*, May 31, 1981, p. 1, 48.

21. Boyer, p. 162.

22. Ibid., p. 163.

23. *Children Out of School in America* (Cambridge, Mass.: Children's Defense Fund of the Washington Research Project, 1974); Kent A. Heller, Wayne H. Holtsman, and Samuel Messick, eds., *Placing Children in Special Education: A Strategy for Equity* (Washington, D.C.: National Academy Press, 1982). (This study was carried out for the Office of Civil Rights (OCR), U.S. Department of Education.); Southern Regional Council and the Robert F. Kennedy Memorial, *The Student Pushout: Victim of Continued Resistance to Desegregation.* (Atlanta: Southern Regional Council, 1974); Task Force on Children Out of School, *The Way We Go to School: The Exclusion of Children in Boston* (Boston: Beacon, 1971); United States Commission on Civil Rights, *Fulfilling the Letter and Spirit of the Law: Desegregation of the Nation's Public Schools* (Washington, D.C.: U.S. Government Printing Office, 1976).

24. Education for All Handicapped Children Act of 1975, *Public Law 94-142.*

25. Ira Berkow, "Goal-Line Stand in Learning," Sports of The Times, *New York Times*, November 26, 1983, p. 19; Harry Edwards, "Educating Black Athletes," *Atlantic Monthly*, August 1983, pp. 31–36; Halberstam, p. 226; "Jersey City Tightening Rules for Sports Eligibility," *New York Times*, November 24, 1983, p. B2; Sheldon Silver, "Athletic Energy for Academic Power," *New York Times*, May 14, 1983, p. S2.

26. Boyer, pp. 245–48, 255–67; Fred M. Hechinger, "92 Schools That Are Overcoming Urban Obstacles," *New York Times*, April 12, 1983, p. C5; IMPACT II, New York City Public Schools, 131 Livingston Street, Brooklyn, New York, 11201; Phi Delta Kappa, *Why Do Some Urban Schools Succeed?* (Bloomington, Ind.: Phi Delta Kappa, 1980); Sara L. Lightfoot, *The Good High School* (New York: Basic Books, 1983); Joyce Purnick, "Rare Success Stories," *New York Times*, December 2, 1983, p. C1.

2 GETTING IT OFF MY CHEST

My first day of teaching almost devastated me. What happened to me that day continues to happen to many new teachers, to many teachers in new positions, and to many teachers working with children with whom they are unfamiliar. However, the key to your success or failure as a teacher still depends upon your constitutional factors—that is, the genes you inherited from your parents and the experiences you had as you were growing and maturing. These factors in turn determine how you will react to your students' testing of your ability to establish order and teach.

My first public school teaching position was at Haaren High School in New York City's Hell's Kitchen. I completed my undergraduate work in three years in industrial arts at New York University's School of Education to make up for the time spent in the Army. After taking both regular and substitute industrial arts teaching examinations, I was offered a position to teach mechanical drawing and blueprint reading at Haaren High School in Manhattan.[1] It was there that I was subjected to and experienced my rite of passage into teaching.

REALITY 1

I went to Haaren and was interviewed by my department chair. He showed me my room, which contained four or five large tables around which my forty-five students would sit. When I suggested taking the T-squares and drawing boards off the tables and putting them away in a closet, ne told me to leave them there and just tell my students not to use them until I gave the word.

11

We next walked to his room, where I noticed that his students had individual work tables. He also told me that I should not give my students too much too fast and not to worry about homework because they were slow.

At the time, I accepted his advice. However, I later came to realize that his advice was either racist or ethnocentric. When anyone suggests that teachers working with minority or poor children not make the behavioral and academic demands that would be made on middle class children, that suggestion is either racist or ethnocentric. More about that later.

As he bid me goodbye and suggested I come in on the following day, he mentioned that I was the sixth substitute this class had had since the regular teacher resigned a few weeks earlier. I started working on Friday, November 3, 1950, ar $13.25 per diem.

I managed to get by the homeroom period and the next double period. After lunch, about ten to fifteen minutes into the first of three periods, I noticed a youngster run out of the back door of my classroom. When I closed the back door, another youngster ran out of the front door of my classroom also leaving it open. After briefly watching some of my students run in and out of the front and back doors, I realized that they were the same ones who were going in and out of the doors.[2] They were not running out and leaving. If you have seen *Up the Down Staircase*, you will see what my room looked like. Though Bell Kaufman did not write her book about Haaren, the movie was shot there.[3]

Next, I discovered a new word: "Teach." One of my students walked up to me and said, "Hey, Teach, we work a period, read comics a period, and then take off the last period—OK?" To which I replied with something like, "Look, I'm a vet, and I'm the teacher now. I intend to stay, and we are going to work all three periods. You guys are not going to drive me out of here the way you drove out all those other teachers."

From then on everything seemed to happen at once. Someone crumpled up a piece of paper and threw it at me. A near miss. I thought of my Psychology I and II courses ("make a joke out of things" or "decontaminate through humor") and said, "If that's the best you can do, you better hang up." Whereupon all hell broke loose. The class showed me they could do better!

Students ran across the table tops throwing T-squares and drawing boards. Others ran in and out of the room. The noise was deafening. T-squares and drawing board missiles flew through the air. The classroom was not only noisy but dangerous. And do you know what I did? You know that section in the teacher's desk where the teacher puts his legs when he sits down? I hid there—in the kneehole.

After what seemed like an eternity, five or six teachers stuck their heads into the room to see what was going on. I looked up sheepishly from my shelter without saying a word. Since the din continued even with their presence, they threw both doors open and my students took off.

I will never forget the weekend that followed. All my life I had known that I wanted to be a teacher. Here was my first chance. I had just spent three years in college getting an education that was supposed to prepare me to teach. I had failed on my first job. What could I do with my life? I was distraught; I actually considered suicide.

Today, some of my university students and some at those attending my workshops or lectures laugh when I talk about my first and second days of teaching. I have to remind them that in 1950 and 1951 you *had* to get a job. There were few, if any, graduate school fellowships or assistantships. And, if not for the World War II GI Bill, it is questionable how many of my generation would have gone to college. At best, it would have taken us many years of night school.

My feelings were not unlike those expressed by Jerome Weidman in his *Fourth Street East.*

The funny thing about growing up in the Great Depression was that while money was the most important factor in your life, because without money you didn't eat, it wasn't really money you worried about. What you worried about was what you were going to be, what you were to do with your life, and whether, by doing what you were doing now, you were on the right track.[4]

After a rather shaky weekend, I went back to Haaren High School on Monday.

REALITY 2

The first student into my homeroom upon seeing me said, "Hey, teach, you back!"

I don't recommend that other new teachers do what I then did with each of my classes. I don't really know why I did it, except for the fact that I was brought up neither to cry nor to scapegoat about my problems, but instead to do something about resolving them. It may also have been the result of my having grown up on the streets of Brooklyn and, to some extent, that I was fighting for my emotional life. If I couldn't make it there, where could I go? What could I do?

What I did was to put my name on the board. Then, when about half of the class was in the room and seated, I waited for someone to make fun of my name by mispronouncing it. As soon as one of the students made fun of my name, I walked to the front of the room, picked up about a two-foot-long stick I had found in the room, and walked up to him. I grabbed his shirt front and picked him up out of his seat. In a calm and moderate voice that somehow did not give away my shaking knees, I said, "Read that name to me."

The class sat transfixed awaiting the outcome—*waiting to join the winner.* Ten to fifteen seconds elapsed; he did not say a word. I dropped him back into his seat, turned my back on him, walked to the board, put down the stick, and started to teach. I repeated this *act* with each of my classes. In none of my classes did any youngster actually read my name to me.

Would you believe that this turned out to be the easiest teaching job, from a discipline point of view, I ever had? Later, as I reflected upon this incident, I realized that in not actually forcing anyone to read my name, I had given the students I had picked up a way out. Each had been provided with a way of saving face with his buddies if he had the need. If his friends challenged him, he could always say that he had never actually read my name.

Fortunately, after the confrontation we all could relax. They had tested me, and I had shown how far I would allow myself to be pushed. I had also shown that I could bounce back; I had shown that I was not afraid physically and that if push came to shove I would be able to hold my own with them physically.

A few years later, as I read Arthur Schlesinger's description of the secret discussions held during the Cuban crisis, that second day of teaching came to mind. The psychology I intuitively had applied during my rite of passage was similar to the thinking that guided our approach to the Soviet Union. If you corner someone and you don't give him a way out, he may be forced to fight you against his will in order to save face with his friends. Schlesinger quotes Governor Harriman as suggesting: "We must give him (Krushchev) an out . . . if we do this shrewdly, we can downgrade the tough group . . . which persuaded him to do this. But if we deny him an out, then we will escalate this business into a nuclear war."[5] Schlesinger also writes of President Kennedy's praising Liddell Hart's *Deterrent of Defense* philosophy.

> Keep strong, if possible. In any case, keep cool. Have unlimited patience. Never corner an opponent, and always assist him to save face. Put yourself in his shoes—so as to see things through his eyes. Avoid self-righteousness like the devil—nothing is so self-binding. Liddell Hart was addressing these remarks to statesmen; they work as well for historians.[6]

And, I should add, for teachers as well.

There is a difference between teachers who once or twice meet their testing challenge as I did and then quickly achieve control and humanize their classroom approach and those who regularly use punitive measures—either corporal punishment or a more covert form of punishment which is often a manifestation of racism and inhumanism.

There are also teachers who are not introspective enough to see what is happening to their classrooms and allow their students to create so much disorder and disruption that no one learns. My students at Haaren understood my reaction because it was on a level with which we were all familiar and secure. It was something they and I had learned in the streets. If I had to do every day what I had done that second day, I would not and should not have continued as a teacher. Actually, the students may not have allowed me to remain, either.

What happened to me on my first day of teaching continues to happen in various ways to new and experienced teachers in all schools. Two factors for such occurrences are (1) the experiences teachers bring with them into the profession and (2) the profession itself—undergraduate teacher education, graduate programs, and in-service education.

Professionally, some of the reasons include:

1. Not enough attention is paid to the teacher's personality and psychological make-up;
2. New teachers are still told that all they need is a good lesson plan;
3. There are few, if any, undergraduate or graduate courses being offered that deal with and cover reality-oriented classroom management and school discipline;
4. Most in-service is a repeat of the too often sterile and unrealistic undergraduate or graduate course work;
5. Where there is reasonable in-service, most often, it is sporadic and rarely ongoing;
6. Rarely does anyone discuss the implications of differences around social class behavior and how it is played out in the classroom;
7. Few graduate educational administration programs provide future administrators with courses in process supervision of staff; and
8. Generally, no one really wants to deal with the ramifications of educator ethnocentric or racist behavior.

New teachers' backgrounds very often consist of being white and having grown up in a mostly white middle class suburban or rural area. Whether black or white, rarely did their parents have as friends anyone from a different social class or ethnic or religious background. Similarly, the teachers themselves have had few friends or even acquaintances from backgrounds different from their own.

This separateness has continued despite the warning of The National Advisory Commission on Civil Disorders that our nation is rapidly moving toward two increasingly separate American societies, one black, one white, separate and unequal. The white society will be located principally in the suburbs, in smaller central cities, and in distinct areas of larger central cities. Meanwhile, blacks are living largely in concentrated large central city areas.[7]

Furthermore, some new teachers bring with them, sometimes unconscious, feelings that cause them to act in racist or ethnocentric ways despite their professed liberality and sincere desire to educate students.

Those new teachers took the usual number of education courses and did a fairly good job of student teaching. Also, as part of their educational foundations course work, they were subjected to quite a number of complaining or *kvetching* books—books that attacked the social order in general and the educational system in particular; books the authors of which blamed the curriculum and the administration, scapegoating their inability to obtain order in their classrooms and to teach effectively; and books the authors of which were so off base that they described their failure to do any classroom structuring and organizing while allowing their students to act in a self-destructive manner.[8]

The ultimate example of this *chutzpa* was written by James Herndon in his book *How To Survive in Your Native Land.* Here was his book, as well as others, being used as guides for changing our schools when he hadn't the slightest idea what the educational process was all about. In his own words:

> I had hoped the kids would show me how to teach. After they did so, I would tell everyone else. But by the end of the year, it was clear the kids didn't know either. Perhaps they'd been hoping all along that I would tell them. We were both waiting around. Together, we amounted to zero. So there, the next year, Arpine and Eileen and I were embarking upon the revolutionary idea that teachers ought to know something about what they were doing. And there was Herb, (Herbert Kohl) yet another year and a half later, allowing as how that was so. It amounted to this: *no eye, no hurricane.*[9]

Many teachers faced their first teaching responsibility weaned on these books that provided a negative, immature, irresponsible, and unprofessional model to emulate.

In the main, most new teachers have never been completely independent of their parents, who up until now, have been administering and providing for all of their needs. Practically overnight, the new teacher is expected to move from his or her dependency role to the supervisory role of a teacher. Although some new teachers know they will not have any problems because they know they will like their students and their students will like them, many are scared to death because no one helped them deal with the real anxieties about their new job and the feeling of "Will I be able to get order and teach?"

REALITY 3

After a short, intensive teacher training program, a woman teacher, in her third week of teaching, experienced a testing that was similar to the testing of many new teachers. While my first day's testing was very aggressive and physical, this teacher's rite of passage was also sexual.

In her teaching methods course, she too was told that a teacher can gain the class's attention by having an exercise on the blackboard and being ready when the students walked into the classroom. As a social studies teacher in an urban high school, this teacher followed that advice with dire results:

> She walked into her freshman class one day and found the board already covered—with four-letter words, threats and a sketch of a nude woman with her name printed below.

When the full class assembled, ... she asked that the "pornographer-in-residence" step forward. Her request met only with silence and a few chuckles. "I don't know who done it," said one student barely containing his amusement. "But they ought to suspend that joker." The room exploded in laughter.[10]

For more than a week, the sketches continued to appear on the board. More time was spent keeping order, and lessons went uncompleted.

Finally, when the teacher caught a student sketching a preliminary "mural" for the next day, she grabbed the sketch from the student's desk. Leaping out of his chair, the student tore the page from her hand and stuffed it into his mouth. He then ran to the toilet and flushed the evidence away.[11]

Unquestionably, this does not happen to everyone. However, what would you do about it? Were such incidents ever discussed in your teacher education courses? Do you panic? Hit the student? Have him suspended? Do you make a joke of what was said and done? Do you start crying? Do you tell him to go to the office? Do you ask him why he did that to you because you want to like him, and you want him to like you. Or do you wonder whether there was something about the way you acted toward the class that caused him to do what he did? Was the confrontation partly of your making? And most importantly, to whom can you go for some empathy, understanding, and guidance.

If you are lucky and show neither fright nor panic, your intuition may help you through the confrontation. You may make it as a teacher in an inner city school, and you may even come to like working there. Or, if you are teaching in a suburban school, you may even come to enjoy working with minority or poor children.

Similar incidents happen every day. They happen often because too many black and white school personnel fail to understand or even recognize what is *really happening from the black streetcorner youngster's point of view.* In addition, school personnel are not aware of their conscious or unconscious conditioned behaviors that may add to the magnitude of the confrontation.

As a result, school personnel are very often frightened and intimidated to the point where some black, poor, or minority youngsters are (1) allowed to disrupt their fellow students' education, (2) allowed to behave in a way that would not be accepted from white middle class children, or (3) suspended or placed in special education programs in numbers out of all proportion to their total numbers in the school district.

Furthermore, because few professional educators (teachers, administrators, higher education professors, researchers, editorial staff, and writers) have the ability to combine idealism and pragmatism, there has not been a realistic discussion of what was once exclusively an inner city school problem. And because there has not been an accurate discussion, we have not been able to solve the real problems. Therefore, the *reality* for many inner city teachers and increasing numbers of suburban and rural teachers is described in this excerpt from a statement of the Ad Hoc Education Committee of the Joint Commission on Mental Health of Children.

5. *Teachers in ghetto schools frequently find the classroom an unmanageable administrative unit for purpose of instruction.*

There is no doubt that the problem of disruptive behavior in the classroom has discouraged large numbers of teachers from planning long professional careers in ghetto schools. It has been responsible in significant measure for the huge turnover rates in these schools and for the crippling morale problems among professionals who stay on for any length of time. The extent to which disruptiveness has spread in inner-city classrooms is not known, but some practitioners estimate that roughly 30 to 35 percent of the school population displays serious behavior disorders. From a mental health point of view, the problem has serious implications despite the fact that its origin may not be intrapsychic.... The teacher is so preoccupied with his tense, disciplinary vigilance that children see him only in that role. He does not have the opportunity to present himself as a companion, critic, an instructor and counselor, and a stimulator of ideas and values.

Efforts at calming the learning environment in ghetto schools have not met with notable success. Experimentors have gone into these classrooms with a sincere desire to establish rapport by demonstrating to the pupils an abiding interest in their innermost concerns. They have worked with the children in small groups and, on occasion, on a one-to-one basis, in order to win their confidence and provide supportiveness in the most permissive manner possible.... The object of (one such) experiment was "to surround children with a team of adults who were sensitive to their needs and concerned with designing learning experiences to meet those particular needs." Unfortunately, these objectives were never met. The project director blamed the bureaucratic rigidity of the school system rather than student misconduct for the defeat of the experiment, while the school principal became disenchanted with the air of permissiveness which he felt led to chaos.... The professionals from the university were no better able to make headway in modifying behavior or stimulating learning than were the school officials. After repeated failure, the spirit of despair began to tarnish initial enthusiasm and the project staff resorted to futile improvisation to quell the disruptive behavior.

Administrative solutions have not fared much better.... From all indications, it would seem that no solution to the problem of disruptive behavior in ghetto schools is currently discernible.... The classroom as we know it may not be manageable enough to sustain ghetto children in learning activity.[12]

Unquestionably, the phenomenon of students testing teachers contributes to these conditions. Traditionally, the rules governing the various testing and challenging games differed in each setting from the inner city to the suburbs. In addition, the lifestyle and expectations of the teachers and students were further apart in the inner city schools than they were in the suburban schools. However, for reasons indicated earlier, these testing clashes between students and their teachers around lifestyles and expectations are similar in all schools.

In cases where teachers and students do not respect the same rules, street-corner students want their teachers to play the game of teaching and learning by the rules and regulations they know and understand and that are important to them, not by the rules that are important to their teachers. These students want teachers to be physically and emotionally tough enough to make them control their behavior, since they, in fact, gain their strength to behave from the emotional strength of their teachers. They want teachers who will "make me work and not let me get away with anything" (told to me and my university students on numerous occasions by inner city school "discipline problems"). This is indicated clearly in the Educational Television movie *The Way It Is*. In the movie, time after time, when teachers ask their students why they misbehave the way they do, they are told, "You are too easy"; "You let us get away with things."[13]

For the teacher to be able to teach, and for the teacher's rules to count, *the teacher must have control of the class. You can not teach in a chaotic atmosphere.* By "control" I mean having enough order so that you can teach. It also refers to the teacher's ability to control nonpunitively the behavior in the classroom so that a student can relax and "allow himself to be motivated to learn."[14] Youngsters can do this only when they sense that their teacher is in charge and no one is allowed to bother them, to steal from them, or to shake them down. This concept is particularly important for children from lower socioeconomic backgrounds and children who have not yet developed their inner controls and still rely on the teacher's strength for controlling themselves.

Until you actually experience streetcorner testing—when all your middle class niceties do not count a damn and you wonder why this kid is doing this to you because you are not prejudiced like the others and you really want to help blacks—it will be hard, if not impossible, for you to understand what I mean. It should be noted here that I may *be talking about only one to three students in a class of thirty.*

Whereas many earlier conflicts in urban schools involved ethnic and religious groups, today's conflicts are exacerbated to a large extent by skin color.[15] White educators, generally unfamiliar with and perhaps even fearful of black students, often allow these children to create a violent and fearful school atmosphere in which learning is impossible. In addition to this, many of these professionals do not make enough academic and behavioral demands on their black, minority, and poor students. In response, some black groups accuse school personnel of practicing mental genocide or "menticide" (miseducation) for allowing black children to get away with behavior they would not accept in white children. White educators (and often black educators as well) then suspend supposedly disruptive children. In response, blacks indict the schools for acts of wanton suspension and for treating black children as colonial subjects.

The charges and countercharges are often made by well-meaning, sincerely interested individuals. At other times, the combatants are only interested in patronage or the maintenance or attainment of position, control, or power. They might also simply be racists (either black or white). The consequences for some school personnel and their students is the creation of a school beset with disorder and disruption; students, teachers, parents, and outsiders physically attacking other students and teachers; shakedowns; false fire alarms; bomb threats; shootings; knifings; sexual assaults; or stealing by small groups of students—all at least interfering with and preventing instruction.[16]

With a little effort on the part of some teachers, administrators, and professors in teacher education and graduate education programs, we can reverse this trend. Although they help, we do not need new buildings, the latest media equipment, the most current books, or the state-of-the-art computers to accomplish this. Unquestionably, money to purchase such things would help. However, money to repeat the same mistakes is not what is needed.

What we need are more teachers and administrators with the skills and sensibilities to be able to recognize and understand (1) the reality of the consequences of institutionalized white racism and ethnocentric behavior, (2) how that reality affects their behavior, and (3) how it prevents them from understanding the self-destructive streetcorner behavior of some of their students. This is what the problem has been about in inner city schools and is fast becoming the problem in so many other schools. It is that simple. We must also understand that it is institutionalized white racism in the form of discrimination in housing, in employment, and in unions that has tolerated deplorable ghetto conditions that, in turn, have given rise to the development and continuation of streetcorner behavior.

Improvements *can* be made in inner city schools. I will discuss how to accomplish this by writing on the affective areas and ideas that to date none of the other books or articles on inner city schools have addressed. I can do this because my experiences have been different from the experiences of most of the others who have written or spoken about inner city schools, with an occasional exception, such as Dr. Esther Rothman's *The Angel Inside Went Sour.*[17] Most of what has been published has been written by those who taught for a year or two in the elementary schools or by professors who have "visited" inner city schools but never taught in them.

Almost all my teaching and administrative experience has been with the urban lower class black, white, and minority youngsters whose streetcorner lifestyle and supposed emotional problems contribute to most of the innter city school problems. Furthermore, my experience has been predominately on the secondary school level, most of it being in the "600" schools, for socially maladjusted and emotionally disturbed youngsters.

What I have discussed so far draws attention to one of the gaps separating many "liberal-minded" teachers from the poor and black children and their parents. In many cases, these same factors separated the immigrants of the 1880s and 1900s from the educational reformers of those eras. What I am referring to is an unwillingness on the part of so many educators and college professors to come to grips with the lower economic class urban ghetto child's lifestyle—a way of life that courts violence and physical aggression. Indeed, many urban lower class black parents are also part of this culture and share in its values; many expect their children's teachers to be tough disciplinarians. More than one black parent has said to me, "You are a man. Why did you let him get away with that?"

There is a big difference between the expectations of parents from a lower economic class background and their children in relation to discipline and the average teacher's concept of his or her role in relation to discipline. Some of my pacifist and "liberal" friends and students have become angry with me when I have suggested the need for teachers working with children from lower economic backgrounds to be tough but humane in establishing control of a class. They feel love, freedom, and permissiveness will solve all their problems. They either refuse to or are unable to face the *reality* of the inner city classroom. For many of them, lower class lifestyle as it is played out in the classroom and the teacher's feelings about such behavior is an off-limits area for investigation or even discussion.

To deal with such issues as violence or even to recognize their existence in the inner city culture is often seen as prima facie evidence of racism. Hence, the conflict between the lower class expectancy of physicalness and toughness in discipline and the middle class ideal of permissiveness, nonviolence, and discussion remains unresolved.

Thus, we have on the one hand students challenging their teachers physically, with their parents having a specific view of how the teacher should respond to this challenge.

The black parent approaches the teacher with the great respect due a person of learning. The soaring expectations which are an important part of the parents' feelings find substance in the person of the teacher. Here is the person who can do for this precious child all the wonderful things a loving parent cannot. The child is admonished to obey the teacher as he would his parents and the teacher is urged to exercise parental prerogatives, including beating. To this the parent yields up his final unique responsibility, the protection of his child against another's aggression. The child is placed in the teacher's hands to do with as he sees fit, with the sole requirement that she teach him. . . . The parent tells of a child both beloved and beaten, of a child taught to look for pain from even those who cherish him most, of a child who has come to feel that beatings are right and proper for him, and of a child whose view of the world, however gently it persuades him to act toward others, decrees for him that he is to be driven by the infliction of pain. . . . [B]lack parents will feel that, just as they have suffered beatings as children, so it is right that their children be so treated.[18]

On the other hand, we have administrators telling teachers, "never touch a youngster under any circumstances," with the higher education academics adding their support to this hands-off position. Neither differentiates between corporal punishment and the physical restraint of a child who has lost control of his behavior and may be threatening a fellow student or teacher and interfering with instruction. Or, teachers becoming physical in desperate frustration or fear. And, how can teachers express physical and emotional strength without hitting their students? What role does the teacher take when challenged physically or sexually?

Instead of facing these questions and attempting to understand and resolve them, we have statements that leave us further in limbo with added feelings of guilt and frustration.

In these last decades of the twentieth century, in this assumed enlightened country, infant and child abuse continues to deform large numbers of our young physically, intellectually, and emotionally. When frequently disturbed or harrassed parents inflict their hostility upon their child it is a sad and criminal act. When a supposed professional, principal, teacher, guidance counselor, or other staff member beats a child, insults, or diminishes a child in any way, that person and the whole system bear responsibility for the act.

An interesting dichotomy of children's feelings is presented in the following quotation. It does not, however, represent their general resentment against those who beat them.[19]

Dr. Jablonsky: What is a good teacher like?

Boy: We have a good teacher. She says she is not doing it for her, but she wants to see us when we grow up, about ten years from now, that we can do things and . . . that we get a good education.

Girl: Like if you don't do your work or something; and your mother sends you to school to work and not to play. If you don't do it, she come over and hit you. And then, if you still don't do your work, so then she start beating you. If you did your work, she'll never do nothing to you.

Dr. Jablonsky: And you say she is a good teacher and she beats you?

Boy: She doesn't beat you. She just hits you to make you do your work.

Dr. Jablonsky: Has she ever hit you?

Boy: Yes.

Dr. Jablonsky: And you still think she is a good teacher because she cares and makes you learn?

Boy: Yes, because when she talk to you she tell you that when you grow up she don't want to see you like ten years from now scrubbing other people's floors, or doing something like that.

Dr. Jablonsky: Is this teacher a white teacher or a black teacher?

Bly: She is black.

Dr. Jablonsky: Do you think that that is another reason why you feel good about her—because she is black?

Boy: No, I like that teacher because she makes us learn.[20]

Unfortunately, we also have in-service programs that run away from touching base with a teacher's true feelings, emotions, and anxieties that in any way relate to the aggression and violence of lower class lifestyles or the teacher's feelings of aggression and violence.

REALITY 4

I was asked to lead a Saturday morning workshop for inner city secondary school teachers in a large city. I led the workshop informally, as we sat in a circle talking and sharing experiences. There were about fifteen teachers and the district's supervisor responsible for my workshop. We were all white.

I discussed student-teacher aggression and lower class lifestyle. When the question of corporal punishment came up, I announced that I was against it. One of the new young male teachers talked about how he hit his students and said that he felt this was an acceptable way to achieve order in his classroom, if not the only way. His words and feelings began to loosen up some of the other participants. Many began to express their feelings quite strongly in agreement with him.

At this point the supervisor became noticeably anxious over the direction of our discussion. After looking at her watch a few times, she informed us that it was time for the coffee break. During the break she cornered me. In an anxious whisper she insisted that we change the direction of the discussion. When we reconvened, she took over and led the conversation in a different direction. The group went to sleep physically and intellectually. It is interesting to note that, since then, only one white administrator in that district has asked me to run a workshop. From what I have heard, he was asked, in no uncertain terms, why he hired me. Black administrators, however, have asked me to run workshops.

Another incident related to this issue of not wanting to deal with reality happened to me recently. In this case, the person involved was a black administrator in a high-power position. Had he chosen to, he could have had a positive influence in providing some top professionals with a greater understanding of the problems they faced or would be facing. Instead, he chose not to.

REALITY 5

Recently, I was asked to give a keynote talk at the annual workshop for the staff of a government agency that mediates problems between schools and their community. The format called for me to speak for twenty minutes concerning the problems I thought this agency might be facing over the next ten years. Two experienced professionals would be responding to my presentation. Following their comments, I was to have the opportunity to react with a question and answer period, after which we would move into workshops to discuss what the three of us said.

I talked about how their staff ought to learn about not only *Ribbin', Jivin', and Playin' the Dozens* but the street language and behavior of our other and newer minority and immigrant groups as well. I emphasized, however, that black streetcorner behavior had spread and was being used by nonblack groups as well. And, many discipline problems had, as their roots, a lack of educator understanding of what was going on when these teachers "reported" students for using the streetcorner behavior.

Therefore, I suggested their staff ought to learn about the streetcorner behavior and language of all groups so that they would have a better understanding of what may have been the root cause of a school/community problem.

The first respondent was white and very conservative. He took me to task for being too liberal. The other respondent was black and a real orator in the tradition of the Reverend Dr. Martin Luther King and the Reverend Jessie Jackson. However, he spoke very much in generalities about blackness and curriculum and what should be done and then told the group that I was "way off base" because "we [blacks] have moved beyond those streetcorner games."

We did not follow the plan, and I was never given a chance to respond to his statements. However, when we finished for the evening, I walked over to him, grabbed his hand to shake it, and would not let go until I had my say and his response.

"Did I hear you say that what I said about streetcorner behavior was no longer true and was no longer going on?" I asked. "Because I don't know where you have been lately, but I see that behavior all over. When I talk with teachers, that is what they all describe as causing them problems." He said that he did not mean that, and he wished he had known I felt that way because he would have told the group that what I had said was correct.

On the streetcorner, what he did publically would have been called "showcasing" or "showboating." I checked around later with some of the staff to see whether my perception of what he said was accurate; most agreed with my observation of what he had said. Later, I felt better when the group discussion reports indicated that my message had gotten through, and a number of black men sat me down to tell me some more Shine and Signifyin' Monkey (see Chapter 6) stories and to discuss with me our observations of the streetcorner.

What was sad about this reality was that here was a black man in a power position giving an important group of professionals an incorrect and inaccurate message about how to help some poor blacks and other minorities. He was doing what so many white administrators had done earlier, and continue to do. He was, for who knows what reason, denying that that behavior was being used in the classroom and that it was causing teacher problems.

Such refusal to face the problems of lifestyle openly and honestly results in a buildup of guilt and frustrations for staff and hampers teaching and learning because the real problem is not being addressed. Chapter 7 will discuss further this quandary of discipline, corporal punishment, nonpunitive physical intervention, and the clash of lifestyle expectations in relation to discipline; and, of course, the question that is basic to any discussion of discipline: Is the teacher's role in teaching passive or is it participatory? Many teachers feel that their role in discipline is nonexistent. Their students should enter their classroom ready to learn; they merely transfer knowledge to them or show them where it can be found.

I finished the term at Haaren and never had any other real problems. I even managed to assist other teachers who were having discipline problems. On one occasion I commented to some students that someone had stolen two of the hubcaps from my car—not near school but home in Brooklyn. The next day when I arrived in school four hubcaps were on my desk.

It was also at Haaren that I experienced my first argument with a teacher about "lowering yourself to their level." I remember at Haaren one of the aloof male teachers always spoke negatively of his students because, according to him, his students couldn't understand what he was trying to teach them.

It was the first of many disputes of this type that I have had with teachers, administrators, college and university professors, laymen, and students. I would suggest that perhaps anyone who thinks that way or even raises the question of "lowering oneself" should not be working with disadvantaged youngsters. Good teachers discipline and motivate their students without worrying about "lowering themselves." *Motivation has to start where the youngsters are, with something they can relate to, not where you wish they were. Otherwise you will never be able to take them where you want them to go.* The good teacher "must relate his teaching to the world of his students as it is, not as he would like it to be."[21]

This question of whether one should "lower oneself" has arisen before in other contexts. One such argument developed at the height of Russian Jewish immigration to the United States between Jewish immigrant radicals and Abraham Cahan, who organized and became the editor of the *Jewish Daily Forward*, a leading Yiddish newspaper in New York City.

According to Ande Manners, Cahan, who could "identify and empathize with the uneducated Jewish immigrants," loved Yiddish, which he saw as

"a veritable linguistic ugly duckling." Yiddish was not even acceptable in early Yiddish theater companies which fastidiously chose a broken-German, broken-Yiddish "refined" blend known as *deitchmerish*, a dialect spoken by the socially ambitious in an attempt to pass as German Jews. Heroes often spoke straight German, and only the low comic spoke Yiddish.[22]

Under Cahan's leadership, the *Forward* was printed in Yiddish "clear as chicken soup." When Cahan and his reporters were reproached for their use of

Yiddish, a language with "no status at all," and for dealing with the real immigrant problems rather than more elevated topics, he often repeated an analogy that suggested his feelings about helping the newly arrived Jewish immigrants adapt to American life: "If you want to pick a child up from the ground, you first have to bend down to him. If you don't, how will you reach him."[23]

No matter how much we don't want to believe it, lower economic class youngsters start with a different frame of reference in relation to discipline than do middle-class youngsters. And teachers must attempt to enter that frame of reference if we are to make contact with them.

If what I did on my second day of teaching annoys you, give me credit for being honest. I had to describe the incident for a number of reasons. The first reason is that since this is an honest book about the way I see teaching in inner city schools, I must tell about the experiences that brought me to what I and others now believe. There are already too many teachers full of guilt because their fellow teachers, supervisors, and college professors (who may not really know) denied that these testing incidents actually happened to them or to anyone. How many teachers, feeling dejected after a tension-filled confrontation with a disruptive student, walk into the teachers' room looking for solace and a little compassion and help, only to be told by a colleague, "I can't understand why that happened to you. He never gives *me* any trouble."

The "official" image presented by the nonprofessional educational critics is that the United States is an all-loving, classless society always engaged in a war against those who do evil. The offspring of the lower classes are represented as "dead-end kids" whose wrongdoing is somehow related to Robin Hood acts. All they need is love, understanding, and some affection, and somehow good intentions will prevail against all evil. Of course this is not true; it is *bullshit*.

There are distinctions in child rearing and family lifestyles between very poor families and those families whose patterns are associated with effective adaptation to the demands of today's society. Reflected in the society are *class differences* rather than *color differences*.[24] There also happen to be quite a number of seriously disturbed and aggressive acting-out youngsters attending our schools. Very often, all it takes is one acting-out youngster in a class of thirty and the average teacher is in trouble. Indeed, in the late 1960s and early 1970s, a handful of acting-out young people brought many of our most liberal and open institutions of higher education to their knees. Although acting out can be a symptom of emotional disturbance, as can quiet withdrawal, *it may be a streetcorner behavior that is being used to test a teacher*; or the particular streetcorner behavior *may be interpreted as acting-out behavior by an unknowing teacher*.

Because the average teacher or administrator is not familiar with lower class streetcorner behavior, the behavior tends to frighten him or her. Very often, though, the educator considers it a manifestation of emotional disturbance or mental retardation and mislabels the child. However, the youngster's behavior may also be a healthy adaptation to the effects of racism and poverty.

To survive discrimination and poverty, many minority group youths adopt a life pattern that in itself perpetuates the cycle of poverty. Motivation is stifled by a society that apparently prefers to support the poor with welfare payments which keep them at a level of bare subsistence, rather than allowing minority groups an equal opportunity within the economic structure. The marginal activities of the ghetto, the reservation, the barrio, or the depressed rural sections are the only social settings in which many opportunities exist for enhancing self-esteem. Large families are at once a burden and a supportive group. Education may correlate with economic advancement, but the school institution tends to push out those children who cannot conform to the goals established by the school. Such life circumstances may be accepted in a pattern of ennui, hopelessness, and despair. A healthier adaptation may be rebellion.[25]

Rebelliously inappropriate behavior in a school, regardless of how adaptive it may be to a life of poverty, is inappropriate and should be treated as such. The key to such a situation, however, is how this inappropriate behavior is perceived and dealt with.

Because idealistic new teachers are not told the truth about how lower class behavior is played out in the classroom to test them, they are not prepared for the rigors of the testing games to which they are subjected. Indeed, even the older, more experienced teacher may not be adequately prepared for the rigors of the same testing. Too many teachers who are now attempting to teach poor, black, and minority children are becoming fixated at the disciplinary level; establishing order and achieving an effective learning environment seem to be beyond their ability. Hence, we continue to dehumanize ourselves while also dehumanizing and discouraging more lower class children from completing their education.

As the Joint Commission on Mental Health of Children has reported, "discipline becomes a major preoccupation of the teacher."

The role of the teacher in a child's life is of vital importance. Not only is a year of the child's education in her hands, but she may also have a crucial effect on his mental health. Many teachers are neither educationally nor emotionally prepared for this responsibility. The behaviors learned by children living in a slum may be repugnant and even terrifying to the teacher. Some teachers become intolerant of ethnic differences after a frustrating year of struggling to teach effectively in a ghetto or barrio school. Others bring to the classroom a stereotyped preconception of what the black, brown, or red child is capable of achieving.[26]

One of the reasons for my telling the story of my first and second days of teaching is that too many in educational leadership positions, and too many editors of the more influential magazines, newspapers, and professional journals, either have not been aware of or have refused to recognize reality. Whether they have acted from political, psychological, or other reasons is a matter for speculation. However, because they control so much of what is discussed and what gets printed—which in turn generates public opinion—we still have not been able to deal with the real problems involved in educating poor children. The publicized rationales have been wrong for the most part. Consequently, we have not been able to solve school problems. Typical of this inability to recognize and come to grips with reality was Bosley Crowther's review of the movie *The Blackboard Jungle* when he wrote:

> Evan Hunter's *Blackboard Jungle*, which tells a vicious and terrifying tale of rampant hoodlumism and criminality among the students in a large city vocational training school, was sensational and controversial when it appeared as a novel last fall. It is sure to be equally sensational and controversial, now that it is made into a film.
>
> For this drama of juvenile delinquency in a high school, which, . . . is no temperate or restrained report on a state of affairs that is disturbing to educators and social workers today, it is a full-throated, all-out testimonial to the lurid headlines that appear from time to time, reporting acts of terrorism and violence by uncontrolled urban youths. It gives a blood curdling, nightmarish picture of monstrous disorder in a public school. *And it leaves one wondering wildly whether such out-of-hand horrors can be* [my emphasis].[27]

At the time of the review, I was already teaching in the New York City "600" schools, and was experiencing incidents like those depicted in the movie. Soon afterward, Claire Booth Luce, our ambassador to Italy, prevented the movie from being shown in an Italian film festival.

More recently, Fred Hechinger, then education editor of the *New York Times*, continued in this tradition when he reviewed the movie version of *Up the Down Staircase*.

> School people are relieved to see that earlier motion picture image of 1955—*Blackboard Jungle*—superseded by something less sensational, more honest. At the time of this violence-packed "portrayal" of an alleged vocational high school, the *New York Times* film critic Bosley Crowther said: "And it leaves me wondering wildly whether such out-of-hand horrors can be."[28]

Although we can excuse Mr. Crowther for his comments because he wrote as a movie reviewer without any special knowledge of inner city schools, Mr. Hechinger is an education editor and should know better. Nor can I understand why Mr. Hechinger and so many others refuse to come to grips with the reality of inner city schools. After all, quite a literature has been developed on the lower class or slum lifestyle. Why hasn't anyone discussed how this lifestyle has always been played out in the classrooms of our inner city schools and now in so many other schools too? For reasons unknown to me, no one seems to be able to take the next logical step that will lead them to the real issues. Of course if they did this, their excuses will have run out.

What is so regrettable about this state of affairs is that this approach generates endless books, articles, and theories that are nothing but smoke screens clouding the real issues and problems. Possibly some of the more militant black critics are right; maybe it is just another manifestation of institutionalized white racism. Indeed, if we continue to talk and write but refuse to deal with the real problems and issues, we can continue to keep blacks, other minorities, and the poor in their present state without too much guilt. Or, perhaps it is the guilt that keeps us from dealing with the real issues.

Another example of this unwillingness to come to grips with the real problems of the schools and thereby help the schools was observed in the reports of the National Commission on the Causes and Prevention of Violence. As far as children and their schools are concerned, the reports were simply another exercise for academicians to contribute, primarily, as a source for an additional listing on a vita or a source for citations for future papers, lectures, books, and speeches.

On June 10, 1968, President Johnson launched the greatest single effort of organized research in the area of violence that has ever been attempted when he issued Executive Order 11412 and established the National Commission on the Causes and Prevention of Violence "to undertake a penetrating search into our national life, our past as well as our present, our traditions as well as our institutions, our culture, our customs, and our laws."[29]

To accomplish their charge, the commission divided its research into seven areas and created a task force to inquire into each area. Included were task forces on: (1) historical and comparative perspectives, (2) group violence, (3) individual acts of violence, (4) assassination, (5) firearms, (6) the media, and (7) law and law enforcement.

An eighth task force was organized to investigate the then violent events on which no other adequate factual records had been made. While the various task forces proceeded, the commission met and studied reports and articles. They held public hearings and sponsored conferences in which the views of more public officials, scholars, experts, private citizens, and religious leaders were heard. More than 140 research projects and special analyses were undertaken for the task forces by outside experts and scholars.

On January 9, 1969, after six months and twenty-nine days, the commission submitted a progress report that *established a relationship between youth and violence.*

The key to much of the violence in our society seems to lie with the young [my emphasis]. Our youth account for an ever-increasing percentage of crime, greater than their increasing percentage of our population.

Recent research suggests the possibility of identifying the youths most prone to violent or antisocial behavior. . . . These . . . youths accounted for the major cost to society from juvenile crimes. Clearly these chronic offenders merit special attention and study, especially as a means for judging when and how society might best take preventive and therapeutic action.

The Task Force is assessing the factors that motivate and stimulate the young to act . . . and the manner in which factors that motivate peaceful behavior might be encouraged.[30]

The commission also investigated and gave special consideration to corrections institutions, rehabilitation of convicted offenders and adjudicated delinquents, and reported that "the theme of the inadequacy of penal institutions as agents for rehabilitation has been reiterated by many of the witnesses appearing before the Commission."[31]

Some of the points made by the commission included: First, the imperativeness of working with the youth of the nation to solve the problems of violence. ("The key to much of the violence in our society seems to lie with the young . . . juvenile arrest rates for crimes of violence are rising . . . rapidly.") Second, we do have reasonably valid tools for identifying potential delinquents. ("Recent research suggests the possibility of identifying the youths most prone to violent or antisocial behavior, especially those prone to commit the more serious crimes.") Third, the longer we wait to help the troubled child, the harder it is to help him. ("It will always be difficult to rehabilitate the young person who had already been in trouble and been labeled a delinquent.")[32]

The commission was also aware of the very high rates of recidivism and wrote:

The Commission has given a great deal of attention to the question of prevention of juvenile delinquency and violence before it happens. . . .
In an F.B.I. survey of a large number of arrests in 1966 and 1967, approximately 75 percent of those arrested for violent crimes were "repeaters."[33]

After reading all the aforementioned and knowing that there were 183 titles that the commission's consultants and experts worked on, how many of those 183 titles do you think were related directly to the largest social agency we have for working with youth—the schools? Would you say thirty, fifteen, five? *Would you believe ONE?* The Task Force on Individual Acts of Violence contracted with the United States Office of Education for a "Review of Education Legislation, Survey of Requirements Necessary to Improve Educational Environment."

Isn't this hard to believe! The final staff report of the Task Force on Individual Acts of Violence also refused to deal with the problems of the schools— except, that is, to suggest the schools' shortcomings. "The public school should be a major institution for the transmission of legitimate values and goals of society. Recent commissions and studies, however, have pointed out that the system is failing to reach all youth equally and is thus contributing to low achievement and school dropouts."[34]

What is interesting is that the Task Force on Individual Acts of Violence, in addition to all the data linking youth and violence, came up with a number of findings that should have suggested a greater effort on their part in investigating the problems related to youth and the schools. The task force reported that "as part of the age cycle, youth has a higher probability than any other period for engaging in protest, overt expression of grievance, or rebellion. Psychologically, and in terms of the sheer distance to biological termination, the young have a greater tendency to strike out vigorously for or against something."[35]

The task force reported also that our correctional system is a failure, and that the "goal of rehabilitation must be given first priority."[36] They also reported

> that if the question of social intervention is posed in terms of the greatest amount of offense reduction registered between groups, it is clear that preventing poor nonwhite boys from committing crimes after their first offense would produce maximum delinquency reduction. By focusing resources and attention on lower-class, nonwhite offenders, not only would the general rate of delinquency be affected, but the incidence of serious violent acts would be most drastically decreased.[37]

Additionally, the task force went back further and even recognized where we should place a larger share of our effort.

> We do know that our public educational system, overburdened and inadequate as it may be for the tasks, remains the major single instrument for opening opportunities for success, influencing patterns of future behavior, and recognizing and answering specific individual problems and needs before they become dangerous. Teacher training, school-community relations, programs for dropouts and educationally handicapped adults, and many other areas of education deserve more research and national support for the roles they can play in diminishing violence in America.[38]

Why did the Task Force on Individual Acts of Violence do exactly the opposite of what they suggested should be done? Why did they not place a greater effort into the schools? After all, no one dictated to them what or where they should investigate. Actually, their charge was open:

> That scholarly research is predominant in the work here presented is evident in the product. But we should like to emphasize that the roles which we occupied were not limited to scholarly inquiry. The Directors of Research were afforded an opportunity to participate in all Commission meetings. We engaged in discussions at the highest levels of decision making, *and had great freedom in the selection of scholars, in the control of research budgets, and in the direction and design of research* [my emphasis]. If this is not unique, it is at least an uncommon degree of prominence accorded research by a national commission.[39]

With this unique freedom to move, it is interesting to note that *no* public school educator was brought in on the initial planning by the commission. "In early July a group of 50 persons from the academic disciplines of sociology, psychology, psychiatry, political science, history, law and biology were called together on short notice to discuss for two days how best the commission and its staff might proceed to analyze violence."[40]

When an official from the Task Force on Individual Acts of Violence called me about a paper I had written, I asked why the task force had not done more on the schools. His response was, "We just didn't think about it." What does *that* tell us?[41]

Perhaps I am being too harsh in my criticism. Possibly those who determine what gets published and those who write most of what gets published are limited in their ability and feelings to deal in concrete terms with educational realities. The insights and understandings required to deal with line level, pragmatic solutions may be beyond the range of their liberal arts education, their training, and their experiences. Their psychological set, their education, and their training may not have provided them with the ability to function at the level of the reality faced by the teacher in many classrooms with poor and minority children.

What I am talking about is analogous to the rear echelon World War II staff officers who were infuriated by Bill Mauldin's realistic front line "Willie and Joe" cartoon characters. The staff officers' interpretation of their experiences kept them from the understanding required to comprehend "Willie and Joe" or to believe that there actually could be real Willies and Joes.[42]

What this book is all about is reality on the teachers' level—not the reality understood at the staff or academic level. Those in academia used to dealing with educational issues on a philosophical level and those in school staff positions might not identify with this book. They might not even understand it. To them it may be something wholly foreign, a fantasy, a dangerous book, even a racist book.

But those teachers who get up early every morning and fight a feeling in their stomachs, as well as most of the teachers who can't wait to get into their classrooms, and the majority of urban blacks, who are at home with their blackness, will recognize the book for what it is: a true statement about the reality of so many of our schools. It is a statement about what I have seen, what I have experienced, and what I continue to see and experience.

Most of the book, therefore, deals with the lower class urban black male's streetcorner lifestyle and how it is being played out more often in the classrooms and schoolyards of our country. The book discusses how teachers and administrators can deal with this behavior in the affective areas to create the safe, secure, relaxed atmosphere necessary for teaching and learning. If school personnel could come to understand and learn to work positively with children possessing this lifestyle, most of our school discipline problems would disappear, and teachers could turn to their role of educating black, poor, and minority youngsters in our schools. Indeed, educating these youngsters would become the primary role of teachers in our schools, and discipline would take on a secondary, taken-for-granted role.

NOTES TO CHAPTER 2

1. Haaren High School was sold to a company that has converted the building into a comprehensive television and film production center. See Edward Schumacher, "Film/TV Center Planned for Haaren High Building," *New York Times*, January 8, 1979, p. B3.
2. When I worked for the New York City Board of Education, the law required that I lock the door to my classroom when neither students nor I was there; you are not allowed to lock the door if a student is in your room. As I became a more experienced teacher, I most often taught with my door open.
3. Bell Kaufman, *Up The Down Staircase* (Englewood Cliffs, N.J.: Prentice-Hall, 1964); Robert Mulligan, dir., *Up the Down Staircase* Warner Brothers, 1967; Bosley Crowther, "Screen: 'Up the Down Staircase' Opens: Crises in a City School Makes Poignant Film," *New York Times*, Late City Ed., August 18, 1967, p. 36.
4. Jerome Weidman, *Fourth Street East: A Novel of How It Was* (New York: Random House, 1970), p. 217.
5. Arthur Schlesinger, Jr., *A Thousand Days: John F. Kennedy in the White House* (Boston: Houghton Mifflin, 1965), p. 821.
6. Ibid., p. 110.
7. The National Advisory Commission on Civil Disorders, *Report of the National Advisory Commission on Civil Disorders* (Washington, D.C.: U.S. Government Printing Office, 1968).
8. Pat Conroy, *The Water Is Wide* (Boston: Houghton Mifflin, 1972); George Dennison, *The Lives of Children: The Story of the First Street School* (New York: Random House, 1969); Edgar A. Friedenberg, *The Vanishing Adolescent* (Boston: Beacon, 1964); Paul Goodman, *Growing Up Absurd: Problems of Youth in the Organizational Society* (New York: Vintage, 1956); James Herndon, *How To Survive in Your Native Land* (New York: Simon & Schuster, 1971); James Herndon, *The Way It Sposed To Be* (New York: Simon & Schuster, 1968); Jonathan Kozol, *Death at An Early Age: The Destruction of the Hearts and Minds of Negro Children in the Boston Public Schools* (Boston: Houghton Mifflin, 1967).
9. Herndon, 1971, p. 147.
10. "Assaults on Teachers," *Today's Education* 61, no. 2 (1972): 30-32, 69, 70-71; Stephen K. Bailey, *Disruption in Urban Public Secondary Schools* (Washington, D.C.: National Association of Secondary School Principals, 1970); Herbert L. Foster, "The Inner-City School: A Different Drumbeat," *University Review* 2, no. 2 (1969): 28-32; Herbert L. Foster, "The Inner-City Teacher and Violence: Suggestions for Action Research," *Phi*

Delta Kappan 50 (1968): 172–75; Herbert L. Foster, "To Reduce Violence: The Interventionist Teacher and Aide," *Phi Delta Kappan* 53 (1971): 59–162.

11. Jim Miskiewicz, "City's Instant Teachers Meet Special Problems," *New York Times Education Magazine*, October 10, 1982, p. 44.

12. Ibid., p. 44.

13. Abraham J. Tannenbaum, *Education and Mental Health* (Washington, D.C.: Joint Commission on Mental Health of Children, 1968), a statement by the Ad Hoc Education Committee. (Unpublished manuscript, October 15, 1968.)

14. "The Way It Is," National Educational Television Journal, Channel 13, New York City, May 1, 1967; Homer Bigart, "N.Y.U. Clinic Stalled in Trying to Improve School," *New York Times*, November 26, 1967, p. 83; Leonard Buder, " 'The Way It Is,' " *New York Times*, May 2, 1967, p. 95; Fred M. Hechinger, "N.Y.U. Adopting a School for Brooklyn Slum Study," *New York Times*, July 17, 1966, pp. 1, 6; Nina McCain, "A School Marriage between N.Y.U. And Junior High," *World Journal Tribune*, October 9, 1966; John C. Robertson and Neil M. Postman," New York University—New York City: Clinic for Learning (New York University, N. D.), p. 6. (Mimeo.) For a description of the school a few years later, see Bob Moore, *Welcome to #57: Four Years of Teaching and Learning in Bedford-Stuyvesant* (New York: G. P. Putnam's Sons, 1974).

15. Herbert L. Foster, "Teaching Industrial Arts to the Emotionally Disturbed Student," *Industrial Arts & Vocational Education* 53, no. 1 (1964): 22–23.

16. Leonard Covello, *The Teacher in the Urban Community: A Half Century in City Schools. The Heart Is the Teacher* (Totowa, N.J.: Littlefield, Adams, 1970), first published in 1958 under the title *The Heart Is The Teacher*; Herbert Gans, *The Urban Villagers: Groups and Clans in the Life of Italian-Americans* (New York: Free Press of Glencoe, 1962); Murray Levine and Adeline G. Levine, *A Social History of Helping Services: Clinics, Court, School, and Community* (New York: Appleton-Century-Crofts, 1970); Angelo Patri, *A Schoolmaster of the Great City* (New York: Macmillan, 1923); Diane Ravitch, *The Great School Wars New York City, 1805-1973: A History of the Public Schools as a Battlefield of Social Change* (New York: Basic Books, 1974).

17. Esther P. Rothman, *The Angel Inside Went Sour* (New York: David McKay, 1970).

18. William W. Grier and Price M. Cobbs, *Black Rage* (New York: Basic Books, 1968), pp. 137–38.

19. Dr. Jablonsky does not make it clear whether this was her perception of the children's feelings or whether they told this to her.

20. Adelade Jablonsky, "Man's Inhumanity to the Young," *IRCD Bulletin* 7, nos. 1 and 2 (1971): 19.

21. Herbert L. Foster, "Teaching Industrial Arts to The Emotionally Disturbed Student."

22. Ande Manners, *Poor Cousins* (New York: McCann & Geoghegan, 1972), p. 275.

23. Ibid., p. 28; Ronald Sanders, *The Downtown Jews: Portraits of an Immigrant Generation* (New York: Harper & Row, 1969), p. 265.

24. Catherine Chilman, *Growing Up Poor*, U.S. Department of Health, Education, and Welfare (Washington, D.C.: U.S. Government Printing Office, 1966); Joint Commission on Mental Health of Children, *Crisis in Mental Health: Challenge for the 1970's* (New York: Harper & Row, 1970), p. 191.

25. Joint Commission, p. 220.

26. Ibid., pp. 231-32.

27. Bosley Crowther, "Delinquency Shown in Powerful Film," *New York Times*, March 21, 1955, p. 21; Evan Hunter, *The Blackboard Jungle* (New York: Dell, 1954).

28. Fred M. Hechinger, "Schools, Teachers, and Images," *New York Times*, August 20, 1967, p. E19.

29. National Commission on the Causes and Prevention of Violence, *Progress Report of the National Commission on the Causes and Prevention of Violence to President Lyndon B. Johnson* (Washington, D.C.: U.S. Government Printing Office, 1969), p. 1.

30. Ibid., pp. 6, A-21.

31. Ibid., p. A-22.

32. Ibid., pp. 6, A-21, A-22.

33. Ibid., p. A-22.

34. Donald J. Mulvilhill, Melvin M. Tumin, and Lynn A. Curtis, *Crimes of Violence: A Staff Report Submitted to the National Commission on the Causes and Prevention of Violence*, Vols. 11, 12, and 13 (Washington, D.C.: U.S. Government Printing Office, 1969), p. xxxiv.

35. Ibid., p. 603.

36. Ibid., p. xlvi.

37. Ibid., p. 611.

38. Ibid., p. xliii.

39. Ibid., p. xvi.

40. Ibid., p. xv.

41. Herbert L. Foster, "The Inner-City Teacher and Violence: Suggestion for Action Research.

42. Bill Mauldin, *Up Front* (New York: Henry Holt, 1945).

3 THE UNRECOGNIZED DILEMMA OF ALL OF OUR SCHOOLS

> Over the mountain,
>   across the street.
> There's a bad mutha fucka,
>   named Stackolee.
> He wore baggie pants,
>   wore hustler's shoes
> Talked more trash
>   than the *Daily News*
>
> —taped in Brooklyn, New York

> The feelings of brotherhood on The Streetcorner never stopped astonishing me.
>
> —Mezz Mezzrow, *Really the Blues*

U.S. public schools have educated successfully masses of children better than any other nation in the world. In particular, our schools have had and continue to have outstanding success in educating children who enter school with the middle class orientation of speaking and behaving in a restrained middle class way and not being too overtly physical or sexual.

However, despite this outstanding educational record, our schools also have always had an "unrecognized dilemma": a problem educating more of the children of first-generation immigrants, of minorities, and of the poor.[1]

The primary reason that we have not been able to educate more immigrant, poor, or minority children is that we either have not had enough of an understanding of racism or we have been unwilling to come to grips with racism and ethnocentrism—a universal and international behavior. Most pointedly, educator racist and ethnocentric behavior, sometimes very unconscious and sometimes very conscious, has never been dealt with over an extended period of time.

It must be stated emphatically that racist and ethnocentric behavior is not just a school problem. Racism and ethnocentrism is as much an international problem as it is a U.S. national problem. Every nation, no matter how homogeneous, has problems around either race, ethnicity, shades of color, tribe, sex, state, province, class, or religion.[2] Indeed, Americans probably have attempted to overcome racism more than any other nation has.

Nevertheless, it is the unconscious or conscious racist or ethnocentric behavior that creates the unrecognized dilemma when educators—not all educators, but too many—refuse to understand, accept, or work with, on other than their rigid terms, many students whose life experiences, dress, speech, and behavior are different from theirs— that is, students who exhibit lower class or blue collar behavior in general and lower class black male streetcorner behavior in particular.

To put it another way, differences in factors of personality, life history, and social background between educators and students can serve to either reduce or increase the effects of teaching and learning. What William Schofield found about psychiatrists, psychologists, and social workers, applies to educators:

> The capacity for and the condition of "understanding" a patient is generally held to be of key importance in the establishment, maintenance, and successful direction of a therapeutic relationship. If it happens that therapist and client have certain identities in their respective social histories there is possibly a spontaneous empathy, a preformed rapport that can facilitate the mutual acceptance of each other and, more importantly, may serve continuously as a catalyst for the stream of communication, spoken and unspoken, which is the medium of therapy [and teaching, too].[3]

However, in his study, Schofield found that if the bulk of the psychiatrists, psychologists, and social workers had their druthers to select an ideal client, the client would "present the 'yavis' syndrome—clients who are youthful, attractive, verbal, intelligent, and successful."[4]

If we can generalize from Schofield's work to education, we can assume that educators would also like to work with "yavis" students. Conversely, we could refer to many immigrant, poor, and minority children as "non-yavis" students with whom many educators would not have any rapport.

These next two realities provide examples of the unrecognized dilemma where educators reacted in either a racist or ethnocentric way. In reality 6 all involved were white, and ethnocentrism played a role. In reality 7 the educators were white, the male adolescent involved was black, and the educators' behavior was unknowingly racist.

A.B. Hollingshead, in his 1949 classic *Elmtown's Youth: The Impact of Social Class on Adolescents*, for which the field work was carried out between

May 1941 and December 1942, described how the social system of an all-white middlewestern corn belt community organized and controlled the behavior of its high school students. His reporting of the social class divisions and resulting affects on the school's social structure, teaching and learning, and, in particular, discipline could still be reported today in communities throughout the country.

He found that Elmtown's prestige structure was stratified into five classes. There was a very strong association between the position of a student's family in the adult class social system structure and his peer group reputation. The student reputational categories included The Elite, The Good Kids, and The Grubby Gang.

Though some parents from all classes were counseled about the work or discipline of their children, there was a big contrast between the frequency of counseling of the two top groups and that of the two bottom groups. Also, though lower class children were given poorer grades, their parents were counseled far more frequently about their children's discipline than they were counseled about their school work. From Hollingshead's reporting on discipline:

> If the stories which circulated can be believed in their entirety, the honors in the graduating classes from both the elementary and high schools are deliberately given to children from the prominent families. According to these stories, the winner is not entitled to the honor under the rules of fair competition; but under the unfair rules imposed by some parents and teachers, these children are sure to win. It is charged that grades are changed, teachers threatened with dismissal, and examinations rigged to achieve this result. . . . There is little doubt that many of the stories are rooted in facts, for the teachers do cater to the prominent families.[5]

Furthermore, "the administration of discipline laid bare the dynamics of the class system in a way that is directly observable but difficult to quantify."[6] Although Hollingshead did not name these dynamics, ethnocentrism certainly would be applicable as per this example.

REALITY 6

While the teachers handled rules related to talking in class, lack of attention, passing notes, and so on, the administration handled problems of tardiness, class attendance, and expulsions. The most constantly violated rule by both the students and the staff concerned tardiness. Often, when the principal was out of his office on official work, four female students would provide admission slips for tardy students. The "office gang," as they were called, very often trapped their enemies by withholding slips while saving friends by issuing slips.

After a few months of school, this situation deteriorated so badly that a teachers' meeting was held, at which time the staff voted unanimously for all the students to be sent to detention with no excuses accepted. The next day, the office gang and all the students were told about the new rule, which was also approved by the student council.

Nevertheless, the second week, Kathy, from a prominent family, violated the detention rule. Instead of going to detention, she kept an appointment to have a permanent wave for the country club dance the next night. The principal called her mother and told her about Kathy's skipping detention.

The next day, he discussed this with the superintendent, who indicated he knew about it because the girl's mother had mentioned the incident to his wife while talking about the church supper. He warned the principal to be careful because there was nothing to be done in this case. When Kathy came in to meet with the principal for her lecture,

> she was dressed neatly in a brushed wool sweater and tweed skirt. She walked coyly to the principal's desk and asked in a naive voice, "Did you want to see me last night?"
>
> The principal looked up and quietly asked, "Did you forget about detention?"
>
> A pause. "No, I had an appointment at Craig's to have my hair set."
>
> "Did you have to go last night?"
>
> "Yes, tonight I have to go to Mrs. Nettle's to get my dress for the dance."
>
> "All right. Go on on to class, but don't let this happen again."
>
> After Kathly left the office, the principal threw a pack of excuses on the desk and muttered, "There it goes again! The next time one of these prominent families puts pressure on me, I am going to raise hell!"
>
> The following Wednesday morning, Frank Stone, Jr. (Class I) parked his father's Cadillac in front of the high school at a quarter after eight, climbed out leisurely, picked up his notebook, and walked into the office and casually remarked, "I guess I'm late again."
>
> The principal looked hard at him and spoke firmly, "What's the story this time?"
>
> "I didn't wake up, I guess."
>
> "This time you are going to detention like everyone else." He wrote young Frank an excuse, placed his name on the detention list, and, as he handed him the excuse said, "This means one hour in detention. I want to see you there at three-fifteen tonight." [7]

At three-thirty, the principal checked detention and found out that Frank was not there. He walked to his office and called Frank Stone, Sr. and said, "I want him [Frank] down here right away." [8]

The superintendent had heard the conversation between the principal and Frank's father through his open office door and asked the principal what Frank's father had said. The principal informed him that Frank's father was bringing him down immediately. However, since he had to leave to practice singing for Sunday's Methodist's Church choir, he would notify the teacher in charge of detention.

About a half hour later, Frank was delivered to school by his father. The superintendent met Frank on the stairs, took him to his office for a brief talk, and then had him sit in the outer office for a while. Later, the superintendent indicated that he had Frank sit in the outer office because he did not want him "in the detention room with the rest of the kids."[9]

Although the principal was enraged over what had happened after he left, there was nothing he could do about it. As a result, from then on, there was practically no enforcement of the detention rule, to a large extent, for children from the upper economic families. And the office gang went back to their old ways of saving friends. However, in the main, for the lower economic students the detention rule was enforced more rigidly, as described in the example that follows.

Just three weeks after the Frank Stone, Jr. episode, a fifteen-year-old class IV boy, "Boney" Johnson, came to school late. Since the English teacher would not admit him without a note, he went to the principal. The principal was sitting at his desk when Boney walked in. Before Boney could say a word, the principal sarcastically barked out:

"So my pretty boy is late again! I suppose it took you half an hour to put on that clean shirt and green tie!" [The principal arose from his desk, walked around, and looked at Boney's trousers and shoes and went on.] "Ha, you have your pants pressed today! I suppose you took a bath last night, too. New shoes, and they're shined."[10]

Though Boney's face became flushed and he bit his lip, he said nothing. The principal gave Boney an admission slip, put his name on the detention list, and told him to go to class and show the girls what a pretty boy he was.

As he walked out of the office, Boney turned his head and said, "I'm not going to your damned detention room tonight or any time."[11]

The principal did not appear to hear him, and he went back to work. A few minutes later, though, he commented to those in the office that Boney was one of the wise guys who thinks he's a hot shot. Also, his old man works out at the fertilizer plant and is just a laborer, and the kid thinks he's someone. If they have the W.P.A. twenty years from now, that kid will probably be working for them. His final comment was that Boney was one person he was going to see put in detention.

That afternoon when school was out, the superintendent, the principal, and two teachers guarded all the doors and patrolled the building. After most of the teachers had gone home and the students had left, the superintendent went to his office and the principal stood outside the front door. Suddenly, the front door was thrown open, there were loud angry voices, and the superintendent rushed from his office to stand at the head of the stairs.

The principal pushed and shoved "Boney" up the stairs and repeated, "You can't get away with that stuff." As they neared the top, "Boney" broke from his grasp and started down the hall toward the side door. The superintendent blocked his path, and "Boney" ran upstairs. The principal leaped and grabbed him by the coat collar with his left hand. "Boney" turned and started to fight. The principal spun him around seized the visor of his cap with his right hand and yanked it down over his eyes. While "Boney" was fighting to get the cap off his face, the principal hit him three times with the heel of his hand on the back of the neck near the base of the skull. "Boney" cursed, struggled, and hit in all directions. Soon he broke free and ran toward the Superintendent, who shook and slapped him three or four times. Both men then grabbed him by the arms and shook him vigorously. The Superintendent angrily screeched, "You're going out of this building. You're never coming back until you bring your father and we talk this over." By this time, the three had reached the front door. "Boney" was shoved outside. He stood there cursing and threatening both men with violence. In a few minutes he composed himself, straightened his clothes, and walked away, muttering to himself.[12]

The superintendent and the principal then walked upstairs to the superintendent's office. The superintendent sat down, and, when he caught his breath, said:

"I can stand a lot of things from kids, but one thing I can't stand is a sassy kid. No kid's going to sass me." . . . The principal said nothing, and the Superintendent resumed, "That boy is a trouble maker. I've had my eyes on him all year. Look at the gang he's running with."

"Yes, I know. They're trouble makers around here. I had trouble with them all last year, and they're starting out again this year. If he wasn't that type, he wouldn't be running with that bunch."

After a pause, the Superintendent composed himself and remarked, "That boy will have to bring his father back here, or he'll not get in this school." The principal agreed, "Yes, I'll stand with you on that. We have got to stop this thing some way."[13]

An interesting point is that Boney was finally tossed out of the building when that was where he wanted to go in the first place. Educators could also learn a lesson from the redirection of all the principal's frustration with the other students onto Boney.

To say that Kathy, Frank, and Boney were treated differently would be an understatement. In fact, the difference in treatment afforded Boney in comparison to Frank and Kathy is an excellent example of ethnocentric behavior on the part of educators. What surprised me and continues to surprise me is that I have not found any mention of this section of the book or that incident in any of the contemporary materials related to schools. It is possible that the unequal and ethnocentric behavior described is still not felt to be wrong. Or, it could be possible that present authors are not as well read as they purport to be.

Incidents similar to those in reality 6 described above by Hollingshead continue to happen in our schools every day. That such things happen in inner city schools is well documented. However, such incidents are happening with more frequency in suburban and rural schools as minority children move into these districts, and blue-collar children pick up and exhibit streetcorner behavior.

This next reality is typical of the way the behavior of minority students is so easily misunderstood to the detriment of the students and, of course, to our society over the long run.

I was presenting a workshop at a national Council for Exceptional Children annual conference and was describing streetcorner behavior in relation to "ditty boppin'," or "pimp walking," which is described in more detail in Chapter 6. For here, though, suffice it to say that ditty boppin' is a way of walking. I have observed the walk in movies, on television, in the theater, on the streetcorner, and at all sorts of athletic events. In fact, I have at times been accused of walking that way myself.

The professional who related this story is a white social worker who works for a county special education agency in the Midwest. The area served by his agency encompasses a fairly affluent suburb of a large midwestern city within which there are two high schools, two junior high schools, and six elementary schools with an overall black population of less than 5 percent.

REALITY 7

"Well, I am a clinical staff member of a program where my actual title is a Behavior Management Specialist. As a result, I'm responsible for attending staffings and looking at students who are being referred to us from the co-operating schools within our cooperative."

"Recently, we had a student who was seventeen years old and referred to us for school problems and possible placement within our program. And, at the staffing, we went through a list of behaviors such as not attending classes regularly, not completing assignments, etc."

"However, there did not appear to be any severe acting-out or aggressive behavior that we were hearing at that time. Two of the teachers who were working with this student felt that one of the problems was that he would *walk through the hallways in a sexually provocative way* [my emphasis]. And, that this was one of the main reasons of concern for referring him to a program that would have ended up costing the school district about $8,000. And, again, its a very restrictive program for severely disturbed young people."

"I was aware of what his walking behavior was. I was sensitive to it. Again, I'm a social worker by training, and I have worked in a kind of multi-ethnic situation in Boston. And, I picked up on it relatively quickly. I just couldn't believe that we were sitting there with two building administrators, two teachers, and one special educator and the way he walked was actually one of the reasons stated for referring a student to this type of a program. I could not see anything else indicated other than non-attendance as a behavioral concern."[14]

The assigning, or attempting to assign, a black adolescent male student to a special education program for ditty boppin' is more common than most readers will realize. I have had many discussions with regular and special education teachers who, for reasons they cannot explain, get annoyed, angry, even livid when they see one of their black male students walking this way. Indeed, in the city of Buffalo, New York, "according to some reports, kids have been suspended for 'walking in an insolent manner.'"[15]

There must be a good deal of deep-rooted feelings around race and sexuality that some whites, and middle class blacks too, have when they see black male adolescents ditty boppin'. (The middle class blacks who react negatively to a black student walking this way might be feeling that it is lowering the standards for blacks in general.)

The conflict between the school's formal rules and the formal rules of the streetcorner is not unlike the problem faced by the late Dr. Martin Luther King, Jr. when he brought his southern, acceptable-to-whites, religious-style civil rights movement to the northern urban black ghettoes. We saw a confrontation between the rules of the ghetto and the rules that guided Dr. King's middle-class-behaviored and middle-class-supported movement. We also saw an expression of male role expectancy as reflected in the ghetto black's feelings toward Dr. King as compared with his feelings toward, for example, Malcolm X. Stephen Henderson pointed this out.

> There was also something in the personality and background of the man—the mere fact that he was a preacher and formally educated man—which, while no obstacle to the loving, suffering black multitudes in the South, made it difficult for the Northern, urban, hip young blacks to identify with him. The abstractions of brotherhood and universal love were difficult to believe in after a day with the Man,[16] or a night with the blues.
>
> Chicago signaled the dimensions of the urban alienation. In addition to a powerful political machine, theology stood in the way. *Nonviolence was not natural. Self-defense was* [my emphasis]. And then we remember the terrible anguish that King endured as he tried to come to grips with the power of black power, we realize that there was some limitation in his early life which precluded his solving the problem in time. *That limitation was insufficient knowledge of black ghetto life* [my emphasis]. Of course, he knew the poverty, and he deliberately subjected himself to it; and he knew immense suffering and anguish. Of course, he sympathized with and loved the poor people, the common people; he was like Langston Hughes in this, and he never tired of quoting the poet's "Mother to a Son," with the line, "Life for me ain' been no crystal stair." And it hadn't been, with his beautiful mind and raw courage and his pride. *But he didn't know the pimps and the whores and the dope pushers* [my emphasis] that black poets both love and hate and try to change—the "konk-haired hipsters wig-wearing whores."
>
> Malcolm X Shabazz knew them. He had been a konk-haired hipster and he had been a pimp and he had been a hustler and a dope addict. But he went through changes. Rough changes! And paid more dues than any man on

record. And he was baptized into blackness and repudiated his slave name (Little—how inappropriate!) and became Malcolm X—indicating the lost part of his life and history. He went through more changes—beautiful changes—and became, after his pilgrimage to Mecca, El-Hajj Malik El Shabazz. In some ways, his death was more tragic than King's, for the Movement had moved North and he had the potential of unifying elements in the black community that King could not reach.[17]

THREE CONCERNS OF STREETCORNER BEHAVIOR

1. The rules, regulations, and conditions of the ritual coping and survival techniques that urban lower class black males have developed and refined to survive in the white racist society.
2. The additional behavior involved in urban lower class black male streetcorner lifestyle—for example, language, mode of dress, running a game, aggression (sometimes only perceived as such by whites and sometimes real), physicalness, putting someone down before he puts you down, the put-on or front, playing either the "cat" or "gorilla," the importance of style, and a flare for drama.
3. The urban lower class black's concept and expectation of men's and women's behavior and role as related to the educator's behavior and role, and the juxtaposition of these expectations with the middle class educator's concept and expectation of his or her teaching role.

The rules governing streetcorner behavior that continue to cause problems for educators obviously also caused problems for Dr. King. These rules are related closely to what Charles Kiel referred to as the "expressive male role within urban lower class Negro culture—that of the contemporary blues-man."[18]

To provide an understanding of the "expressive male role" as it applies and relates to black schoolchildren and educators, we must look at three concerns that have their roots in lower class behavior in general and urban lower class black males' streetcorner lifestyle in particular.

To point up the degree to which these three areas affect teaching and learning in our schools, four categories of student behavior are suggested as operating in secondary school classrooms housing large numbers of urban lower class black children. It is through these four categories of student behavior that the rules, regulations, behaviors, and style embodied in the above three areas of concern set the informal rules governing much of this behavior. These four categories of student behavior, however, should not be thought to suggest a similarity to the urban lower class black adult population.

1. Youngsters with middle class lifestyle and behavior.
2. Youngsters who have adopted the lifestyle and behavior of the streetcorner but have the potential for middle class lifestyle and behavior.

3. Youngsters who are emotionally or physically handicapped or both. Because of the inner city environment, the disturbed inner city child often exhibits an aggressive acting-out syndrome.[19]
4. Youngsters who are entertainment and sports world oriented and youngsters who are religious or politicized.

There is some movement by youngsters among categories 1, 2, and 4. The behavior of youngsters on any particular day may depend upon their teacher or teachers, their home situation, what may have happened on the way to school, or how they feel on that day; and, of course, how the teacher feels that day. (Chapter 7 will go into this in more detail.)

Though the parameters of behavior are somewhat fluid, there are central tendencies of behavior within each category. Additionally, the unknowing educator might improperly classify youngsters who exhibit this streetcorner behavior as emotionally disturbed, socially maladjusted, learning disabled, or even retarded. In the New York City "600" schools, I found many youngsters classified as emotionally disturbed or socially maladjusted who were just tough streetcorner black or minority youngsters. Furthermore, a graduate student who took a number of graduate courses with me had been classified as CRMD (Classes for Children with Retarded Mental Development) when an adolescent in the New York City schools. This improper classification of black and minority children has been and continues to be a historical national problem.

To explain my hypothesis of differentiated inner city classroom behavior, a brief explanation of the four classifications of student behavior follow which should provide the reader with insight into the consequences and importance of understanding lower class black male streetcorner behavior. It should also make the reader aware that there are actually large differences in student behavior in inner city classrooms, though most of the students may be black and poor.

1. Youngsters with Middle Class Lifestyle and Behavior

This behavior will be discussed briefly because middle class black and white youngsters behave pretty much the same. The youngsters who behave this way usually learn regardless of the teacher or his or her methods. However, these youngsters learn very little, if anything, when they are in schools with large numbers of urban lower class black youngsters. This is because these classrooms and schools are chaotic and disruptive because (1) our society has not opened up to provide them with the motivation for achieving in spite of the disruptive ones and (2) racism has prevented their parents from moving into middle class neighborhoods. However, these middle-class-behaviored children are sometimes in trouble in suburban and rural schools too when unknowing or racist educators react negatively to their color, social class, or city background.

As noted earlier, middle class behavior is compatible with the way the schools are organized presently. It is also the behavior with which most of our teachers, guidance counselors, and administrators feel secure. This is the behavior that is reflected in the ability of the youngsters to sit still for reasonably long periods of time, to use and be secure with pen and pencil, to understand the importance of time and structure, to be oriented toward the importance of reading and writing, and to be conversant in Standard English. This is the behavior that tends to inhibit and internalize aggression, physicalness, and sexuality.

The middle class youngster is still fearful of a "blue slip" or whatever other system is used for reporting misbehavior. These youngsters usually behave when you threaten to call their parents. This is also the group that must be educated to develop a black middle class. If pressure of law, court action, militant physical action, and growing numbers can continue to force economic opportunities and accompanying middle class or suburban housing for this group, our schools will be integrated through social and economic movement instead of busing. To add support to the possibility of this contention, a 1971 survey found more white ethnic Americans favoring integration than ever before, even though they continue to oppose busing.[20]

Another important point is that this group has the behavior compatible with middle class white American behavior. Their moving to the suburbs or better neighborhoods, after initial fear and some selling by whites, will begin to show whites who have never known blacks on their own social, educational, or economic level personally, that the middle class lifestyle of blacks and whites is similar except for skin color. I would suggest that one of the contributors to inner city school problems is the institutionalized white racism that has prevented most black and white middle class Americans of similar social, educational, and economic level or background from meeting and knowing one another. Black and white school personnel with three or more years of teaching in inner city schools estimate this group of youngsters as representing approximately 17 percent of the black inner city school population.

2. Youngsters Who Have Adopted the Lifestyle and the Behavior of the Streetcorner but Have the Potential for Middle Class Behavior

This is the behavior that most black and white educators neither understand, nor relate to, nor even know exists. This is the behavior that many youngsters use to test their teachers. It is the behavior that many white school personnel consider to be symptomatic of emotional disturbance or social maladjustment, often resulting in the improper placement of these youngsters in programs for the emotionally disturbed or, sometimes, the retarded. It can also be argued that these school personnel act out of guilt, racism, ignorance, or ethnocentrism.

This is also the behavior read about in books[21] and seen in many of the plays of Ed Bullins, Immamu Amiri Baraka (Le Roi Jones), and J. E. Franklin,[22] and in Melvin Van Peebles's movie *Sweet Sweetback's Baadasssss Song* and in his play *Ain't Supposed to Die a Natural Death*.[23] This is also sometimes the behavior that urban blacks use to "run a game on the man." It is the defensive behavior that some blacks have been forced to adopt to help them survive in a white racist society.

Although the behavior takes place on streetcorners in the black ghetto; is depicted in books; is acted out in plays; is presented in nightclub acts; is found in songs and records;[24] was seen by many in the movies *M*A*S*H*, *Putney Swope*, and *Stir Crazy*; and takes place in almost all of our schools, there is very little in the educational literature discussing this behavior from an organized point of view.[25]

Roger Abrahams, John Dollard, and Thomas Kochman must be credited with providing the best material to date by placing aspects of this behavior in some perspective and order.[26] However, even they have not placed streetcorner behavior in an inner city or other school setting. The only organized literature placing streetcorner behavior in a school setting is the first edition of *Ribbin'* and Richard Maratto's dissertation.[27] This is true despite the fact that "it would be ... difficult to imagine a high school student in [an] inner city school not being touched by what is generally regarded as 'street culture' in some way."[28]

Such a literature should (1) describe and report it as an organized behavior with guidelines, (2) place it in a school setting and perspective, (3) offer suggestions to the educator to assist him or her to cope with the behavior, and (4) suggest methods and techniques for using the behavior to increase time on task and teaching and learning.

Despite the paucity of reporting of streetcorner behavior, the streetcorner is where many lower class blacks are really educated. H. Rap Brown talks about the importance of the streetcorner as the locus for educating black youngsters.

> Sometimes I wonder why I even bothered to go to school. Practically everything I know I learned on the corner. . . . If you were going to stay in control, you had to be in the street. . . .
>
> The street is where young bloods get their education. I learned how to talk in the street, not from reading about Dick and Jane going to the zoo and all that simple shit. The teacher would test our vocabulary each week, but we knew the vocabulary we needed. They'd give us arithmetic to exercise our minds. Hell, we exercised our minds by playing the Dozens. . . . And the teacher expected me to sit up in class and study poetry. . . . If anybody needed to study poetry, she needed to study mine. We played the Dozens for recreation, like white folks play Scrabble.
>
> In many ways, though, the Dozens is a mean game because what you try to do is totally destroy somebody else with words. It's the whole competition thing again, fighting each other. . . . Those that feel humiliated humiliate others. The real aim of the Dozens was to get a dude so mad that he'd cry or

get mad enough to fight. You'd say shit like, "Man, tell your mama to stop coming around my house all the time, I'm tired of fucking her and I think you should know that it ain't no accident you look like me." And it could go on for hours sometimes. Some of the best Dozens players were girls.[29]

Playing the dozens, for example, is one of the prime streetcorner contributers to school discipline problems.[30] I have observed youngsters playing the dozens in innumerable ways to test teachers. I have witnessed the dozens being played by students and ending in some horrible fights and classroom disruptions. At other times, it had no negative effects whatsoever because the teacher knew the game and how to handle it.

Realities 8 and 9 are two examples of the dozens being played in school. In Reality 8, the dozens was played with an almost deadly result. In Reality 9, it had very little negative effect because the student teacher upon whom it was being played had been taught about the dozens as part of his undergraduate teacher education program.

REALITY 8

The dean of boys was in his office talking with a student. Suddenly, there was loud screaming and cursing coming from the other end of the building. The noise grew louder. One of the seniors was running through the hall cursing, screaming, and crying. Students and teachers gave him a wide berth. In one hand he held a whisky bottle, jagged edges showing where the top had been broken off; in his other hand he held two four-foot sticks. "I'm gonna kill that mutha fucka who sounded on my moms," he screamed. He was seventeen and stood about six one.

The dean ran from his office and grappled with the youngster. When he realized that the youngster didn't really want to fight him, he grabbed the youngster's hand that held the bottle with both his hands, twisting and hitting it against the top of a bench back, forcing the youngster to drop the bottle. The youngster was then isolated in the dean's office and held for about twenty minutes until he gained control of himself.

After the youngster had calmed, he explained his action as retaliation against another boy who had said something about his mother.

REALITY 9

The student teacher was working his way around the room helping children with their work. It was an eighth grade social studies class. As he neared the back of the room, one of the bigger students said, "Hey, I saw your mother on Jefferson Avenue last night."[31] A number of the nearby students stopped working and listened.

"I don't play that dozens game," the student teacher responded.

"You know how to play the dozens?" the student said slowly with his eyes wide open.

The students nearby who had been listening chuckled. One of them pointed a finger at the student involved and said, "Hey, he got you."

Everyone went back to work—including the youngster who had asked the question.

Streetcorner behavior is expressed in many ways in addition to playing the dozens. Some of the additional streetcorner behavior is demonstrated through such verbal games as "signifying," "shuckin' and jivin'," and "ribbing." The streetcorner is also where some young blacks learn to "run a game," to act in a physical way to achieve something, to "put someone down," or to play on someone's fears or fantasies for personal, emotional, financial, or sexual gain, or for other kinds of exploitation.

Another aspect of streetcorner behavior that causes problems in school is the physicalness that can explode or be provoked into acting-out aggressive or sometimes violent acts. Claude Brown wrote of the street pressures that put many young blacks into the position of always having to act tough and crazy and to be willing to fight *from the jump.*

> They'd ask me, "You kick anybody's ass today?" I knew that they admired me for this, and I knew that I had to keep on doing it. This was the reputation I was making, and I had to keep living up to it every day that I came out of the house. Every day, there was a greater demand on me. I couldn't beat the same little boys every day. They got bigger and bigger. I had to get more vicious as the cats got bigger. When the bigger guy started messing with you, you couldn't hit them or give them a black eye or a bloody nose. You had to get a bottle or a stick or a knife. All the other cats out there on the streets expected this of me, and they gave me encouragement.[32]

> Fighting was the thing that people concentrated on . . . we all had to make our reputations in the neighborhood. Then we'd spend the rest of our lives living up to them. A man was respected on the basis of his reputation. The people in the neighborhood whom everybody looked up to were the cats who'd killed somebody. The little boys in the neighborhood whom the adults respected were the little boys who didn't let anybody mess with them.[33]

H. Rap Brown also wrote of growing up and always fighting to survive or to get ahead.

> Once I'd established my reputation, cats respected it. . . . If I went out of my neighborhood, though, it was another story. I'd be on somebody else's turf and would have to make it or take it over there. So there was always a lot of fighting and competition among the young brothers.[34]

If you acted like a child, you didn't survive and that's all there was to it. Hell, you be walking home from school and up comes some high school dude who'd jack you up and take the little dime your mama had given you to buy some candy with. So what'd you do? Jump some dude who was younger and littler than you and take his dime. And pretty soon you started carrying a razor blade, a switchblade or just a pocketful of rocks so you could protect yourself as a man. You had to if you were going to survive.[35]

According to Nathan Heard, there are few options of behavior available to someone who is black and poor and living in a black ghetto. "For in a black slum if one is not loud-mouthed and aggressive, then one is mean, a square or a punk.[36]

Additionally, for the highly mobile ghetto youngster, moving back and forth from one neighborhood to another takes on the additional problem of always having to prove yourself physically in each new neighborhood. Piri Thomas relates the problems he encountered as he moved again—back to 104th Street, Spanish Harlem: "You're torn up from your hard-won turf and brought into an 'I don't know you' block where every kid is some kind of enemy. Even when the block belongs to your own people, you are still an outsider who has to prove himself a down stud with heart.[37]

He went on to describe how he planned to fight his way into acceptance on the block where he knew he had to take on the leader of the local gang. "*I've got to beat him bad and yet not bad enough to take his prestige all away.*" They fought—they punched and bit. Then it was time to talk peace.

I had to back up my overtures of peace with strength. I hit him in the ribs, I rubbed my knuckles in his ear as we clinched. I tried again. "You deal good," I said.
Then it was over, almost as soon as it had started.
"You too," he muttered, pressuring out. And just like that, the fight was over. No words. We just separated; hands half up, half down. My heart pumped out. *You've established your rep. Move over, 104th Street. Lift your wings, I'm one of your baby chicks now.*[38]

Streetcorner behavior appears to be more highly developed in the western and northern urban areas. White racism in urban areas appears to perpetuate the streetcorner behavior and lifestyle, causing it to become such a destructive school force. Whereas members of most of America's earlier ethnic and religious groups, after initial overt bigotry, were allowed to move out and up economically and educationally, because of racism, this has not been the case with blacks. Hence, in frustration, many blacks have tended to direct their drives and energies into developing streetcorner behavior and lifestyle.

Furthermore, those who become involved in the streetcorner behavior would become at least aggressive salesmen, businessmen, or politicians under the conditions experienced by the earlier white ethnic and religious minorities. But to understand the depth of racism we must realize that earlier ethnic and religious minorities eventually controlled the crime in their neighborhoods. Blacks, however, have not even been allowed to achieve this degree of autonomy.[39] Hence, because of a lack of successful middle class adult models to emulate, too often the black child's model for emulation becomes the hustler, the pimp, the murphy man, the preacher, the athlete (only recently), and the bluesman. Tom Wolfe wrote:

> In the ghettos the brothers grew up with their own outlook, their own status system. Near the top of the heap was the pimp style. In all the commission reports and studies and syllabuses you won't see anything about the pimp style. And yet there it was. In areas like Hunters Point boys didn't grow up looking up to the man who had a solid job working for some company or for the city, because there weren't enough people who had such jobs. It seemed like nobody was going to make it *by working*, so the king was the man who made out best by *not working*, by *not* sitting all day under the Man's bitch box. And on the street the king was the pimp. . . . The pimp is the dude who wears the $150 Sly Stone-style vest and pants outfit from the haberdasheries on Poll and the $35 Lester Chambers-style four-inch-brim black beaver fedora and the thin nylon socks with the vertical stripes and drives the customized sun-roof Eldorado with the Jaguar radiator cap. The pimp was the aristocrat of the street hustle. [He] . . . might be into gambling, dealing drugs, dealing in stolen goods or almost anything else. They would truck around in the pimp style, too. Everything was the street hustle. When a boy was growing up, it might take the form of getting into gangs or into a crowd that used drugs. . . . The pimp style was a supercool style that was much admired or envied.[40]

Keil, in writing about lower class Negro life, adds to the importance of the hustler's life in the ghetto.

> On the basis of my own limited research into lower class life, I would go further, suggesting that the hustler (or underworld denizen) and the entertainer are ideal types representing two important value orientations for the lower class Negro and need not be distinguished from the lower class as a whole. Both the hustler and the entertainer are seen as men who are clever and talented enough to be financially well off without working.
>   Most ways of making good money without working are illegal, and Henry Williamson has explored many of the ways in *The Hustler*. The most striking thing about his autobiography is not the thoroughly criminal character of his life, from the white American point of view, but that within his culture he is very well adapted, successful (when out of jail), and even enjoys "doin' wrong."
>   . . . Aside from hustlers, entertainers, and rare individuals like Malcolm X (who began his career as hustler) or Reinhardt (the archetypal preacher-hustler in Ellison's *Invisible Man*), few Negroes wear their image in real com-

fort. Those black men who are comfortable in this sense become logical career models for those who aren't. If we are ever to understand what urban Negro culture is all about, we had best view entertainers and hustlers as culture heroes—integral parts of the whole—rather than as deviants or shadow figures.[41]

Even Malcolm X turned to hustling when his drives were thwarted. However, his later short-lived leadership of ghetto blacks reflected his brilliance that was earlier devoted to hustling. In his autobiography he wrote of the night he turned to hustling: On the night I had started on my way to becoming a Harlemite. I was going to become one of the most depraved parasitical hustlers among New York's eight million people—four million of whom work, and the other four million of whom live off them.[42]

John Horton interviewed twenty-five black males who had sporadic unsatisfactory work and unemployment. Many turned to hustling whenever necessary or possible.

When I asked the question, "When a dude needs bread, how does he get it?" the universal response was "the hustle." Hustling is, of course, illegitimate from society's viewpoint. Street people know it is illegal, but they view it in no way as immoral or wrong. It is justified by the necessity of surviving. As might be expected, the unemployed admitted that they hustled and went so far as to say that a dude could make it better on the street than on the job. "There is a lot of money on the street, and there are many ways of getting it" or simply, "This has always been my way of life." On the other hand, the employed, part-time hustlers, usually said, "A dude could make it better on the job than on the street." Their reasons for disapproving of hustling were not moral. Hustling meant trouble. "I don't hustle because there's no security. You eventually get busted." Others said there was not enough money on the street or that it was too difficult to "run a game" on people.

Nevertheless, hustling is the central street activity. It is the economic foundation for everyday life. Hustling and the fruit of hustling set the rhythm of social activities.[43]

According to L.A. Dennis, "hustling, as a profession, has been adopted by many black men as a way of life, a means of survival, requiring a degree from the streets."[44] Although hustlers have varied educational backgrounds, "they believe the only relevant education is that which is learned in the streets."[45] Hustling offers the black man who has his desires blocked the avenue for acquiring all the material accouterments and symbols of white middle class American success. Indeed, this can be accomplished by the full-time qualified hustler without having to " 'work,' that is work defined in terms of holding a regular legitimate job."[46]

Dennis also reported that the "qualified" hustler usually participates in two or more of the five major categories of hustling: loan sharking, playing the con game, pimping, drug sales, and the selling of stolen goods. Dennis also suggested that "hustling offers an oppressed man a chance to advance financially. It gives him an opportunity to feel and be important among his peers. The hustler must demonstrate his success through his material gains in order to remain on top in his profession."[47]

Certainly, some black youngsters who are exposed to the hustler will envision him as a role model to emulate. Therefore we can expect some of these young- sters to practice their hustling ability by running their hustling game on their teachers and fellow students. Indeed, the youngster who successfully hustles his teachers will gain the respect of his peers.

If you look at the streetcorner closely, there is not much difference between the desires of the streetcorner man and the desires of the middle class man; they both want basically the same things. The difference comes about in what each perceives as a logical road to travel to reach the objectives his subculture has set as a concept for "making it" or "gettin' ova."

Many streetcorner students share in the desires and actions of streetcorner men. Heard described Jackie spelling out where students of the streetcorner are at.

> "Do you know that if you gave any one of the people you see a hundred dollars, he wouldn't buy food if he was hungry? The whores'd give it to their pimps and the men'd go buy a suit and a pair of long shoes."
>
> ". . . Y'see, long shoes are success. They're the keen-toed design, right for kickin' a whore in the behind with when she comes up with short money or gits outta line. Some of the guys that got whores do kick 'em in the ass. The ordinary cat, though, is just satisfied to show off the shoes and quote the high price of 'em. It'd take too long to really run it down to you, man. Just say that long shoes means that the cat wearin' them is into somethin', er, if he ain't an outright pimp, he's doin' good, dig?"
>
> ". . . Like I was saying about the hundred bills: the suit and shoes would run about eighty bill, right? So he'd have twenty left, which his rent would take if he'd pay it all. But he wouldn't do that: he'd give the landlord maybe ten, then he'd bring the other ten to Howard Street and party with it. As for eatin'—he can always beg a sandwich somewhere. Anything that ain't showy don't impress him, see? He's got three main ambitions . . . one is to drink and look sharp; two is to fuck as much as he can; and three is to have as much dope as he wants without working' for the money to buy it with. In a word, his ambitions is to ball."[48]

The style and abilities required for success on the streetcorner and in hustling suggest that the participants are gifted. Accordingly, it is hypothesized that had not racism forced black males to develop and exploit this illegal outlet for the preservation of masculinity and ego, and the wherewithall for monetary reward, many of the players would have shown extreme giftedness in their pursuit of middle class, socially acceptable means for gaining economic success.

We could say that the high-pressure television or automobile salesman is really a hustler. The difference is that his method of hustling or his hustle is socially acceptable. The parallel development, to some extent, of black and white societies in the South supports this contention. Indeed, where black males have been allowed to earn economic rewards through middle class endeavors and rewards, a highly organized streetcorner society appears not to have developed; whereas in the urban areas of the North and West, a highly organized street-corner society has developed.

It is also hypothesized that those blacks who left the South may have had more drive and ambition than those blacks who remained. Consequently, when the black man's drive for middle class economic success within the overall north-ern communities was thwarted by racism, the streetcorner lifestyle evolved and developed as an outlet for these drives. Some support for this overall argument can be found in nine inmates earning high school diplomas and a black prisoner, Victor Taylor, earning an undergraduate degree *magna cum laude* at a U.S. peni-tentiary at Merion, Illinois.[49] He earned a normal four-year undergraduate degree in twenty-one months with cumulative grade point average of 4.89. Dr. Walter G. Robinson, Jr. claims that "there are Vic Taylors at every institution," and "there is an abundance of brain power sitting out there behind those walls."[50] Victor Taylor may be a typical example of the intelligent black man who be-comes thwarted by racism or imagined racism and turned to extreme street-corner behavior: crime.

> In his talk, Taylor recalled family fights, frequent separations and constant poverty. He also recalled the torment of integrating a posh Jesuit high school in Dallas, spending three years envying his classmates' convertibles while he rode public buses—and then quitting school.
>
> He recalled how he wanted to be a Navy pilot but was disqualified because of his slight color-blindness. Feeling that the Navy had deceived him, he and a buddy held up a Navy bank and were caught in Mexico. After four years in jail, he was paroled back to Dallas, where his peers "already had college degrees, wives and families, embarked on successful careers."
>
> Within 90 days he went on a robbing spree ("I guess I was trying to get myself killed"). The resultant jail term was so long that he tried to escape twice.[51]

Mezz Mezzrow, a white clarinetist jazzman and one of the few whites accepted by black jazzmen, described his feelings about the giftedness of streetcorner hip-sters. His reporting brought to life the street language and feelings of the 1930s and 1940s as an outlet for blocked dreams and desires.

> Once and for all, these smart Northern kids meant to show that they're not the ounce-brained tongue-tied stuttering Sambos of the blackface vaudeville routines, the Lazybones' of the comic strips, the Old Mose's of the Southern plantations. Historically, the hipster's lingo reverses the whole Uncle Tom attitude of the beaten-down Southern Negro. Uncle Tom believes he's good-for-nothing, shiftless, sub-human, just like the white bossman says he is. Uncle Tom scrapes and bows before his ofay 'superiors,' kills off all his self-respect and manliness, agrees that he's downtrodden because he doesn't

deserve any better. Well, the kids who grew up in Northern cities wouldn't have any more of that kneebending and kowtowing. They sure meant to stand up on their hind legs and let the world know they're as good as anybody else and won't take anybody's sass. They were smart, popping with talent, ready for any challenge. Some of them had creative abilities you could hardly match anywhere else. Once they tore off the soul-destroying straitjacket of Uncle Tomism, those talents and creative energies just busted out all over. These kids weren't schooled to use their gifts in any regular way. So their artistry and spirit romped out into their language. They began outlingoing the ofay linguists, talking up a specialized breeze that would blow right over the white man's head. It gave them more confidence in themselves.

Deny the Negro the culture of the land? O.K. He'll brew his own culture—on the street corner. Lock him out from the seats of higher learning? He pays it no nevermind—he'll dream up his own professional doubletalk, from the professions that *are* open to him, the professions of musician, entertainer, maid, butler, tap-dancer, handyman, reefer-pusher, gambler, counterman, porter, chauffeur, numbers racketeer, day laborer, pimp, stevedore. These boys I ran with at The Corner, breathing half-comic prayers at the Tree of Hope, they were the new sophisticates of the race, the jivers, the sweet-talkers, the jawblockers. They spouted at each other like soldiers sharpening their bayonets—what they were sharpening, in all this verbal horseplay, was their wits, the only weapons they had. Their sophistication didn't come out of moldy books and dirty colleges. It came from opening their eyes wide and gunning the world hard. Soon as you stop bowing your head low and resting your timid, humble eyes on the ground; soon as you straighten your spine and look the world right in the eye, you dig plenty. . . . Their hipness, I could see, bubbled up out of the brute scramble and sweet living. If it came out a little too raw and strong for your stomach, that's because you been used to a more refined diet. You didn't come of age on the welfare, snagging butts out of the gutter. You can afford the luxury of being a little delicate, friend.

You know who they were, all these fat-talking kids with their four-dimensional surrealist patter? I found out they were the cream of the race—the professionals of Harlem who never got within reaching distance of a white collar. They were the razor-witted doctors without M.D.'s, lawyers who never had a shingle to hang out, financiers without penny one in their pokes, political leaders without a party, diplomatless professors, and scientists minus a laboratory. They held their office-hours and made their speeches on The Corner. There they wrote prose poems, painted their word pictures. They were the genius of their people, always on their toes, never missing a trick, asking no favors and taking no guff, not looking for trouble but solid ready for it. Spawned in a social vacuum and hung up in mid-air, they were beginning to build their own culture. Their language was a declaration of independence.[52]

In reading this section on streetcorner behavior in the schools, the reader must understand that we are talking about a percentage of students. Exactly how many we do not know, although estimates by inner city black and white school personnel with three or more years of experience in inner city schools put the number at 60 percent. I would put the number at 10 percent or less.

However, we must be realistic and understand that if a teacher has only two or three youngsters in a class who exhibit this behavior and adhere to its standards, the teacher may be in trouble if he or she cannot cope with the testing techniques. When this happens and the teacher starts to panic, other students join in playing the disruptive game, and no one in the class learns. The teacher becomes involved in discipline only. Sadly, it is almost a self-destructive action on the part of black youngsters. What we are doing is allowing black schoolchildren to use their creativeness to destroy themselves and one another. It is the same destructiveness that H. Rap Brown wrote about when he said, "It's one of the things that keeps us fighting ourselves instead of the enemy. Black people have always been ready to shoot and cut each other up. The weekend is always wartime in the Black community. Every week when Friday rolls around, you know that somebody is goin' to get killed before church time Sunday morning.[53]

2a. The Urban, Suburban, and Rural Youngsters Who Are Equivalent to the Inner City Streetcorner Youngster

In most schools in the United States, as in Elmtown, students are treated differently depending upon where they live, their parent's income or position, or even how their parents dress. Those students treated negatively usually are poor, and their experiences, style, behavior, dress, speech, and sexuality do not fit the staff's class mold.

These urban, suburban, and rural youngsters, most often, however, are white, and many of the boys have picked up on some of the black streetcorner behavior. In addition, these boys are, just as is the black inner city streetcorner youngster, most often disciplined, most often suspended, most often expelled, or most often placed in special education or vocational education programs.

Such boys dress differently from the preppies in L.L. Bean or other status brands of clothing. The non-yavis boys usually wear jeans,[54] wide leather belts with big buckles, the name and emblem of a hard rock group printed on their dark T-shirts, leather studded bracelets and unlaced work boots, and biker or trucker wallets.

The preppie girls are usually dressed in button-down shirts, turtleneck shirts under crew neck sweaters and vests. Their jean skirts (with pleats and side vents) or jeans (with pleats) now sport stripes and patterns. Their shoes are flats, boots, topsiders, boat shoes, or Jelly Bean shoes.

The non-yavis girls, meanwhile, are usually bra-less wearing strands of beads hanging from their low-cut blouse fronts, leather jeans and vests, long dangling ear rings, and high heeled and pointed boots.

Additionally, these youngsters are isolated further from the main stream of students through assigned names. For example, Hollingshead, in his study of Elmtown found seven groups of students that were combined into three "reputational categories": 1) the Elite, 2) the Good Kids, and 3) the Grubby Gang.[55]

The Elite group consisted of those students involved in extracurricular student activities, church work, social affairs, or youth groups. They saw themselves as leaders, and the adult leaders, the teachers, and the ministers relied on them for helping to form and promote organized adolescent activities.

The Good Kids came to school and, though they did their work, they did not distinguish themselves with either notoriety or glory. This category consisted of two-thirds of the students.

The Grubby Gang were set off from the other students for such reasons as personality traits, unfortunate family connections, living in the wrong part of town, or a lack of cooperation with teachers. Grubbies were considered "nobodies" by nongrubbies. Also, nongrubbies considered grubbies poorly groomed, unclean, troublemakers without any interest in school affairs. Many supposedly were uncooperative and sassy school skippers and cheaters. Also, some of the girls were considered grubbies because they broke the school's sex taboo.[56]

In a suburban school near Buffalo, New York, according to students, there are three categories of students: (1) Rats—Sewer Rats or Burn Outs, (2) Preps or Heads, and (3) Jocks. The Rats use drugs and usually are representative of the suburban and rural poor, minorities, or youngsters alienated from their middle class parents. They are often placed in special programs and usually do not graduate. The Preppies wear all brand name clothes (i.e., Adidas, Izod, Polo, OP, L. L. Bean) and study a lot. The Jocks are all sports minded.

Recently, three books by novelist Susan E. Hinton were produced as movies: *Tex, The Outsiders*, and *Rumble Fish*. These books and the resulting movies highlighted the tensions and fights between groups of teenagers—the underprivileged "greasers" and the affluent "Socs."[57]

Greasers were further publicized by the Fonz and the "Hey there all you greasers. It's time for Sha Na Na," greeting by Bowzer. The movie *Suburbia* depicted "a bunch of young dropouts who call themselves 'The Rejected' or, for short, the TR's."[58] On the higher education level, the competition and feelings between the "Cutters" and the college kids in the movie *Breaking Away* will be recalled.[59] Also, most television viewers will remember Cotter's "Sweathogs."

Since the first edition of *Ribbin'*, while speaking throughout the United States and Canada, I collected the following names designating those youngsters not accepted into the mainstream of our schools and often in trouble. Some of the reputational categories or names by which they are known may have changed or been replaced by another name. They might also be very specific in describing a place where they live or a special program they are in. However, most readers will recognize some of the names from their high school days.

Animals, Baits, BAS (BOCES Animals), Bo Bos, Bubas, Burn Outs, Corner Kids, Derelicts, Dirts, Drakes, Dregs, Druggies, Fifties, Fog Heads, Freaks, Gear

Heads, Gingerillos, Graters, Grave Yard Kids, Greasers, Grits, Hard Kids, Hard Guys, Hard Rocks, Hood Hill Kids, JDs, Lint Heads, Hitters, Jitterbugs, Motor Heads, Muckers, Odd Squad, Project Kids, Pukes, Red Necks, Resource Room Kids, Rocks, Rumps, Scrapple Hundred, Scruffs, Surfs, Potter Rodents, Techies, Torquers, Toughs, Vegees, Vokies, Wagon Burners, Wet Backs, and Wrenches.

3. Youngsters Who Are Emotionally Handicapped, Physically Handicapped, or Both

Prior to Public Law 94-142: The Education for All Handicapped Children Act, it was impossible to carry out accurate research on the numbers of handicapped children in the U.S. Public Law 94-142, however, declared that there were more than 8 million handicapped children in the United States, and set a cap of 12 percent of all children aged five to 17 which states could count for federal reimbursement.

Since the required reporting of state Child Find data for the 1976-77 school year as a result of Public Law 94-142, the handicapped children received special education services has risen each year since the first child count in 1976-77. The numbers of children receiving special services, however, have begun to level off and have never reached the 12 percent cap.

According to the act, participating states have been required to provide all handicapped children with a free and appropriate public education since 1980. Despite the law, there still are some law suits concerning compliance.

In 1976-77 there were 3,708,588 handicapped children receiving services under Public Law 94-142 and Public Law 89-313 of a total public school enrollment of 44,317,000 for a total of 8.37 percent.[60] The 1982-83 total was 4,298,327 served which was an increase of 65,045 over the previous school year, and 16 percent since 1976-77. The number of handicapped children served in proportion to the number of children enrolled in preschool through 12th grade rose from 10.47 percent in 1981-82 to 10.76 percent in 1982-83.[61]

There still were variations in the number of children served within the different handicapping categories. Large increases were reported for the learning disabled and the emotionally disturbed but there were decreases in the number of children served in most other categories.

There were 1,627,344 learning disabled children served in 1981-82, and 1,745,871 served in 1982-83. These numbers represented 4.3 percent of the school-age enrollment and more than 40 percent of all the children receiving special education services. The learning disabled population since 1976-77 has grown by 948,658 children, for an increase of 119 percent.[62]

Some of the reasons for this increase of learning disabled children being served include social acceptability, liberal eligibility criteria, and a lack of general education alternatives for children who experience problems in regular classes. Furthermore, 68 percent of the increase in learning disabled children being served between 1981-82 and 1982-83 came from New York State. Two reasons were suggested for the increase. First, a definitional change brought children who had been listed as neurologically impaired and counted as health impaired into the learning disabled category. Second, many of the new children in special education in New York City were classified as learning disabled.[63]

The emotionally disturbed was the next group of handicapped children that increased noticeably between 1981–82 and 1982–83. This group increased by 3.4 percent or from 341,786 to 353,431. This increase was attributed to the school's efforts to serve this population formerly served by non-school agencies.[64]

It would be interesting to see the racial or ethnic breakdowns of the children served in each of the handicapping areas. An educated guess would find black, poor, and minority children in programs for the retarded and the emotionally disturbed, and white children and the children of influential blacks in programs for the learning disabled.

Of course, the point raised a number of times already is whether middle class personnel unfamiliar with streetcorner behavior can accurately diagnose, or differentiate, streetcorner behavior from either emotionally disturbed, socially maladjusted, or mentally retarded behavior—particularly the borderline child's behavior.

Differentiating between Streetcorner Behavior and Emotionally Handicapped Behavior. The third area to be considered is the question of whether school personnel who were brought up and educated in a racist and ethnocentric environment and are unfamiliar with streetcorner behavior can diagnose accurately and differentiate between streetcorner behavior and emotionally handicapped or retarded behavior.

Many of the black youngsters I became friendly with in the New York City "600" schools were either big and tough or small and tough. All were wise in the ways of the streets. When these youngsters were with teachers who were not physically afraid of them, they generally behaved well and also learned their school skills. This is interesting when you consider that so many of these youngsters had been assigned to the "600" schools for overt acts of verbal or physical aggression and assaults against teachers. However, when you understand streetcorner behavior and the workings and conditioning of racism and ethnocentrism, you observe incidents precipitated every day. You see the black youngster involved being penalized for acting in a streetcorner way toward a teacher, an administrator, other school personnel, or even a fellow student. In school, most often the youngster's streetcorner behavior draws a reaction from school personnel that is different from the reaction it would draw in the street. Very often, the school personnel overreact or underreact because of factors varying from fear, to racism, to ethnocentrism, to a lack of knowledge, to a lack of understanding, to complete panic. Often, one incident leads to another and a youngster soon develops a "loser" syndrome, because of being punished out of proportion to the supposed misdeed. I refer to this as the Emmett Till syndrome.[65]

What is so sad is that he should have been so severely punished for the first negative act. In so many cases, if the teacher had known how to cope positively with his actions, he would not have been reported in the first place. The following anecdotes will provide the reader with some illustrations.

REALITY 10

This incident took place in a northern inner city elementary school. Those involved included a fifth-grade black male student and an exceptionally attractive white female teacher, a southerner who had resided in the North only a few years. She was a personable young teacher and spoke with a decided southern drawl. A number of the youngsters recognized her southern dialect and talked with her about where she came from and developed a good relationship with her.

One day as she was walking in the hall, one of the youngsters she was friendly with called to her, "Hi, Country," and she waved back to him smiling.

The principal heard the youngster call out, "Hi, Country," and suspended him from school. The teacher found out about the suspension and interceded to clear the case. However, not all children are this lucky.

The point here is that the expression "country" is used to refer to someone who is newly arrived in the city.[66] It is not necessarily an insulting or threatening term. The term often is used as a kidding term. In this incident, it was used with feeling and affection. The principal, lacking an understanding of the street-corner lifestyle and language of his pupils, saw this friendly exchange as some form of insult that deserved punishment.

The following background information is provided to give the reader some insight into Reality 11.

George is a junior high youngster who runs in the streets. In the streets he has learned that physical behavior has brought him and his friends rewards. George is also quite involved in using females in the way streetcorner men use them. According to Elliot Liebow, the streetcorner man views himself as an economic and sexual exploiter and user of women. "In a world where sexual conquest is one of the few ways in which one can prove one's masculinity, the man who does not make capital of his relationship with a woman is that much less a man.[67]

Additionally, according to Liebow, the streetcorner man is often reinforced for acting physically and forcefully with women.

The husband who sometimes responds to this testing and challenging by slapping his wife's face or putting his fist in her mouth is frequently surprised at the satisfactory results. . . . Leroy . . . was going home to see what "Mouth" (Charlene) wanted. She probably wanted a whipping, he said; she seems to beg him to beat her. Afterwards, she's "tame as a baby, sweet as she can be. . . ."

For Charlene, like Lorena, wanted some tangible evidence that her husband cared about her, about them as a family, and that he was willing to fight to establish and protect his (nominal) status as head of the family. She openly envied Shirley who, when things were going tolerably well for her and Richard, took pleasure in boasting to Charlene, Lorena and other women that Richard pushed her around, insisted she stay off the street, and enforced the rule that she be up early every morning, dress the children and clean the house. For evidence of this kind of concern, Charlene would gladly pay the price of a slap in the face or a pushing around.[68]

Furthermore, Liebow reported that the streetcorner man was always ready to look elsewhere for sexual gratification, even though he might already have a good sexual relationship with a willing partner, be it his wife or someone else.

One of the most widespread and strongly supported views the men have of themselves and others is that men are, by nature, not monogamous; that no man can be satisfied with only one woman at a time. This view holds that, quite apart from his desire to exploit women, the man seeks them out because it is his nature to do so. This "nature" that shapes his sex life, however, is not human nature but rather an animality which the human overlay cannot quite cover. The man who has a wife or other woman continues to seek out others because he has too much "dog" in him.[69]

With this background suggested as George's frame of reference, we should look at the reporting of Reality 11. Before we do this, however, one further point dealing with discipline. This point relates to the effects of conditioning and will be discussed in greater detail in Chapter 9.

A former Green Beret killed his friend in a barroom brawl where "dazed and thinking he had just killed an attacking Viet Cong, was stripping the body so that it could not be rigged with booby traps."[70] The veteran was eventually acquitted. His acquittal was based on the testimony primarily of Harvard Sociologist Charles Levy, who reported on interviews with returning combat veterans who experience a "kind of psychological disorientation . . . after returning from Southeast Asia."[71] Levy reported that "he discovered a common tendency on the part of his subjects to carry into civilian life the unbridled violence that served them well in combat. They have learned to react violently, spontaneously and with premeditation . . . it's a situation that keeps them alive over there but gets them into prison back here."[72]

Levy also found that often veterans learned to "admire the courage and skill of the Communists, and often vent their anger against their South Vietnamese comrades, whom they see as inept, and against their own officers, sometimes brutally injuring or killing them." Then, when discharged and home, "some of the veterans still treated allies like enemies. Relatives and friends often took the place of officers and South Vietnamese as targets for misdirected hostility." Levy conceded that some of his veterans were probably violent before they entered the armed forces. However, he found that their violence after returning "has no boundaries."[73]

What is being suggested is that there are some behavioral similarities between these veterans and some inner city schoolchildren. Many of the schoolchildren are conditioned to act in certain physical, aggressive, and sexual ways. They are also used to a strong physical control. Their behavior has also been conditioned and reinforced to act this way. Therefore, when such youngsters come to school and their teachers do not act in the way they expect a man or woman to act, they are disoriented and do not understand the behavior. If the situation becomes sticky or crisis, most often they will revert to their streetcorner behavior; they act out in the way they have been conditioned to act. This should be kept in mind when reading Reality 11 and the rest of this book.

REALITY 11

School has just ended. George is sitting on the steps in the school running a strong rap with a number of girls. A female teacher comes down the steps and hears him say, "How about a kiss, baby?"[74]

The teacher's face reddens and she slaps his face. He, in turn, kicks her backside. She is white; he is black.

Investigation reveals that the teacher was a good teacher who had a rough week. She had accidently been knocked down by a running student while she was walking in the hall and experienced a few other unsettling incidents. George, for his part, said he was talking to one of the girls.

George, who had had a reasonably good school record, was acting in typical street fashion for which, we must realize, he has been reinforced with the street rewards he and his peers value. The teacher, because she had had a rough week, acted the way her background had taught her to act. The principal, knowing the need to support teachers, did what he felt he had to do—suspend the youngster. Assault charges against the youngster were drawn up, too. At the last moment, however, the teacher decided not to sign the charges.

If the teacher had not been out of sorts, she could have parried his repartee and no one would have considered it an incident worth much more than talking about in the lunch room or in some graduate course, if at all.

This may not excuse the youngster's asking, "How about a kiss?" loud enough for the teacher to hear, which was what he probably intended. However, it must be understood that from his frame of reference, it was not meant as a threat but more likely a form of compliment.

Actually, if the female teacher were a "scab" or a "fish" the student probably would have ignored her. This teacher, however, was a "phat tip." By making a big play in front of the girls, he was paying her a compliment.[75]

Realities 12, 13, and 14 will provide the reader with insight into how three adult white males reacted to a reasonably similar incident. The actions of the youths in these incidents are typical of the way streetcorner youngsters may physically test a new teacher or almost anyone who is unknown to them—a test of the machismo of someone he knows or who he may think is weak. The action reflects the streetcorner, where "might makes right" and where you must put the other person down first or he will put you down.

REALITY 12

A new teacher was walking the hall on his way to his room from lunch. As he turned a corner, two students came toward him. When the student closest to him was about a foot from him, he suddenly reached out and put his hand against the wall. The teacher said, "Hey, what are you trying to do?" The student responded by keeping his hand on the wall and leering at the teacher.

The teacher, not sure of what was happening except that he felt uncomfortable and fearful, was unsure as to whether he should bend and walk under the outstretched arm or walk around both boys. He opted to go under the boy's arm (actually I have observed teachers doing both); whereupon, teacher and students went on their way.

The next time the boys saw the teacher, they greeted him with, "Hi, faggot." Before too long, most of the school population called the teacher Mr. Faggot rather than by his proper name. He soon left the school after too many classroom problems.

Before this teacher transferred, he told everyone in the school that he did not come here to hit kids. When asked, "Who do you see hitting kids?" he could not name anyone. What he was saying was that he was afraid physically of the students.

Because the teacher reacted improperly, a number of negative behaviors were reinforced for the teacher and the two students. The teacher's and students' negative feelings about each other were reinforced; all black kids are "animals" and all whites are "faggots." The students were allowed to continue learning how to manipulate their environment or life space both negatively and physically. They were allowed to use their creative powers to contribute to their own destruction. When the teacher reacted the way he did, he reinforced the youngsters' manipulative behavior, and the youngsters, observing the incident, saw this behavior reinforced.

REALITY 13

This incident started out about the same as Reality 12. However, when the teacher asked what they were doing and they continued to laugh and leer, the teacher panicked. He hit the youngster who had his arm against the wall. This youngster, in turn, punched the teacher in the face. The incident resulted in the student's being suspended. Of course, it was never brought out that the teacher hit the youngster first. As in Reality 12 both the teacher's and the student's negative feeling about one another and how one is supposed to act were reinforced.

REALITY 14

This example is similar to Realities 12 and 13 except that the teacher was more experienced and reacted differently. An experienced inner city school teacher was walking in the hall of a junior high school. As he walked, six students came toward him. The first youngster in line moved over close to the wall to block the teacher's path. He smiled, grabbed the youngster's outstretched arm while pressing his thumb into the pressure point, moving him to the side out of the way, and in a loud clear voice said, "Excuse me," while smiling and walking on.

The biggest student in the group observing this incident saw that the teacher's "game" was the stronger and joined his side. He indicated this by saying to his friend so that everyone could hear, "Hey Jiiim, what you tryin' to do to that man? You tryin' to make him walk around you?" With that everyone laughed and continued on his respective way.

In this incident neither the youngsters' nor the teacher's negative feelings about each other were reinforced. Additionally, the students did not see any positive reinforcement for their friend's behavior, and the student involved was not allowed to use his creativity to destroy himself. The situation was handled without any negative or punitive aggression, violence, or reporting of the student.

Actually, this youngster is now ready to listen to this adult because the adult gained his respect for the way he carried himself in the streetcorner machismo competition. Additionally, the youngster's negative behavior was stopped in a way that did not make him lose face. The student, therefore, does not have the need to retaliate with an even more aggressive act.

Another point must be mentioned but cannot be explored in depth here. This is the type of testing that teachers in inner city schools are being subjected to. To some extent, this testing has reached the point at which it may be in violation of the civil rights of teachers and of the students whose education is being interrupted by the resulting disruption.

Because teachers are being tested so physically and because they are unprepared to deal with it, we have an unhealthy teaching-learning environment. Do we blame streetcorner youngsters for testing the way they do? Or do we blame the teachers for their inability to pass the tests the students impose on them? This question is discussed further in Chapter 9.

Black and white school personnel with three or more years of teaching in inner city schools estimated that 18 percent of their students are emotionally or physically handicapped.

4. Youngsters Who Are Entertainment and Sports World Orientated and Youngsters Who Are Religious or Politicized

Youngsters who are entertainment and sports world orientated are a new category who have, to a large extent, supplanted the religious and politicized students. In most cases, the entertainment- and sports-minded groups have not caused many real school problems.

These students look to achieve overnight money and prestige in the manner of Eddie Murphy, Michael Jackson, Darrel Strawberry, or Herschel Walker; they see neither education nor time as necessary to their achieving monetary and material rewards.

Usually, in school the sports-minded youngsters dress in Izod polo shirts; the entertainment-oriented youngsters dress to resemble their entertainment idol. In class, in the halls, and anywhere else in or around school, the entertainment-oriented youngsters can be observed walking, dancing, or singing with their Walkmans hooked up and playing or their box blasting away. This behavior often gets them in trouble. Teachers and administrators often use the word "temerity" to describe the way the entertainment youngsters behave in school.

Punk rock appears to have spawned a punk student group that is sometimes in trouble in schools. These youngsters do not appear to fit into any existing student group. The punk youngsters appear to be from upper and middle-class families, to be bright and articulate, and many relating to their parents better than to their teachers and administrators.

The youngsters who are religious or politicized do not appear to have as much of an effect upon the average inner city school today as they did ten to fifteen years ago. Many of their earlier requests and demands have been met or are no longer important. However, in some schools, these youngsters are involved in some school problems. Most often, though, it is a school in an area where time has finally caught up. Consequently, only brief mention will be made of those students who were religious or politicized and were involved in school problems in the 1960s and 1970s. The reader who wishes to know more about these youngsters should research notes 76 through 81 in this chapter and pages 54 through 63 of the first edition.

The youngsters who are or were religious or politicized fell into any of at least five categories. The first two categories are those who may have belonged to the Black Panthers or the Black Muslims. The third category included youngsters who may have acted politically and had some formal political or religious affiliation other than the Black Panthers or the Black Muslims. The fourth category consisted of those youngsters who were regular churchgoers. And the fifth category included those youngsters who were organizationally uncommitted but militant and antagonistic to whites or to the system.

All five groups of students would affect the school's teaching and learning in many ways. The first three groups—Black Panthers, Black Muslims, and affiliated politicized students—may have affected the school through similar types of actions. They may even have received assistance in the form of political expertise and advice, strikers, and propaganda, fliers from outside sources such as white college, or high school, Third World, radical, or Communist students.

The fourth group of students, conventional churchgoers, may have affected the teaching and learning in a completely different way. They may have become the butt of jokes, pranks, and physical abuse because of their middle class behavior, dress, and actions. Hence, they may have caused problems not because of any particular overt actions but rather as targets for the acting out of the frustrations of others. Similarly, some youngsters may have been bullied because their parents belong to the Jehovah's Witnesses, Seventh-Day Adventists, or other religious groups that support middle class lifestyles.

Elenore Lester, in discussing the works of J.E. Franklin and Ed Bullins, wrote of the frustration, helplessness, and self-hate that makes ghetto "hoods" and others act out against symbols of upward mobility. "The implicit concept in . . . Ed Bullins' play, *Clara's Ole Man*, for example, . . . typically makes the young college man in a suit the victim of a brutal attack by young hoodlums who view his gentle manners, school attendance and fondness for poetry as symptoms of Uncle Tomism."[76]

The first three groups affected some schools in any number of ways. Youngsters who were Black Muslims may have wanted soul food served in the school's cafeteria or alternative meals made available whenever pork was served. They may have wanted to wear a fez in school or refused to stand and salute the flag. They may have also wanted the school closed to commemorate the birthday of the Reverend Martin Luther King, Jr. or other black leaders. Interestingly, in many areas of the country, schools, public offices, and public institutions are now closed to commemorate his birthday. Others may have organized protests to compel the establishment of black studies programs or demand that a teacher they considered racist be fired despite his or her tenure.

Additionally, certain nonaggressive acts may have been construed as threatening by unknowing white personnel. For example, the black student's pride in his or her blackness may, of itself, have frightened and continue to frighten many white and middle class black suburban school personnel who look upon Afros, dashikis, and other black styles as signs of aggression against them. In many forms, this problem continues.

This interpretation of nonovert acts as being aggressive, threatening, and frightening also takes place outside of school. In one example, a black stewardess with United Airlines lost her job because she refused to cut her Afro. According to *Newsweek*, "Some whites fearfully see Afro hair-do's . . . as a symbol of anger and rebellion. But United says it was simply a matter of enforcing the airline's traditional standards of good grooming." [77]

More recently, Afros have become shorter, more blacks are processing their hair again, and more blacks are corn-rowing or braiding their hair. Some readers will recall Bo Derek's braided version in the movie *10*.[78] Interestingly, what was sexually attractive on a white beauty was considered "inappropriate" for a black television reporter.

> San Francisco (AP) — Reporter Dorothy Reed returned to work Tuesday at KGO-TV wearing a modified cornrow hairstyle — a style that caused her to be suspended for two weeks.
>
> After public protests and intervention by Ms. Reed's union, the ABC-owned station agreed to reinstate Ms. Reed, who is black and who charged racism was involved the action. . . .
>
> Jim Osborn, general manager of the station, had said the braided style was "inappropriate" for an on-air reporter and that racism was not involved.
>
> A station spokesman said a "compromise" had been reached. Ms. Reed's new style doesn't have colored beads interwoven into the ends of the braids.[79]

In some schools, youngsters wished to fly the red, black, and green flag of the Republic of New Africa alongside of or in place of the flag of the United States on the stage, in classrooms, in the halls, or on the school's main flagpole. Of course, readers must also remember that many other black and white teachers and students have also been involved in protests concerning saluting or standing for the Pledge of Allegiance as well as singing the "Star Spangled Banner." These acts are not a black militant phenomenon.[80]

Sometimes, even where administrative and teaching decisions were sound, outside-of-school problems may have impacted negatively upon the school. For example, many community organizations in inner city areas went through internal schisms that often resulted in confrontations and violence.[81] A school located in a large inner city area may have had students whose families, relatives, or friends were involved with opposing factions fighting for control of the various community organizations, and many of these students brought these community conflicts into the school. These problems involving outside-of-school organizations, therefore, sometimes affected the school's teaching and learning despite sound educational policy.

The last and most important point related to this classification of behavior is that the politicized and religious students often used streetcorner behavior to achieve their goals. The behavior of black militant adult groups was not lost on the school-aged youngsters; they had learned their lessons well. More about this in Chapter 6.

The fifth and last category of politicized or religious youngster is the one who was organizationally uncommitted but militant and contemptuous of whites or less militant blacks. These youngsters did not belong to any religious, politicized, or civil rights group. They were ready, nevertheless, to take on any administrator or teacher whom they felt was racist, often feeling that all whites were racist until they had proved they were not. Quite often, these youngsters came from intact homes where:

1. Parents may have been active in a militant organization that was contesting the white political structure openly.
2. They may have been affected by the step-by-step advance of the civil rights movement from legal cases, to sit-ins, to marches, to street confrontations.
3. They may have become resentful of their middle class parents whom they felt had denied their black heritage by playing "the man's" game.
4. Their middle class parents had just discovered their blackness and were attempting to make amends by a hatred of whites, which they passed on to their children.
5. Their parents, who always looked negatively at their blackness or never expressed their true feelings about racism, had begun vicariously to relive their lives through his acting out against the schools and the system.

CONCERNING MIDDLE CLASS VALUES
AND BEHAVIOR

Whenever I present my four classifications of student behavior in inner city class-rooms to university students or to teachers, there are always some who accuse me of making a value judgment that middle class behavior is more desirable than lower class behavior. They also say that the trouble has been that we have been forcing middle class values down the throats of black kids.

When these accusations are made, I plead *nolo contendere* to the charge that middle class behavior and values are more desirable than are lower class behavior and values and ask my accusers to list the negative aspects of middle class life or values that they are referring to. Their response usually refers to the supposed middle class drive to accumulate money and the subsequent purchase of material goods.

I then remind everyone that the poor black men and women whose ghetto existence they are romanticizing desire all the material items the middle class talk about denying while wallowing in them. After all, if they have these items, why deny them to the poor? Additionally, ghetto residents lead fearful lives trying to keep their children free from drugs and from becoming victims of violence. If ghetto life is so exemplary, why are we so involved in trying to improve the conditions of the poor or disadvantaged?

These students and teachers then figure they can get me by asking me to list the middle class values or skills that I think are so good. Whereupon, I list or call off such salable skills and values as learning how to read so that one can read a street sign to get off a bus and get to work, or to read street signs and numbers to make a delivery, or to be able to read a plan or blueprint, or to be able to read well enough to advance to a better job. I also mention getting to know how to use an alarm clock to get up to go to work or learning how to use a bank account to save money.

These students and teachers then respond with, "Then maybe we ought to change the system. Why should we continue to perpetuate this system?" To which I suggest, "Good idea, but *you* change the system. Don't use black youngsters to change your system. It sounds to me as though you are trying to keep them from getting the material things you have."

It is amazing how many teachers with middle class skills, bank accounts, and even job tenure, want to use black youngsters to change the system instead of teaching them how to read, write, and do mathematics so that they can take advantage of the good of the system. Once inner city youngsters grow into adulthood knowing how to read, write, and do arithmetic, they have the option to do as they please with their salable skills. It is the teachers' job to provide them with these skills.

To get back to the charge that we have been forcing middle class values down the throats of black kids, I would suggest that these young people are confusing the plight of inner city black students with their conflicts of growing up in a family amidst an abundance of material goods without ever having had to assume any responsibility. What they are really talking about is racism that has neither taught nor allowed that black is also beautiful and that blacks should be prideful too.

In actuality, these radical students and teachers are acting in a racist way toward the black children they profess to help. They are doing this by not pressing black children to learn, to read, to write, to do math, to do homework, and to study. In spite of their paternalistic rhetoric, they are saying that black youngsters really are slower than whites and therefore we don't have to pressure them to learn and do all the academic things we expect from middle class white youngsters.

Many of these white college students and teachers—the offspring of materially dominated, middle and upper class homes—are still caught up in the dilemma of growing and maturing into adulthood, and tend to take the stance that (1) glorifies and romanticizes the pimps, the whores, the hustlers, and the abject proverty of ghetto blacks and rural poor; (2) talks of doing away with poverty and racism; and (3) attacks *all aspects* of middle class life while unable to verbalize any comprehensive meaning of middle class life, all while they indulge themselves in academic lives of some study, summers abroad, unlimited hi-fi equipment, and automobiles that their parents' middle class behavior has provided for them. Or they might have the opportunity to "drop out" in England or somewhere else for a year or two "to find oneself" rather than going to work, to school, or to the armed forces. The new teacher frequently sports a new car, and Christmas, Easter, and summer vacations based on the pay scales secured by the establishment they condemn.

Sadly, many of these "idealistic" or "unhappy" students or teachers cannot separate their insecurities and feelings from their teaching role, and they try to spread these insecurities and conflicts to their students, who continue to pay the bills long after they have gone on to graduate school, to write a book about their experiences, or to something else. Unquestionably, older teachers, too, have these problems. In addition, some younger professors and teachers themselves, caught up in their own conflicts and uncertainties, rhetorically feed their students' insecurities.

What is needed are more professors and educators who are understanding, empathic, warm adults willing to help young people into adulthood with some of their idealism still intact. This responsibility and need was pinpointed in Richard Schickel's review of *The Last Picture Show.*

> [W]hat the picture says, ever so softly and ever so intelligently, is that the way out of adolescence that always carries with it the threat of becoming perpetual is through decent connections with those few adults who, whatever their other problems, have at least made this journey successfully and are willing to show and tell what it's like. The movie says what we all know—that too few adults are willing to perform these vital initiatory functions—but it adds a point that, in our present romanticizing of rebellious youth, we often forget that a youth has to reach out to them, make known in some civil way his pain and need.[82]

SUMMARY

Almost all schoolchildren challenge their teachers. However, when some youngsters challenge their teachers with streetcorner behavior, most school personnel become frightened and react improperly. Most often, this improper reaction to their students' testing escalates a testing game into ongoing disorder and disruption. The resulting disruption and disorder prevents youngsters from learning as much as they are capable of learning, if anything at all.

Whether schoolchildren should be condemned for their testing games that result in disorder, or whether the educational staff should be condemned for allowing this state of affairs to continue, is questioned. One is inclined to ask, Since educators are the adults, when will they take the first real step to solve the problem? The Emmett Till syndrome of negatively marking and stigmatizing youngsters for small misdeeds continues to be perpetuated, and the destruction and waste of additional humans is continued.

Educators have not solved the problem of educating more lower class, black, or minority children because neither they nor the professors have come close to understanding what is causing this problem. Sadly, most kindergarten through twelfth grade and university educators have neither an understanding nor appreciation of lower class black male social behavior. Too often, where there is some knowledge, the response is either contempt or, at the other extreme, romantic idealization. They are not aware that the behaviors affecting every aspect of inner city school life and now so much of suburban and rural school life are derived from the streetcorner. Consequently, until they learn to understand these informal rules and regulations governing streetcorner behavior and learn to use them for educational change and advantage, they will not be able to educate more black, poor, or minority children.

The discussion in this chapter—the game of teaching and learning in our schools as related to the manner in which the three concerns of streetcorner behavior are played out in the classroom through at least four categories of student behavior—should not be thought to suggest that all school personnel must play the game by streetcorner rules.

Just as each teacher should develop his or her teaching style based on his or her personality, so should each teacher relate his or her personality to the playing of streetcorner games. Those who can play and teach that way, may; those who cannot play and teach that way should not. All teachers, however, must become aware of and learn the rules and regulations of the games they are involved in every day in their schools. If this can be accomplished, school personnel might not be so upset by their students' actions. And, hopefully, we could then increase the teaching and learning in our schools.

My reporting of only the negative aspects of urban lower class black youths is done for a reason. However, readers must be reminded again that there are many black youngsters with middle class behavior in inner city, suburban and rural classrooms. These youngsters, by and large, are not the perpetuators of the testing and disruptive tactics; they are rather the ones who are being deprived of the education to which they are legally and morally entitled. Consequently, the emphasis must be placed on understanding and reaching those who are involved in the tactics or games that are creating the disruption that is interfering with the time on task for teaching and learning. Educators must learn to hear and understand that different drumbeat to which the inner city, urban, suburban, or rural streetcorner poor or minority youngster responds.

NOTES TO CHAPTER 3

1. Leonard Covello, *The Social Background of the Italo-American School Child: A Study of the Southern Italian Family Mores and Their Effect on the School Situation in Italy and America* (Leiden, Netherlands: E.J. Brill,

1967); Leonard Covello, *The Teacher in the Urban Community: A Half Century in City Schools* (Totowa, N.J.: Littlefield, Adams, 1958); Murray Levine and Adeline Levine, *A Social History of Helping Services: Clinic, Court, School, and Community* (New York: Appleton-Century, 1970); Diane Ravitch, *The Great School Wars: New York City, 1805-1973, A History of the Public Schools as Battlefield of Social Change* (New York: Basic Books, 1974); Diane Ravitch, *The Troubled Crusade: American Education, 1945-1980* (New York: Basic Books, 1983); Maxine Seller, "The Education of Immigrant Children in Buffalo, New York 1890-1916," *New York History* 57 (1976): 183-99; Sarah Schmidt, "From Ghetto to University: The Jewish Experience in the Public School," *American Education* 2, no. 2 (1978): 23-26; Meyer Weinberg, *The Chance to Learn: A History Of Race and Education in U.S.* (Cambridge: Cambridge University Press, 1977); Bernard J. Weiss, ed., *American Education and the European Immigrants: 1840 to 1940* (Urbana, Ill.: University of Illinois Press, 1982).

2. R. W. Apple, Jr., "Iran's Baha'is: Some Call It Genocide," *New York Times*, February 27, 1983, p. E9; "Around The World," *New York Times*, September 21, 1984, p. A7; William Borders, "Britain Debates Immigration and Race," *New York Times*, February 8, 1981, p. 3; William Borders, "Britain Discovers a Race Problem To Its Surprise," *New York Times*, April 19, 1981, p. 4E; "Britain, Facing a Multiracial Future: A Worried White Majority Confronts the Stress of Change," *Time*, August 27, 1979, pp. 50-51; Alan Cowell, "Reporter's Notebook: South African, '4th class'," *New York Times*, September 17, 1984, p. A2; Alan Cowell, "Split by Victory in Zimbabwe, Ex-Allies Wage a Bitter War," *New York Times*, February 18, 1983, pp. 1, A14; Alan Cowell, "Zimbabweans Won Their War but Are Losing the Peace: Under Independence, Politics is Tribal," *New York Times*, February 27, 1983, p. 2E; "France Will Extradite 3 Basques," *New York Times*, September 24, 1984, p. A3; Sanjoy Hazarika, "Foes of Sikhs Clash with Police in Delhi," *New York Times*, April 5, 1984, p. A3; Sanjoy Hazarika, "Sikh Raiders Burn Punjabe Stations: Caller Threatens More Action after Gangs of Terrorists Hit Dozens of Buildings," *New York Times*, April 16, 1984, p. A4; Pamela G. Hollie, "Australian Town Is Shaken by a Racial Clash," *New York Times*, November 7, 1982, p. 15; Per Isaksson, "Officials Fret as Swedes Sour on Immigrants," *Buffalo Evening News*, September 7, 1982, p. A-5; Simcha Jacobovici, "Ethiopian Jews Die, Israel Fiddles," *New York Times*, September 15, 1984, p. 23; Marguerite Johnson and Dean Brelis, "India, 'This Is All So Painful': Hindus and Muslims Clash in Bloody Rioting around Bombay," *Time*, June 4, 1984, p. 36; Michael T. Kaufman, "Canada Admitted Few Jews: Book Showing That Only 5,000 Were Accepted from 1933 to 1945 Is a Best Seller," *New York Times*, January 2, 1983, p. 12; Michael T. Kaufman, "A Case of Honor in Canada: Redress for Its Japanese," *New York Times*, November 22, 1982, p. A2; Michael T. Kaufman, "Case of 6 Serbs Signaling Crackdown," *New York Times*, September 28, 1984, p. A10; Anthony Lewis, "On the Edge in Zimbabwe," *New York Times*, February 27, 1983, p. E17; Andrew H. Malcolm, "Slaying in Toronto

Increases Tensions: Conflict between Police Force and Immigrant Groups Is Growing after Shooting of a Black," *New York Times*, February 9, 1979; p. 4; Judith Miller, "Upset by 'Sadat,' Egypt Bars Columbia Films," *New York Times*, February 2, 1984, pp. 1–C17; John Nielsen, Gary Lee, and John Saar, "Rising Racism on the Continent: Immigrants Face Economic Hardship and Increasing Prejudice," *Time*, February 6, 1984, pp. 40–41, 44–45; Walter Pitman, *Now Is Not Too Late* (Toronto: Municipality of Toronto, 1977); David K. Shipler, "Jews and Arabs of Israel: Worlds That Don't Mingle," *New York Times*, December 27, 1983, pp. 1, A8; David K. Shipler, "Arabs and Jews of Israel: The Bigotry Runs Deep," *New York Times*, December 28, 1983, pp. 1, A8; Terence Smith, "South Lebanon Militiamen Said to Kill 13 Shiites," *New York Times*, October 21, 1984, p. A14; Lawrence Van Gelder, "New Faces: Ben Cross and Ian Charleson, What Makes Two Olympic Heroes Run in the British 'Chariots of Fire'," *New York Times*, October 2, 1981, p. C10; John Vinocur, "Swedes Discover Their Dark Side: Racism," *New York Times*, February 24, 1980, p. E9; "Voting Brings Murderous Days To Assam State," *New York Times*, February 27, 1983, p. 2E; Ray Wilkinson, "Ethiopia" The Reign of King Mengistu," *Newsweek*, July 6, 1981, pp. 46–47.

3. William Schofield, *Psychotherapy: The Purchase of Friendship* (Englewood Cliffs, N.J.: Prentice-Hall, 1964).

4. Ibid., p. 133.

5. August B. Hollingshead, *Elmtown's Youth: The Impact of Social Classes on Adolescents* (New York: John Wiley, 1949), p. 184.

6. Ibid., p. 185.

7. Ibid., p. 188.

8. Ibid.

9. Ibid., p. 189.

10. Ibid., p. 190.

11. Ibid.

12. Ibid., p. 191.

13. Ibid.

14. Personal taped interview with Ronald Crayton, April 26, 1984.

15. Charlie Breinin, "Too Many Suspensions? Why Not 'Magnetize' Instead?" *BTF Provocator*, January 1981, p. 11.

16. In jive talk, the Man is the white man. The term may refer to anyone from an employer to a policeman to white society as a whole.

17. Stephen E. Henderson, "Survival Motion," in Mercer Cook and Stephen E. Henderson, eds., *The Militant Black Writer* (Madison, Wis.: University of Wisconsin Press, 1969), pp. 110–11.

18. Charles Keil, *Urban Blues* (Chicago: University of Chicago Press, 1966), p. 1.

19. These youngsters may fit Ulf Hanner's "swingers" classification, In his ethnographic study of a black neighborhood in Washington, D.C., Hanners found four descerrible lifestyles within the ghetto social system: mainstreamers, swingers, street families, and streetcorner men. As many of these youngsters achieve adulthood, they will undoubtedly fall within his streetcorner men category.

20. Joseph P. Fried, "Study Finds Steady Rise in Whites' Acceptance of Integration," *New York Times*, December 8, 1971, p. 34.
21. Claude Brown, *Manchild in the Promised Land* (New York: Macmillan, 1965); Cecil Brown, *The Life & Loves of Mr. Jiveass Nigger* (New York: Farrar, Strauss & Grioux, 1969); Ed Bullins, *The Reluctant Rapist* (New York: Harper & Row, 1973); George Cain, *Bluechild Baby* (New York: McGraw-Hill, 1971); Nathan C. Heard, *Howard Street* (New York: Dial, 1968); Michael Herr, *Dispatches* (New York: Knopf, 1978); Elliot E. Liebow, *Tally's Corner: A Study of Negro Streetcorner Men* (Boston: Little, Brown, 1966); Louise L. Meriwether, *Daddy Was a Number Runner* (Englewood Cliffs, N.J.: Prentice-Hall, 1970); Robert D. Pharr, *The Book of Numbers* (New York: Doubleday, 1969); Daniel Smith, *A Walk in the City* (New York: World, 1961); Piri Thomas, *Down These Mean Streets* (New York: Knopf, 1967); John A. Williams, *The Man Who Cried I Am* (Boston: Little, Brown, 1967); Tom Wolfe, *Radical Chic and Mau-Mauing the Flak Catchers* (New York: Strauss & Giroux, 1970); Richard Wright, *Lawd Today* (New York: Walker, 1963); Sol Yurick, *The Warriors* (New York: Holt, Rinehart & Winston, 1965). Also, see notes to Chapter 2.
22. Imamu A. Baraka, *Dutchman and the Slave: Two Plays* (New York: Morrow, 1964); Imamu A. Baraka, *Four Black Revolutionary Plays, All Praises to the Black Men* (Indianapolis: Bobbs-Merrill, 1969); Imamu A. Baraka, *The Motion of History and Other Plays* (New York: Morrow, 1978); Imamu A. Baraka Le Roi Jones, *Selected Plays and Prose of Amiri Baraka* (New York: Morrow, 1979); Ed Bullins, *The Electronic Nigger, and Other Plays* (London: Faber, 1970); Ed Bullins, *Five Plays: Goin'n A Buffalo; In the Wine Time; A Son, Come Home; The Electronic Nigger; Clara's Ole Man* (Indianapolis: Bobbs-Merrill, 1969); Ed Bullins, *For Dynamite Plays* (New York: Morrow, 1972); Ed Bullins, *The Theme Is Blackness, "The Corner" and Other Plays* (New York: Morrow, 1973); J.E. Franklin, *Black Girl: A Play in Two Acts* (New York: Dramatists Play Service, 1971).
23. Clive Barnes, "Stage: Ghetto Life of 'Ain't Supposed'," *New York Times*, October 21, 1971, p. 55; Melvin Van Peebles, dir., *Sweet Sweetback's Baddasssss Song*, Cinemation Industries, 1971; Roger Greenspun, "Screen: Ideas for Cliches," *New York Times*, April 14, 1971, p. 17.
24. For example, George Carlin, *Occupation: Foole*, Little David, LD 1005, 1973; Oscar Brown, Jr., *Sin & Soul*, Columbia, CS 8377, 1960; Rudy Ray Moore, *The Rudy Ray Moore Album: Eat Out More Often*, Comedians, Inc., COM S 1104, n.d.; Rudy Ray Moore, *The Second Rudy Ray Moore Album*, Kent, KST-002, n.d.; Lou Rawls, *The Best of Lou Rawls*, Capital, SKAO 2948, 1968; Melvin Van Peebles, *Aint Supposed to Die a Natural Death*, AM Records, SP 3510, n.d.
25. Robert Altman, dir., *MASH*, 20th Century Fox, 1970; Roger Greenspan, " 'MASH' Film Blends Atheism, Gore, Humor," *New York Times*, January 26, 1970, p. 26; Sidney Poitier, dir., *Stir Crazy*, Columbia Pictures, 1980. Vincent Canby, "Movie: Pryor and Wilder Inside in 'Stir Crazy'," *New York Times*, December 12, 1980, p. C10; Robert Downey, dir., *Putney*

Swope, Cinema V, 1969; Vincent Canby, "Screen: Putney Swope, 'A Soul Story'," *New York Times*, July 11, 1969, p. 10.

26. Roger D. Abrahams, *Deep Down in the Jungle . . . : Negro Narrative Folklore from the Streets of Philadelphia* (Chicago: Aldine, 1970); Roger D. Abrahams, *Positively Black* (Englewood Cliffs, N.J.: Prentice-Hall, 1970); John Dollard, "The Dozens: Dialect of Insult," *American Imago* 1, no. 5 (1939): 3-5; Thomas Kochman, " 'Rapping' in the Black Ghetto," *Trans-Action* 6, no. 4 (1969): 26-33; Thomas Kochman, *Rappin' and Stylin' Out* (Chicago: University of Illinois Press, 1973); Thomas Kochman, "Toward an Ethnography of Black American Speech Behavior," in Norman E. Whitten, Jr. and John F. Szwed, eds., *Afro-American Anthropology: Contemporary Perspectives* (New York: Free Press, 1970), pp. 145-62.

27. Herbert L. Foster, *Ribbin', Jivin', and Playin' the Dozens: The Unrecognized Dilemma of Inner City Schools* (Cambridge, Mass.: Ballinger Publishing Company, 1974); Richard A Marotta, " 'Posin' To Be Chosen': An Ethnographic Study of Ten Lower Class Black Male Adolescents in an Urban High School," *DAI* 39 (1978), 1234-A (State University of New York at Buffalo).

28. Kochman, "Toward an Ethnography of Black American Speech Behavior," p. 162.

29. H. Rap Brown, *Die Nigger Die!* (New York: Dial, 1969), pp. 25-27, 30.

30. See Chapter 6 for an explanation of the dozens.

31. Two points: (1) Jefferson Avenue is the main street in the black community of Buffalo, New York, and (2) the statement implied that the student teacher's mother was out whoring or hooking the night before. Interestingly, since David Milch, who grew up in Buffalo joined the writing team of "Hill Street Blues," many of Buffalo's streets and sections are mentioned regularly on the show.

32. Claude Brown, p. 259.

33. Claude Brown, p. 256.

34. H. Rap Brown, p. 15.

35. H. Rap Brown, p. 18.

36. Heard, p. 26.

37. Thomas, p. 47.

38. Ibid., p. 50.

39. There is some indication that certain areas of dope traffic and the like, are gradually moving into the hands of blacks, though the higher levels of crime are still under white control. Indeed, even playing the numbers has been co-opted as a game within the New York State Lottery program.

40. Wolfe, pp. 130-31.

41. Keil, p. 20.

42. Alex Haley, *The Autobiography of Malcolm X* (New York: Grove, 1969), p. 75.

43. John Horton, "Time and Cool People," in Lee Rainwater, ed., *Soul* (Chicago: Aldine, 1970), pp. 37-39.

44. L.A. Dennis, "The Hustler," *Black America* 2, no. 6 (1972): 16.

45. Ibid., p. 57.

46. Ibid., p. 18.
47. Ibid., p. 19.
48. Ibid., p. 177.
49. "9 Tombs Inmates Awarded High School Diplomas," *New York Times*, October 12, 1972, p. 51.
50. George Vecsey, "A Scholar in the New Alcatraz," *New York Times*, October 2, 1972, p. 1.
51. Ibid., p. 60.
52. Mezz Mezzrow and Bernard Wolf, *Really the Blues* (New York: Signet, 1964), pp. 193-94.
53. H. Rap Brown, p. 17.
54. Rick L. Jennings and Carl S. Davis, "Attraction-Enhancing Client Behaviors for 'Non-Yavis, Jr.'." *Journal of Consulting and Clinical Psychology* 45 (1977): 135-44.
55. Hollingshead, pp. 220-21.
56. Ibid.
57. Stephen Farber, "Directors Join in the S.E. Hinton Fan Club," *New York Times*, March 20, 1983, p. H19; S.E. Hinton, *The Outsiders* (New York: Dell, 1967); S.E. Hinton, *Rumble Fish* (New York: Dell, 1975); S.E. Hinton, *Tex* (New York: Dell, 1979). Movies and reviews—Francis Coppola, dir., *The Outsiders*, Warner Bros., 1983, Vincent Canby, "Film: 'Outsiders,' Teen-Age Violence," *New York Times*, March 25, 1983, p. C3; Francis Coppola, dir., *Rumble Fish*, Universal Pictures, 1983, Janet Maslin, "Matt Dillon in Coppola's 'Rumble Fish'," *New York Times*, October 7, 1983, p. 10; Tim Hunter, dir., *Tex*, Buena Vista Dist, Co., 1982, Janet Maslin, "Tex: Parentless Boys in Oklahoma'," *New York Times*, September 28, 1982, p. C17.
58. Penelope Spheeris, dir., *Suburbia*, New Horizons, 1984; "Screen: Down-and-Out Youths in 'Suburbia'," *New York Times*, April 13, 1983, p. C10.
59. Peter Yates, dir., *Breaking Away*, 20th. Century Fox, 1979; Janet Maslin, "Film: 'Breaking Away,' A Classic Sleeper," *New York Times*, July 18, 1979, p. C22.
60. "Number of Handicapped Students Leveling Of, Ed Official Says," *Report on Education Research*, July 6, 1983, pp. 5-6.
61. U.S. Department of Education, *Sixth Annual Report to Congress on the Implementation of Public Law 94-142: The Education for All Handicapped Children Act* (Washington, D.C.: U.S. Government Printing Office), p. xiii.
62. Ibid., p. 7.
63. Ibid.
64. Ibid., p. 7.
65. Emmett Louis Till was a fourteen-year-old black youngster from Chicago who went to Mississippi to visit with his relatives. While visiting, he was lynched for not "knowing his place"; according to "2 Held for Trial in Slaying of Boy," *New York Times*, September 7, 1955, p. 15, "Till's body, a bullet in his head and a 100-pound cotton gin tied to his neck to weight him down, was pulled from the Talihatchie River Wednesday. The

boy . . . was kidnapped three days earlier from his uncle's home where he had been vacationing. Young Till allegedly whistled or made 'ugly remarks' to Mrs. Bryant"; Although Mrs. Bryant, a twenty-one-year-old white woman, never testified about what Emmett Till allegedly did, according to John N. Popham, "State Rests Case in Youth's Killing," *New York Times*, September 23, 1955, p. 15, Till entered her store and, "made a purchase and when she held out her hand for the money he grabbed her hand, and she had to tug to get free. She said he followed her to the cash register, grabbed her around the waist and said 'How about a date? I've been with white women before.' " Later, according to Popham, Till was pulled out of the store and onto the porch by another black youngster where Till "wolf-whistled" at Mrs. Bryant. Roy Bryant, twenty-four, and his half-brother J.W. Milan, thirty-six, were indicted for murdering Till. However, the all-white jury in LeFlore County, Mississippi acquitted them for murder and refused to indict them for kidnapping.

66. See 12th and Oxford St. Gang, dir., *The Jungle*, Churchill Films, 1968; Judy Stone, "The Best Things We Knew Was Gang War," *New York Times Magazine*, October 13, 1968, p. 16D.
67. Elliot Liebow, p. 150; also see above Nelson C. Heard; Lou Rawls, "The Street Hustler's Blues," *The Best of Lou Rawls*, Capital, SKAO 2948, n.d.
68. Liebow, pp. 134–35.
69. Ibid., pp. 120–23.
70. "The Violent Veterans," *Time*, March 13, 1972, pp. 45–46.
71. Ibid., p. 45.
72. Ibid., p. 46.
73. Ibid.
74. The earlier definition of "rapping" or "running a strong rap" had sexual connotations. The object was for the rapper to get the girl's nose. When a male has a female's nose, she is in his power, which usually means she is his to do with as he pleases sexually.
75. In jive lexicon or street language, a "fish" or "scab" is an ugly girl. A female who is a "Phat Tip" is a beautiful girl or woman. The letters in "phat" stand for "pussy," "hips," "ass," and "tits," or a "pretty hole at times." I am sure that there are also other definitions. In Buffalo, New York, "tip" means a girl or woman. See Chapter 6 for further explanation of streetcorner behavior as related to cat and gorilla roles.
76. Elenore Lester, "Growing Up Black and Female," *New York Times*, July 11, 1971, p. D5.
77. "A Question of Style," *Newsweek*, October 6, 1969, p. 104.
78. Blake Edwards, dir., *10*, Orion, 1979; Vincent Canby, "Screen: '10' Spoofs Pursuit of Happiness in L.A.," *New York Times*, October 5, 1979, p. C6.
79. "TV Reporter Modifies Hair," *Buffalo Evening News*, December 11, 1981, p. 2.
80. U.N.I.A. Black Liberation Flag. The flag came into contemporary use about twenty years ago. The "Liberator" tristar originated with Marcus Garvey's black nationalist movement; "Black Flag," *Time*, December 13,

1972, p. 10; Leonard Budder, "Education Board Curbs Use of Nonofficial Flags," *New York Times*, December 10, 1970, p. 56; Florida Teacher Tries to Keep Job Lost in Fight on Flag Oath," *New York Times*, December 27, 1970, p. 41; "Jersey Slates Hearing on Black Flag Issue," *New York Times*, January 11, 1972, p. 41; "Michigan Reinstates Teacher Who Sat During Anthem," *New York Times*, April 30, 1972, p. 14; John I. Sinn, "Pledge of Allegiance Causes School Problem," *Buffao Courier-Express*, April 4, 1971, p. 43; "Principal Accused of Pledge Coercion," *New York Times*, December 12, 1970, p. 18; "State School Chief Overrules Newark on Black Flag Plan," *New York Times*, January 27, 1973, p. 1; J.F. Sullivan, "Argument Heard on Black's Flag," *New York Times*, January 15, 1972, p. 35; "Teacher Suspended Over Flag Pledge: Community Stirred," *New York Times*, October 24, 1971, p. 95; "Teacher Upheld on Flag Pledge," *New York Times*, February 28, 1971, p. 43.

81. Paul Delaney, "Internal Struggle Shakes Black Muslims," *New York Times*, January 21, 1972, p. 1; Scott Thompson, "A Perspective on Activism," in Richard L. Hart and J. Galen Saylor, eds., *Student Unrest: Threat or Promise* (Washington, D.C.: Association for Supervision and Curriculum Development, N.E.A., 1970), pp. 35–45; National School Public Relations Association, *High School Student Unrest* (Washington, D.C.: author, 1969).

82. Richard Schickel, "Some Lessons in Growing Up. The Last Picture Show," *Life*, October 15, 1971, p. 14; Vincent Canby, "Screen: Life In a Shabby Texas Town," *New York Times*, October 4, 1971, p. 51; Peter Bogdanovich, dir., *The Last Picture Show*, Columbia, 1971.

4 A HISTORICAL PERSPECTIVE CONCERNING INNER CITY AND LOWER ECONOMIC CONDITIONING EXPERIENCES

In his high-crime neighborhood, Mr. Anthony has seen children playing around dead bodies as the police tried to determine the who, what, where, when and why of the crime.

He has seen men with guns in their hands weave their way through groups of screaming boys and girls. And he has seen children doped up with the latest out-of-control substance.

Mr. Anthony chose to work nights so he could keep an eye on his boys during the day. He makes sure they are in the house before he leaves for his job. They are as close as brothers can be. When one is in a brawl, the other jumps in to defend him.

—Sheila Rule[1]

It is a community where rage always lurks just below the surface and often erupts in acts of seemingly mindless violence. It is a place where a dissenter at a meeting of a model cities policy committee was murdered by being dragged into the street and thrown under a moving car. It is where a youngster outside intermediate school No. 155 on Jackson Avenue in Mott Haven was nearly stomped to death in an argument over a bottle of soda pop.

—M. Tolchin[2]

In some neighborhoods boys went to and from school in parties, to insure safety against attack by gangs of enemies or toughs slightly older. Tenth and Fourteenth Warders on opposite sides of the Bowery were hereditary enemies. A boy from one ward ventured into the other only at the risk of black eyes, split lips, and ruined clothing. Pitched battles were fought across the frontier along the Bowery itself; and when word flashed up and down the

81

street, "De Tent' and Fourteent' is fightin' again!" loyal partisans joyously hastened from all quarters to the fray. Stones, brickbats, and oyster shells flew like hail, to the great menace of noncombatants—until at last came the crash of a merchant's window or a cry of "cheese it, de cop!" and the armies vanished like a fog before the sun.

—A. F. Harlow, *Old Bowery Days*[3]

As suggested in Chapter 3, there are at least four classifications of students in inner city classrooms housing large numbers of lower class or poor urban black children. It must be emphasized, however, that many of these children are very middle class.[4] Also, much of the streetcorner behavior of some of these black children is misunderstood and misinterpreted by school personnel.

All inner city and, to some extent, even poor children are exposed to some degree of negative conditioning experiences that include, among others, ethnocentrism, racism, delinquency, gangs, poor housing, crime, violence, drugs, and lower class physical problemsolving.

Unquestionably, many inner city and poor children are also exposed to positive conditioning experiences. We must realize, however, that continual exposure to the maladies associated with lower class and slum lifestyle must have some effect upon the child's behavior, particularly as it is played out in the classroom.

Those lifestyles that are most predominant among the very poor tend to be damaging to a child's mental health. Although these lifestyles are adaptive to poverty living, "the patterns interact with many stresses of economic deprivation and tend to limit the growing child's opportunity for positive mental health."[5] An overview of research findings suggests that very lower economic people, more so than others, "often fail to adopt child-rearing and family life style patterns which research indicates are associated with children judged to be mentally healthy in our society."[6]

With this in mind, we must realize that many inner city and poor children will not, at outset, behave as do middle class children. They will bring their lower class street lifestyle and behavior into the classroom. This is particularly true in the early student/teacher classroom testing and crisis or unfamiliar situations where those involved in the altercation or misunderstanding may revert to their more familiar behavior or provoke others to do so. Harrison Salisbury, writing about gang problems, pointed out how uncertainty about this behavior can affect teaching and learning.

[W]hen you have large numbers of these youngsters in a school, when they have, like Pavlov's dogs, been subjected to so many bewildering shocks by life that their reaction patterns become erratic, unpredictable and frequently dangerous to themselves and others, you introduce a very uncertain factor into the classroom. Trouble may break out at any time—and for no reason which even an alert teacher necessarily observes. It may have a source far away from the study section. Knowledge that she is conducting her lessons in a situation which may suddenly explode can unnerve a teacher—to the point that she herself triggers the outburst by revealing a lack of certainty of control.[7]

It is because we have denied the possibility that this streetcorner lifestyle is being played out in the classrooms that we have contributed to our problems in inner city schools. We have been influenced too much by the advocates of the simplistic "there are no bad boys," or "all you need is a well planned lesson," or "that is not our responsibility. Suspend them." We have to become more realistic and pragmatic in our attempts at educating inner-city or poor youngsters. To this end we must look at three negative factors that affect the inner-city youngster's lifespace—the factors, in addition to his family, that mold and shape his behavior and which, in turn, affect his classroom behavior: (1) gangs, (2) juvenile delinquency and crime, and (3) physicalness and violence. These are also the areas that appear to cause consternation among middle class adults and school personnel. Hence, they cause problems in school that interfere with instruction.

GANGS

There is disagreement over the amount of crime and violence for which juvenile gangs and groups are responsible. Nevertheless, the Task Force on Individual Acts of Violence reported significant involvement by gangs in certain areas of crime and violence.

> These figures are crude, and more refined work is obviously necessary. When combined with the foregoing literature, however, the information does lead us to believe that gangs and groups are responsible for a very small proportion of the urban criminal homicides and aggravated assaults in this country, but that they are involved in a significant percentage of all robberies and, to a lesser extent, of all forcible rapes. The implication, in turn, is that the dominant form of serious violence committed by juvenile or youthful gang is much more likely to be robbery than murder, assault, or rape.[8]

However, gang violence appears to follow a cyclical pattern through the years with some differences in each cycle. In the early 1950s we had the "bopping" or fighting gangs with mass fights or "rumbles" between gangs as they guarded their turf. In the mid 1950s, drugs and street workers appeared to be taking over and the gangs supposedly began to wane.

According to Walter Miller, however, "the urban adolescent street gang is as old as the American City.[9]

> Gangs in the 1910's and the 20's were attributed to the cultural dislocations and community disorganization accompanying the mass immigration of foreigners; in the 30's to the enforced idleness and economic pressures produced by the Great Depression; in the 50's to the emotional disturbance of parents

and children caused by the increased stresses and tensions of modern life. . . .
[T] he existence of gangs is widely attributed to a range of social injustices;
racial discrimination, unequal educational and work opportunities, resentment over inequalities in the distribution of wealth and privilege in an affluent society, and the ineffective or oppressive policies of service agencies such
as the police and the schools.[10]

In discussing the gangs of the late 1950s, Salisbury also noted some earlier
New York City gangs. The Navy Street Boys, the Red Hook Boys, the Coney
Island Boys, and the Garfield Boys used bricks, sticks, and fists to rule their
areas. "They used to haul ashcans of cinders and broken glass up to the roofs of
the four-story houses and dump them on passersby."[11]

Historically, there were gangs in New York City as early as 1728. White boys
formed the Vly gang (from the Vly Market), the Broadway Boys, and the Bowery Boys. Negro boys formed the Fly Boys and the Long Bridge Boys, the name
for the latter coming from either the bridge at the foot of Wall Street, the
Coffee House Bridge, or the bridge over the sewer at the foot of Broad Street.
The reporting of the earlier gang fights sounds similar to the reporting of gangs
of later and probably earlier generations of gangs, though the weapons are
different.

> There were great hills of tanbark in the swamp district which the warriors
> utilized as lookouts and redoubts. Their conflicts, especially when they
> fought with slings and stones, sometimes became a serious menace, not only
> to their own persons but to those of innocent bystanders. When they clashed
> in Pearl Street or Maiden Lane, shopkeepers hastily put up shutters over their
> windows and pedestrians fled for their lives.[12]

Just as they do today, gangs organized alliances to ward off encroaching powers. The Broadway Boys gang allied with the Smit's Vly Boys to fight the Bowery Boys gang from the north,

> with whom they had each separately contended, the dissemination of whose
> principles they dreaded, and whose strength, from the rapid increase of popu-
> lation in that quarter, threatened to overwhelm their southerly and more
> civilized neighbors. The battles between the allies and the Bowery Boys were
> frequently fought on and around Bunker Hill, sometimes with armies of
> twenty to fifty on a side. The Grand Streeters and the Spring Streeters were
> two other youthful clans who fought many a lively skirmish in the early dec-
> ades of the century.[13]

During the first ten to fifteen years of its existence, the Five Points area was a
relatively peaceful and decent place: One policeman could preserve order. By
about 1820, however, "a regiment would have been unable to cope with the tur-
bulent citizenry of Paradise Square, and rout the gangsters and other criminals
from the dens and burrows. Respectable families began to leave the area and

freed slaves and "low class" Irish began to move in as part of the first big wave of post-Revolutionary War immigration. "They crowded indiscriminately into the old rookeries of The Points, and by 1840 the district had become the most dismal slum in America."[14]

The tenements, dance halls, and saloons were the genesis of the original Five Points gangs. About 1825, greengrocery speakeasies opened, and in their back rooms these gangs were organized into working gang units. "This room became the haunt of thugs, pickpockets, murderers, and thieves. The gang known as the Forty Thieves, which appears to have been the first in New York with a definite, acknowledged leadership, is said to have been formed in Rosanna Peers' grocery store, and her back room was used as a meeting-place, and headquarters by . . . eminent chieftans."[15] Such gangs as the Kerrigonians (from County Kerry, Ireland), the Roach Guards, the Chichesters, the Plug Uglies, and the Dead Rabbits were organized and met in various grocery stores, "and in time these emporiums came to be regarded as the worst dens of the Five Points, and the centers of its infamy and crimes."[16]

Just as today's gangs wear the "colors," the Five Points gangs had their colors too. The Dead Rabbits wore a red stripe on their pantaloons and when they went into battle a guidon (flag) with a dead rabbit was carried. The Roach Guards adopted only the red stripe on their pantaloons as a battle uniform. The uniform of the Shirt Tails obviously was shirt tails hanging outside their trousers. The Plug Uglies, mainly big Irishmen, received their name from the enormous wool and leather stuffed plug hats they wore pulled down over their ears to serve as a battle helmet. In the ranks of the Plug Uglies were some of the toughest fighters of the time.[17]

> Even the most ferocious of the Paradise Square eye-gougers and mayhem artists cringed when a giant Plug Ugly walked abroad looking for touble, with a hudge bludgeon in one hand, a brickbat in the other, a pistol peeping from his pocket and his tall hat jammed down over his ears and all but obscuring his fierce eyes. He was adept at rough and tumble fighting, and wore heavy boots studded with great hobnails with which he stamped his prostrate and helpless victim.[18]

Most of the gang members were young men, some of them being mere boys.[19] Gradually, the Bowery superseded the Five Points as an amusement area, and gangs began to form in the Bowery too. The O'Connell Guards, the True Blue Americans, the American Guards, the Atlantic Guards, and the famous Bowery Boys were the most important gangs in the Bowery's early days, according to Asbury. The primarily Irish gangs of the Bowery were not as ferocious as were the Five Points gangs, although they were good fighters.

During the 1850s such street gangs as the Forty Thieves, the Hudson Dusters, the Plug Uglies, the Dead Rabbits, and the Slaughter Housers, held whole areas of New York City in their grips. Savage battles were fought by these gangs in the streets in which it was not uncommon for fifteen to twenty to be killed. The police were often fearful of entering some of their neighborhoods. The police were sometimes unable to stop the gang fights and had to call for the aid of the National Guard or the Army.

The Dead Rabbits and the Bowery Boys had many bitter fights, and maintained a vicious feud. Rarely did a week pass without at least one brawl. These gangs participated in the greatest gang fights of the nineteenth century.

> Sometimes the battles raged for two or three days without cessation, while the streets of the gang area were barricaded with carts and paving stones, and the gangsters blazed away at each other with musket and pistol, or engaged in close work with knives, brickbats, bludgeons, teeth, and fists. On the outskirts of the struggling mob of thugs ranged the women, their arms filled with reserve ammunition, their keen eyes watching for a break in the enemy's defense, and always ready to lend a hand or a tooth in the fray.[20]

June Lazare, in her "Folk Songs of New York City," sings of the fight between the Dead Rabbits and the Bowery Boys.

> They had a dreadful fight, upon Saturday night,
> The papers gave the news accordin',
> Guns, pistols, clubs, and sticks, hot water, and old bricks,
> Which drove them on the other side of Jordan.
>
> Then pull off the old coat and roll up the sleeve,
> Bayard is a hard street to travel.
> Pull off the old coat and roll up the sleeve,
> The Bloody Sixth is a hard ward to travel, I believe.
>
> Like wild dogs they did fight, this fourth of April night,
> Of course they laid their plans accordin'.
> Some were wounded, and some killed, and lots of blood
>   was spilled
> In the fight on the other side of Jordan.
>
> The new police did join the Bowery boys in line,
> With orders strict and right accordin',
> Bullets, clubs, and bricks did fly, and many groan and die.
> Hard road to travel over Jordan.
>
> When the police did interfere, this made the Rabbits sneer,
> And very much enraged them accordin'.
> With bricks they did go in, determined for to win,
> And drive them on the other side of Jordan.
>
> At last the battle closed, yet few that night reposed,
> For frightful were their dreams accordin'.
> For the devil on two sticks was a marching on the bricks,
> All night on the other side of Jordan.[21]

Many of the women were ferocious fighters. During the Draft Riots the women inflicted some of the most horrendous and fiendish tortures upon the soldiers, policemen, and Negroes who were unlucky to be captured by the mob. The women sliced their flesh with butcher knives, ripped out tongues and eyes, and "applied the torch after the victims had been sprayed with oil and hanged to trees."[22]

In the slums, the gang boy's elders also were organized into gangs. Although these groups were small at first, they soon grew in size. These gangs started as petty thieves who also fought for their neighborhoods for the fun of fighting. Gradually, however, some of them became very much involved as predators and as tools of politicians.[23]

In the early days before the Civil War, the composition and objectives of the gangs began to change. In the 1830s district and ward political leaders began to purchase saloons, dance houses, and the greengrocery speakeasies in which many of the gangs congregated, while also taking houses of prostitution and gambling under their protective wings. Hence we had the beginning of the amalgamation of the underworld of the gangs with the politicians.

The underworld thus became an important factor in politics, and under the manipulation of the worthy statesmen the gangs of the Bowery and Five Points participated in the great series of riots which began with the spring election disturbances of 1834 and continued, with frequent outbreaks, for half a score of years. In this period occurred the Flour and Five Points riots, and the most important of the Abolition troubles, while there were at least two hundred battles between the gangs, and innumerable conflicts between volunteer fire companies.[24]

From about 1731, when the first two fire engines were brought to New York City from England, until 1865, when the New York City fire department was municipalized, there appear to have been ongoing physical and violent conflicts between various volunteer fire companies,[25] gangs, and guard target groups. Most often, the gangs were members of the fire companies, while many of the guard groups grew from the fire companies. According to Botkin, the fire company rivalries heightened during the 1830–1850 riot era when election and abolition disturbances and outbreaks by the criminal gangs of the Bowery and the Five Points tore New York City.

The volunteer fire companies were an odd lot. In addition to their membership of Bowery, Five Points gangs, and other area gangs, their membership consisted of many eminent personages. Indeed, the volunteers were powerful politically. In addition to the gang members, important politicians such as William M. (Boss) Tweed also belonged to the volunteer fire brigades. And for a short period while he resided in New York City, George Washington was head of the New York Department.[26]

Augustine Costello reported on the political power of certain politicians who refused to punish those who had caused problems for the fire brigades. In particular, he wrote about Chief Carson's 1843 report, that was

> mainly taken up with the troubles existing among certain inharmonious bodies of fire brigades. From this it appears that William M. Tweed, the one-time boss, and then foreman of Engine Company No. 6, was expelled for leading in an attack on Hose Company No. 31, and his company suspended for three months. The Common Council, however, to the deep disgust of Chief Carson, failed to ratify this sentence, and Mr. Tweed was let off with a suspension of three months.[27]

Another complaint of Chief Carson was against "the outrageous spirit of rowdyism of certain clubs of desperate fighting men called 'Short Boys,' 'Old Maid's Boys,' 'Rock Boys,' etc. . . . " Apparently these gangs or clubs were patterned after similar groups in London and Paris. They appeared to have spent a goodly amount of time attacking the firemen. According to Chief Carson, these clubs

> make deliberate and bloody attacks on our firemen while going to and returning from fires, destroying the apparatus, and often, by stratagem, putting certain companies in collision with each other, individual members against each other, and creating in every way endless broil and confusion in the Department. . . . I have had many of these villains . . . arrested for upsetting our engines, cutting the hose, beating our firemen almost to death, etc., but they were no sooner in prison than the captains of police, the aldermen, and judges of police, would discharge them to commit fresh attacks on the firemen the following night. . . . "But why," he asks, desperately, "recount these daily and daring outrages, when these bloodthirsty creatures are thus encouraged and liberated by aldermen, on whose conscientious watchfulness and unsullied integrity the people rely for the incarceration and severe punishment of these abandoned and heartless fiends."[28]

In the summer of 1842, suggestions were made to prevent young men and boys who were not members of the department from interfering with the firemen performing their duties. Even where some volunteer companies were disbanded for fighting and rioting, their members attached themselves to other companies and there, too, caused problems.

In an attempt to overcome such outrages against the firemen, Chief C. V. Anderson requested the establishment of a twenty-man fire police group. However, nothing seemed to help. The volunteers fought over everything. They fought as they ran to the fires, and they even fought over the hydrants. According to Benjamin Botkin, the firemen organized special groups of tough fighters who would run to the fire ahead of their engine. Once at the fire, they would place a small barrel over the hydrant or cistern to wait until their crew arrived. Needless to say, the firemen often spent more time fighting one another than they did fires.[29]

In one battle on July 26, 1846, five companies of volunteer firemen fought.

> The battle had raged all the way to Canal and Hudson Streets, and attracted an immense crowd of citizens. . . .
>
> But of late three attacks had been made. In one case Engine Company No. 41 was proceeding at great speed to a fire, when they were set upon by these miscreants with clubs, slung-shots, and stones. . . . Another, . . . [was] attacked while attending to their duty, the men driven away, and the carriage upset in the street. The third was an attack . . . by a gang of rowdies. It was useless to look to the police justices for redress, for it was well known they dared not grant it, the political influences of the gangs being so great. . . .
>
> There were many fights, and hot ones, too, in the old department, but they grew out of a natural emulation and were not lacking in a certain rugged element of chivalry which promoted manhood, though somewhat at the expense of public order. The murderous revolver and assassin-like disposition which now mark its use were unknown in those days. The combats were fair hand-to-hand fights between man and man, and he who resorted to any other weapon than those which nature supplied was accounted a ruffian or a coward.[30]

In addition to fighting and rioting, some of the volunteer firemen also participated in thievery. According to Campbell, when there was a fire, the firemen would strip many of the stores in the neighborhood of their contents, particularly if one of the stores happened to be a clothing store. It was just thievery on the part of Bowery "roughs," "toughs," or "Bowery b'hoys" that helped legislate the volunteer fire departments out of existence.[31]

The Gulick Guards, who took their name from Chief Engineer James Gulick, had as their motto "Firemen with Pleasure—Soldiers at Leisure." From 1855 through 1861, guard groups going on target "excursions" were a great feature in New York City. When the Civil War call to arms came to New York City, in 1861, there existed a "considerable hodgepodge of militia and of unofficial military and target companies, in various stages of drill and equipment."[32]

As noted, many of these guard units had their origins with various fire companies and dated back to the 1840s. And many of the Bowery and Five Points gangs assumed names such as the American Guards and the O'Connell Guards.[33] Herbert Asbury reported on a fight between them:

> The Bowery gang known as the American Guards, the members of which prided themselves on their native ancestry, was soon devotedly attached to the Native Americans party, and responded joyfully to the appeals of its ward heelers and district leaders. During the summer of 1835, about a year after the election riots, bitter enmity developed between this gang and the O'Connell Guards, which had been organized under the aegis of a Bowery liquor

seller, and was the particular champion of the Irish element of Tammany Hall. These gangs came to blows on June 21, 1835, at Grand and Crosby Streets on the lower East Side. The fighting spread as far as the Five Points, where the gangsters of Paradise Square took a hand and the rioting became general throughout that part of the city. The Mayor and the Sheriff called out every watchman in the city, and for the force managed to stop the fighting without the aid of soldiers, although several companies were mustered and remained in their armories overnight.[34]

John Allison immortalized the "goings-on" of the various pre-Civil War gangs, volunteer firemen, and guard groups through his song "The Bowery Grenadiers."

We're a gal-lant bunch of he-roes,
We've been or-ganized ten years,
We're known a-bout the cit-y as the BOWE-RY GREN-A-DIERS.
We've had three fights with the Hoo-li-hans
And won ten-thou-sand cheers, . . .
  We can lick the Brook-lyn guards
  If they on-ly show their cards,
We can run like the dev-il (When the ground is lev-el) for about
    four hun-dred yards . . .
(Should the) la-dies be in dan-ger
When the flames a-round them roar,
We're the lads who fight through fire and smoke for a res-cue safe
    and sure.
But when we march of Sun-day
And the Mul-li-gans beat tatoo,
We're good old stock with a cob-cle rock and a length of gas
    pipe too. . . .
We're the toughs with the cuffs,
We're THE BOWE-RY GREN-A-DIERS![35]

While the members of the Dead Rabbits, Bowery Boys, and similar gangs were often thieves, and occasionally murderers, they were primarily street fighters and brawlers and partook of their battling openly in the streets. The newer gangs, however, were thieves and killers first.

Following the post-Revolutionary War wave of immigration, by about 1840 the wealthier residents had already moved northward. Rows of rundown tenements replaced the mansions of the wealthy. By 1845, the Fourth Ward was a hotbed of crime. River gangs such as the Patsy Conroys, Short Tails, Swamp Angels, Hookers, Buckoos, Daybreak Boys, Border Gang, and the Slaughter Housers ravaged all who entered the area. According to Asbury, "no human life was safe, and a well-dressed man venturing into the district was commonly set upon and murdered or robbed, or both, before he had gone a block."[36]

Howlet and Saul, who became captains of the Daybreak Boys in 1850 and terrorized the East River until 1859, had joined the gang when they were fifteen and sixteen. Many of the other gang members were even younger, some as young as ten and twelve. None of the gang members was older than twenty years when they had already gained reputations as cutthroats and murderers. The police finally succeeded in driving the gangsters and gangs out of the Fourth Ward by the end of the Civil War. By 1900 the Steamboat Squad, which was organized in 1876, had managed to drive the organized gangs out of the waterfront.[37]

As the United States grew through immigration, and ecological use changes came about in the cities, new gangs arose, remained awhile, and then disappeared. In some cases, remaining gang members joined up with the newer gangs, became independent criminals, or took over the leadership of criminal groups.

There were the Honeymoon gangs that operated in the middle East Side's Eighteenth Ward in 1853. And in 1855 it was estimated that 30,000 men were aligned with the gang leaders and through them to the corrupt political leaders of Tammany Hall, Native American Party, or Know Nothing Party as they plundered the New York City treasury.[38]

Those who are appalled by yesterday's and today's gang actions or the numerous rioting incidents during the 1960s and 1970s should look at our early history. For example, in the mid-nineteenth century New York City rioting was endemic to the social process. For most of New York's unskilled workers, conditions were hard, life was drab, and drink was the greatest comfort; life was lived "permanently on the edge of destitution." Most women workers were degraded and exploited, and because of their low wages, many turned to crime and prostitution to survive. Living in such a way, people became brutalized. Violence became a release, a way of expression, an entertainment, and a form of adaptive behavior.[39]

> Riot was an integral part of the activities of the slum gangs and some of the volunteer fire companies, the native forms of association of the poor. The gangs, based on ethnic, communal, or local groups, were characteristically made up of young men between sixteen and thirty. Most of them were employed, and though many were simply unskilled laborers, it was by no means uncommon to find gang members who were skilled artisans or tradesmen. The gangs were not usually criminal, and they did not, as a rule, use guns or knives, preferring instead to rely on bare knuckles ad brute strength. Their main concern was fighting other gangs or the police, and a famous gang might be able to turn over a thousand members, ready for battle.[40]

There were sixteen major civil disturbances and innumerable minor disorders between 1834 and 1874; the most famous of these was the Draft Riot in New York City in July 1863.[41] The Draft Riot lasted five days and started when some of the members of the Black Joke Engine Company No. 33 attempted to burn and to destroy the draft records and wheel used in picking several members of their volunteer company.[42]

Despite a mythology concerning an estimated 50,000 to 70,000 rioters and the numbers killed, and though the mobs who battled the troops and police were large, there did not appear to be more than 300 "hard-core street fighters gathered in one place at any one time during the riots." There were only 2,000 to 3,000 real rioters, and the large crowds filling the streets were, to a large extent, spectators.[43] However, amassed against the rioters were 2,297 men of the Metropolitan Police Force, and between 7,000 and 10,000 Army and National Guard troops. Also included were approximately a dozen artillery batteries that poured grape and canister (shot) into the mobs surging through Manhattan.[44]

According to arrest records, 352 people were identified as rioters. If every doubtful case were included, the death toll for the riots reached 119. Of the rioters who could be identified, the overwhelming percentage were Irish. Interestingly, the actual rioters were a fair cross-section of the working class of New York City. It must also be pointed out that there were antidraft disturbances outside of New York City as well. And, there were very specific killings, beatings, and looting of homes of Negroes.[45]

In New York City after the Civil War, the Whyos gang arose, supposedly from the Chichesters of the Old Five Points, and lasted into the mid–1890s. The gang was made up of sneak thieves, burglars, pickpockets, and murderers. The Whyos also advertised murder and mayhem for money. For example—punching for $2.00; stabbing for $25.00; and doing the "big job $100.00 and up."[46]

During this period, New York had such gangs as the Rag Gang, the Hartly Mob, and the Molasses Gang. In about 1868, the Hell's Kitchen Gang was organized. Meanwhile, such gangs as the Stable Gang, the Silver Gang, and Potashes, and the Boodle Gang were operating on the lower West Side of Manhattan.

From many of the ethnic and racial gangs in immigrant neighborhoods came the criminals and hoods of the next generation. In the early 1900s, under Tim Sullivan, there arose two great racial mobs, Jews under Monk Eastman operating from the Bowery, and Italians under Paul Kelly operating in the Fourth and Sixteenth Wards just west of the Bowery. "Out of these two groups came the majority of the vicious criminals who pestered and disgraced New York during the first two decades of the century" and who educated the next generation of thugs and criminals.[47]

Unquestionably, the adult gangs had an effect on the footloose children of the immigrants who roamed their neighborhoods. Asbury, writing in 1927, reported an "enormous increase in the number of juvenile gangsters, who were to provide material for street gangs of the nineties and the early part of the present century."[48] Prior to the Civil War, adult and juvenile gangs operated largely in the Bowery, the Five Points, and the Fourth Ward,

> simply because these were the congested and poverty stricken areas of the city; as the slums increased in extent, gangsters of all types and ages multiplied in numbers and power. By 1870 the streets throughout the greater part of New York fairly swarmed with prowling bands of homeless boys and girls actively developing the criminal instinct which is inherent in every human being. While all of these gangs chose their titular leaders from their own

ranks, a majority were at the same time under the domination of adult gang-sters or professional thieves, who taught the children to pick pockets, snatch purses and muffs, and steal everything they could lay their hands upon, while they masked their real business by carrying bootblack outfits, baskets of flowers, or bundles of newspapers. They lived on the docks, in the cellars and basements of dives and tenements, and in alleys and area ways; and when their masters could not feed them, which was often, they ate from swill bar-rels and garbage pails.[49]

The Reverend J. F. Richmond, although not mentioning gangs per se, also wrote about the large numbers of children roaming the streets of New York City and about the institutions responsible for juvenile delinquents.

Every great city contains a large floating population whose indolence, prodi-gality, and intemperance are proverbial, culminating in great domestic and social evil. From these discordant circles spring an army of neglected or ill-trained children, devoted to vagrancy and crime, who early find their way into the almshouse or the prison, and continue a life-long burden upon the community. It becomes the duty of the guardians of the public weal to search out methods for the relief of society from these intolerable burdens, and the recovery of the wayward as far as possible.[50]
  The children who come under the care of the society are between the ages of five and fourteen, and may for the sake of brevity be divided into two gen-eral classes. First, the truant and disobedient; secondly, the friendless and neglected. The first are either voluntarily surrendered by their parents for discipline, or committed by the magistrates for reformation. The second class found in a state of friendlessness and want, or of abandonment, or vagrancy, may be committed by the mayor, recorder, any alderman or magistrate of the city. . . .
  The correctives applied are mainly moral, the rod being very rarely em-ployed.[51]

Richmond also reported on the institutions on Hart Island in New York City. One was The Industrial School and The School Ship.

The number of vagrant, vicious, and adventurous children around New York is so great, that a new institution for their correction and reformation springs up every few years, . . . the buildings are always full, and the supply well nigh inexhaustible. For years past a class of large vicious boys have been thrown on the hands of the Commissioners of Charities and Corrections, for whom it has been difficult to well and suitably provide. . . . The school began late in the year 1868, and on the 31st of December, 1868, the warden reported the reception of 504 boys. The utter neglect under which they had thus far grown up appears in the fact that seventy-five per cent of them could neither read nor write, fifteen per cent able to read only, leaving out ten per cent in tolerable possession of the rudiments of an education. . . . During the last year 972 boys were received into the school.

Many boys in each generation are wild and adventurous in their natures, fond of excitements and dangers, and who will not sober down to the quietudes of ordinary industry. Neglected, they become the roughs, harbor thieves, pirates, and fillibusterers of the world. As early as 1812, Rev. Dr. Stanford, chaplain of the penal institutions of New York, recommended the separation of the youthful criminals from those more advanced, and urged the importance of training this adventurous class in a nautical ship for service on the sea. . . . The boys, whose features for the most part show their foreign origin and treacherous tendencies, are all clothed in bright sailor's uniform, and governed on the apprenticeship system of the United States Navy.[52]

The Reverend L. M. Pease arrived in the Five Points in 1850 and found a connection between the fighting and thieving adult gangs and the juvenile gangs. The Dead Rabbits had their Little Dead Rabbits, The Forty Thieves had their Little Forty Thieves, and the Plug Uglies had their Little Plug Uglies, all emulating the older gang members in action, speech, and, wherever possible, dress. Along the waterfront in the Fourth Ward youngsters of eight to twelve were in the Little Daybreak Boys. Most of these youngsters strove to emulate and aid their elders in their criminal activities and act as lookouts, participants, and decoys.[53]

With the Civil War over less than ten years, the slums of New York grew beyond the Bowery and the Five Points and so did the Juvenile gangs. On the lower West Side, around Washington and Greenwich Streets, a group of sneak thieves and small beggars made life miserable for the householders and merchants.

Of course, the adult and juvenile gang activity had some effect upon the schools too. Alvin Harlow reported on some of the problems faced by youngsters who wanted to go to school. "In some neighborhoods boys went to and from school in parties, to insure safety against attack by gangs of enemies or roughs slightly older. Tenth and Fourteenth Warders on opposite sides of the Bowery were hereditary enemies. A boy from one ward ventured into the other only at the risk of black eyes, split lips, and ruined clothing."[54]

Asbury summed up the actions and activities of the pre-1900 gangs of New York City:

The character of the juvenile gangs changed in proportion to the increased activity of welfare agencies, better housing conditions, greater efficiency of the police and, especially, to reforms in the educational system which permitted effective supervision and regulation of the children of the tenement districts. It is quite likely that there are as many juvenile gangs in New York today as there have ever been. For forming in groups and fighting each other is part of the traditional spirit of play, but in general they have become much less criminal. . . . In many parts of the city, particularly the Harlem and upper East Side districts, the boys fought with wooden swords and used wash-boiler covers for shields. But invariably the excitement of battle overcame them and they resorted to bricks and stones, with the result that a few heads and many windows were broken.[55]

Most of the criminals and racketeers of the years from about 1900 to the 1930s spent their formative years prowling and fighting with juvenile gangs. Al Capone, for example, was born in Brooklyn, in 1899, and joined the waning Five Pointers while in his mid-teens.[56]

The stark reality of gang activities and fighting is something that most urbanites and suburbanites fear but have very little experience with. Most of their experience has been vicarious. Sometimes the vicarious experience was visual and auditory, such as observing the Jets and the Sharks battling on the stage and screen in the musical *West Side Story*. The theory of social causation of gang participation was satirized as gang members analyzed themselves in "Gee, Officer Krupke!"

> Dear kind-ly Ser-geant Krup-ke,
> You got-ta un-der-stand,
> It's just our bring-in' up-ke
> That gets us outa hand.
> Our moth-ers all are junk-ies,
> Our fath-ers all are drunks.
> Gol-ly Mo-ses, nat-cher-ly we're punks!
> Gee, Of-fi-cer Krupke,
> We're ver-y upset;
> We nev-er had the love that ev-'ry child ought-a get.
> We ain't no de-lin-quents,
> We're jus mis-un-der-stood.
> Deep down in-side us there is good![57]

Transcriptions from some of my own tapes made with Brooklyn gang members in the 1950s sound different.

> On the Corner of Honky Tonk Street
> Out jumped the Chaplains in a black sedan
> Pull out a shotgun ready to cheat
> Make a Corsair cop a bad plea.
>
>   . . .
>
> In a 1941 the mighty Bishops
> They had just begun.
>
>   . . .
>
> 1, 2, and 3, 4,
> We are the Chaplains,
> Mighty, Mighty, Chaplains
>
>   . . .
>
> Bishops on the corner
> Three Four Five
> Doin' what we wanna.

A very realistic presentation of gang activity and fighting ("20 minutes and 14 seconds of uncompromising ugliness and waste") is a movie called *The Jungle*. *The Jungle* was written, acted in, and directed by black street gang youngsters from 12th and Oxford Streets in Philadelphia.[58]

Richard Sorenson taped "six boys in trouble" singing gangland and street rhythms. One of the gangland rhythms is entitled "gang fight" and ends with,

> We never . . . . , We never go without a fight,
> Because we can't lose any fight,
> That's why they call us the Teen . . . Teen Agers,
> The Alligator Lords,
> We rumble, we tumble, we fight all night,
> We never, we never, we never give up,
> We always fight, we never lose,
> We always get somebody 'fore we go,
> Because we are the winner Teen Ager Lords.[59]

In the late 1960s and early 1970s, gangs, fraternities, cliques, organizations, and "rat packs" were reported. New York, Chicago, Los Angeles, and Philadelphia reported an increase of street gangs. One of the supposed differences between the 1970s gangs and the gangs in the 1950s is that the gang members of the 1970s were older—some in their early thirties and some Viet Nam veterans.[60]

Where the gangs of the 1950s used knives, clubs, zip guns, chains, and fists, the 1970s gangs were reported to have arsenals consisting of such additional weapons as "molotov cocktails, rifles, shotguns, and, say youth workers, hand grenades and machine guns." Additionally, Vincent Wright reported "sophisticated" shotguns and automatic pistols replacing the zip guns of the 1950s.[61]

Another difference is that as "the racial composition of America's slums has shifted from white to black, so has the makeup of America's gangs."[62] As indicated earlier, just about all the earlier immigrant groups that came to the United States experienced a rite of passage that included poor and overcrowded housing, drugs, street gangs, prostitution, poverty, long working hours, problems in the schools, rats, and so on. Though blacks were brought here as slaves, since the Civil War, because of racism, they have been kept in a state of immigration continually experiencing all of the above and more.

Another example of this immigration rite of passage syndrome applies to the Chinese. My generation was brought up being told that there were never any problems related to crime or gangs in Chinese families. In fact, in 1967, William A. McIntyre wrote an article claiming that "Chinese families follow a pattern of life that breeds virtually no juvenile—or any other kind of—delinquency."[63]

However, after earlier Chinese immigration to the United States was stopped by such laws as The Chinese Exclusion Act of 1882, the Scott Act of 1888, and The National Origins Law of 1924, which based future immigration on a "national origins" quota, there was very little Chinese immigration. Finally, in 1965

President Johnson signed the Immigration Act abolishing the discriminatory national origins quota system, and Chinese immigrated legally to the United States for the first time in decades.[64]

New York City's Chinese population jumped from 20,000 in 1960, to 200,000 in 1982. Many of the new Chinese immigrants were marginally poor and lacked American salable skills. Consequently, the result was family and juvenile problems experienced by earlier occidental and white immigrant groups and Chinese street crime, Chinese gangs, other problems, and even public protest.[65] As a result, in May 1981, District Attorney Robert M. Morgenthau of Manhattan formed a special unit to concentrate on Chinese gangs.[66]

However, for many other Chinese who immigrated from a very middle class skilled background, there were good jobs and schools where their children achieved and are achieving at the top of their class.

Salisbury pointed out a misconception concerning the comparisons of the ages of more recent gang members with the ages of the earlier gang members.

There is an impression today that the street gangs of the past were "adult" gangs whereas those of today are "adolescent" gangs. This is a misconception. One hundred years ago little distinction was made between the adolscent and adult. A boy strong enough to work was regarded as an adult. Boys of fourteen or fifteen started out in life on their own. Physical maturity and strength, not chronological age, were the test. The street gangs of the last century were made up of the same age groups as those of today. This is not the first era in which society, particularly the adolescent segment, has been badly disturbed and shaken up.[67]

It is obvious that the gangs have some effect on the inner city communities within which they range, upon the schools that are located within the inner city area, and on the schools to which inner city youngsters are bussed.

In the city of Buffalo, during the 1970s, gangs had a definite effect upon the schools. In some cases, the threat of sudden gang incursions so permeated the school that the staff and students were in a constant state of fear. Often, rumors would spread through the school that it was about to be raided by a particular gang. At times, gangs would bring all teaching and learning to a halt as they would surround a school suddenly. Then, just as suddenly, they would leave, with rumors spreading that they were on their way to another school.

In some cases, gang presidents sometimes speak with school authorities concerning the conduct of a gang member, thus taking on the *in loco parentis* role. Additionally, gang ethos sanctions the use of force as a means for solving problems and grievances. Although gangs do not generally operate in schools, schools have been paralyzed and operations disorganized by the fear of gang reprisals. Misdemeanors go unreported; assault charges are not filed; students who should be suspended are not; school resources are diverted from educational considerations; and extracurricular activities are curtailed.[68]

Many students have reported being shaken down. Some parents have transferred their children because they were afraid they would be shot or stabbed. At other times, gangs actually entered schools in a very violent way. Reality 15 describes an inner city schoolteacher's experience with a gang from another school. He was on morning duty near the door to give out late passes.

REALITY 15

"My early morning assignment went regularly until one of my students warned me of an imminent invasion by a youth gang known as the Manhattan Lovers. The gang supposedly was armed with broom handles, chains, knives, and so on. Since the student in question had a very poor attendance record— he was absent from school at least 120 days up to that time — and since he did absolutely no work for me, nor for any of his other teachers, I did not place much confidence in his information. Indeed, I initially laughed it off and dismissed the young man. . . .

"As the homeroom period slowly drew to a close I decided to tell our principal what I had been told. . . . I went to see the principal to report my news. But he was unavailable. . . .

"As I was leaving the main office, I noticed a group of boys approaching our school from the direction of —— Junior High School. The boys were armed with broomsticks, bats, chains, and so on. Since at this time I was in the relative safety of the main office, for some reason . . . I saw fit to try to intercept the young men and lock the front door to prevent their entering.

"When I reached the hall, I was too late. The boys already had entered and I saw one youngster pick up my briefcase, which was heavy with books and reports, and slam it into one of our display cases which housed trophies and various articles.

"The glass shattered and the noise . . . brought many people into the halls to see what the problem was. At this moment, I was out of the main office directly in the path of the invaders. I had no time to dash back to the main office. Therefore, I made a right turn and sought the safety of the elevator. Unfortunately, the elevator was on a different floor and the door was locked.

"At this time the boys all passed me. At no time did I approach, speak to, or try to prevent any of them from entering our school. . . . Since I was alone, . . . I did not feel I was in any position to prevent their progress into the school.

"As the boys went by me, . . . no youngster made a threatening gesture to me nor did they look at me in any dangerous way. However, the last youngster in line had a black glove on. As he approached me, I saw out of the corner of my eye that he was swinging at my face. I decided to . . . prevent this from happening. . . . I brought my right elbow up to protect myself, and as I did so, his punch missed my mouth area and nose . . . and just grazed my right upper cheek area. In fact, my blocking action prevented pretty much serious injury to this part of my face. A swelling developed which was . . . taken care of by an ice pack provided by our office nurses.

"After the boys had passed by me, they proceeded to the second floor. . . . They attacked a teacher who had opened his door to see what the commotion was. . . . A youngster hit him in his eye and caused a cut and some injury. . . .

"After the boys had entered the second floor, they decided to leave the building. . . . The police arrived about ten minutes after the boys left the building.

"One of our assistant principals took me and the other teacher to the hospital where extensive x-rays were taken.

"The next day, many of our teachers in the school, fearful of their safety and health, did not report."[69]

In the 1960s and early 1970s in some Buffalo high schools where black youngsters were being bussed, black and white gangs, clubs, and fraternities, often goaded by parents, sometimes battled one another. At other times, the gangs kept everyone in a state of fear in anticipation of renewed hostilities.

Because of the threat of gangs, some PTAs found it impossible to have evening meetings, parents being fearful of venturing out at night. One school had to turn to Saturday morning meetings, which, by the way, proved very successful.

In some schools, because parents feared for their children's safety at afterschool remedial and advanced programs, the attendance at these programs fell off. When rumors circulate through a neighborhood that gangs have invaded a particular school, many parents rush to the school to take their children home.

Further reporting has found additional school-gang problems affecting the teaching and learning in New York, Philadelphia, Los Angeles, and Chicago. For example, gangs attacked children going to and from school. At some high schools, parents kept children home; other parents transferred their children to parochial and private schools.[70]

Pupils in some schools are afraid to go to the toilet for fear of being assaulted or robbed. Additionally, some principals have suggested that teachers not remain alone in their classrooms. Across the country, innumerable schools now employ security guards. Furthermore, many principals have to take teachers from their teaching responsibilities to have them patrol in and around the school.

Reportings of gang/school-related problems have included (1) a school closed for lack of police protection after repeated assaults and muggings of students by gang members; (2) school lavatories locked so that school security guards have less area to cover; and (3) stabbings, assaults, robberies, and acts of intimidation going on in and outside of schools.[71]

Additional gang-related problems have included youngsters being beaten if, for example, they did not carry a leaf or similar item in a certain pocket. Sometimes gang members would force nongang members to carry their knives or guns into school. In the late 1950s and early 1960s, some gang members stopped carrying weapons. However, they would walk close to the curb. If attacked, they would break off a car antenna and use it as a weapon. Gang and nongang members have often threatened teachers, with "I'll get my gang after you." Recently, in some cases, gangs reported break-dancing competitions rather than gang fights.

For me, two incidents out of many with gangs or students who belonged to gangs stand out. They stand out because of the numbers of school-aged youngsters involved and because of what could have happened if I had not been so lucky.

REALITY 16

Our school was on West 93rd Street and Amsterdam Avenue in New York City. We had just opened the school after closing the one for drug users on North Brothers Island.

The principal called me into the office and introduced me to a detective, who informed me that one of the students on my going-home line was the war counselor of a gang responsible for the stabbing of a youth from another gang. The stabbed youth had just been released from the hospital and would probably try to retaliate against the student on my line. Should my student spot him, I was supposed to nofity the principal, who would call the police.

About two days later, another teacher and I started our fifteen students toward the subway. Just as we left the school building one of our students yelled, "There he is!" and pointed to one of a group of about eight teenagers standing there.

I called to the fellow they had pointed to, "What do you want—this is still school property?"

"Fuck you!" he yelled.

As he ran toward me holding a bat that I had not noticed earlier; suddenly about thirty more teenagers popped up from behind parked cars. I turned and shouted to the other teacher, "Call the cops!" I tried pushing and yelling at our students to go back the fifteen feet or so to the school.

One of our bigger students ran off to the side, reached into his inside jacket pocket, pulled out a large serving spoon, and yelled, "Come on mutha fuckas—over here." The gang leader and two others then ran past me to get to him. When two of them reached the sidewalk, they bent down and picked up a bat and metal window frame they had stashed, and went after him. Almost unbelievably, he beat the three of them off.

He probably saved my life, or at least saved me from getting a good beating by attracting the three boys to him and away from me.

For the next few minutes, I still don't know how long, we all cursed, screamed, dodged, ran, punched, shoved, kicked, and swung out. Then suddenly, as quickly as it started it was over; the attackers took off running.

The police arrived about fifteen minutes later and told us to go to the station house while they hunted for the other gang. While we were sitting in the station house waiting, one of my students turned to me and asked, "Hey, what would you have done if he had hit you in the head with the bat?"

"What do you mean?" I asked.

"Man, when you turned around and told us to get into school, he missed your head by about that much with the bat as he ran by you," he responded, holding two fingers about an eighth of an inch apart.

After a wait of about twenty minutes, the police brought in four members of the gang and asked us to identify them. Although the gang leader had been less than twenty feet from me, I was not sure. I turned to one of my students and asked, "That him?"

He nodded.

I turned to the policeman and said, "That's him." They were booked, and I ran to catch my car pool.

A month later we were called to Family Court on 23rd Street. We went before the judge and all the reports were read. The judge asked whether I had been hit or hurt with the bat. When he was told no, let let all four go without even a reprimand. Interestingly, we learned the gang leader was playing hooky from another "600" School the day they jumped us.

As we were leaving, the judge called the three students who were with me as witnesses. He leaned across the table, pointed his finger at them, and snarled, "If I see you punks down here again, I'll put you all away."

As we walked away, I turned to my students, shook my head, and apologized.[72]

REALITY 17

We were on the G. G. Independent Subway on our way to Red Hook Stadium for an afternoon of track and field events with about sixty students from our after-school program. Six teenagers loped through the train eyeing everyone.

They halted and pointed at two brothers among our students. "You Eagon's brother?" one of them asked.

Before either of the brothers could answer, they ran to the next car, had a quick and excited conversation, and got off the train at the next stop. Our seven staff members got together to talk over what had happened as our students began to get fidgety. One of the staff informed us that our students' brother was an important member of a Brooklyn fighting gang; he had beaten up someone from another gang the week before.

We got off the train at Smith and 9th Street and began about a six-block walk to Red Hook Stadium. We walked hurriedly, everyone looking about apprehensively. As we neared the stadium, about twenty teenagers then nearly two blocks away, came toward us. They carried sticks, pipes, chains, bottles, and anything that would make a good weapon.

We filed into the stadium and sent someone to call the police. When the gang kids reached the stadium, they stopped outside so we decided to go on with our track meet. Our students sat in the stands. We seven faculty went down to the track to organize things. We have just finished our opening ceremonies when we noticed our students moving away from the Eagon brothers.

As if by signal, the gang had come into the stadium through a hole in the chain link fence and entered the stands. They formed a line from the bottom of the stands to the top and began walking toward our students.

I was dead on my feet. I was scared. I thought, "Shit, what the hell am I doing here—I have a kid now."

Suddenly one of our staff, a short wiry guy, yanked his jacket off, grabbed a bat, yelled "Come on," and took off running for the stands. The rest of us faculty moved after him. He turned and faced the gang as they walked slowly toward him. We lined up on either side of him and formed a line between the gang and the two Eagon brothers and our students.

The teacher who had moved first began to shout and gesture with the bat. The gang was then about seven or eight feet from us.

"You mother fuckers," he yelled, "touch one of our kids and we'll kick everyone of your fuckin' asses! This is a school function and we'll defend the two brothers."

The gang president must have realized we were serious. He took the smart way out. "We didn't know it was a school meet. We'll get them some other time."

In almost a single file, the gang walked to the top of the stadium and tossed their weapons over the stadium wall. They slowly walked out of the stadium and hung around on the outside.

By then, two police cars had arrived, and the policemen agreed to take the brothers out of the neighborhood. However, the brothers refused to go until they ran in their races. We therefore rearranged the schedule and ran their race. The brothers won their races, got into the squad cars, and were on their way out of the neighborhood. When the gang saw them leave, they left too.

This was the first time that our students had not stuck together. And, this was the last time we went to Red Hook.

The youngsters who belong to gangs may fall into any of my four categories of behavior. The middle class student may join a gang because his survival on his or nearby streets necessitates joining. The streets in his neighborhood may be controlled by a gang, and peer gang pressures as well as the need to walk the streets in his or other neighborhoods may require his joining a gang. Also, the gang may give him the security, the belonging, and the action he craves and needs.

This reminds me of a newspaper story I read twenty years ago. At a social worker conference, the participants were arguing over defining a neighborhood.

After listening for about forty-five minutes, a Puerto Rican social worker took the floor.

"I don't know about you guys," he said. "But where I come from a neighborhood is the place that if you walk out of it you get beat up."

Of course, whether gangs really fight or not becomes of little consequence. The fearful atmosphere they create permeates the community and its schools, interfering with the teaching and learning and sometimes tying up the downtown administrators for weeks. This is true for many cities where gangs guard their territory physically or pose the threat of violence. Indeed, the gangs' continued existence is also noted by their graffiti markings on the school buildings that declare their territory or turf (see Chapter 5).

JUVENILE DELINQUENCY AND CRIME

Unquestionably, there is underreporting of the misdeeds of middle class children. However, even this underreporting would not alone explain the high rates of delinquency on the part of lower class males.

Studies by John Conger and William Miller indicated higher delinquency rates among certain lower class groups, particularly those in socially disorganized areas. Whether or not delinquency and emotional disturbance should be equated is still being debated. However, even where such subgroup behavior is considered "normal," it is not likely to produce emotionally healthy results.[73]

Despite the biases in reporting of youthful crime and delinquency, there appear to be some substantial conclusions. In a staff report to the National Commission on the Causes and Prevention of Violence, some perspectives were presented concerning crime.

> The conclusions nonetheless emerged that the true rate for each of the four major violent crimes—homicide, rape, assault, and robbery—appears considerably higher for those aged 18–24 and 15–17 than for the other age groups. The juvenile and youthful population is growing at a greater rate than other age groups; thus, we found that about 12 percent of the increase in the rate of the major violent crimes combined between 1950 and 1965 was attributable merely to increases in the population aged 10–24.[74]

However, recent reported FBI statistics found a drop in certain crime attributed to a drop in the numbers in the eighteen to twenty-five age group. Hence, there does appear to be a relationship between numbers of juveniles and the amount of crime.[75]

Further reporting on crime by the Task Force on Individual Acts of Violence concerning race, sex, and the inner city found,

> Most youthful offenders are male, and there is a disproportionate representation of Negroes. FBI estimates in 1967 suggested a reported criminal homi-

cide arrest rate for the Negro 10–17 age group of 22 per 100,000, approximately 17 times greater than the white 10–17 age group. The reported forcible rape rate for Negro juveniles was 12 times higher than the corresponding rate for white juveniles; the reported robbery rate 20 times higher, and the reported aggravated assault rate 8 times greater. Even when considerable reporting problems are taken into account, these figures imply large differentials in the true rates of juvenile violence when broken down by race.[76]

Also,

The locus of delinquency and youth violence is more likely to be the urban ghetto than any other place. A 1960 study of Minneapolis showed that ghetto delinquency rates were twice as high as in the rest of the city. The same differential appeared when the Hough area was compared to Greater Cleveland in 1961. A 1961 study conducted in a St. Louis ghetto area, where 60 percent of the population is Negro, showed a delinquency rate 3 times higher than in the rest of the city. In 1962, the delinquency rate for Harlem was 109 per 1,000 population between the ages of 7 and 20, while New York City taken as a whole the rate was 46 per 1,000 for the same age group. In 1963 statistics gathered in a ghetto area of greater Boston where most of the city's Negro population resides showed delinquency to be four times greater than for Boston as a whole.[77]

The commission, in reporting these figures, realized that there is some aspect of bias in arrests and in the reporting of ghetto crimes as compared with middle class white crime. However, taking this into consideration they found that "there is some bias in these figures because, among other things, slum offenders are more likely to be arrested than urban or rural offenders. Although it would be naive to say that inner-city youth have a monopoly on violence when middle- and upper-class delinquency are considered, it is still safe to conclude that delinquency remains primarily a slum problem."[78]

Crime appears to be committed most often by the poor in slum areas. It is interesting to speculate how much of this adolescent crime could be prevented if more educators could overcome their historical ethnocentric and racist behavior to provide a more positive school environment and more of an experiential learning curriculum that would include socially acceptable risk taking, challenge, and adventure.[79]

VIOLENCE AND PHYSICAL AGGRESSION

That National Commission on the Causes and Prevention of Violence documented the relationship between youth and crime in general and youth crime in poor areas.

The commission also made an interesting point in relation to the instigation of ethnic and religious violence in the United States.

Ethnic and religious violence has also occurred frequently in the United States, involving the Irish, Italians, Orientals, and—far most consequently—Negroes. Only in the last decade, however, has it become common for such ethnic groups to initiate violent conflict. Historically the violence resulted when groups farther up the socioeconomic ladder resisted the peaceful upward progress of particular ethnic and religious groups toward higher positions in the social order. Those who felt threatened by the prospect of the new immigrant or the Negro getting "too big" and "too close" resorted to defensive violence.[80]

Criminal and violent attacks upon citizens are not committed by the emotionally disturbed only. However, there is a great deal more crime and physical assault in lower class socioeconomic areas when compared with middle class or upper class areas. A staff report to the National Commission on the Causes and Prevention of Violence reported a difference between ghetto residents' contact with physical assault as compared with suburbanites' contact with physical assault: "A recent survey in Chicago concluded that the chances of physical assault for a Negro ghetto dweller were 1 in 77, while the odds were 1 in 10,000 for an upper middle-class suburbanite.[81]

The FBI uniform crime report for 1971 established that in the fifty-seven cities with populations greater than a quarter-million people, crimes of violence rose 7.5 percent over 1970. The suburbs for the same period experienced a rise in violent crime of 13.4 percent.

Although the rate of increase for crimes of violence was greater in the suburbs, the suburban population is greater than the big-city population by 56.9 million to 42.6 million. Therefore, in relation to a person's chances of being exposed to a violent crime these figures show that "for every 100,000 people in the suburbs, 206 were victims of violent crimes. In the large cities the number was 1,048."[82]

Dr. Marvin E. Wolfgang, director of the Center for Studies in Criminology and Criminal Law at the University of Pennsylvania, offered a possible reason for the high rates of robbery and murder in the slums as contrasted with the rest of New York City.

"In some of these communities," he said, "a subculture of violence had developed. In addition to the drug scene and the unbelievable poverty, there is a life-style of organized violence and physical aggression sometimes looked on as machismo or manliness.

"It's sort of corny to say," Dr. Wolfgang added, "but there is a violence born into generations. Life has become terribly cheap."[83]

When a university professor was mugged and killed near Columbia University in New York City, a resident's comments expressed the acceptance of violence as part of the routine of living in that area: "[T]here are so many muggings and purse-snatchings in daylight on the street that such incidents have become part of the neighborhood scene, like the sound of the cars and trucks."[84]

In a hot dog establishment frequented by prostitutes, pimps, and junkies just off New York City's Times Square, knife wielding has become so common that even the police ignore it. "It's normal, said the restaurant supervisor. . . . 'It wouldn't be normal if someone didn't come in here with a naked knife.' And even as he spoke, in low, guarded tones, another man walked in, also wielding a knife. Within an hour, a third man walked in waving a knife."[85]

From another point of view, in the United States the pathology of the black urban slum has developed over long years and many ecological pattern changes. The slum culture provides some black disadvantaged children with a frame of reference or code of behavior that is different from that of the middle class teacher or the middle class black child.

The disadvantaged children's lower class life is violent, hostile, aggressive, anxious, and unstable. Often they turn their aggression on themselves, their peers, and authority figures. They learn to fight for everything; they learn that might does indeed make right. As children their discipline tends to be physical and custodial, with the use of threats and punishment as common means of control rather than the gentler psychological and emotional approaches of the middke class.[86]

If you have read Claude Brown's *Manchild in the Promised Land* and Piri Thomas's *Down These Mean Streets*, which deal with growing up in Harlem and Spanish Harlem, you will recall how, time and time again, the authors make the same point: To make your reputation and not succumb, you had to act crazy and prove yourself with your fists.[87]

Brown wrote,

Fighting was the thing that people concentrated on. In our childhood, we all had to make our reputations in the neighborhood. Then we'd spend the rest of our lives living up to them. A man was respected on the basis of his reputation. The people in the neighborhood whom everybody looked up to were the cats who killed somebody. The little boys in the neighborhood whom the adults respected were little boys who didn't let anybody mess with them. . . . It seemed as though if I had stayed in Harlem all my life, I might never have known that there was anything else in life other than sex, religion, and violence.[88]

Finally, there is physicalness in lower socioeconomic groups. Whereas middle class youngsters, in both subtle and unsubtle ways, are taught to sublimate or hold back their feelings, emotions, and attitudes concerning physicalness, lower class youngsters are not. Consequently, many lower class children are very physical. Aggression and violence are lower class problemsolving techniques. Most often, this physicalness frightens members of the middle class, particularly school personnel. Quite often, the educator interprets physicalness as aggression; and it is normal for an adult to fear an aggressive child.

Such lower class physicality is depicted in such works as Mary Greene and Orletta Ryan's *The Schoolchildren: Growing up in the Slums*; Herbert Kohl's *36 Children*; Le Roi Jones's off-Broadway production of *The Toilet*; the TV special and now movie entitled *The Way It Is*, which depicted the N.Y.U.-Jr. High School fiasco in Brooklyn; and James Herndon's *The Way It Spozed To Be*. Anyone who has lived in an inner city, lower class neighborhood or worked in an inner city school has also experienced or observed such behavior.[89]

Samuel Tennenbaum's "The Teacher, The Middle Class, The Lower Class," described how one house of lower class inhabitants unknowingly terrified and frightened an entire block of middle class residents on the west side of Manhattan.

Boys and girls mixed and it was difficult to think of them as single, individual children. They shouted, they screamed, they pushed, they fought. In the midst of play, they would suddenly get into individual fights and collective fights. Violence, aggression, play and friendliness seemed all mixed up. Every wall on the block was used, either to play ball on or throw things at. The streets became cluttered with debris, especially broken glass. . . . [W]hat frightened them, was the violent, hostile way in which lower-class families found their amusement. An almost palpable atmosphere of aggression and violence hovered over the street. The children would attack an automobile—literally attack it as locusts attack a field—climb on top of it, get inside, and by combined, cooperative efforts shake and tug until they left it a wreck. . . . [E]ven their innocent, friendly play was violent. Suddenly, strong, tall, gangling adolescent boys would dash pellmell down the street, like stampeding cattle, shrieking and screaming, pushing, shoving, mauling each other.

Like my neighbors, teachers remain in a perpetual state of fear of these children, at their acting out, their defiance of discipline, their destructivensss and vandalism. . . . Many teachers feel trapped, frightened, helpless.[90]

Harry Brill, reporting on a rent strike, added support to the view of a lower class black lifestyle that is threatening, aggressive, and loud; they were expressive but not effective. They appeared to be continually searching for stimulation which begot behavior that was frantic, highly impulsive, sometimes frightening, and also dramatic.[91]

The middle class educator who is secure with his or her sexuality and physicalness is better able to deal with this physicalness. Given certain positive personality attributes and attitudes, this professional has the potential for becoming a good inner city teacher. Because this person is more secure with physicalness and his or her body, he or she is usually capable of separating hostile aggressive acts from playful lower class physical activity or streetcorner behavior. Additionally, the physical teacher may not be fearful of another physical person or may not feel threatened and insecure by a student's physical actions. These feelings are often instinctual reactions on the part of this professional who is physical. Also, the physical child senses the teacher's physicalness. (Chapter 9 discusses this point.) Reality 18 is an example of lower class physical activity that did not frighten two middle class teachers and ended positively.

REALITY 18

Two male teachers were standing and talking at the bottom of the steps in an inner city, all-black, junior high school. A male student was standing a few feet from them. Suddenly, another male student let out a banshee scream and leaped, as though propelled, at least five or ten steps onto the back of the other youngster. They started pummeling one another.

The teachers barely took time from their conversation. One of them, however, turned to the supposed battling youngsters and said, "Hey fellas, give it some slack."

The youngsters looked at the teachers, flung their arms around one another's shoulders, and walked down the hall talking.

The majority of teachers and administrators however, are frightened and repelled by such physically aggressive behavior. Hence, all physical activity becomes a threat to them; and their fears create problems. Reality 19 is just such an example. It is identical to Reality 18 except in its outcome.

REALITY 19

Two male teachers were standing and talking at the bottom of the steps in an inner city, all-black junior high school. A male student was standing a few feet from them. Suddenly, another male student let out a banshee scream and leaped the last five or ten steps onto the back of the other youngster, whereupon, they started pummeling one another.

The teachers stopped their conversation and yelled at the boys to stop. When the boys continued their roughhousing, one of the teachers ran over to them and attempted to stop them physically, whereupon, they both ganged up on him. There was a lot of cursing, hollering, and threats, when suddenly, the boys broke away, ran down the hall, and yelled, "Fuck you, you white fuck."

Too often, the teacher who has the positive instinctual feelings about the streetcorner physical behavior ends up feeling guilty about his instincts to become physical with his students in a positive, nonpunitive way. What this person needs is a good college or in-service course, or contact with a good supervisor who will help him or her (1) feel good and not guilty about his or her physical instincts, (2) help him or her develop this physicalness in a teaching style, and (3) help him or her to be at ease with lower class streetcorner behavior.

You may argue that our entire society is becoming more violent. There is a difference, however, between the violence of the middle class and that of the lower class. For those in the middle class or upper class, most violence is experienced vicariously, safely, and at a distance by the half hour or hour from movies, reporting of crime and war on TV, and Sunday afternoon professional football. For many disadvantaged children, violence is a way of life. It is very real, and to cope with it is to survive.

Realities 20, 21, 22, and 23 describe my personal experience with lower class physicalness that may provide the reader with additional insight into what is being referred to as physicalness and how it affects those from the middle class.

REALITY 20

I was directing a large day campgrounds within which were sixteen decentralized day camps. My elder daughter, at the time about eight years old, wanted to go to one of the camps, I picked the camp with the best director and program for her to attend.

The camp drew its population from a neighborhood that was in flux. Most of the middle class inhabitants had moved and had been replaced by lower class black and Puerto Rican families, whose children now made up the majority of the campers.

After two days in camp my daughter demanded vehemently to be taken out. No amount of talking or questioning on my part could either get her back or uncover the reason for her departure. It wasn't until months later that I found out why she had refused to go back to camp.

Her reasoning went something like this: "You know, Daddy, everytime my counselor put out cookies or crayons or milk, or anything else, all the kids were rough and would fight and yell and shove and grab and I would never get any milk or cookies or crayons or anything, and the counselor never did anything about it."

Because my roots were in the city streets and because of my experiences in the "600" schools, the physicalness of the black and Puerto Rican campers seemed natural to me. Not so, however, to my daughter, accustomed to a quiet, calm, suburban, almost rural, lifestyle. It frightened her, and she didn't want any part of it.

REALITY 21

My family was in Manhattan one weekend visiting with relatives in the West 80's. My daughters and I decided to cross Broadway to purchase some ices at one of the pizza places on the east side of Broadway. Traffic was not too heavy as we crossed to the east side. suddenly, as we came close to the east side sidewalk, my daughters pressed close to me holding my hands tightly. It was as though they were trying to climb into my pockets.

I looked at them and then around to see what was going on. They tried to get closer to me as we walked south on Broadway. Suddenly, I realized what was happening. All around us were dozens of kids of all sizes and shapes. They were running, pushing, shoving, laughing, jumping, yelling, and generally playing as urban lower class youngsters do. No one was being beaten or hurt, but many had dirty faces and hands, their shirts or tee shirts were torn or open, dirty and flapping as they ran. All the physicalness had frightened my middle class suburban daughters.

In relation to Realities 20 and 21, it was not the blackness of many of the youngsters that my daughters feared. We had middle class black friends with children with whom we exchanged visits; therefore, blackness was not something my daughters feared. But constant aggressive physical behavior was something that frightened them, as they could not relate to it.

This clash of divergent socioeconomic lifestyles is the phenomenon that has been causing many of our school problems. For some reason, we fear unfamiliar lifestyles. In addition to the middle class fear of aggressive physicalness, we also have differences in dress that cause fear and problems. Jeff Greenfield made this point as he described his "terror" in visiting the unfamiliar ground of the Brooklyn Paramount to see a rock show.

REALITY 22

Terror. Perhaps you think you can define it. It is sitting in a jet fighter cockpit, plummeting to a crash landing in a hostile country. It is losing footing on a mountain ledge in the midst of a blizzard. It is walking down a deserted city street in the dead of night, with the sudden sound of footsteps behind you.

No, that is not terror. I will tell you what terror is. Terror is waiting on line at 6:30 in the morning on a school holiday in 1957 for the Brooklyn Paramount to open for Alan Freed's rock and roll revue.

You have been up since 5:30 on your first day of vacation. Christmas or Easter (Hanukkah or Passover in my set). You have staggered into the darkness, found your friend Alan (another normal, neurotic Jewish kid) and weaved your way into the subway. There you pass interminable time, speeding past unfamiliar stops, emerging into the sullen dawn in downtown Brooklyn (downtown Brooklyn?). There, about a block away, is the Brooklyn Paramount, a huge movie palace built to hold the thousands who do not go out to movies anymore. On the marquee are big red letters: "Ten Days Only! Alan Freed's All-Star Rock 'n' Roll Revue!"

You walk to the theater, past the shuttered luncheonettes and cheap clothing stores. There is already a knot of kids waiting on line, even though the doors will not open for 2 hours and 45 minutes. And now you will begin to learn the meaning of fear.

There people are different. They do not look the way I do. They do not talk the way I do. I do not think they were born the same way I was. All of the males are six feet, seven inches tall. The last six inches is their hair, carefully combed into a pompadour. They are lean, rangy, even scrawny (except for one who is very, very fat). They have the hard faces of the children of the working poor. They read auto specs at night, not college catalogues. They wear St. Christopher medals, white T-shirts with their cigarette packs held in the left sleeve which is rolled up to the muscles. They have muscles.

The girls are all named Fran. They have curlers in their hair and scarves tied around their heads. They chew gum. They wear jeans and sweaters, and their crucifixes bounce on their breasts, some of which are remarkable examples of stress under pressure.

The conversation is guttural, half-sentences and grunts, with innuendos and veiled hints of lubricity. "Eh, that party, eh, Fran? Remember, heh, heh? Han, she don't remember nuthin." Fran is giggling, blushing. There is about these people an overwhelming sense of physical force, the same sense exuded by the students of Ascension High who chased the Jews home from school every afternoon: they hit other people a lot. Every joke, every insult, every question, is followed by open-handed jabs to the face, punches on the arm, slaps which barely miss being punches. It is like watching Leo Gorcey and Huntz Hall in the Bowery Boys movies.

At this point, there is only one stark thought in my mind: what in God's name am I doing here? These people are going to kill me and steal my five dollars and I will not be found for days. Consequently, the strategy of waiting on line at the Paramount is clear. You do not talk with your friend about your grades on the Social Studies test. You do not talk about where you are going to college. You do not engage in precocious argument about socialism. You keep your big mouth shut.

The vow of silence makes time go slowly, so you look at the posters over the theatre entrance, the pictures of the stars blown up on cardboard, the names spelled out in letters glittering from the gold and silver dust. There is Buddy Holly and the Crickets; the Cleftones, in white dinner jackets and red slacks; Jo Ann Campbell, "the blonde bombshell" who wears high-heeled shoes and very tight skirts, and whose biggest hand comes when she turns her back to the audience.

If you talk at all, it is in grunts to the others. "Yeah, Frankie Lyman, I saw him—seen him—last year. You heard the new Fats Domino?" You wait for the doors to open, for the sanctuary of the dark theater, for the Terror to go away.[92]

Here we saw terror resulting not only from the phenomenon of divergent socioeconomic lifestyles, but also from a different speech pattern, dress, and even hair style. These problems resulted from differences within white groups; blacks were not even involved. The divider was lifestyle and social class—not color.

Reality 23 came about as my wife and I observed another instance of the contrast between lower class and middle class lifestyles when we walked along the crescent-shaped shore of Lake Welch in the Bear Mountain Harriman State Park.

REALITY 23

At one end of the lake, we observed bathers in what appeared to be less expensive bathing suits, milk in glass containers, people sitting on towels or occasionally beach blankets, a preponderance of adult females. The water was in endless turmoil as kids with few adults around yelled and screamed, jumped and shoved, and ran after one another screaming. No one was really hurt or crying, though.

As we continued along the water's edge and neared the middle of the crescent-shaped beach, we observed a different order. On the beach were men, women, and children sprawled on chaise lounges or on big towels or blankets. The bathing suits looked more expensive. Food was continually being withdrawn from large ice chests and eaten. Juice, iced tea, and iced coffee poured from insulated coolers, not glass jars. In the water there were a noticeable number of adults, particularly fathers playing with their children. If by some slip of the mind a father lifted his child onto his shoulders or someone flipped some water at someone else, the life guard's whistle soon brought them back to the middle class reality and they ceased breaking the rules.

When fear of physicalness is combined with a fear of blacks, the fear can become hate. Norman Podhoretz explained his special "twisted" fear, envy, and hatred of Negroes as compared with other immigrant groups. While growing up in Brooklyn in the 1930s, he alternately envied, feared, and hated blacks because they "were tougher than we were, more ruthless, and on the whole they were better athletes." And, they "do not seem to be afraid of anything," and "act as though they have nothing to lose."

What mainly counted for me about Negro kids of my own age was that they were "bad boys." There were plenty of bad boys among the whites—this was, after all, a neighborhood with a long tradition of crime as a career open to aspiring talents—but the Negroes were *really* bad, bad in a way that beckoned to one, and made one feel inadequate. *We* all went home every day for a lunch of spinach-and-potatoes; *they* roamed around during lunch hour, munching on candy bars. In winter *we* had to wear itchy woolen hats and mittens and cumbersome galoshes; *they* were bareheaded and loose as they pleased. *We* rarely played hookey, or got into serious trouble in school, for all our street-corner bravado; *they* were defiant; forever staying out (to do what delicious things?), forever making disturbances in class and in the halls, forever being sent to the principal and returning uncowed. But most important of all, they were *tough*; beautifully, enviably tough, not giving a damn for anyone or anything. To hell with the teacher, the truant officer, the cop;

to hell with the whole adult world that held *us* in its grip and that we never had the courage to rebel against except sporadically and in petty ways.[93]

Even today, Podhoretz points to aspects of physicalness as being central to his feelings toward blacks.

> But envy? Why envy? And hatred? Why hatred? Here again the intensities have lessened and everything has been complicated and qualified by the guilts and the resulting over-compensations that are the heritage of the enlightened middle-class world of which I am now a member. Yet just as in childhood I envied Negroes for what seemed to me their superior masculinity, so I envy them today for what seems to me their superior physical grace and beauty. I have come to value physical grace very highly, and I am now capable of aching with all my being when I watch a Negro couple on the dance floor, or a Negro playing baseball or basketball. They are on the kind of terms with their own bodies that I should like to be on with mine, and for that precious quality they seem blessed to me.[94]

SUMMARY

The object of this chapter is to demonstrate the additional conditioning experiences that poor or inner city youngsters are exposed to whenever they are in their neighborhoods. Certainly, continual exposure to the negative conditioning of gangs, juvenile delinquency, crime, and violence must have an effect on inner city children. Therefore, when you talk about inner city schools you must consider the social and economic realities of their community.

It must also be remembered that inner city youngers' willingness to become aggressive and violent has not been lost on either black ghetto children or their teachers. From a historical point of view, this willingness to become aggressive and violent is, to some extent, positive, for a study of U.S. history will reveal that almost all ethnic, religious, and racial groups had to go through a period of violent confrontation with those who preceded them as one of the final steps required for achieving economic and political power.

The pictures of the violence and the disturbances in the ghettos accompanied by racist fantasies linger in the minds of school personnel; many come to school fearful of blacks. And many black children come to school with their fantasies, fears, and expectations of whites. This fear, dislike, and sometimes hatred of poor blacks by school personnel is rather obvious to the poor black child. In turn, these feelings expressed by school personnel provoke the streetcorner-conditioned youngster to act out even more. For ghetto living teaches you to take advantage of, manipulate, abuse, or even destroy those who are weaker than you or who fear or dislike you.

Another point that must be remembered is that, historically, as the earlier Irish, Italian, Jewish, and other ethnic and religious immigrants struggled through their urban immigration rite of passage, to a large extent, they had similar incidents and experiences to those reported in this chapter. Though blacks were nonvoluntary immigrants, racism has kept them in an economic, legal, and social state of immigration since the American Civil War. Therefore, the incidents of crime, gangs, and overcrowded housing are manifested and perpetuated by social class behavior and racism rather than by one's blackness.

NOTES TO CHAPTER 4

1. Sheila Rule, "A Man Sweeps Floors, and Dreams," *New York Times*, September 6, 1984, p. B1.
2. Martin Tolchin, "South Bronx: A Jungle Stalked by Fear, Seized by Rage," *New York Times*, January 15, 1973, p. 19.
3. Alvin F. Harlow, *Old Bowery Days: The Chronicles of a Famous Street* (New York: D. Appleton, 1931).
4. By middle class I am referring to those children who, though they may come from a one-parent family and be on welfare, have their television viewing limited; if there is some money, they may be taking music lessons; when someone visits their apartment they have to recite something for the guests; they are taken to the zoo, to museums, and to other cultural activities; their homework is insisted upon; and they are disciplined by being "grounded" rather than by being hit. They can sit quietly for a while, and they are verbally and physically restrained. They may even dress as do typically middle class children.
5. Joint Commission on Mental Health of Children, *Crisis in Child Mental Health: Challenge for the 1970's* (New York: Harper & Row, 1969), p. 265.
6. Ibid.
7. Harrison E. Salisbury, *The Shook-Up Generation* (New York: Harper & Brothers, 1958), p. 136-37.
8. Staff Report Submitted to The National Commission on the Causes and Prevention of Violence, *Crimes of Violence*, Vol. 12 (Washington, D.C.: U.S. Government Printing Office, 1969), pp. 609-10.
9. Walter B. Miller, *Trans-Action* 6, no. 10 (1969): 11.
10. Ibid., p. 12.
11. Salisbury, p. 9.
12. Harlow, p. 185.
13. Ibid., p. 186.
14. Herbert Asbury, *The Gangs of New York: An Informal History of the Underworld* (New York: Capricorn, 1970), p. 9.
15. Ibid., p. 12.
16. Ibid., p. 22.
17. Ibid., p. 13; A rabbit was a rowdy in the slang of that time. Originally, the Dead Rabbits were a faction of the Roach Guards. During a stormy meeting of the Roach Guards, marked by internal dissention, a dead rabbit was

thrown into the center of the meeting room. Whereupon, one of the dissident factions took it up as their name and standard.

18. Ibid., p. 22; The term "plug ugly" has carried over to today's slang. According to Harold Wentworth and Stuart B. Flexner, *Dictionary of American Slang* (New York: Crowell, 1960), p. 398, a "plug ugly" is "a hoodlum; a tough or ugly-looking ruffian . . . a strong, ugly, uncouth man; a rowdy; a tough guy."

19. Joel T. Headley, *The Great Riots of New York 1712 to 1873: Including a Full and Complete Account of the Four Day's Draft Riot of 1863* (New York: Dover, 1971), p. 131.

20. Ibid., p. 29.

21. June Lazare, "Dead Rabbits Fight with the Bowery Boys," *Folk Songs of New York City*, Folkways, FH 5276, 1967.

22. Asbury, p. 19.

23. Harlow.

24. Asbury, p. 37.

25. Benjamin A. Bodkin, *Sidewalks of America* (New York: Bobbs Merrill, 1954), p. 251.

26. Asbury, p. 31.

27. Augustine F. Costello, *Our Friends: A History of the New York City Fire Department: Volunteer and Paid* (New York: author, 1887), p. 19.

28. Ibid., p. 118.

29. Bodkin.

30. Costello, pp. 134, 172.

31. Helen Campbell, *Darkness and Daylight: or Lights and Shadows of New York Life, a Woman's Story of Gospel, Temperance, Mission, and Rescue Work* (Hartford, Conn.: Worthington, 1892).

32. Harlow, p. 337.

33. Costello, p. 190.

34. Ibid., p. 38.

35. "The Bowery Grenadiers," *Mitch's Greatest Hits*, Columbia, CL 1544, 1961; A personal correspondence with Mr. John Allison, who was eighty-eight years old in January 1973, reported that "the item done by Mitch Miller is a patched together job from the memories of both my friends Ted Dibble and myself. He and I heard it back in about 1924 as done by a Dr. Holmes in Englewood, New Jersey. The doctor used to bat it out in his key-of-C chords on the Holmes piano for the amusement of us youngsters. . . . I have no idea where Dr. Holmes heard the song—it may even be that he dated back to those days of the fire laddies."

36. Asbury, p. 49.

37. Ibid., p. 67.

38. Ibid., pp. 104-5.

39. Adrian Cook, *The Armies of the Streets: The New York City Draft Riots of 1863* (Lexington, Ky.: University of Kentucky Press), 1974).

40. Ibid., pp. 28-29.

41. Ibid., p. 19 and Notes p. 274. Election Riot, 1834; antiabolitionist riots, 1834 and 1835; Stevedores' Riot, 1836; Flour Riots, 1837; Election Riot,

1842; Astor Place Riots, 1849; Labor Riots, 1850; Kaine Riots, 1852; Forth of July Riots, 1853; Police Riots, 1857; Dead Rabbits-Bowery Boys Riots, 1857; Draft Riots, 1863; Orangeman's Day Riots, 1870 and 1871; and the Tompkins Square Riots, 1874.

42. Cook, pp. 56-57.
43. Ibid., p. 198.
44. Asbury, pp. 169-70.
45. Cook, 194-97.
46. Asbury, p. 28.
47. Harlow, p. 501.
48. Asbury, p. 238.
49. Ibid., p. 238-39.
50. Rev. J. F. Richmond, *New York and Its Institutions, 1609-1873*, 7th ed. (New York: E. B. Treat, 1873), pp. 328-29.
51. Ibid., pp. 330-31.
52. Ibid., pp. 572-73.
53. Asbury, p. 239.
54. Harlow, p. 444.
55. Asbury, p. 246.
56. John Kobler, *Capone: The Life and World of Al Capone* (New York: G. P. Putnam's Sons, 1971).
57. Leonard Bernstein, "Gee, Officer Krupke!," *West Side Story*, Columbia, OL 5230, 1957.
58. Judy Stone, "The Best Things We Knew Was Gang War," *New York Times Magazine*, October 13, 1968, p. 16D; 12th and Oxford Street Gang, dir., *The Jungle*, Churchill Films, 1968.
59. E. Richard Sorenson, *Street and Gangland Rhythms: Beats and Improvisations by Six Boys in Trouble*, Folkways, FD 5589, 1959.
60. Donald Janson, "Gangs Face Drive in Philadelphia," *New York Times*, February 13, 1972, p. 30; Donald Janson, "Violence by Youth Gangs is Found Rising in 3 Cities," *New York Times*, April 16, 1972, pp. 1, 58; "Southwide Story," *Time*, April 3, 1972, pp. 17-18; Shane Stevens, "The 'Rat Packs' of New York," *New York Times Magazine*, November 28, 1971, pp. 29-29, 91-95.
61. "Southwide Story," p. 18.
62. "Return to Rumble," *Newsweek*, September 8, 1969, pp. 51-52.
63. William A. McIntyre, "Chinatown Offers Us a Lesson," *New York Times Magazine*, October 6, 1957, pp. 49, 51, 55-56, 59.
64. Susan Jacoby, "Immigration Is at Its Highest Point in Half a Century," *New York Times*, June 8, 1975, p. E7; Jack Yen, *The Chinese of America* (New York: Harper & Row, 1981).
65. Martin Arnold, "Where Violence Is Part of Life's Routine," *New York Times*, September 22, 1972, p. 48; Melinda Beck and Peter Rinearson, "A Massacre in Chinatown," *Newsweek*, February 28, 1983, p. 24; Richard Bernstein, "Tourists' Image of Chinatown Marred by Tensions and Violent Youth Gangs," *New York Times*, December 24, 1983, p. B2; "Beware the Wah Ching!," *Newsweek*, August 20, 1971, pp. 63-64; "Foreign-Born Gang Terrorizing Chinatown in San Francisco," *Buffalo Evening News*,

October 27, 1971, p. 34; Robert R. Hanley, "Unrest Vexes Youth in a Torn Chinatown," *New York Times*, January 31, 1972, p. 37; Douglas E. Kneeland, "Young Hoodlums, Scorning Tradition of Hard Work, Plague San Francisco's Chinatown," *New York Times*, September 5, 1971, p. 29; Dena Kleiman, "American Dream of Chinese Family Turns Bittersweet," *New York Times*, October 1, 1982, p. B1; Selwyn Raab, "New Militancy Emerges in Chinatown," *New York Times*, June 8, 1975, pp. 1, 48; Nathaniel Sheppart, Jr., "Chinatown Fears Renewed Violence," *New York Times*, October 18, 1976; "Shooting of Restaurant Manager Spreads Fear in Philadelphia's Chinatown," *New York Times*, August 21, 1983, p. 28; "6 in Gang Seized in Rape-Murder," *New York Times*, October 21, 1982, p. B6; "Squad Reduces Chinatown Violence on Coast," *New York Times*, September 23, 1983, p. A14; "Surge in Immigration Now Means Chinese Are Largest Asian Group in U.S.," *New York Times*, July 30, 1981, p. A12; Joseph B. Treaster, "More Chinatown Youth Gangs Pledge to End Street Fighting," *New York Times*, August 14, 1976, p. 19; Wallace Turner, "13 Slain at Club in Seattle's Chinatown," *New York Times*, February 20, 1983; Wallace Turner, "20-Year-Old Is Convicted in Deaths of 13 in Seattle," *New York Times*, August 25, 1983, p. A12; Frederick M. Winship, "U.S. Chinatowns Now Torn by Gang Violence," *Buffalo Courier-Express*, July 15, 1973, p. 28.

66. Joseph P. Fried, "New City Unit Combats Chinese Gangs," *New York Times*, June 10, 1981, p. B7.

67. Salisbury, pp. 9-10.

68. Alvin Hart, "Street Gangs," *New York University Education Quarterly* 4, no. 2 (1973): 30-31.

69. Transcribed from a taped interview.

70. Donald Janson, "Violence by Youth Gangs Is Found Rising in 3 Cities," *New York Times*, April 16, 1972, p. 58.

71. Frank Fasso and Roger Wetherington, "Nine Stabbed in Fighting at a Junior High," *New York Daily News*, June 9, 1972, p. C 3; Gene I. Maeroff, "Anxiety Growing at Stevenson High Over Gangs and Violence at School," *New York Times*, March 21, 1972, p. 36; James M. Markham, "Stabbing of Washington High School Student Points Up a Resurgence of Youth-Gang Violence in City," *New York Times*, April 19, 1972, p. 29; Paul Montgomery, "P.L. School Closing Over Gang Threat Asked in Bronx," *New York Times*, December 21, 1971, p. 22.

72. In the "600" schools, students were escorted to the bus or to the subway to make sure they were on their way out of the neighborhood of the school. Supposedly, the "600" schools were organized in nongang neighborhoods so that the gangs would have to travel quite a distance to attack anyone in the school.

73. John J. Conger and William C. Miller, *Personality, Social Class, and Delinquency* (New York: Wiley, 1966).

74. Staff Report, p. 607.

75. Alan Dershowitz, "Statistics on Crime Misleading," *Buffalo News*, October 29, 1984, p. C-3; "F.B.I. Says Serious Crimes Declined by 5% in First Half of '84," *New York Times*, October 28, 1984, p. 27; "FBI Statistics

on State's Cities Show Crime Drop in Early '84," *Buffalo News*, October 28, 1984, p. A-16.

76. Staff Report, p. 607.

77. Ibid.

78. Ibid., pp. 607-8.

79. Herbert L. Foster, "A Personal and Professional Challenge: Socially Acceptable Risk Taking, Challenge, and Adventure, *Forum* 8, no. 4 (1982): pp. 22, 24-28.

80. The National Commission on the Causes and Prevention of Violence, *Progress Report of the National Commission on the Causes and Prevention of Violence to the President Lyndon B. Johnson* (Washington, D.C.: U.S. Government Printing Office, 1969), p. A-5.

81. Staff Report, p. 707.

82. Linda I. Greenhouse, "Violent Crimes Rise in Suburbs," *New York Times*, October 9, 1972, pp. 12, 1.

83. David Burnham, "A Wide Disparity Is Found in Crime throughout City," *New York Times*, February 14, 1972, p. 1.

84. Arnold, p. 48.

85. "Knife-Wielding is Reported Common at Site of a Midtown Slaying," *New York Times*, October 8, 1972, p. 42.

86. Susan Keller, *The American Lower Class Family* (Albany, N.Y.: State Division for Youth, 1965).

87. Claude Brown, *Manchild in the Promised Land* (New York: Macmillan, 1965); Peri Thomas, *Down These Mean Streets* (New York: Knopf, 1967).

88. Brown, p. 281.

89. Leonard Buder, " 'The Way It Is'," *New York Times*, May 2, 1967, p. 95; Homer Bigart, "N.Y.U. Clinic Stalled in Trying To Improve School," *New York Times*, November 26, 1967, p. 83; Mary F. Green and Orletta F. Ryan, *The Schoolchildren: Growing Up in the Slums* (New York: Pantheon, 1966); Fred M. Hechinger, "N.Y.U. Adopting a School for Brooklyn Slum Study," *New York Times*, July 17, 1966, p. 1; James Herndon, *The Way It Spozed to Be* (New York: Simon and Schuster, 1963); Herbert Kohl, *36 Children* (New York: New American Library, 1967); Leroi Jones, "The Toilet," *Kulchur* 3, no. 9 (1963): 25-39; Nina McCain, "A School Marriage between N.Y.U. And Junior High," *World Journal Tribune*, October 9, 1966, p. 4; "The Way It Is," NET Journal, Channel 13, May 1, 1967.

90. Samuel Tennenbaum, "The Teacher, The Middle Class, The Lower Class," *Phi Delta Kappan* 45 (1963): 82-86.

91. Harry Brill, *Why Organizers Fail: The Story of a Rent Strike* (Berkeley: University of California Press, 1971).

92. Jeff Greenfield, " 'But Papa, It's My Music, I Like It,' " *New York Times*, March 7, 1971, Section 13, p. 1.

93. Norman Podhoretz, "My Negro Problem—And Ours," *Commentary* 35 (1963): pp. 93, 94, 97-98.

94. Ibid., p. 99.

5 JIVE LEXICON AND VERBAL COMMUNICATION

If you signify, you qualify.

—Streetcorner philosopher

The heavy thing in the black community is the con and the conversation.

—A black student

The only language of education is the language which people can understand—no matter where it originates.

—Leonard Covello, *The Heart Is the Teacher*[1]

Come let us go down, and there confuse their language that they may not understand one another's speech.

—Genesis

We Jews of the village of Golinsk were all plain talkers and long-winded. We spoke as we felt and our hearts were always full and what we said never came out dainty or grammatical; yet our own everyday language, our Yiddish, our treasured tongue in which we could speak safely, held for us the daily comfort of a mother's song. Because of this, any two Golinsker Jews in a hurry could stop to say hello in the afternoon and still be a-talking until time for evening prayers.

—Peter Martin, *The Landsmen*[2]

Teacher-student communication is vital to the teaching-learning process. This communication may come about through such modes as language in the form of verbal symbols or words modified by tone and emphasis, nonverbal body movements, motions, gestures, shrugs, head movements, facial expressions, or the touching of one person by another.

Our schools, however, are highly developed verbal institutions where language consisting of Standard English verbal symbols is the main instrument of communication.

When people from the same social class or region of the country communicate, differences in dialect cause little difficulty. However, when members of different social classes or different sections of the country interact, dialectical differences may cause communication problems. Additionally, because our schools are middle class Standard English verbal institutions, the middle class child's language and lifestyle are compatible with the way our schools are organized. Accordingly, most middle class children succeed in school regardless of the teacher and methods.

For disadvantaged and poor children, however, their language and lifestyle work against school success. Their environment ill prepares them for the rigorous Standard English demands of our schools. Despite their verbal problems in school, however, they are able to communicate without apparent problems at home, with their peers, and in their neighborhood.

It appears that these problems existed between the children of earlier immigrant groups, too. There were, for example, the problems faced by Italian immigrant children in Greenwich Village in New York City from 1920 through 1930:

> The literary material to which the child was exposed often lacked reality. . . . While children drew the bulk of their experience from movie attendance, the subjects and the attitudes contained in the movies were ignored by the schools. The same was true of language and speech. All the schools of the locality reported that they laid special stress on the teaching of English—"the teachers almost break themselves trying to make the children talk right" because of the importance of having children from foreign homes learn the English language. But the language which is taught was not that which had vitality for the children—the accent of the street, the diction of the movies, and the vocabulary of the tabloid press. To talk in the manner prescribed at school was to act the part of a "sissy" or to "put on airs."[3]

A major source of problems in inner city, and now in almost all of our schools and out-of-school situations, is the breakdown in communication that often results from the differences in interpretation and understanding of the verbalizing and social-class-taught behavior of those involved. Though this communication breakdown was and still is precarious in many inner city schools, the same problem now exists in other schools because educators, used to working only with middle class white children, are now suddenly working with poor and middle class black children, working class children, and other children with whom they are unfamiliar and with whom they have little in common.

Basil Bernstein, writing about English working class children, pointed out that "this may lead to a situation where pupil and teacher each disvalues the other's world and communication becomes a means of asserting differences."[4] The words of Ben Bagdikian are also appropriate and related.

Nothing in the usual background and training of the American schoolteacher prepares her for the special problem of the slum child. Nothing in the background of the child prepares him for the teacher. They are strangers to each other, commanded by law to be mutually present a certain number of hours a day, but they part, usually, still strangers and even bitter enemies. When by chance there is established the communication needed to teach and learn it is a tenuous line easily broken.[5]

In this chapter, I will discuss communication in general and how differences in definition and knowledge of Black and Standard English have caused and continue to cause teacher-student problems, particularly as related to double or nonstandard word meanings and nonstandard language usage in crisis or emotional stress situations. I will combine the theoretical and the empirical but will not get technical.

First, all of our schools must unconditionally accept black, disadvantaged, urban children's dialect (I will discuss primarily their nonstandard vocabulary, which I refer to as his "jive lexicon") as the first step toward their acceptance of the school. Second, we must teach these youngsters Standard English, without denigrating their nonstandard speaking system, so that they will have the knowledge and skills for using the appropriate language for the appropriate social situation. One of the biggest parts of our job is to provide these youngsters with the middle class salable skills that are needed for upward economic and social mobility.

Realities 24 and 25 are examples of the breakdown of teacher-student communication resulting from the teacher's ignorance of jive lexicon (discussed later in this chapter). Both examples are related to the word "trim." Reality 24 was described to me by a teacher after hearing my talk on jive lexicon in which the double meaning of trim was discussed.

REALITY 24

A black, middle-class, middle-aged, female teacher was conducting a lesson on poetry with her black inner-city students. The teacher was giving the students the correct pronunciation of the different terms used to measure a line of poetry.

The teacher said, "A line of poetry with two measures or two feet is called dimeter and it is pron ounced dim-e-ter. Now class, repeat each syllable." The class repeated the term. Then she went on.

"The line of poetry with three measures or three feet is called trimeter—trim-e-ter. You know how to say trim-e-ter, I'm sure. '

The class began to giggle and whisper among themselves and it took some time for the puzzled teacher to get the class to order again.

REALITY 25

This incident took place in an inner city junior high school language arts class about a week before the Christmas vcation. During a lull, two black male students approached their white female teacher and asked, "Miss Frank, what does "trim" mean?"

Miss Frank, unsuspectingly, responded with, "Oh, I guess to hang ornaments on the Christmas tree."

With that, one youngster turned to his friend, grinned, put out his hand for some skin, and the class burst into laughter.[6]

In this incident, too, it took the teacher quite some time to get the class to order again.

Now let us see what meaning "trim" had that could cause these two classroom incidents.

According to the *Random House Dictionary of the English Language*, there are thirty-two definitions for the word "trim." The most common definition is "to put into a neat orderly condition by clipping, paring, pruning, etc."[7] According to Howard Wentworth and Stuart Flexner, trim is "to defeat an opponent or opposing team, as in a game, esp. to defeat by a narrow margin."[8] These dictionary definitions aside, in the jive lexicon of the students in the realities above, "trim" means anything from sexual intercourse to vagina. Had either of the teachers been familiar with jive, jazz, or blues vocabulary, they would have understood the game the youngsters were "running" on them.

H. L. Mencken, reporting on jive and jazz vocabulary, said "Trim is sexual intercourse enjoyed by bedding down."[9] Additional published definitions include: (1) "To possess (a woman sexually)";[10] (2) "a woman's sexuality; to have sex with a woman";[11] and (3) "Female genitalia."[12]

Of course, there are examples of teachers who understand and are not threatened by their students' games and nonstandard language. For example, in Reality 26, the teacher was white, teaching in a suburban high school, and a doctoral student of mine.

REALITY 26

She was teaching remedial reading and, as part of her teaching, had her students take books home for certain periods of time. One of her students, who happened to be black, did not return his book as he should. She spoke with him about the book, and he told her that he had left the book at the "crib" and just sat there. Instead of getting into a verbal game with the student, she let his comment pass and called me that evening to find out the definition of crib.

Upon the student's returning after having been suspended for several weeks, she asked him the whereabouts of another book. He was slouching down in his chair when she asked him where this book was. Again he replied, "It's at the crib."

Whereupon, she very calmly said, "Its not doing us any good at your house."

He then sat strait up in his seat and said, "How do you know what that means?"

Laughingly, she continued, "George, I know everything."

The next day, he brought his book to school and returned it; his game had been exposed.

DIALECT AND JIVE LEXICON

When I lecture about student-teacher communication problems in our schools and elsewhere, I usually use my Foster's Jive Lexicon Analogies Test—Series IIA as a motivational tool.[13] My talk usually goes something like this:

"You shouldn't have any problems with this test. After all, most of you have at least two degrees, and all of you have at last one degree. And, as you know, in most cases, you must pass a standardized aptitude or achievement test to get into most graduate programs."

"An analogy test is often used as a separate test or as an important part of a battery of tests. Analogy questions are important parts of such well-known testing instruments as the College Entrance Examination (Scholastic Aptitude Test), The Graduate Record Examination, Medical College Admission Test, and Miller Analogy Test.

"Remember, the major variables in analogy test items include vocabulary, relationships, and word associations. Analogy questions test your ability to see relationships to additional words and ideas. The test indicates your vocabulary knowledge and your ability to think things through clearly, based on the influence of your past associations.

"Some of the relationships analogy tests ask you to think through include: (1) antonym, (2) synonym, (3) part-whole, (4) part-part, (5) cause-effect, and so on. To test these relationships, analogy test items are usually designed so that the correct response is secured through: (1) true or false, (2) multiple choice, (3) blank space, or (4) matching answers.

"I might add that I am working on the University of Buffalo's testing service people to have my test replace the Miller Analogy Test as a requirement for admission to our graduate programs. I already require it of my students.

"Oh, one more point. As you know, the argument has been presented that our standardized tests are culturally biased. The words, experiences, and ideas used in the makeup of these standardized achievement tests suggest a white, middle class frame of reference. Therefore, when the disadvantaged child is tested on the standardized test model, he is being tested on an unfamiliar model.

"Supposedly, members of any disadvantaged population would score higher if tested on references to their experiential background. Whether blacks would score higher than whites on tests reflective of the black experiential background is another question that appears not to have been really tested."

Instructions are then given for taking the test. Participants are given twenty minutes. Here is an example of one of the questions from Foster's Jive Lexicon Analogy Test, Series I:

CHUMP CHANGE is to YARD as TOGETHER is to:

(1) tack
(2) fox
(3) freak
(4) work

This item requires an answer related to opposites. "Chump Change" means small change. "Yard" refers to $100. Hence, "together," which means good or a person who is all right or dressed stylishly, requires an opposite response. The proper response is, therefore, "tack," which is used to describe someone who does not know what is going on.

Once the test is undertaken, blacks in the group usually begin to smile and chuckle. Most of the whites look disgusted, uncomfortable, annoyed, and some laugh nervously. The group is asked for their feelings when the test is completed.

Invariably, a few sullen white teachers argue that the test is phony and that the words do not exist. In a middle school with a majority of black students where I gave the test to the staff, one white male teachers jumped up, waved his hand at me, and yelled. "Look, I've been working with black kids for twelve years; eight years in this place. I never heard one of these words. You trying to tell me that these words exist and these kids know them?" When this happens, I usually suggest he not take my word, but that he ask one of the black teachers. "Why don't you ask him?" I suggest, pointing to one of the black teachers I had noticed smiling during the test. Most often, the white teacher then asks, "Do the kids in this school really know and use words like those on the test?"

The black teacher usually responds with, "They use them—they sure do," while his face says *if you really liked these kids you would have heard some of these words.*

Everyone usually then starts yelling and talking at once. When everyone is calm, I steer the discussion toward the recognition that all languages could be considered a dialect consisting of: (1) phonology—the way we pronounce words, (2) syntax—grammar, and (3) lexicon—word meaning and vocabulary.

The group is provided with an example of phonology when those from New York City, Utica, Rochester, and Buffalo are asked to pronounce "apple," demonstrating the difference between an up-state and a down-state pronunciation. The group is also reminded of the way our presidents have spoken with their regional dialects.

Two of the many phonological characteristics of Black English that are mentioned briefly are: (1) sometimes the *r* is dropped before vowels—example: Carol-Cal; and (2) some final consonant clusters are simplified—*t, d, s,* or *z*—example: hold-hol.

Syntax or grammar is discussed next. A number of examples of syntactical differences between Black English and Standard English are offered—for example: (1) I been washin' the dishes, (2) I be washin' the dishes, and (3) I wash the dishes.

The point is stressed that educators working with disadvantaged youngsters must be aware of these differences between black and standard English for communication as well as curriculum. I then suggest a number of books that can be read for insight into Black English.[14]

We next get to the urban, black, disadvantaged child's functional peer vocabulary, which I call jive lexicon but which has also been referred to as slang, cant, idiom, metaphor, Afro-Americanism, colloquial expression, patois, and vernacular, to name a few.

To bring the lexicon discussion closer to home, I use the overhead projector to show a bottle of soda, ice cream on a stick, and a common flying insect. Everyone is asked what they call these items. Usually some folks call ice cream on a stick a pop; to others it is the soda that is called pop. The insect is called any number of names such as a darning needle, dining needle, ear sewer, and so on.

As one moves from one region to another, improper use of regional expressions can sometimes prove discomfiting. This begins to get the realization across that our vocabulary may depend upon where we grew up, where we lived, or where we live now. From here the group becomes a bit more receptive to the concept of Black English and even begins to admit that it exists. The audience is then provided with the answers to the test, and hopefully a good discussion ensues.

We discuss the fact that vocabularies of the black and white teacher and student are "borrowed" from many sources. Their Standard English vocabulary includes regionalisms and, most often, other distinctive vocabularies. For example, most social, religious, ethnic, professional, and trade groups have distinctive vocabularies that operate within the framework of Standard English and are understood primarily by members of that group. Educators and members of most professions and organized sports also have their particular vocabularies. For centuries, criminals and drug users have used secret argots and lingos. With each war, each advance in technology, or each development of new industries also come new vocabularies. For example, space flight enthusiasts know that "burn" is the firing of a spacecraft's rocket engines in flight, and that EVA is a space walk or extravehicular activity.[15] As a particular sport achieves prominence and a following, a special language is often born. Surfers know that a "wipe-out" is what happens when you are knocked off your board, and the "curl" is the top of a wave when it crests.[16] Currently, a whole new language has been born around computers. In many schools and areas outside of school "hackers" are busy.[17]

The Department of Defense published an eleven-page mimeographed pamphlet to provide returning Vietnam prisoners of war with "a head start" to "perhaps bring you up to date, on the current slang expressions being used by the young people of America." The glossary was compiled from the slang expressions suggested by the prisoners' sons, daughters, and wives.

Our nation's immigrants, too, have contributed borrowings from their language to today's American English vocabulary. From the Dutch we have borrowed "sugar," "butt," and "waffle"; from the Spanish, "mosquito," "calaboose," and "corral"; from the French, "chowder" and "levee"; from the Germans, "kindergarten," "burger," and "delicatessen"; from the Italians, "spaghetti"; from the Jews, "bagel" and "blintz"; from the Turks, "chisel"; from the Chinese, "chow mein"; and from the Swedish, "smorgasboard," to name a few. We are indebted to the American Indian for "hickory," "hooch," "pow-wow," "moccasin," and "skunk."[18]

These examples suggest that the teacher speaks a form of Standard English that includes any number of vocabularies. These vocabularies may include: (1) a regional form of Standard English; (2) a language used in his or her profession; avocation, hobby, or sport interest; (3) an earlier language shared with childhood, adolescent, or college peers; or (4) an earlier ethnic or religious vocabulary brought from the home country of parents or grandparents. In addition, the middle class speakers know the appropriate social situation in which to use each vocabulary. They acquired this facility through a middle class conditioning process of imitation and correction through the mediating forces of parents, brothers, sisters, relatives, and teachers; that is, from their total milieu.

Although some middle class urban black children possess typically middle class Standard English vocabularies, personal observations and a review of the pertinent literature suggest that a large proportion of urban blacks do not. These youngsters have a fully developed and structured linguistic system containing a nonstandard lexicon. Moreover, although middle class teachers' vocabulary includes many lexicons, the words and definitions in their vocabulary are often different from the words and definitions contained in their disadvantaged black students' jive vocabulary. For example, the white male teacher may say, "She's a sharp lookin' chick (or broad)." His black student may say, "Jim, she fly," or "She a phat chib," or "She a boss tip."

It is important to realize that the black disadvantaged child's jive lexicon may be the only language he or she possesses. There may be no additional stock of vocabulary words from which to choose. Therefore, at certain times and under certain conditions, it is possible that the child's and the teacher's vocabulary are incompatible.

On July 12, 1979, U.S. District Judge Charles W. Joiner issued a ruling that the Ann Arbor schools must provide for their teachers (1) to learn more about the dialects of their students and (2) to teach their students Standard English, the language used in the arts, the sciences, the professions, and the commercial world.[19] This was a very misunderstood decision. Many educators thought the judge had ruled that the students be taught nonstandard English.

The lawsuit was filed by eleven black students in the Martin Luther King Junior Elementary School in Ann Arbor, Michigan against the Ann Arbor School District Board. The suit argued that the litigants were unable to participate equally in the school's educational program with other students because of their speaking a dialect of English referred to as "Black English," "black dialect," or "black vernacular."

DOUBLE OR NONSTANDARD WORD MEANINGS AND UNKNOWN WORDS

The teaching-learning process is often interrupted when either the teacher or a student, either purposely or unknowingly, uses a word that is unknown or has a double meaning. In some cases, teachers innocently use a word for which their students know another meaning, often with a sexual connotation. On the other hand, students often use such words either to test playfully their teacher's hipness or to destroy deliberately the teacher's composure and effectiveness by student ridicule. At other times, a word spoken innocently or published as part of the curriculum may also cause a problem. Thus, problem situations may come about when:

1. The teacher does not know all the meanings or nuances, known to students, of certain words he or she is using.
2. There are words in self-made or purchased curriculum materials that have second meanings unknown to the teacher.
3. Children purposely use particular words to embarrass or test the teacher or to wrest control of the class from the teacher.
4. Students use certain words to insult, taunt, or make fun of other children.
5. Children unknowingly use words that cause problems.
6. Students do not know what a Standard English word means.
7. Students do not have another word in their repertoire to use in a particular situation.

There is precedence in Afro-American culture for black urban youngsters' applying a second (often sexual) meaning to a Standard English word. The blues, which to a large extent is based on black folk songs, is replete with double meanings of a sexual nature.

Guy Johnson divided the double meanings into two general groups: "(1) those meanings pertaining specifically to the sex organs and (2) those relating to the sex act or to some other aspect of sex life."[20] Though his breakdown is into two groups, there is continual overlapping.

Robert Gold wrote that throughout the history of jazz there runs an opposition and rejection of the "dominant modes of thinking and feeling" and that this was often expressed through the "deliberate and significant reversal of the conventional connotations" of certain vocabulary. Gold feels that this usage by Negro jazz men expresses their belief in the hypocracy of conventional white morality. Therefore, the terms with which the white man expresses his morality must be also hypocritical.[21]

[I]n addition, the puritanical equation of sex with sin has reinforced the Negro's suspicion that the in-group is supremely mistaken in its judgments of good and bad, and that standard designations of disapproval have been attached to things that are, by sensible standard, perfectly good—for example, earthiness and virility. Hence, the Negro retains the standard terms of designation, but gives to these an interpretation which reverses their value.[22]

For example, the term "to jazz" has an American folk speech definition of participating in sexual intercourse.[23] According to Paul Oliver, the recorded blues was seldom an outspoken song of protest. Negro self-assertiveness, however, was often manifested through sexual concepts in the blues.

Above all other subjects there is in blues a preponderance of lyrics about sexual love, or merely sex. A complex language of metaphors, often domestic or culinary, camouflaged a multitude of sexual references. "I want my biscuits in the daytime and my jelly at night,' declares one singer. "My stove's in good condition, this is the stove to brown your bread,' his woman replies. A swaggering list of the singer's physical attributes was common, with women no less than with men. "I'm a big fat woman with meat shakin' on the bone, and every time I shake it a skinny woman leaves her home." Sexual virtuosity is the subject of scores of blues and the singer played a game with the censor and hence with "the Man" when he sang *The Dirty Dozen* or *Shave 'Em Dry*. His words were heavily bowdlerized but were clear enough to his listeners. Sometimes a more specific code would be used—the number combinations of the "policy racket"—a kind of "housey-housey"—in which the figures $3 - 6 - 9$ would mean excreta or $4 - 11 - 44$ would mean a phallus. In his sexual prowess, real or imagined, a man could realize himself; he knew and asserted the maturity as a man which segregation and race legislation deprived him of within the total society. In sexual blues the spirit of revolt was canalised; the blues singer did not care whether he was fitting popular stereotypes about the Negro: "I'm blue, black, and I'm evil; and I did not make myself," he declared coldly.[24]

Few symbols are found for sex organs in the blues. Where one is found, however, it is usually "worked to the utmost." One of the most commonly used of these terms is "jelly roll." The term refers to the vagina, the female genitalia, or sometimes sexual intercourse.[25] On a reissue of Bessie Smith's earlier records the reader can hear her "Nobody in Town Can Bake a Sweet Jelly Roll Like Mine," "I Need a Little Sugar in My Bowl," and others.[26]

The term "transvaluation" is used by Roger Abrahams to describe the process of assigning a definition and feeling to a word that is "sometimes diametrically opposed to the accustomed (Standard English) meaning." Abrahams points out that the techniques of using words in this way is a dramatic trait in a "performer-centered word play." The use of such words is an important attribute of a good talker's repertoire because of the affective value. The audience must listen closely to decipher the tone of voice as well as the context to gain the full meaning of the story or presentation.[27]

According to William Grier and Price Cobbs, the slaves brought to America were divided so that none speaking a similar African tribal dialect would be together. This arrangement was made to prevent slaves from communicating and conspiring. Additionally, slaves were not allowed to learn to read or write. Therefore, what English words they learned were garbled and mispronounced and usually understood only by those on the same plantation.

The slaves, however, reversed the purpose of the language as it was given to them, which was what the slave owners did not want. Though the slaveowners laughed at their slaves' misunderstandings and mispronouncements, a secret language began to be developed from the "patois."

Language was used with a particular emphasis on double meanings. In fact, multiple meanings were imposed on language, as, for example, in the spirituals. To the uninformed listener the words spoke of religious longing; the singing provided a harmonious accompaniment to their work, and to the viewer all was piety and submission. The true meaning of the spirituals, however, involves a communication from one to another regarding plans for escape, hostile feelings toward the master, and a general expression of rebellious attitudes.[28]

"Inversion" is the term Grace Holt used to describe the verbal defense mechanism developed by blacks to fight white psychological and linguistic domination. Blacks gradually developed this inversion process as their way of resisting the white man's domination through the use of his language. Furthermore, since the whites' language was also an expression of their caste system, blacks, by mastering the system, would "in effect . . . consent to be mastered by it through the white definitions." By using the inversion process blacks were able to take advantage of the unknowledgeable white opponents.[29]

Blacks took standard words and phrases and reversed or changed their function and meanings. Because the whites were unaware of the dualism, denotations, and connotations that blacks were developing linguistically, whites were unaware of the new interpretations. Consequently, the black and white understanding of a linguistic event were dissimilar. Therefore, blacks were and are able to, at times,

> deceive and manipulate whites without penalty. This protective process, understood and shared by blacks, became a contest of matching wits, the stake in the game being survival with dignity. This form of linguistic guerrilla warfare protected the subordinated, permitted the masking and disguising of true feelings, allowed the subtle assertion of self, and promoted group solidarity. The purpose of the game was to *appear to but not to*.[30]

According to Joseph White, any discussion of language and the black experience is complicated because historically words were used simultaneously to conceal and express meaning with hidden meanings, nuances, and intuition. Some ideas had to be conveyed to slaves while being hidden from the slavemasters. "The slavemaster . . . listening to . . . 'steal away, steal away to Jesus, steal away home" were deceived into believing that the [slaves] were thinking only about Heaven. The real message was about stealing away and splitting up North.[31]

William Schechter also discussed the double meanings attached to Bible stories and jazz terms. He wrote that "Negroes transformed the accepted (e.g., Bible Stories) into their own unique culture." He uses the term double-entendre to describe the indecent blues expressions that "often approached or reached obscenity." Because the words were known to blacks and unknown to whites, blacks laughed when whites unknowingly used any of these expressions.[32]

In addition, blacks used music and humor as outlets in their spirituals and slave work songs where "courageous *double-entendre* lyrics . . . provided a small measure of comic relief from the cruelty and hardships of slavery." Drums, rhythms, and slave work songs also carried ominous warnings and important messages.[33] With the aforementioned in mind, the reader may begin to understand how the following incidents resulted in classroom disruption of the teaching learning processes.

REALITY 27

The following incident took place in a junior high school language arts class being taught by a young white female teacher. A number of female students were at the board practicing sentence structure skills. One of the students wrote, "Everybody knows Jean is a ho."

Jean jumped up, yelled, "See what she wrote about me!" and attacked the writer. A wild hair-pulling, cursing, and punching fight raged through the school's halls, as a result.

In this incident, a female student taunted her classmate by using a word the teacher knew nothing about. Had the teacher known that "ho" meant a whore or prostitute, she could have interceded immediately on behalf of the wronged youngster and the wild, upsetting race through the halls might have been avoided, to say nothing of the loss of another forty-five minutes of instruction.

Actually, had the teacher read Nathan C. Heard's *Howard Street*, she would have found: 'Whut is you? Nuttin' but a 'ho! Seem like t'me you oughta be glad t'have a man want you fuh his woman 'steada his 'ho."[34]

Another form of testing practiced by many students is to ask new experienced teachers who think they're hip what a certain word means. Sometimes, if the word has an off-color meaning and the teacher is too embarrassed or becomes angry, the children have won even if the teachers knows the definition.

REALITY 28

In this incident, handled successfully by a guidance counselor, two junior high school male students asked their guidance counselor, "Do you eat at the 'Y'?"

He responded by playfully pushing them out of his office and saying, "Do you think I was born yesterday!"

Of course, everyone knows that "Y" is short for either Young Men's or Women's Christian Association (Y.M./Y.W.C.A.) or Young Men's or Women's Hebrew Association (Y.M./Y.W.H.A.). As used by these youngsters, the question meant "Do you practice cunnilingus?" Had they asked the question of a female teacher they would have been referring to fellatio. This phrase has been observed in use by both blacks and whites.[35]

In Realities 29 and 30, a disadvantaged black high school youngster did not understand the Standard English word used by a middle class school administrator.

REALITY 29

The student had worked for many weeks completing an excellent woodworking project. The teacher picked up the project and called the youngster, as he started for the principal's office. Once in the office, the teacher praised the youngster for his work and complained that the youngster would not allow him to place the project on display. Suddenly, the youngster grabbed his project, bolted from the school, and went home. The next day, after a lengthy conversation, it was discovered that the youngster did not know what the word "display" meant. He thought that the woodworking teacher wanted to keep the project that he had worked on for so long.

REALITY 30

A youngster was being questioned by a school administrator concerning a rash of incidents of urinating on the radiators. The suspected youngster was uncooperative and gave the questioning administrator a rough time. Upon questioning the youngster later, it was ascertained that he thought he was being charged with stealing, as he did not know what the word "urinate" meant.[36]

REALITY 31

This incident describes a black disadvantaged junior high school student unknowingly creating a problem for himself by using the word "crib." With permission, he walked into the office and politely asked the secretary (who also happened to be black), "Do you mind if I call the crib?"

The harried secretary responded with, "What did you say?"

"May I please call the crib?" he responded.

She turned and asked whether he thought he was a wise guy. Luckily, a knowledgeable teacher came by and explained to the secretary that "crib" meant the youngster's home.

REALITY 32

In this next incident, the student did not have another word readily available to use that would describe what he was talking about. He was making a speech as a candidate for school office and ended his presentation with, "No matter what I say, you guys gonna vote for the fellas you *down with*."

The next day when asked what he meant by "down with," he responded, "You know, the guys they drink with, smoke pot with."

When asked why he didn't use another word, he said, "Man I don't know no other word. And, anyway, those cats know what I meant."

Reality 33 provides examples of how two teachers handled the same incident where a word caused an interruption of the teaching-learning process. In the first example, the teacher lost the class completely. In the second, because the teacher knew the lexicon, she was able to recoup and get on with the lesson.

REALITY 33

The junior high school language arts teacher was using a commercially purchased ditto master to conduct a class on critical reading. She distributed the dittoed copies to her students and signaled for them to start reading.

After a few minutes, students began to laugh and giggle. The teacher tried to calm the class but finally gave up in desperation. Her students joked and played for the remaining class time. To this day, she is still not sure of what happened.

The material she was using told the story of an Indian chief and his raiding party returning from an unsuccessful raid. Many of his braves had been killed. "The chief was very sad. He was returning to his village in disgrace. He had no booty; he had no scalps."

An innocent appearing sentence? The word "booty" caused the upset. Probably, the average teacher would define booty as spoils taken from an enemy in war, pillage, or plunder. However, the youngsters involved in Reality 33 defined booty as either someone's buttocks or sexual intercourse.

A second teacher, using the same material, was aware of the students' definition, reacted differently, and there was no time lost from instruction. When the class started to giggle and make comments about the word booty, she said, "Look, I am sure this is not talking about *that* definition." After a few more chuckles, the class got back to work.

Interestingly, the movie *The Adventures of Buckaroo Banzai: Across the 8th Dimension* has a character named "Big Booté."[37]

Reality 34 was told to me by a young white male teacher after a workshop I did for the New York State Division for Youth.

REALITY 34

He was working in a school program for migrant children in Florida and was trying, without success, to teach his students addition with carrying a number. During a break, while he was carrying one of his students on his shoulders, another of his student's said, "Look, he totin' Miguel."

This gave him an idea. Instead of using the word "carry," he used the word "tote." It worked beautifully. He was able to teach his students how to carry numbers.

Again, it must be pointed out that problems created by the misunderstanding of words happens outside of school, too. For example, in 1901, in Texas, Sheriff Morris and Romaldo Cortez were killed because the Anglo-Texan interpreter was not able to differentiate between a mare (*yegua*) and a horse (*caballo*) and then turned a question into a threat.[38] On December 1, 1974, a Trans World Airlines Boeing 727 crashed while approaching Dulles International Airport. Eighty-five passengers and seven crew members were killed when the plane crashed into a mountain about twenty-five miles from Dulles. Investigation determined that the problem that lead to the crash came about when there was a misunderstanding of various terms between the air traffic controllers and the crew of the aircraft.[39] And, David Tom, who is Chinese, spent thirty-one years in a mental institution in Illinois because no one could understand his native Taiwanese dialect.[40]

EMOTIONAL STRESS OR CRISIS SITUATIONS

This area can sometimes be frightening because of the tensions and feelings prevailing in some inner city schools, schools with bused in children, or, more recently, suburban and rural schools with newly arrived black, minority, immigrant, or poor children. Within many of these schools, because of the prevailing conditions around race, social class, ethnicity, national origin, and so on, calm, unemotional, nonracist, or nonethnocentric good intentions can inadvertently deteriorate into crisis and violence. One of the factors working against conflict resolution in these situations is the possibility of linguistic switching or the misreading of cues under emotional stress or crisis.

Among the psycholinguistic factors that may cause problems in this area are the following:

1. There might be too large a difference between the teacher's language and the student's language, which may lead to alienation and behavior problems;[41]
2. In crisis or emotional stress, those involved might revert to their native, more secure language or lexicon;[42]
3. For conflict resolution, continual communication is imperative regardless of the topic;[43] and
4. One may be able to express oneself only through a nonstandard dialect or lexicon.[44]

These psycholinguistic factors must be considered as they interact with the prevailing lifestyles of the children in our schools. For example, many poor and disadvantaged children's lifestyles are poverty stricken, hostile, violent, aggressive, anxious, and unstable.[45] Further, lower class children "refer more to violence" when compared to upper and middle class children.[46]

Because the student's lifestyle cannot be kept out of the school, confrontation and crisis have always been a way of life in some of our schools. Therefore, the ramifications of psycholinguistic behavior in crisis and emotional stress situations can play a crucial role in either the resolution or the escalation of an already volatile school atmosphere.

What could be considered classic examples of an escalation of crisis in a black and white situation because of the inappropriate use of the word "punk" by whites was explained in Chapter 1. Actually, the incidents described there reflected the interaction of language and social class with ethnic overtones. As racial, economic, and immigrant groups continue to mix, there will be even more possibilities for misunderstood lexicons and for tempers to reach boiling points. The next few realities provide further examples of the problem.

REALITY 35

A white high school administrator, giving a late pass to a black student who appeared tired and red eyed, said, "Boy, you look beat up and tired."

Whereupon, the young man jumped back, threw up his hands and yelled, "Who's beat up?"

The comment, innocent from the administrator's point of view, was interpreted as a challenge to the manhood of the youngster. He interpreted the comment to mean that he had just been beaten up in a fight. Luckily, the school administrator did not overreact to the youngster's challenge. Instead, he questioned him and then explained what he had meant.

REALITY 36

In this incident, a black student was annoying his teacher when his teacher said, "Stop buggin' me."

The youngster responded by running into the hall, throwing off his coat, and challenging the teacher to a fight by yelling, "You better check yourself before you wind up by yourself."

The teacher became fearful and words and threats began to be exchanged. An administrator came by and calmed the incident. It was resolved when he elicited from the youngster the fact that "buggin" in his neighborhood meant "let's go — let's fight."

REALITY 37

In a similar incident, a school administrator was trying to straighten out a mistake made in a student's program when the young man began verbally to harass the administrator. Whereupon, the administrator said, "Come on, I'm not playing now."

With this, the student jumped up out of his seat, ran into the hall, and yelled that he was ready to fight. The administrator, who had been on reasonably good terms with the youngster, calmed him down and found that the youngster had interpreted "I'm not playing now," as a challenge to a fight.

In Reality 38, a white female guidance counselor could have prevented what started out as a low-key verbal encounter for escalating into a regrettable incident had she understood her student's language.

REALITY 38

Two black female students in a special college skills program were engaged in a verbally aggressive argument. The guidance counselor realized that something was wrong and walked between the girls. However, as the argument heated, the girls lapsed further into their dialect, using a lexicon which the counselor did not understand. The counselor just watched without knowing how threatening to each other the girls had become. The resulting fight, during which one of the girls were severely hurt, took her completely by surprise.

REALITY 39

This incident took place in a high school for emotionally disturbed youngsters. A white teacher was working with a student when the door burst open and one of his students rushed into the room and demanded his coat, which was locked in a metal closet. Since it was too early for the student to go home, the teacher told the youngster to wait until he finished his work with the other student.

The youngster then lost control of his behavior and began kicking and smashing the metal closet doors while pulling the closet from the wall. The teacher rose from his seat, pushed the closet back against the wall, turned, and started to speak to the out-of-control youngster.

He jumped back and said, "You gonna *off* me?"

Since the teacher knew the lexicon, he responded with, "If I have to."

Whereupon the youngster sat down and waited calmly.

The word "off" was popularized a few years ago in such usages as "off the pigs." Off can mean anything from kill, beat up, destroy, to "waste" (lexicon to beat up or kill). In the above incident it meant that the teacher would have intervened by physically restraining the youngster. The school where the incident took place forbade corporal punishment, while staff used nonpunitive physical restraining techniques. In this incident, the situation was ameliorated because the teacher knew his student's lexicon.

Two interesting examples of linguistic switching are reported in Realities 40 and 41.

REALITY 40

As a teacher was describing an incident, she became excited and switched her linguistic style to her earlier dialect. When she had completed the story, she was asked whether she realized that she had switched linguistic styles?

She responded, "When I get hot, I don't have time to think—I say the first thing that comes to my mind."

This second example is similar to the first in many respects. A teacher was describing to me a school incident when she said, "I tol' im, I'd hit 'em on the butt."

I looked at her and said, "Do you realize you used the word 'butt'?"

She responded by saying, "When they get me provoked, I don't have time to say 'behind'! I don't have time to think. I was talkin' that way all my life."

Linguistic switching can be observed not only in an overt crisis situation, but also in the classroom as students and teachers become positively involved in an emotional discussion. In Sol Yurick's *The Bag*, one of the main characters switches his linguistic style as he deteriorates emotionally.[47] Very often, black civil rights leaders will switch to their dialect when giving an emotional speech. In labor bargaining sessions in the French areas of Canada, the bargaining begins in English. However, as the discussions become heated, linguistic switching takes place and French becomes the language.[48] Edward Frazier reported that when his maternal grandmother, who came to this country as a slave and who could speak the African language, "became angry, no one could understand what she said."[49] Interestingly, when Moise Tshombe, the late former president of the Congo, was brought to Algeria and injected with sodium pentothal, he confounded his captors by speaking in his tribal dialect.[50]

Apparently, there is a difference between the anxiety of an athletic contest and the anxiety generated in a court of law. A well-known All-American black basketball star went before a judge for a speeding ticket. Although the judge thought she was taking the athlete's basketball schedule into consideration when she fixed a trial date, she set a wrong date. According to the newspaper report, supposedly the following verbal switching occurred:

REALITY 41

At this point Lanier, acting as his own lawyer, should have worked up an objection to the date with such phrases as "Your honor," and "May it please the court," and other time-sworn stereotyped expressions.

Instead, he blurted out: "I won't be here, baby."

This brought a broad smile from Judge Mikoll, who usually goes about her work with a rather set solemn manner.

"I am not your baby," she answered.[51]

The following anecdote describes how a Polish-speaking Jew lived through Gestapo torture and was not deported to a gas chamber.

He was passing for a Christian when a former neighbor informed the Gestapo that he was Jewish. In such cases, it was Gestapo practice to torture the suspect until the pain became so unbearable that he could no longer control his language and would cry out in Yiddish, which was the primary language of most East European Jews. In this instance, however, though the person was Jewish, Yiddish had not been spoken in his upper class Warsaw home. Consequently, even under torture he continued to cry for help in Polish. Having schooled himself to behave like a Christian, he repeatedly called out to Jesus, Mary, and the Christian Saints, convincing the Gestapo that he was not Jewish. He was eventually released and survived the war.[52]

ADDITIONAL CONSIDERATIONS

The language we use to communicate and to be understood can be called an arbitrary system of vocal symbols. What is appropriate or inappropriate depends upon the social group and context within which we are attempting to communicate. Because of many factors, most black disadvantaged youngsters do not possess either Stokely Carmichael's or the late Dr. George Wiley's middle class ability to switch to the appropriate verbal code, and hence social role, as described.

> In the four months that I traveled with him I marveled at his ability to adjust to any environment. Dressed in bib overalls, he tramped the backlands of Lowndes County, Alabama, urging Negroes, in a Southern-honey drawl, to register and vote. The next week, wearing a tight dark suit and Italian boots, using the language they dig most—hip and very cool. A fortnight later, jumping from campuses to intellectual salons, where he was equally damned and lionized, he spoke with eloquence and ease about his cause, quoting Sartre, Camus and Thoreau.[53]
>
> "We demand $35,000. We demand it now and that's that." A moment later, talking to a reporter, Dr. Wiley shifted from anger to a scholarly calm that belied the tense atmosphere in the convention hall, as it reflected his academic background.
>
> And then, turning next to the Negro youths who were still barricading the hall because Dr. Wiley had not yet told them to desist, he slipped into the vernacular of the street, obviously retaining their confidence with it.
>
> The ease with which the 38-year-old leader established the several relationships illustrated one of the major assets of a black militant who speaks with mounting national power for an increasing number of impoverished Americans.[54]

For many black disadvantaged youngsters, their dialect, and particularly their lexicon, may be their only mode of verbal communication. Their language is an integral part of them; to deny their language and its use is to deny them. Language is egocentric. Some hypotheses can be made in relation to lexicons:

1. The social structure and attitudes of a group are reflected in its lexicon;[55]
2. Lexicons are developed, at times, by subcultures to maintain or develop privacy, selectivity, and/or status;[56]

3. Lexical terms and definitions change and may vary according to city, area, neighborhood, or even from school to school or class to class;[57]
4. Some forms of lexicon are used by all levels of society, professions, and occupations;[58]
5. A nonstandard lexicon may, in some cases, be the only verbal language known to a particular individual;[59]
6. The use of a special vocabulary is perfectly acceptable and often the only method of verbal communication in certain subcultures;[60] and
7. With time, certain words of a group's nonstandard lexicon may become acceptable English.[61]

Furthermore, lexicons are always in a state of flux.

1. Words change meaning.
2. New words are born.
3. Some words lie fallow only to grow in use at a later date.
4. Word usage and definition sometimes differ from city to city—even neighborhood to neighborhood.
5. The definition of a word may depend upon who is using it and the context of the conversation in which it is being used.
6. The way a word is pronounced, and even the syllable on which the emphasis is placed, may also have to be considered before certain words can be defined.
7. With time, some words become shortened.
8. A school youngster's definition or understanding of a word may vary from that of a more sophisticated adult, of an older or younger child, or even that of the child's parents. As stated in *Manchild in the Promised Land*,

"Sometimes I would try to tell Mama things in the slang terms. They had their down-home slang expressions. I couldn't understand theirs too much and they couldn't understand ours. The slang had changed. In this day when someone would say something about a bad cat, they meant he was good."[62]

Despite these lexical variations, students' language and, in particular, their lexicon, must be considered as being integral to improving student-teacher communication. I have used my students' lexicon successfully in curriculum materials, the binding of student-teacher relationships, the easing of student-teacher and student-peer tensions, and the improving of teacher-student articulation.

Many of the riots in the black ghettos over the years were to some extent caused by the inability of white officers to differentiate between a real threat and ghetto rhetoric. Similarly, the fuse for the Attica prison riot in New York State, was ignited when a guard misinterpreted streetcorner behavior.

The at one time top-ranking black police officer in Detroit, Deputy Chief Inspector George Harge, pointed up the problem white officers face in differentiating between repartee and a real threat, saying, "Language is the biggest barrier. White policemen find it hard to differentiate between riot language and horseplay language. Some black talk implies an imminent riot to whites, but to blacks it is a way of life. A rash decision by a patrolman based on language that he believes is offensive can precipitate instead of quash a riot."[63]

Another manifestation of this controversy was brought out when *Time* reported on the disagreement between the FBI and Ramsey Clark, then the attorney general. The FBI wanted to bug the Panthers and Clark turned them down as a "local law-enforcement problem, not as a national menace. . . . 'Life,' said one veteran of those days, 'is full of chances. The question is whether you're going to exhaust yourself guarding against dangers that don't exist.' "[64]

However, John Mitchell's Justice Department looked upon the Panthers as more of a national threat. "If a Hilliard threatens the President, said one Panther specialist there, we can't afford to sit back and say, "That's just rhetoric." They have the capability of killing any government official, and I'm not going to get into the position of having to walk around apologizing after they do it."[65]

In the same article, *Time* pointed out that the Panthers were engaging in "guerrilla theater masterfully done—so masterfully that, at a point, everybody began to believe them and to be frightened of them."[66] (See Chapter 7 for more on this subject.)

In my doctoral dissertation I studied the effect of introducing nonstandard English dialect and lexicon upon the black disadvantaged tenth grade high schools student's ability to comprehend, to recall, and to be fluent and flexible in providing titles for verbal material.[67]

Examination of the data revealed the students scored higher in response to nonstandard English stories than they did to the Standard English stories. Furthermore, the results, at least as they relate to recall, flexibility, and fluency, suggest that the subjects obviously think better in their language when they are: (1) cued in some semblance of their language, (2) not limited to preset written responses, and (3) allowed to respond verbally, freely, and to interpret as they proceed. The test also suggested that in an uninhibiting situation, the black disadvantaged youngster can be more verbal and intellectually creative in his own language than he can be in Stand English.

STREET CULTURE, GRAFFITI, AND CURRICULUM

Graphic arts, which I taught, was an ideal subject for including my students' street culture and interests into the school's curriculum. These past years working at the university with undergraduate and graduate students has also pointed up the high motivation quality of bringing student street culture into just about all areas of the curriculum. Three of the many street-related areas I worked with were (1) woof (wolf) tickets, (2) party announcements and tickets, and (3) graffiti.

Illustration 5-1.

Woof Tickets

About 1964, my students started using the expression "woof" or "wolf" interchangeably in a number of ways. When these tickets were first printed, they were printed as Wolf Tickets because I was not astute enough to realize that my students were actually saying woof instead of wolf. However, after *Ribbin'* was published, I had Woof Tickets printed to publicize the book.

A student might say, "Mr. Foster, he's woofin' on me," which might mean anything from "he is challenging me to a fight," to "he is making fun of my clothing or my mother." Accepting a "woof ticket" was accepting a challenge to fight (see Chapter 6).

One of my students cut a wolf's head out of linoleum, another set some type, and thousands of wolf tickets were printed. Printing wolf tickets gave my shop status with students. Thus, (1) working in my shop took on new meaning, (2) many students increased their work in the shop, and (3) some ended up working in the graphic arts industry. Of course, students had to master preliminary skills before they were allowed to print the tickets.

Party Announcements and Tickets

My students printed invitations and announcements that usually contained a rhyme announcing their parties, sessions, sets, or gigs (Illustration 5-2).

Taking pictures of Harlem graffiti, I came across a rhyme on a wall similar to those printed on the above cards (Illustration 5-3).

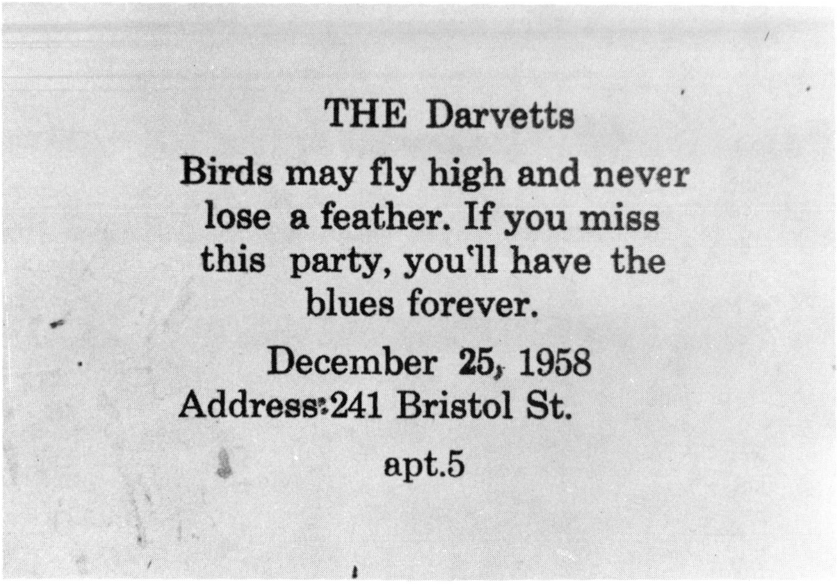

THE Darvetts
Birds may fly high and never lose a feather. If you miss this party, you'll have the blues forever.
December 25, 1958
Address:241 Bristol St.
apt.5

Illustration 5-2.

MY NAME IS COFFEE
CAUSE I GRIND
So Fine
COME to my PARTY
AND HAVE A
Good TIME
the Lights ARE Low
the Music is Fine
COME ON OVER
AND COP A GRIND
ALRIGHT
Twiggs
PAT

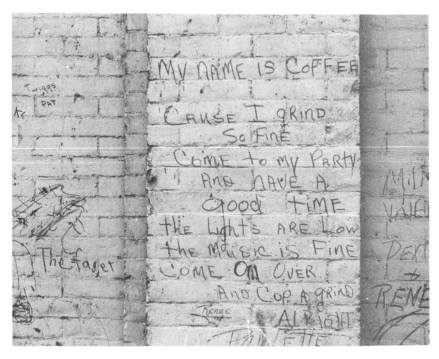

Illustration 5-3.

Later, as I read Negro history, I discovered that the rhyming cards had historical significance. A southern custom, the Friday night fish fry or house rent party, moved north during prohibition and the Great Depression. In Chicago, these parties were called a "parlor social," "gouge," "struggle," "percolator," "too terrible party," or the "skiffle." Most often though, they were just called a house rent party or a boogie. During the worst of the depression days these parties "provided a substitute for open saloons, being mounted in back-rooms in ten thousand apartments all over the South Side.[68]

In Harlem, the parties were also referred to as whist parties or dances. They were held to raise rent money, and "to have a get-together of one's own, where you could do the black bottom with no stranger behind you trying to do it, too.[69]

Langston Hughes wrote that these parties

were often more amusing than any night club, in small apartments where God knows who lived—because the guests seldom did—but where the piano would often be augmented by a guitar, or an old cornet, or somebody with a pair of drums walking in off the street. And where awful bootleg whisky and good fried fish or steaming chitterlings were sold at very low prices. And the dancing and singing and impromptu entertaining went on until dawn came in at the windows.[70]

These parties were usually advertised or announced by "brightly colored cards stuck on the grills of apartment house elevators. Some of the cards were

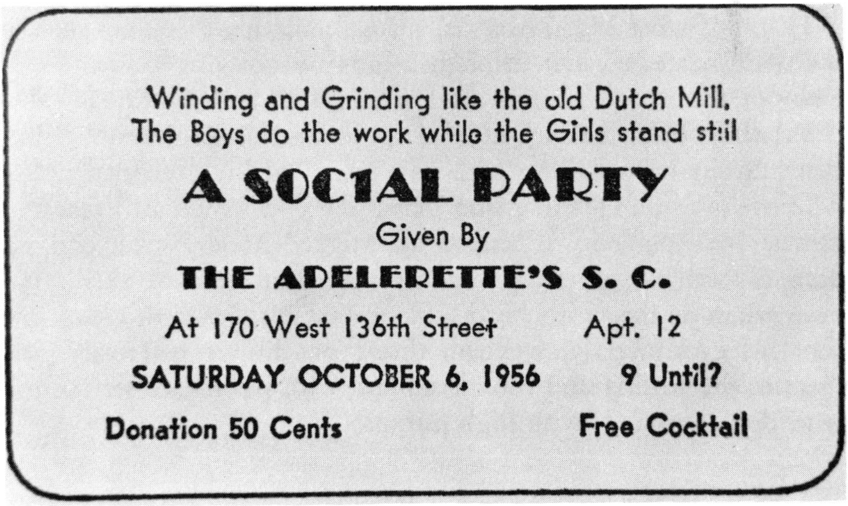

Illustration 5-4.

highly entertaining in themselves."[71] According to Hughes, the cards were called House Rent Party Cards and they were placed on bars and sometimes distributed in the streets. Eventually, the cards became simply cards announcing "pay frolics."[72]

Malcolm X also reminisced about the "rent-raising parties," and people giving out little cards announcing the parties. One that he went to had about thirty to forty guests eating, dancing, sweating, drinking, and gambling. They were all together in a run-down apartment, "the record player going full blast, the fried chicken or chitlins with potato salad and collard greens for a dollar a plate, and cans of beer or shots of liquor for fifty cents."[73]

Graffiti

I became interested in graffiti when one of my students printed a card that caused a stir. My policy allowed anyone who printed a card to tack it up for all to see. One youngster printed a card with his name and the letters L.A.M.F. (Illustration 5-5). This card was up for two weeks when I realized that it was causing some snickering and guffawing. Upon investigating, I discovered that L.A.M.F. meant "Like a Mother Fucker." Further investigation, however, disclosed a different type of meaning from that related to fornication.

This youngster was boasting in his street culture way that he was proud. Since then, I have seen L.A.M.F. affixed to individual and gang names or even in such contexts as "black-L.A.M.F." Often, when used with gang names, L.A.M.F. is accompanied by D.T.K. which means "down to kill" (Illustration 5-6). I have also found the same L.A.M.F. − D.T.K. in other than black neighborhoods.

L.A.M.F. has shown up in number of other places: A rock record entitled *Bunky & Jake L.A.M.F.*[74]; The *New York Times* and the former *Herald Tribune* ran pictures of walls with L.A.M.F.[75]; The *Star Journal* reported, as part of a button craze, students at Queens College in New York City wearing buttons with L.A.M.F. According to button wearers, L.A.M.F. meant "Let's All Make Friends," and "Look At My Face."[76]

In its own way, the L.A.M.F., and D.T.K. graffiti may compare with the blustering masculine epic yell, roar, brag, boast, holla, scream, or boasting chant of the Mike Finks as well as the streetcorner toast, the Davy Crocketts, and the hosts of raftsmen, cowboys, riverboat men, mountain men, bullies, and pseudo bad men of the American frontier.

> West of the Mississippi the scream of the backwoods boaster and bully passed into the howl of the pseudo or mock bad man, who, in his boasting chants and yells, proclaimed his intestinal fortitude with more and more weird anatomical details. . . .
>
> No one liked to play bad man more than the cowboy on a spree; . . . .

Illustration 5-5.

Illustration 5-6.

On the frontier, . . . "apparent rage" and "vigorous language" had their uses in bluffing or blustering one's way out of a tight place as well as in letting off steam.[77]

"Bad men," of the "I eat humans for breakfast" kind functioned in the presence of tenderfoots by fierce looks and snorts, by savage remarks, and sometimes by the recital of speeches ferocious in phrase and committed to memory. These men would "wild up" whenever they obtained an impressionable audience, and their braggadocio often was picturesque, even though made up at least in part from strings of stereotyped Western anecdotes.[78]

Typical of this form of bravada was David Crockett's brag.

I'm that same David Crockett, fresh from the backwoods, half-horse, half-alligator, a little touched with the snapping-turtle; can wade the Mississippi, leap the Ohio, ride upon a streak of lightning, and slip without a scratch down a honey locust; can whip my weight in wild cats—and if any gentleman pleases, for a ten dollar bill, he may throw in a panther—hug a bear too close for comfort, and eat any man opposed to Jackson.[79]

Bragging or boasting has always been part of the make-up of the folk hero. The same holds for the streetcorner youngster. The fantasy and transparent world of the streetcorner is similar to Benjamin Botkin's feelings about the backwoods boaster. He "seemed more interested in making claims than in living up to them. Moreover, since boasting, like bombast, contains in itself the seeds of its own travesty, it became hard to distinguish bragging from windy laughing at bragging and serious from mock or burlesque boasts."[80]

Although graffiti (1) can tell you who is going with whom, who claims the territory, the turf, or the neighborhood of the school, and what someone's nickname is; (2) can be used to boast without any immediate put up; and (3) is usually found all over the school, there is not too much that has been reported in the professional literature. Few educators are able to decipher graffiti.

In *The Warriors*, Yurick described Hinton making his graffiti mark: "Hector told Hinton to leave their mark. Hinton took out the Magic Marker and put the Family sign on the tomb, Dominators, LAMF, DTK and told the Junior, 'I leave this for them ghosts.' "[81]

Joseph Wambaugh, in his *The New Centurions*, dramatically and realistically described the actions of members of the Los Angeles Police Force. His writing takes officers to the Mexican barrio, where officers also observe graffiti.

This was a gang neighborhood, a Mexican gang neighborhood, and Mexican gang members were obsessed with a compulsion to make their mark on the world. . . . Serge read the writing on the wall in black and red paint from spray cans which all gang members carried in their cars in case they would spot a windfall like this creamy yellow irresistible blank wall. There was a heart in red, three feet in diameter, which bore the names of "Ruben and

Isabel" followed by *"mi vida"* and there was the huge declaration of an Easy-
streeter which said *"El Wimpy de los Easystreeters,"* and another one which
said "Ruben *de los Easystreeters,"* but Ruben would not be outdone by
Wimpy and the legend below his name said *"De los Easystreeters y del mun-
do,"* and Serge smiled wryly as he thought of Ruben who claimed the world
as his domain because Serge had yet to meet a gang member who had ever
been outside Los Angeles County. There were other names of Junior Easystreeters and Peewee Easystreeters, dozens of them, and declarations of love
and ferocity and the claims that this was the land of the Easystreeters. Of
course at the bottom of the wall was the inevitable "CON SAFOS," the crucial gang incantation not to be found in any Spanish dictionary, which declared that none of the writing on this wall can ever be altered or despoiled
by anything later written by the enemy.[82]

In New York City, early subway graffiti was primarily confined to station
advertising and playcards. Then, in the early 1960s, graffiti began to spread in
the subways and all over the city. The Taki award, spawned by the *New York
Times*, reported on a seventeen-year-old high school graduate named Taki (Taki
is a traditional Greek diminutive for Demetrius, his real first name) who lived on
183rd Street in Manhattan and who, using Magic Markers, wrote "Taki 183" all
over New York City. He started leaving his mark in the summer of 1970, when
he began sneaking his name and street onto ice cream trucks in his neighborhood.[83] Chew 127, Frank 207, and Julio 204 were also early graffiti writers
whose marks appeared on walls, public monuments, stoops, and then into subway stations.[84] The writing spread to entire walls and entire subway trains, and
the writers developed rules, styles, and titles of honor.[85]

For the city of New York, the fight against graffiti has been unending. In
1970 the MTA estimated it cost $300,000 to clean graffiti from the subways.[86]
In 1980 the graffiti clean-up cost was $5 million.[87] Attempts at prevention and
clean up have included (1) $18 million to fence in the train yards, (2) $200,000
a year for guard dogs, (3) graffiti-resistant paint at $2,200 a car, (4) legislation,
and (5) radio and television commercials and subway posters.[88]

My early work and dissertation reported definitions of some graffiti, D.T.K.,
and L.A.M.F.[89] Herbert Kohl and, more recently, Craig Castleman have provided excellent books on graffiti.[90] The movies *Beat Street, Breakin*, and *Wild
Style* depicted the adventures of rappers, breakers, and graffiti artists.[91]

Harrison Salisbury referred to graffiti as "a living newspaper of the streets."
"Here are the threats and taunts of rival gangs, the challenges and defiances.
Here is word of neighborhood romance, old flames and new loves. Here bids
are staked for leadership. Here bulletins are posted on the rumbles."[92]

U.S. Army officers in Germany read latrine graffiti "to learn if dangerous
[racial] conflicts were building up beneath the surface."[93] When I visit a school,
I read the graffiti and desk inscriptions to provide insight into student relationships and the school's atmosphere. A knowledgeable educator can interpret the

graffiti just as an archeologist discovers bones and artifacts located in various horizons. Dolores Stocker, Herbert Kohl, and Carl Bonuso have even suggested school curriculum using graffiti.[94]

LANGUAGE ARTS

Though all teachers should know black dialect and jive lexicon, the language arts teacher *must* have this facility. In addition, many schools have black studies or Afro-American studies programs and have books by black authors on their reading lists and in their libraries. Also, some teachers take their black and white students to see plays and movies by or about Afro-Americans. Many works by black authors are based on their streetcorner experiences. Also, as indicated earlier, many white authors describe and use black streetcorner language and experiences.

Tom Wolfe described an English class at San Francisco State where the white female "Peter, Paul, and Mary-type" intellectual instructor read aloud to her predominately liberal white students from Eldridge Cleaver's *Soul On Ice.*[95] She read in "pure serene tone." When finished, she closed the book just like a preacher closing the bible. Her eyes shone, her chin was up, and she had a soulful look on her face. She had read with heavy emotion, letting it all sink in. She had her students all thinking they were in a college cell block, and that revolution was the only thing that could change the damn system.

She asked for comments. A ghetto blood raised his hand to speak, and she recognized him "with the most radiant brotherly smile the human mind imagines and says, 'yes?' " The brother put her and all the white students down and told them that ghetto folks would probably laugh at what she just read.

> You try coming down in the Fillmore doing some *previously dabbling* and talking about Albert Camus and James Baldwin. They'd laugh you off the block. That book was written to give a thrill to white women in Palo Alto and Marin County. That book is the best su*burb*an jive I ever heard. . . . and don't preevy-dabble the people with no split-level Palo Alto white bourgeois housewife Buick Estate Wagon backseat rape fantasies . . . you know?[96]

He completely destroyed their "black hero trip" before they really had a chance to get into it. They were really confused; they couldn't talk against what he just said because he looked and talked like real ghetto. "So mostly this fellow is trying to blow their minds because they are being smug and knowing about The Black Man. He's saying, "Don't try to tell *us* who our leaders are, because you don't know."[97]

Reading the story related above reminded me of a story a black woman college student told me about a language arts class she had in high school. Her white female teacher was reading some prose about the British soldiers during the American Revolution.

REALITY 42

"This teacher was reading us this story, and she came to, "The soldiers in their red uniforms and black *boots, boots, boots!*"[98]

"All the guys and girls started cracking' up and laughing." "She just stood there and couldn't figure out what had happened that we were all laughing."

"Why didn't someone tell her why you were all laughing?" I asked.

"Oh, I don't know," she responded, "We were kind of ashamed to do it. We had tried to tell her other things but she just would look at us."

Reality 43 was part of a taped conversation I had with a black high school student who was both laughing and disgusted about all the books in his school by blacks and about blacks but that were unintelligible to his white teachers, thereby almost making everything useless because the white language arts teachers could not interpret or even understand many of the writings.

REALITY 43

"You know, killing the monkey to feed my habit. . . . And, she swears this means killing the white man to survive in a racist society. This is not it. It's not it at all! . . . You know, to kill a monkey, to feed my habit—it is slang for a junkie, . . . but you can't convince her of it."[99]

What is going on in some schools is a reversal of the usual role of the English teacher. Traditionally, the teacher knows and the student does not know the context clues. However, if the English teacher is not knowledgeable of Afro-American literature, her black students will understand the context clues, and she will not.

Too often, language arts teachers feel their responsibility to their students ends when they put the black-authored books on their reading list to provide the books. Real involvement goes beyond this token approach. Real involvement means reading the books and learning what they are saying. Not enough teachers are able to do this.

Reality 44 is part of another taped conversation with a black high school youngster. The conversation concerned a book that the teacher had provided for the class but did not understand. It took place in an urban high school in New York State.

REALITY 44

Student: "Well this was one that they produced at ——— High School. They were laughing at the teacher for . . . because he didn't even understand what we were really getting across to him."

Adult: "Was the book made by the youngsters at ⎯⎯ High School?"
Student: "No, this is one [that] one of the teachers had given to the kids.
. . . The kids were laughing at him because they, you know, they would get to
various slang words and various expressions and the teacher couldn't explain it."

Many books by black, white, and other authors have been published in the
past two decades that contain jive lexicon.[100] There are also books, such as Bernard Malamud's *The Tenants*, where you have to know jive talk and Yiddish.[101]

In addition to jive lexicon, the language arts teacher should also know what
such sentences as " 'Lesser, I have to pull your coat about a certain matter,' "
or, what words such as *megillah, shiksa*, and *chutspah* mean. If you are listening
to records by black authors, how would you interpret "When the man runs his
game, he sure runs it mean"?[102]

Many black poets are using and have used jive talk as an expression of blackness. "By the end of the 1960s there were indications that Black artists and
intellectuals were picking up Black English and making it a symbol of Black
unity. Today an impressive school of Black poets is producing poetry in Black
English and expressing pride in the expressive power of the language."[103]

Imamu Amira Baraka (LeRoi Jones) used jive lexicon and Black English creatively as a form of expression. Some of the jive lexicon used includes "vine,"
"main man," "fly," and "a do rag."[104] According to Ron Welburn, Baraka uses
language and Fundi uses images that blacks understand and whites have problems understanding.

The language is rich, but never inflated or esoteric; it abounds with verbal
images that only blacks are likely to interpret effectively. There are no con-
cessions made to the nonblack reader. . . . Couched in the language of the
streets and intoned with the rhythms of jazz, it is both an expression and evo-
cation of the rudiments of blackness, which whites may find perplexing.[105]

Welburn also pointed out to the nonblack reader that the title of the book *In
our Terribleness* "is derived from black slang, in which reversing the white standard, 'bad' and 'terrible' are synonymous with 'good' and 'superb.' "[106]

In LeRoi Jones and Larry Neal's *Black Fire: An Anthology of Afro-American
Writing*, jive lexicon is used throughout in the poetry and short stories. Such jive
words and expressions as "toms," "grey," "gimme five," "outta sight," "stone,"
"fox," "run it down," "shades," and "buns" are used.[107] James T. Stewart
uses "half a man" and "buns."[108] Marvin E. Jackman employs such jive lexicon
as "hittin'," "stone fox," "rapped," "run it down to me," "gimme some slack,"
and "light'n up on me."[109]

John O. Killens wrote of the conflict a young black female experiences as she
tried to find her black identity while being pressured to fulfill her mother's
bourgeois aspirations. The author-narrator stated he must write in Afro-Ameri-
canese, using a rhythm, an idiom, nuances, a style, truths, and exaggerations that
are all black.[110]

Paul Carter Harrison and Ed Bullins used the black idiom to do more than entertain their audience. In *Tabernacle*, Harrison's selection of language articulates the verbal aggression ghetto blacks experience and sometimes express. Bullins also used jive vocabulary to illustrate the counterculture and consciousness of blacks[111]

Bullins, in "Goin'a Buffalo," provided the reader with a picture of the aggression and violence of prison life. To help paint the picture, he used such black lexicon as "agitatin'," "signifyin'," "rank," "ofays," "sucker," "jive-sucker," "shit started really going down," and "got themselves together."[112]

Stephen Henderson presented one of LeGraham's poems and wrote that it "shouts his own black beauty in his own black language." In discussing further LeGraham's "The Black Narrator" and Sonia Sanchez's "Righteous Brothers," he wrote,

> There should be no doubt in anyone's mind that these poems are not intended for white readers and white audiences, that their purpose was direct address to the black community, to get us together to TCB. If there is any doubt in anyone's mind, Don L. Lee dispels it. He states that his poetry is not directed to "white boys and girls" but to black people. . . . His poetry speaks for them and to them—to "the man with the wine bottle and processed hair"—about rat-infested slums and the spiritual corruption they breed. His poetry is a weapon for his people at the same time that it draws upon them for strength. It is "like daggers, broken brew bottles, bullets, swift razors from black hands cutting through slum landlords and Negro dope pushers." It will confront "pimps and prostitutes and aid in the destruction of their actions." He says, "Black poems are a part of the people: An energy source for the people's life style."[113]

HISTORY OF JIVE LEXICON

There appears to be some controversy concerning the origins of jive lexicon. Dan Burley, former editor of Harlem's *Amsterdam News*, reported that Negroes began to use jive about 1921 in Chicago, to play the dozens. It meant to scoff, to taunt, to sneer—it was an expression of sarcasm. "Like the tribal groups of Mohammedans and people of the Orient, Negroes of that period had developed a highly effective manner of talking about each other's ancestors and hereditary traits, a colorful and picturesque linguistic procedure which came to be known as 'putting you in the dozens.' Later, this was simply called 'Jiving' someone."[114]

Eventually, ragtime musicians adopted the term and it soon began to mean any number of things. Since the 1930s, the "jitterbug" population has used the term jive as the trade name for "swing." The dozens concept of jive no longer exists today; it is no longer a term of opprobrium related to one's appearance, one's parents, or one's knowledge. Today, jive is "a term of honor, dignity—class."[115]

Burley also suggested that "jive talk came into being because of the paucity of words and inadequacy of the vocabularies of its users."[116] Jive is also the result of slang parlance from the hamlets, the villages, and the cities wherever Negroes come together. The jive lexicon undergoes a continual "purifying process" in which expressions are used and retained or tried and discarded.

Jive has been in the process of evolution from the early years following World War I. The Prohibition Era, the Gangster Period, the Age of Hardboiled, Quick-shooting Heroes, and their seductive molls contributed to it. So did the decade known as the Great Depression. All this led inevitably to the Age of the Jitterbug, a spasmodic era with a background of World War II and swing music contributing to its use and popularity.[117]

But most important, jive is a rebellious and different way of speaking.

Jive is language in motion. It supplies the answer to the hunger for the unusual, the exotic and the picturesque in speech. It is a medium of escape, a safety valve for people pressed against the wall for centuries, deprived of the advantages of complete social economic, moral and intellectual freedom. It is an inarticulate protest of a people given half a loaf of bread and then dared to eat it; a people continually fooled and bewildered by the mirage of a better and fuller life. Jive is a defense mechanism, a method of deriving pleasure from something the uninitiated cannot understand. It is the same means of escape that brought into being the spirituals as sung by American slaves; the blues songs of protest that bubble in the breasts of black men and women believed by their fellow white countrymen to have been born to be menials, to be wards of a nation, even though they are tagged with a whimsical designation as belonging to the body politic. Jive provides a medium of expression universal in its appeal. Its terms have quality, sturdiness, rhythm and descriptive impact. It is language made vivid, vital and dynamic.[118]

Earl Conrad wrote that the origin of jive probably goes back into the very bowels of the Negro–American experience—as early as slavery times when Negroes had to sing, speak, and think in a sort of code.

We know that the Negro's music grew up out of his revolutionary experience, that his spirituals reflected his struggle, his "escape to the North." Jive talk may have been originally a kind of "pig Latin" that the slaves talked with each other, a code—when they were in the presence of whites. Take the word "ofay." Ninety million white Americans right now probably don't know that that means "a white," but Negroes know it. Negroes needed to have a word like that in their language, needed to create it in self-defense.[119]

Furthermore, jive is another of the Negro Americans' contributions to the United States. It began to evolve when white America forced a new and foreign language on African slaves. "Slowly, over the generations, Negro America, living by and large in its own segregated world, with its own thoughts, found its own way of expression, found its own way of handling English, as it had to find its own way in handling many other aspects of a white, hostile world. Jive is one of the end-results."[120] According to Louise Pound, many of the words used by Negroes were survivals of words used by seventeenth and eighteenth century Englishmen who settled here.[121]

Ruth Banks differentiated in the use of what she calls idioms of the present-day American Negro. She felt that some of the idioms were found in the swing magazines and easily adopted for general use, while another group of words was used almost exclusively by urban Negroes. She also pointed out that many of the words are "common English words" that are given new meaning. And where the words are adequate and clever, they remain. Also, the expressions are often quickly discarded, which prevents the average white American from learning the special inflection of the voice needed to pronounce these words effectively.[122]

Lou Shelly called the vocabulary "jive talk" and wrote that the language was picked up from the whites and was embellished with racy and rich idioms by the negro who traveled to Harlem from Africa. He also felt that the jive is incomprehensible to all but those who are "hep."[123]

Marcus Boulware published *Jive and Slang of Students in Negro Colleges* and called the language both slang and jive. Although Boulware was not sure where the word jive originated, he felt that it made its appearance with swing music. And just as jazz became swing, so has slang become jive.[124]

"Colored English" or "Spoken Soul" is what Claude Brown called the vocabulary. He claimed that its roots were over three hundred years old. Starting with slavery and aided by malapropisms, colloquialisms, fractured and battered grammar, and quite a bit of creativity, the sound of soul or Colored English evolved. He pointed out further that spoken soul is less a language and more a sound.

> It generally possesses a pronounced lyrical quality which is frequently incompatible to any music other than that ceaseless and relentlessly driving rhythm that flows from poignantly spent lives. Spoken soul has a way of coming out metered without the intention of the speaker to invoke it. There are specific phonetic traits. To the soulless ear the vast majority of these sounds are dismissed as incorrect usage of the English language and, not infrequently, as speech impediments. To those so blessed as to have had bestowed upon them at birth the lifetime gift of soul, these are the most communicative and meaningful sounds ever to fall upon human ears.[125]

Brown also differentiated between soul and slang. Whereas slang lends itself to conventional English, soul does not. When Negores do adopt words from the white vocabulary, they become "soul words" and take on a different meaning. The concept of words with double meanings is discussed further in this chapter and may be related to the double meanings in many blues songs.

Schechter referred to the lexicon as soul vocabulary or vernacular that Negroes have invented for themselves. The syntax and vocabulary have moved from "slave riddles to blues slang to jive and into the current Soul vernacular." He felt that soul vocabulary is more open, more humorous, has more irony, and is more socially aware than past Negro expressions and is reflective of today's blacks openly seeking identity and full equality.[126]

According to Jack Daniel, survival for blacks meant their developing a private and secret patois, or private public language with which they could communicate privately.[127] Jack Schiffman wrote that the Negroes' language originated with the code or patois that slaves created to keep their white masters ignorant of their discussions.[128]

Grier and Cobbs use the term patois to refer to the jive and hip language that has developed. They suggest that the language served an adaptive function in slavery days and today. It was and is "used as a secret language to communicate the hostility of blacks for whites, and great delight is taken by blacks when whites are confounded by the language."[129]

Mez Mezzrow, a blue-eyed Jewish jazz musician, reported on hearing the jive language in its early stages on the South Side of Chicago, It was a different language; different from the traditional language of the southern Negro. The hipster's jive language was a knitting together of "tight secret society . . . which resents and nourishes its resentment, and is readying to strike back." The jive is not only an escape valve or a defense mechanism of the traditional southern Negro, " . . . it's a kind of drilling academy too, preparing for future battles."[130]

Mencken wrote that the "queer jargon called jive" emerged in the early '40s and was a mixture of Harlem's Negro slang, the drug addicts' and pettier sort of criminals' argot, plus some additions from the theatrical gossip columns and the high school campus. At its inception jive also appeared to be in use by jazz musicians. Furthermore, though jive varies from city to city, "it manifests a surprising uniformity for an idiom that is almost exclusively spoken, not written."[131]

Wentworth and Flexner in their Dictionary of American Slang, reported that though some jive terms originated outside of Harlem, the peak of jive popularity was around 1935.[132]

Robert Gold, in his A Jazz Lexicon, suggested that the language of the jazz world is a fusing of the languages of the jazz musician and the Negro people.

So we get a people in rebellion against a dominant majority, but forced to rebel secretly, to sublimate, as the psychologist would put it—to express themselves culturally through the medium of jazz, and linguistically through a code, a jargon. But as the music developed from New Orleans marches and early Dixieland through the blues-and-rhythm cycle and the swing era on its bop and modern, or progressive, jazz, an immense change took place in the life of the Negro. He became more urbanized and the life of the streets peppered his language, and so filtered into jazz parlance, which to this day is highly interrelated with Negro life. Always close (though hardly by choice) to the most squalid aspects of big-city life, the Negro assimilated the jargon of the rackets—dope peddling, prostitution, larceny, gambling—and the more interesting of these terms spilled over into jazz lingo. Then, too, the high frequency of Negro impressment into Southern chain gangs was another, unhappy source of Negro slang, much as it was a source of Negro work songs and folk songs.

The totality of his experience in America stamped the Negro with a psychology demanding not only a unique and rebellious music, but a unique and rebellious way of speaking.[133]

JIVE LEXICON AND COMMUNICATION

Discipline continues to be a problem in many schools, and the hip urban streetcorner youngsters or their suburban or rural equivalents appear to be involved in these discipline problems. Intervention and prevention of these problems would indicate improving educator understanding and communication with these youngsters. Educators, therefore, must understand the motivation and context of these students' verbal behavior.

We know that urban, hip, streetcorner youngsters are usually aggressive, physical hustlers, wise in the ways of street survival. They know how to "run a game," to "signify," to "woof," to "loud talk," to "shuck and jive," and to "sound." They know how to do all of these and more; they know how to "run a game" to get what they desire from people. One of the most important parts of their game is their verbal ability, reports of lower class black youngsters being nonverbal to the contrary. Additionally, Paul Lerman's study of black and Puerto Rican youth argot reinforced the findings of linguists that "people who share modes of verbal communication are likely to share participation in a social and cultural community as well."[134] Thus, the teacher should begin to think of his or her streetcorner students' talking and acting as a performance with their audience, their fellow students. If teachers will accept this concept, they will be on their way to understanding and coping with their streetcorner students' behavior. Abrahams pointed out that "there is an integral relationship between the speaking system and the social structure of any community," and that "each speaker has in his repertoire, different codes which arise in response to different situations." The reader must remember that school is included in the streetcorner youngster's social structure.[135]

On the black streetcorner, the good streetcorner performer is respected whether the performance is verbal or otherwise. Additionally, the performance is judged in relationship to the performer's ability to achieve audience participation "and how well the utilization of these high affect actions is capable of producing the desired result for the performance." Usually, verbal performance contains a good deal of kinetic and verbal interaction with the audience. These performances or encounters contain a good deal more verbal repartee than do usual middle class verbal encounters.[136] In addition, these verbal encounters are more stylized and related to ceremonial procedures. Most importantly for discipline, this repartee is often verbally aggressive and related to machisimo in reputation and identity. Furthermore, verbally aggressive repartee is a phenomenon of lower class behavior in general. The need to express one's masculinity, to act "tough," is, at other times, also expressed through language and physical interaction by men of all lower classes.[137] In particular, Herbert Gans reported on the verbally aggressive behavior of lower class Italians in Boston's Roxbury in the mid-1950s.[138]

Hopefully, the reader is beginning to relate what is being written to a classroom communication scene. If students respect the good and forceful speaker and the verbal interaction considered a performance, the teachers must know how to relate on this dramatic and verbal level to gain their students' respect. Middle class teachers unfamiliar with lower class language style are too often overcome and their teacher role impaired or destroyed because of their ignorance of the verbal requirements.

This statement by Abrahams described what is going on in our classrooms— a reality that is understood by few educators.

> Because of the focus on talk—as performance, a feeling develops that the talker is potentially 'on' all of the time—that is, verbal behavior will be judged as if it were a performance and the speaker judged as if he were on stage. This means that virtually any conversation may turn into a routine or something else equally dramatic. But being "on" like this also means that, to a certain extent, the entire expectation pattern of the performance is invoked, including the special relationship between the performer and the audience.[139]

One of the most important tools in the streetcorner performer's arsenal is the use of "strong words and hyperbolic expressions." And, according to Abrahams, "the most obvious of these is the use of slang and colloquialisms, in-group terms which self-consciously show the speaker to be in verbal control, and by extension, in control of the social environment. Slang is more characteristic of urban BE (Black English) because of the heightened importance of peer-grouping in the *hip* city environment."[140]

There is a style and technique in the use of black lexicon in relation to high affect with the audience. These generally fall into three categories:

1. Words with double meanings. Often the second nonstandard meaning is in no way related to the standard meaning. Most often, as mentioned earlier, students use Standard English words with sexual connotations to upset their teachers—especially female teachers.
2. Discussion of the behavior of others that emphasizes their nicknames rather than their given names.
3. Words used to describe those items that are considered important to maintain one's prestige and style with the "in" group—the reference points of a culture. These would include black lexicon for such items and activities as cars,

clothing, girls, sexual intercourse, parts of the body, alcoholic beverages, drugs, entertainment, and parties.[141]

The above-described behavior that includes style, technique, strong words and hyperbolic expression, talk as a performance, and playing to the audience can be recalled by the reader in relation to, in particular, the early eays of the career of Muhammad Ali—then Cassius Clay—and the reaction of the average white American.

Also, for those who were not part of or a witness to the 1960s civil rights movement, television brought the 1984 election campaign and the Reverend Jesse Jackson into many homes that had never seen anything like it before.

The Jackson campaign is likely to be remembered for the oratorical flourish it added. . . . It was a style rich in metaphor and biblical allusions, conventions common to Baptist churches and blacks' slang. All combined to make listening to a Jackson speech a change from the usual fare of the stump.[142]

The argument has now been made that inner city streetcorner youngsters are verbal, that often when they talk they are putting on a performance for their teacher and fellow students with some manipulative objective in mind. Often, this manipulative verbal behavior creates discipline problems. Additionally, their black lexicon is extremely important in peer identification and communication. The next step, therefore, is to look at some of the psychosocial and affective implications of language in general and black lexicon in particular, specifically as related to schools.

PSYCHOSOCIAL IMPLICATIONS

The right language at the proper time can serve as a socializer, a relaxing agent, and a positive catalyst to enhance communication. Conversely, the wrong language or the improper time, or the improper interpretation of language, can cause communication problems. Realities 45 and 46 are two examples of where language was used as a relaxer to enhance communication. Reality 45 is taken from the literature; Reality 46 is the report of a personal experience.

REALITY 45

"I am there, once again at my office at Franklin. I see the careworn face of a little Puerto Rican woman, aged beyond her years from the poverty and hard work in the fields of her native island. She has come to see me on some matter relating to her son.

"Señora," I say to her in Spanish, 'sit down. Make yourself comfortable and we will talk about Miguel and his future.'

"And to the boy, also in Spanish, 'You sit down over there and do not interrupt us while I talk to your mother.'

"The only language of education is the language which people can understand—no matter where it originates. To this simple Puerto Rican woman I have suddenly become more than the principal of an English-speaking high school. I am a human being who understands and is trying to help her. In the eyes of the boy I have given respect and status to his parent. The process of education has been translated into human terms."[143]

I observed Reality 46 while with a friend who was then an assistant principal in a Harlem junior high school serving a black and Puerto Rican student population. The reactions of those described in Reality 46 are similar to those reported above.

REALITY 46

As we were leaving school one afternoon, an elderly Puerto Rican gentleman approached us and addressed us in a halting Spanish and English. His face reflected discomfort and distress.

My friend, who happened to be a Sephardic Jew, responded easily and openly, in Spanish. The man's face broke out into a smile as he burst forth speaking in Spanish. His problem solved, the man left smiling. It was a warm and beautiful happening.

In the reality of the life outside the school, the proper language is the language that brings people together and succeeds in accomplishing an objective. Politicians are notorious for winning votes by eating lox and bagels and wearing a yarmulke, by eating pizza, lasagna, or manicotti at an Italian block party, or speaking in the language of any group they are trying to win over. Alfonso Narvaez provided an example of what is so common and accepted in big-city politics.

REALITY 47

"*Kumt arois un zugt sholom aleichem tzu eyer nexten Senator fun de stut fun New York,*" blares a loudspeaker atop a car in the Borough Park section of Brooklyn.

Inside the car Isaac Steinheim, a campaign worker for Leonard Silverman, the local Democratic candidate for the Assembly, exhorted passers-by in "New York Yiddish" to come and meet Representative Richard L. Ottinger, the party's candidate for the Senate.

Mr. Ottinger, accompanied by Representative Hugh L. Carey and Mr. Silverman, walked along 13th Avenue in the predominately Jewish and Democratic area and was greeted enthusiastically.[144]

As the director of the Mildred Goetz Day Camp of the Henry Kaufmann Campgrounds, I participated in the filming of a portion of a TV fundraising commercial for the Federation of Jewish Philanthropies of New York City. The filming took place at the campgrounds alongside our lake. The movie was to point up a senior citizen day camp program as one of the many programs supported by the federation. The short film centered on singer Steve Lawrence speaking with a number of senior citizens.

REALITY 48

As the lighting and cue cards arrangements were worked out, the senior citizens sat obviously ill at ease. Suddenly, by what appeared to be intuition, Steve Lawrence spoke two words in Yiddish (I do not remember what they were). It was a different ball game. The senior citizens smiled with pleased surprise *"E' is a Yiddish boychical?"*[145]

They almost had to be restrained from petting him to death. Filming was then completed with ease.

A few years ago, I participated as a guest lecturer in a preservice education program for teacher aides in a large city. My topic was classroom communication. The majority of the approximately sixty aides were black. Their reaction to my presentation was similar to the aforementioned incidents.

REALITY 49

The aides sat stiffly, stonefaced, staring at me. After a brief introduction, I gave out Foster's Jive Lexicon Analogy Test and *A Lexicon of Words with Standard and Non-Standard Meanings.*

As the aides picked up these items and began to read, the room appeared to come alive. They started to laugh, move in their seats, and talk. I could hear murmurings in dialect. The jive test was familiar to most of the aides, and they related to it.

The white assistant director of the program rushed over to me, a broad grin on his face, and said, "This is the first time these aides have smiled and relaxed since the program began."

When the workshop session was over, many of the black aides approached me, shook hands, and stayed to talk awhile.

The aides' response reminded me of something I read in Jane Phillips's *Mojo Hand*. Miss Phillips depicted a society tea covered by photographers from the local black newspaper. The photographers had left and the ladies sat about like "china dolls . . . dressed in all the grotesque finery at their disposal" listening to classical music. Someone hunts through the stack of records, finds an old 78 blues recording, slips it onto the record player, and it begins to scratch forth its sounds.

> *"I want to know if your jelly roll's fresh, or is it stale, I want to know if your jelly roll's fresh or is it stale? Well, woman, I'm going to buy me some jelly roll if I have to go to jail."*
> Almost immediately she heard shouts and shrieks from the other room.
> " . . . Oh, yeah, get to it! . . . Laura, woman, how long since your husband's seen you jelly roll?"
> "Gertrude, don't you ask me questions like that. Eh, how long since your husband's seen you?"
> Eunice went back downstairs. Everyone had relaxed. Some of the women were unbuckling their stockings, others were loosening the belts around their waists. Someone had gotten out brandy and was pouring it into the tea cups.
> "Give some to the debs," someone said, "show them what this society really is."
> Eunice sat down. The record ground on and on, and it was then that she knew that she had to go find the source of herself, this music that moved her and the others, however much they tried to deny it.[146]

Sister Elizabeth Ann Donnelly took a graduate course with me. As a course project, she administered my jive test to a hospital employee population of ninety-five—forty-two blacks and fifty-three whites. Though the black subjects scored higher than did the whites, what is important were the aftereffects vis-à-vis the improved communication with the subjects. The conclusion to Sister Donnelly's paper is worth reporting:

> In this large hospital where I resided this summer very often I would meet the personnel in passing. Before meeting the people to whom I gave the test, when I passed them in the corridors there was a slight nod or such. After I had given the test I noted a sort of transformation, especially among the black persons. They would always call to me and had something to say as I passed them. It seemed as though just this effort to get to know them better and their manner of communicating meant something to them. Their reaction was really a study in itself.[147]

Another interesting outcome of language differences was reported by Herman Lantz. He reported that blacks were in some cases more acceptable to white miners because they spoke English as compared with the foreign language of the immigrants. Because the miners could not understand the foreign languages, they were fearful and suspicious of the foreigners. The wife of a miner had this to say:

> You couldn't understand the language of the foreigners. Why, I would just as soon live alongside a nigger family as some of these foreigners. I think that

the niggers are whiter than the foreigners are because at least they speak your own language. Why, if you lived next door to a foreigner, they would be plotting to kill you and you wouldn't even know it. At least you can understand the nigger's language.[148]

Claude Brown wrote about the Negro male's choice of the words "man" and "baby" as vicarious expressions of manliness and vehicle for comradery and blackness. He also reflected on the importance of certain words to communicate feeling.

The first time I heard the expression "baby" used by one cat to address another was up at Warwick in 1951. . . . The term had a hip ring to it, a real colored ring. The first time I heard it, I knew right away I had to start using it. It was like saying "Man, look at me. I've got masculinity to spare." It was saying at the same time to the world, "I'm one of the hippest cats, one of the most uninhibited cats on the scene." . . . If you could say it, this meant that you really had to be sure of yourself, sure of your masculinity. . . .

The real hip thing about the "baby" term was that it was something that only colored cats could say the way it was supposed to be said. I'd heard gray boys trying it, but they couldn't really do it. Only colored cats could give it the meaning that we all knew it had without ever mentioning it—the meaning of black masculinity.[149]

I think everybody said it real loud because they liked the way it sounded. It was always, "Hey, baby. How you doin,' baby?" in every phrase of the Negro hip life. As a matter of fact, I went to a Negro lawyer's office once, and he said, "Hey, baby. How you doin'?" I really felt at ease, really felt that we had something in common. I imagine there were many people in Harlem who didn't feel they had too much in common with the Negro professionals, the doctors, and lawyers and dentists and ministers. I know I didn't. But to hear one of these people greet you with the street thing, the "Hey, baby"—and he knew how to say it—you felt as though you had something strong in common.[150]

Though the debate continues as to whether school personnel even should learn or speak Black English, or in some cases whether it even exists, some workers have reported positive results from its use. Pearl Berkowitz and Esther Rothman have written that on some occasions emotionally disturbed children expect their teacher to operate on their perceptual and emotional level. At this time, teachers may "indulge in colloquial speech patterns, meeting the child with his own language and responding and participating with enthusiasm in the child's activities.[151] Paul Crawford, Daniel Malamud, and James Dumpson reported that the New York City Youth Board workers became accepted by the language of the gangs.[152] Cohn holds that the teacher who "is unhampered by moralistic and snobbish attitudes, can help children overcome their ambivalence toward language expression."[153] Narvaez, in writing about the activities of the Preventive Enforcement Patrol (P.E.P.), a special squad of black and Puerto Rican policemen in Harlem, reported police officers rapping with the people and kids in their own language.[154]

One of the most important yet little-known studies supporting the importance of black lexicon as a mode of communication for the urban black street-corner youngster, came out of the New York State Training School for Boys at Warwick, New York. An attempt was made at Warwick to gather information relative to attitudinal changes toward the training school that appeared to take place when new boys were placed into the main program. The first phase of the study concerned depth interviews with fifteen training school youngsters. The findings were interesting.

> The response to two of the interview questions, "What do new boys learn about the Training School from other boys in the Orientation Program?" and "What do new boys learn about the Training School from boys in the Regular Program?" led to the second phase of the pilot study—*A psycholinguistic analysis of the subculture language.*
>
> Most of the boys interviewed said that the first thing they learned from other inmates was how to talk at State School. When asked for examples of this language, they gave such terms as "boody," "boppin'," "capped," "chickee-boy," "lap," "slop drop," and similar linguistic confabulations. From listening to tape recordings of these interviews, it became increasingly evident that a further exploration should be made of this language from the psychological and motivational point of view.[155]

The role and the importance of Black English and jive lexicon as modes of communication in and out of school have become, to a large extent, accepted, and there is now a related out-of-school literature to help educators.[156]

CONCLUSION

This chapter argues the importance of educators' unconditionally accepting any youngster and his or her language as the first step toward helping him or her accept the school. This is particularly important in the United States today, where once again we are experiencing large numbers of immigrants.

The second argument is that educators, without question, must teach all children Standard English. Indeed, the school's responsibility is to teach the way to speak, to behave, and to dress appropriate to the social situation. This is of particular importance for disadvantaged children whose environment does not usually provide these early learning experiences.

In the main, however, educators must be aware of the role of their language and their students' language in school communication. When there is too great a difference, problems may arise.

Language of teachers [is] too remote from the child's developmental level, or from the native tongue ordinarily used on his social plane. If that is the case, the child feels out of place, not really wanted, or even looked down upon, and begins to show signs of social-outcast reactions and protest.[157]

Unquestionably, the teacher speaking in dialect can be interpreted as being paternalistic, racist, or insulting. However, just as school personnel should develop their teaching style based on their personality, so may school personnel judiciously use Black English.

Some teachers can use Black English positively; others cannot. In some situations, the use of jive lexicon would be proper; in others it would be inappropriate. However, without a question, all personnel should know and understand Black English, particularly the jive lexicon.

Finally, Negro slaves have not been credited with having contributed many words to the American vocabulary from their various African dialects.[158] However, since the 1960s, black lexicon has traveled from the United States to Great Britain and returned through the medium of the Beatles, the Rolling Stones, and other British rock groups.[159] Hence, a lexicon that appears to have started out as urban Negro streetcorner jive talk has now spread throughout the United States, if not the world. Jive lexicon words appear to have surpassed the contributions to our vocabulary made by American Indians and earlier ethnic, religious, and immigrant groups.

GLOSSARY

This glossary of words, some with double meanings, is provided to give educators and others some examples. The glossary is only a foundation to be built upon. It is in no way all-inclusive. In addition, the definitions, or even the existence of a word, may depend upon where one lives.

Word	*Definition*
apple, the big apple	New York City
attitude	to get mad without a good reason
bad, baaad	good
balling	sexual intercourse; having a good time, or partying
basting	making a derogatory or ridiculing remark about someone
bat	a job, an ugly girl
bear	an ugly girl
booCoo	many
book	to leave
break	to make fun of someone, or to yell at someone
breeze	to leave
bugged, or bug out	annoying, crazy, or entertainingly crazy, see "trip"

buns	buttocks
bush	to allow your hair to grow naturally
cakes	buttocks
cheeks	buttocks
chill, chill out	to take it easy
click	a gang, a club
crib	house, home, apartment
crying buddy, cut buddy	best friend
cut	to remain out of sight or to be unobtrusive
cuz	best friend, see "home boy"
deal	to fight
deep	nice, smart, used as a superlative to describe almost anything
dig	to understand
dike	a lesbian
dip	a party, a dance
dog, dag, dot it	shucks, darn
dozens	a method of verbally insulting, degrading and/or vilifying someone's female relatives with lewd and obscene remarks that usually degrade or negatively reflect upon the masculinity of someone present
ease	to leave
five	see "skin"
fly	nice, pretty, high fashion
forget you	used to disguise "fuck you"
fox	a pretty girl
fresh	oustanding, stylish, see "stone," "fly," and "bad"
fronts	clothes
fur	a woman
game	a line of talk given someone
grease (greeze)	to eat
grind	a slow sensual dance
grit	to eat
hawk	a cold wind, a powerful person; the term hawk may derive from Coleman Hawkins
heart	courage
heifer	a prostitute, a loose woman
hip	to be knowledgeable, resourceful, see "wit-it"
hoe, ho	whore
home boy	best friend
ice	to stab someone
jeff	a white

Jew	the boss
joey	a white
johnson	penis
joke	penis
jones	penis, a job
kicks	shoes
knit	a Banlon or imported Italian knit shirt
knot	a person's head
lamb	a fearful person, someone who does not know what is going on
lame	a person who is "out of it"
lid	hat
lizard	lizard shoes
loud	to make fun of someone, to yell at someone
man, the	the police, the boss, whites
nose	to have someone's attention, to have someone under your control
nut	to act crazy
off	to kill, destroy, or beat up
oscar	penis
people	your friends, your gang
pig	last year's Cadillac, the police
private	penis
process	straightened hair
rags	clothing
rank	to insult someone
rap, rapping	talking, giving a female a smooth line to get her into bed
scab	an ugly female
shades	sunglasses
short	an automobile
sides	records
silks	a silk suit
skin	slapping each other's palms
slave	a job
smack	sexual intercourse
snack	penis
solid	good, all right
split	to leave
squash it	to forget it
static	to give someone trouble
stone	the best, outstanding, very good
suction	to give someone a hard time

swift	good
swipe	penis
tack	a person who does not know what's going on
taste	whiskey, wine
T.C.B.	take care of business
threads	clothes
through	see "tack" and "weak"
tight	best of friends
tip	a girl, to leave
together	good, to be dressed well
train	when two or more males have sexual intercourse with one female
trim	a female, sexual intercourse, vagina
trip	a positive description of someone's behavior, not a drug trip
turf	territory, neighborhood
turk	territory, neighborhood
vines	clothing
walk	see "weak"
waste	to beat someone up, to kill
weak	something that is phony, out of fashion
wit-it	to be knowledgeable, see "bad" and "hip"
wheels	a car
wolf, wolf'n, woof	can mean anything from making fun of someone to challenging someone to a fight, a powerful person
woord	I agree
work	to fight, to dance with fervor

NOTES TO CHAPTER 5

1. Leonard Covello, *The Teacher in the Urban Community: A Half Century in City Schools. The Heart is the Teacher* (Totowa, N.J.: Littlefield, Adams, 1970).

2. Peter Martin, *The Landsmen* (Boston: Little, Brown, 1952), p. 1.

3. Caroline F. Ware, *Greenwich Village 1920-1930* (New York: Harper Collophon, 1965), p. 338.

4. Basil Bernstein, "Some Sociological Determinants of Perception—An Inquiry into Subcultural Differences," *British Journal of Sociology* 9 (1959): 169.

5. Ben H. Bagdikian, *In the Midst of Plenty—The Poor in America* (Boston: Beacon, 1965), 185–86.

6. To give some "skin," "five," or "dap," is to slap the palms of one another's hands. The viewer of television sporting events will often observe

black athletes, and whites too, now giving a newer version referred to as "high five" after a home run, a touchdown, or at the start of a basketball game.

Giving skin is a physical gesture of approval, agreement, paying a compliment, a greeting, or even parting. It could be considered equivalent to a slap on the back or a pat on the shoulder.

According to Burley, giving skin originated in Chicago in 1939, at the time of the Tony Galento-Joe Louis fight, and jive-conscious blacks almost universally understood it.

> The act of "Gimme-some-skin" involves some theatricals, an intricate sense of timing, plenty of gestures. For example: You are standing on the corner, You see a friend approaching. You bend your knees halfway and rock back and fourth on your heels and toes with a swingy sway like the pulsing of a heartbeat. You hold your arms closely to your sides with index fingers pointing rigidly toward the sidewalk. You say to your friend as he comes up: "Watcha know ole man, whatcha know?" He answers:
>
> "I don't know, ole man, whatcha know?" Then he says: "Gimme some skin, ole man: gimme some of that fine skin!"
>
> You bend your knees in a gentle sag. Your upper right arm is held close to your side, but the forearm with the palm of the hand open, is thrust out like a motorist flagging on a left turn. You both swing around and your palms collide in a resounding whack.

Dan Burley, *Dan Burley's Handbook of Jive* (New York: Jive Potentials, 1944), pp. 59-60.

Malcolm X described going back to visit Michigan. "My appearance staggered the older boys I had once envied; I'd stick out my hand, saying 'Skin me, daddy-o!' . . . wherever I went, I was the life of the party. 'My'man! . . . Gimme some skin!' "

Alex Haley, *The Autobiography of Malcolm X* (New York, Grove, 1966), p. 79.

For a pre-high five exposition of giving or getting skin, see Benjamin G. Cook, "Nonverbal Communication among Afro-Americans: An Initial Classification," in Thomas Kochman, ed., *Rappin' and Stylin' Out* (Chicago: University of Illinois Press, 1972), p. 32-64.

7.   Jess Stein, ed., *The Random House Dictionary of the English Language*, unabridged ed. (New York: Random House, 1966), p. 1514.

8.   Howard Wentworth and Stuart B. Flexner, *Dictionary of American Slang* (New York: Thomas C. Crowell, 1960), p. 554.

9.   Henry L. Mencken, *The American Language: An Inquiry into the Development of English in the United States*, Raven I. McDavid, Jr., ed., abridged edition (New York: Knopf, 1963), p. 745.

10. Robert Gold, *A Jazz Lexicon* (New York: Knopf, 1964), pp. 327-28.

11. Clarence Major, *Dictionary of Afro-American Slang* (New York: International, 1970), p. 116.

12. Edith A. Folb, *Runnin' Down Some Lines: The Language and Culture of Black Teenagers* (Cambridge, Mass.: Harvard University Press), p. 258.

13. Herbert L. Foster, Foster's Jive Lexicon Analogies Test Series IIA—Post High School Level (Williamsville, N.Y.: author, 1972).

14. Alfred C. Aarons, ed., "Back Dialect Issue," Florida FL Reporter 10, no. 1 and 2 (1972); Roger D. Abrahams, Talking Black (Rowley, Mass.: Newbury House, 1976); John Baugh, Black Street Speech: Its History, Structure, and Survival (Austin, Texas: University of Texas Press, 1983); Ila W. Brasch and Walter M. Brasch, A Comprehensive Annotated Bibliography of American Black English (Baton Rouge: Louisiana State University Press, 1974); Joey L. Dillard, All-American English: A History of the English Language in America (New York: Random House, 1975); Joey L. Dillard, Black English: It's History and Usage in the United States (New York: Random House, 1972); Alan Dundes, Mother Wit from the Laughing Barrel: Readings in the Interpretation of Afro-American Folklore (Englewood Cliffs, N.J.: Prentice-Hall, 1973); Joan Fickett, Aspects of Morphemics, Syntax, and Semology of an Inner-City Dialect (Mexican) (West Rush, N.Y.: Meadowood, 1970); Geneva Smitherman, Talkin and Testifyin: The Language of Black America (Boston: Houghton Mifflin, 1977); Harold J. Vetter, Language Behavior and Communication: An Introduction (Itasca, Ill.: F. F. Peacock, 1969); Frederick F. Williams, ed., Language and Poverty: Perspectives on a Theme (Chicago: Markham, 1970).

15. "Glossary of Terms Used in Space Flight," New York Times, March 4, 1969, p. 15.

16. Steve Cady, "Stoked Surfers Thrill Hodads at Gilgo Beach's Title Meet," New York Times, September 11, 1966, p. S6.

17. William D. Barbach, "Cracking Down on Hackers," Newsweek, October 24, 1983, p. 34; Phillip Elmer-Dewitt, "Let Us Now Praise Famous Hackers: A New View of Some Much Maligned Electronic Pioneers," Time December 3, 1984, p. 76; Robert T. Grieves, "In Pittsburgh: Hacking the Night Away," Time May 9, 1983, pp. 13, 15; Steven Levy, Hackers: Heroes of the Computer Revolution (New York: Doubleday, 1984).

18. Roger W. Shuy, Discovering American Dialects (Champaign, Ill.: National Council of Teachers of English, 1967); Wentworth and Flexner.

19. Geneva Smitherman, ed., Black English and the Education of Black Children and Youth: Proceedings of the National Invitational Symposium of the King Decision (Detroit: Wayne State University Center for Black Studies, 1981).

20. Guy Johnson, "Double Meaning in the Popular Negro Blues," Journal of Abnormal Social Psychology 22, no. 1 (1927): 13.

21. Gold, p. xviii.

22. Ibid., p. xix.

23. Mencken, p. 742.

24. Paul T. Oliver, The Story of the Blues (Philadelphia: Chilton, 1969), p. 104.

25. Johnson.

26. Bessie Smith, The Worlds's Greatest Blues Singer, Columbia, GP 33, 1970.

27. Abrahams, p. 33.

28. William H. Grier and Price M. Cobbs, *Black Rage* (New York: Basic Books, 1968), p. 123.

29. Grace S. Holt, "Inversion' in Black Communication," in Thomas Kochman, ed., *Rappin' and Stylin' Out*, p. 154.

30. Holt, p. 154.

31. Joseph J. White, "Toward a Black Psychology," *Ebony*, September 1970, p. 50.

32. William Schechter, *The History of Negro Humor in America* (New York: Fleet, 1970), pp. 60, 69.

33. Ibid., p. 26.

34. Nathan C. Heard, *Howard Street* (New York: Dell, 1968), p. 95.

35. This ploy is also used by teachers to taunt new teachers. Two incidents that I know of involved suburban school staffs.
A sign was placed on the teachers' room bulletin board—"ALL THOSE WHO WANT TO EAT AT THE Y, SIGN BELOW."
In the second incident, a male teacher sent a student to new female teachers with a note asking whether they would like to eat at the Y.

36. See Mary B. Rowe, "Science and Soul," *Urban Review* 4, no. 2 (1969): 31–33, for an article that reports on inner city and suburban youngsters' verbalizing their observations of guppies defecating.

37. W. D. Richter, dir., *The Adventures of Buckaroo Banzai: Across The 8th Dimension!*, Twentieth Century Fox, 1984; Vincent Canby, "Film: Sci-Fi Farce, 'Buckaroo Banzai'," *New York Times*, October 5, 1984, p. C8.

38. Chris Chase, "At the Movies," *New York Times*, October 28, 1983, p. C8; Janet Maslin, "Film: 'Gregorio Cortez'," *New York Times*, October 14, 1982, p. C6; John J. O'Connor, "When Public TV Excels," *New York Times*, June 12, 1981, p. H27; Americo Paredes, *With His Pistol In His Hand: A Border Ballad and Its Hero* (Austin: University of Texas Press, 1958), p. 61.

39. "The 'Black Box'—Why All the Furor," *U.S. News & World Report*, October 3, 1983, p. 9; Personal correspondence with David R. Kelley, Chief, Operational Factors Division, National Transportation Safety Board, Washington, D.C., 10594, May 19, 1983.

40. "Facing World after 31 Silent Years," *New York Times*, January 4, 1983, p. A12.

41. George v. Sheviakov and Fritz Redl, *Discipline For Today's Children*, revised edition Sybil K. Richardson (Washington, D.C.: N.E.A., Association of Supervision and Curriculum Development, 1956).

42. William J. Edwards, *Twenty-Five Years in the Black Belt* (Boston: n.p., 1918); E. Franklin Frazier, *The Negro Family in the United States*, revised and abridged edition (Chicago: University of Chicago Press, 1966), p. 11; Katherine E. D'Evelyn, *Meeting Children's Emotional Needs* (Englewood Cliffs, N.J.: Prentice-Hall, 1957); "Tshombe Talks in Tribal Tongue after Injection," *Buffalo Evening News*, October 6, 1967, pp. 1–2.

43. Elton B. McNeil, "Personal Hostility and International Aggression," *Journal of Conflict Resolution* 5 (1961): 279–90; Fritz Redl, "The Concept of Life Space Interview," *American Journal of Orthopsychiatry* 29 (1959):

1-18; Fritz Redl, "Strategy and Techniques of the Life Space Interview," in Ruth Newman and Marjorie M. Keith, eds., *The School-Centered Life Space Interview* (Washington, D.C.: Washington School of Psychiatry, 1964), pp. 13-17.

44. Werner W. Cohen, "On Language of Lower-Class Children," *School Review* 67 (1959): 435-40; David W. Maurer, *A Correlation of the Technical Argo of Pick-Pockets with Their Behavior Patterns* (New Haven, Conn.: College and University Press, 1964); Donald Clemmer, *The Prison Community* (Boston: Christopher, 1940); Truman R. Temple, "A Program for Overcoming the Handicap of Dialect," *New Republic*, March 1967, pp. 11-14.

45. Joint Commission on Mental Health of Children *Crisis in Child Mental Health: Challenge for the 1970's* (New York: Harper & Row, 1969); National Commission on the Causes and Prevention of Violence, *Commission Statement on Violent Crime: Homicide, Assault, Rape, Robbery* (Washington, D.C.: U.S. Government Printing Office, 1969); Michael Harrington, *The Other America* (Baltimore: Penguin, 1965); Suzanne Keller, *The American Lower-Class Family: A Survey of Selected Facts and Their Implications* (New York: Division For Youth, 1965).

46. Jeremy D. Finn, "Patterns in Children's Language," *School Review* 77 (1969): 108-27.

47. Sol Yurick, *The Bag* (New York: Trident, 1968).

48. Told to me by a friend who was involved in many of the bargaining meetings.

49. Frazier, p. 11.

50. "Tschombe," pp. 1-2.

51. Tom O'Grady, "Cager Was on Unfamiliar Court," *Buffalo Evening News*, August 29, 1969, p. 31.

52. Told to me by the survivor.

53. Gordon Parks, "Whip of Black Power," *Life*, May 19, 1967, p. 77.

54. William Borders, "Cool Welfare Militant: Dr. George Alvin Wiley," *New York Times*, May 27, 1969, p. 32.

55. Clemmer; Albert H. Marckwardt, *American English* (New York: Oxford University Press, 1958); Edward Sapir, *Language and Personality* (Berkeley: University of California Press, 1966).

56. Bernstein; John M. Brewer, "Hidden Language": Ghetto Children Know What They're Talking About," *New York Times Magazine*, December 25, 1966, pp. 32, 34-35; Charles J. Calitri, "The Nature and Values of Culturally Different Youth," in Arno Jewett, ed., *Improving English Skills of Culturally Different Youth in Large Cities* (Washington, D.C.: U.S. Government Printing Office, 1964), pp. 1-9; Clemmer; Folb; Mary A. Guitar, "Not for Finks," *New York Times Magazine*, November 24, 1963, pp. 50, 52, 54; Pearl B. Heffron, "Our American Slang," *Elementary English* 34 (1962): 429-34, 465; Christopher Hibbert, *The Roots of Evil* (Boston: Little, Brown, 1963); Geneva Smitherman, *Talkin and Testifying*).

57. Claude Brown, *Manchild in the Promised Land* (New York: Macmillan, 1965); Bergen Evans and Cornelia Evans, *A Dictionary of Contemporary*

American Usage (New York: Random House, 1957); Folb; Herbert L. Foster, "A Pilot Study of the Cant of the Disadvantaged, Socially Maladjusted, Secondary School Child," *Urban Education* 2 (1966): 99–114; Herbert L. Foster, "A Pilot Study of the Cant of the Negro Disadvantaged Student in Four Secondary for the Socially Maladjusted and Emotionally Disturbed," in *C.E.C. Selected Convention Papers: 1967* (Washington, D.C.: Council for Exceptional Children, 1968), pp. 139–43; Smitherman.

58.   Evans and Evans; William M. Kelley, "If You're Woke You Dig It." *New York Times Magazine*, May 20, 1962, pp. 45, 53.

59.   Miriam L. Goldberg, "Adapting Teacher Style to Pupil Differences: Teachers for Disadvantaged Children," *Merril-Palmer Quarterly* 10 (1964): 161–78; Kelly.

60.   Maurer.

61.   Hibbert; Lawrence Nelson, "Language Has Personality," *Clearing House* 38 (1964): 543–47.

62.   Brown, p. 28.

63.   "The Anguish of Blacks," *Time*, November 23, 1970, pp. 13–14.

64.   "The Panthers and the Law," *Newsweek*, February 23, 1970, p. 30.

65.   Ibid., p. 30.

66.   Ibid.

67.   Herbert L. Foster, "Dialect—Lexicon and Listening Comprehension," *Dissertation Abstracts*, 31 (1971); 674 (Columbia University Teachers College); Herbert L. Foster, "Dialect—Lexicon and Listening Comprehension" (Doctor of Education dissertation, Columbia University Teachers College, 1969), of which Dillard wrote: "The lengthiest treatment of ethnic slang known to me is a dissertation at Columbia University Teachers College by Herbert Foster, who was steered onto the subject as a study of the 'cant' of 'emotionally disturbed' youngsters and discovered that it was not cant and that the youngsters were culturally different rather than emotionally disturbed," (p. 241).

68.   Oliver, p. 83.

69.   Langston Hughes and Arna Bontemps, *The Book of Negro Folklore* (New York: Dodd, Mead, 1966), p. 596.

70.   Ibid., p. 597.

71.   Ibid.

72.   Langston Hughes, ed., *The Book of Negro Humor*," (New York: Dodd, Mead, 1966), p. 123.

73.   Haley, p. 76.

74.   *Bunky & Jake, L.A.M.F.*, Mercury, SR 61199, n.d.

75.   Steven V. Roberts, "My Whole Family Said, 'Leon, You Is Lazy.' " *New York Times*, March 26, 1967, p. D17; "No Landlord—Tenants Run Slum Tenement," *Herald Tribune*, July 1, 1972, p. 3.

76.   "Button Bit Builds Bank Balance," *Star Journal*, November 2, 1965, p. 6.

77.   Benjamin A. Botkin, *A Treasury of American Folklore* (New York: Crown, 1944), pp. 51–52.

78.   Ibid., p. 60.

79.   Ibid., p. 56.

80. Ibid., p. 3.
81. Sol Yurick, *The Warriors* (New York: Pyramid, 1966), p. 50.
82. Joseph Wambaugh, *The New Centurions* (Boston: Little, Brown, 1970), pp. 111-12.
83. " 'Taki 183' Spawns Pen Pals," *New York Times*, July 21, 1971, p. 31.
84. Craig Castleman, *Getting Up: Subway Graffiti in New York* (New York: Cambridge, Mass.: MIT Press, 1982), p. 53; Richard Goldstein, "This Thing Has Gotten Completely Out of Hand," *New York Magazine*, March 26, 1973, pp. 34-39; "The Graffiti Hit Parade," *New York Magazine*, March 26, 1973, pp. 32-33; Frank J. Prail, "Subway Graffiti Here Called Epidemic," *New York Times*, February 11, 1972, p. 39.
85. Craig Castleman; "Fight Against Subway Graffiti Progresses from Frying Pan to Fire," *New York Times*, January 26, 1973, p. 39; David L. Shirey, "Semi-Retired Graffiti Scrawlers Paint Mural at C.C.N.Y. 133," *New York Times*, December 8, 1972, p. 49.
86. " 'Taki 183' Spawns Pen Pals."
87. Caryl S. Stern and Robert W. Stock, "Graffiti: The Plague Years," *New York Times Magazine*, October 16, 1980, p. 44.
88. Susan Heller Anderson and Maurice Carrol, "Greek Power to Battle Graffiti," *New York Times*, August 30, 1984, p. B9; "Antigraffity Paint Found for Use on Subway Cars," *Buffalo Courier-Express*, July 18, 1976, p. 79; Ari L. Goldman, "City Is Losing Another Battle in Graffiti War," *New York Times*, April 8, 1983, p. B1; Clyde Haberman, "New York Plans Graffiti Drive," *New York Times*, February 5, 1982, pp. 1, B6; Ronald Smothers, "Koch Calls for Dogs in Fight on Graffiti," *New York Times*, August 27, 1980, p. B3; "Lindsay Signs Bill to Combat Graffiti," *New York Times*, October 29, 1972, p. 79; "Stiff Antigraffiti Measure Passes Council Committee," *New York Times*, September 16, 1972, p. 41; "Subway Graffiti Going to the Dogs," *Newsweek*, January 24, 1983, p. 9; "Thwarting Graffiti," *New York Times*, October 24, 1982, p. 41.
89. Foster, *Pilot Study*; Foster, *Dialect-Lexicon*.
90. Castleman, *Getting Up*; Herbert Kohl, *Golden Boy as Anthony Cool: A Photo Essay on Naming and Graffiti* (New York: Dial, 1972); Herbert Kohl and James Hinton, "Names, Graffiti, and Culture," *Urban Review* 3, no. 5 (1969): 24-37.
91. Charles Ahearn, dir., *Wild Style*, Film Society of Lincoln Center, 1983; Vincent Canby, "Film: 'Wild Style,' Rapping and Painting Graffiti," *New York Times*, March 18, 1983, p. C8; Stan Latham, dir., *Beat Street*, Orion, 1984; "Movie: 'Beat Street,' " *New York Times*, June 8, 1984, p. C10; Joel Silberg, dir., *Breakin'*, MGM/United Artists, 1982; Vincent Canby, "Film Break-Dancing Stars," *New York Times*, May 5, 1984, p. 17.
92. Harrison E. Salisbury, *The Shook-Up Generation* (New York: Harper & Row, 1958), p. 4.
93. "Army Reads Race Bias on Walls," *Buffalo Evening News*, November 24, 1977, p. 12.
94. Carl A. Bonuso, "Graffiti," *Today's Education* 65 (1976): 90-91; Herbert Kohl, "The Writing's On The Wall—Use It," *Learning* 2, no. 9 (1974):

10-15; Dolores S. Stocker, "The Ghetto Child Can Relate to the Graffiti Fence," *Phi Delta Kappan* 52 (1971): 456.
95. Tom Wolfe, *Radical Chic & Mau-Mauing the Flak Catchers* (New York: Farrar, Strauss & Giroux, 1970); Eldridge Cleaver, *Soul On Ice* (New York: Ramparts, 1968).
96. Wolfe, p. 128.
97. Wolfe, p. 129.
98. "Boots" is used to refer to blacks or Negroes, usually in a pejorative sense.
99. The term "monkey on my back" was popularized in the late 1940s and early 1950s by Nelson Algren's *Man With the Golden Arm*. A movie was produced based on the book, which dealt with heroin addicts.
100. Frank Bonham, *Cool Cat* (New York: Dutton, 1971); Cecil Brown, *The Life and Loves of Mr. Jiveass Nigger* (New York: Farrar, Strauss & Giroux, 1969); Glaude Brown, *Manchild in the Promised Land*; George Cain, *Blueschild Baby* (New York: McGraw–Hill, 1970); Morton Cooper, *Black Star* (New York: Bernard Geis, 1969); Alex Haley; Nathan C. Heard, *Howard Street* (New York: Dial, 1968); Michael Herr, *Dispatches* (New York: Knopf, 1978); Fletcher Knebel, *Trespass* (New York: Doubleday, 1969); Milton Mezzrow and Bernard Wolf, *Really the Blues* (New York: Signet, 1964); Robert F. Pharr, *The Book of Numbers* (New York: Doubleday, 1969); Jane Phillips, *Mojo Hand* (New York: Pocket Books, 1966; Ishmael Reed, *Mumbo Jumbo* (Garden City, N.Y.: Doubleday, 1972); Jean Stein and George Plimpton, eds., *Edie: An American Biography* (New York: Knopf, 1982); Iceberg Slim, *Trick Baby* (Los Angeles: Holloway House, 1967); Shane Stevens, *Way Uptown in Another World* (New York: Putnam's, 1971); Wallace Terry, *Bloods: An Oral History of the Vietnam War by Black Veterans* (New York: Random House, 1984); Piri Thomas, *Down These Mean Streets* (New York: Knopf, 1967); Alice Walker, *The Color Purple* (New York: Washington Square, 1982); Joseph Wambaugh, *The New Centurions*; John E. Wideman, *Brothers and Keepers* (New York: Holt, Rinehart & Winston, 1984). An early book introducing Negro dialect into American fiction was Hugh H. Brackenridge's *Modern Chivalry*, Part I (Cincinnati, N.Y.: American Book Co., 1972). Tremaine McDowell, "Notes on Negro Dialect in the American Novel to 1921," *American Speech* 5 (1930): 291-96, spelled Negro with a small n and also used the word "negress."
101. Bernard Malamud, *The Tenants* (New York: Farrar, Strauss & Giroux, 1977).
102. Malamud, pp. 55, 43, 33, 29; Melvin Van peebles, *Aint Supposed To Die A Natural Death: Tunes From Blackness*, AM Records, SP 3510, n.d.
103. Dillard, *Black English*, p. 114.
104. Imamu A. Baraka and Fundi, *In Our Terribleness* (New York: Bobbs-Merril, 1970).
105. Ron Welburn, "In Our Terribleness: Reviving Soul in Newark, N.J." *New York Times Book Review*, February 14, 1971, p. 11.
106. Welburn, p. 10.

107. LeRoi Jones and Larry Neal, eds., *Black Fire: An Anthology of Afro-American Writing* (New York: Morrow, 1968).

108. James T. Stewart, "Announcements," in Jones and Neal, p. 202.

109. Marvin E. Jackmon, "Flowers for the Trashman," in Jones and Neal, pp. 541–58.

110. John O. Killens, *The Cotillion: Or, One Good Bull is Half the Herd* (New York: Pocket Books, 1972).

111. Paul Carter Harrison and Ed Bullins, "Tabernacle," in William T. Couch, ed., *New Black Playwrites* (New York: Avon, 1971), pp. 71–152.

112. Ed Bullins, "Goin'a Buffalo," in Couch, p. 188.

113. Stephen E. Henderson, " 'Survival Motion': A Study of the Black Writer and the Black Revolution in America," in Mercer Cook and Stephen E. Henderson, eds., *The Militant Black Writer in Africa and the United States* (Madison, Wis.: University of Wisconsin Press, 1969), p. 78.

114. Burley, p. 62.

115. Ibid.

116. Ibid., p. 66.

117. Ibid., p. 63.

118. Ibid., p. 11.

119. Earl Conrad, "Foreword," in Burley, p. 6; "Ofay: a white person (from pig Latin for foe)," Mezzrow, p. 308.

120. Conrad, in Burley, p. 5.

121. Louise Pound, "Survival in Negro Vocabulary," *American Speech* 12 (1937): 231–32. In this article, the word Negro is sometimes spelled with a small n. I am not sure whether this was intentional or whether it was sloppy proofreading. He also wrote that "darkies are people that of necessity keep to themselves and maintain old ways."

    The word Negro was not always capitalized. It was on March 7, 1930 that the *New York Times* announced that it would thereafter capitalize the word Negro. Furthermore, it was not until three years later that the *Style Manual of the Government Printing Office* followed suit with the capitalization (Henry L. Mencken, "Designations For Colored Folk," *American Speech* 19 (1944): 166–74). Interestingly, since the 1960s some of the more militant black authors have spelled Negro with a small n.

122. Ruth Banks, "Idioms of the Present-Day American Negro," *American Speech* 13 (1938): 313–14.

123. Lou Shelly, ed., *Hepcats Jive Talk Dictionary* (Derby, Conn.: T.W.O. Charles, 1945).

124. Marcus H. Boulware, *Jive and Slang of Students in Negro College* (Hampton, Va.: Marcus H. Boulware, 1947).

125. Claude Brown, "The Language of Soul," *Esquire*, April 1968, p. 88.

126. Schechter, p. 159.

127. Jack L. Daniel, "Black Folk and Speech Education," *Speech Teacher* 19 (1970): 123–29.

128. Jack Schiffman, *Uptown: The Story of Harlem's Appolo Theatre* (New York: Cowles, 1971).

129. Grier and Cobbs, p. 125.

130. Mezzrow and Wolfe, p. 191.

131. Mencken, *The American Language*, pp. 739, 745.

132. Wentworth and Flexner, p. xvii.

133. Gold, p. xiv.

134. Paul Lerman, "Issues in Subcultural Delinquency," *Dissertation Abstracts* 27 A (1966), 3131 (Columbia University, School of Social Work): 42.

135. Roger D. Abrahams, " 'Talking My Talk': Black English and Social Sementation in Black Communities," *Florida FL Reporter* 10, nos. 1 and 2 (1973): 29.

136. Abrahams, p. 31; Roger D. Abrahams, *Talking Black* (Rowley, Mass.: Newbury House, 1976); Folb; Smitherman.

137. Walter B. Miller, "Lower-Class Culture as a Generating Milieu of Gang Delinquency," *Journal of Social Issues* 14, no. 3 (1958): 5-19.

138. Herbert Gans, *The Urban Villagers: Group & Clans in the Life of Italian-Americans* (New York: Free Press of Glencoe, 1962).

139. Abrahams, "Talking My Talk," p. 31.

140. Ibid., p. 32.

141. Ibid., p. 32-33.

142. Gerald M. Boyd, "Reporter's Notebook: Jackson's Brand of Politics," *New York Times*, June 15, 1984, p. B7.

143. Covello, pp. XII-XIII.

144. Alfonso A. Narvaez, "Democrat Visits Brooklyn," *New York Times*, 29 October, 1970, p. 49.

145. "Is he a Jewish boy?"

146. Jane Phillips, *Mojo Hand* (New York: Pocket Books, 1970), p. 32-33.

147. The test population consisted of five categories of workers: (1) seventeen Manpower students working toward nurse's aide certification; (2) seventeen Manpower students working toward practical nurses certification; (3) thirty-one who had completed practical nurses training, (4) twenty who were registered nurses; and (5) ten who were registered nurses with B.S. degrees; Black's performed significantly better than did whites in 99 out of 100 cases; Sister E.A. Donelly, *The Inner-City School: Teacher Testing by Pupils*, July 31, 1972. (An unpublished paper for course TED-518, Teaching in Inner-City Schools.)

148. Herman R. Lantz, *People of Coal Town* (New York: Columbia University Press, 1958), p. 47.

149. Claude Brown, *Manchild in the Promised Land*, pp. 164-65.

150. Ibid., p. 165-66.

151. Pearl H. Berkowitz and Esther P. Rothman, *The Disturbed Child* (New York: New York University Press, 1960), p. 142.

152. Paul L. Crawford, Daniel I. Malamud, and James R. Dumpson, *Working with Teenage Gangs: A Report on the Central Harlem Street Club Project* (New York: Astoria Press, 1950); New York City Youth Board, "Street Jargon Has a Flavor All Its Own," October 16, 1964. (Mimeo.)

153. Cohen, p. 435.

154. Alfonso A. Narvaez, "New Police Patrol a Hit in the Slums," *New York Times*, November 19, 1969, p. 49.

155. Richard B. Trent, *An Exploratory Study of the Inmate Social Organization*, vol. 5 (Warwick, N.Y.: Warwick Child Welfare Services Project, New York State Training School for Boys, 1954–1957), p. 41.
156. Abrahams, *Talking Black*; Malachi Andrews and Paul Y. Owens, *Black Language* (Los Angeles: Seymour–Smith, 1973); Howard C. Brooks, *Soul Dictionary* (Buffalo, N.Y.: E. Marie Mays, 426 Moselle Street, 1971); David Claerbaut, *Black Jargon in White America* (Grand Rapids, Mich.: William B. Eerdmans, 1972); Dillard, *Black English*; Joey L. Dillard, *American Talk: Where Our Words Come From* (New York: Random House, 1976); Folb; Bruce Jackson, *Get Your Ass in the Water and Swim Like Me: Narrative Poetry from Black Oral Tradition* (Cambridge, Mass.: Harvard University Press, 1974); Kochman, ed., *Rappin' and Stylin' Out*; Clarence Major, *Dictionary of Afro-American Slang* (New York: International, 1970); Hermese E. Roberts, *The Third Ear: A Black Glossary* (Chicago: Better-Speech Institute of America, 1971); Smitherman, *Talkin and Testifyin*; Paul Stoller, ed., *Black American English: Its Background and Its Usage in the Schools and in Literature* (New York: Delta, 1975); Dennis Wepman, Ronald B. Newman, and Murray B. Binderman, *The Life: The Lore and Folk Poetry of the Black Hustler* (Philadelphia: University of Pennsylvania Press, 1976); Robert L. Williams, ed., *Ebonics: The True Language of Black Folks* (St. Louis: The Institute of Black Studies, 1975); Paul K. Winston, prod., *The Dialect of the Black American*, Western Electric, 1970.
157. Sheviakov and Redl, p. 46.
158. Maximilian S. DeVere, *Americanisms: The English of the New World* (New York: Scribner, 1872); Donald J. Lloyd and Harry R. Warfel, *American English in Its Cultural Setting* (New York: Knopf, 1956); Mencken, *The American Language*; Thomas Pyles, *Words and Ways of American English* (New York: Random House, 1952); Shuy.
159. Dillard, *American Talk*, p. 134.

6 RIBBIN', JIVIN', AND PLAYIN' THE DOZENS
Classroom Contests

Found most often in bars or in pool halls in urban areas, or outside a crossroads store in the plantation country with a bunch of fellows, or late evenings on the stoops of down-home shacks, men with prodigious memories swap tales, songs, and ballads.

—Langston Hughes, *The Book of Negro Humor*[1]

Those young brothers came out of this woofing, diddy-bopping and raising hell period. They had won this confrontation. They had met "the man" and found out that when you start being controlled by fear, then the people you were once afraid of are afraid of you.

—H. Rap Brown, *Die Nigger Die!*[2]

If your sneakers slip and slide,
get the ones with the stars on the sides.

—Heard in a Brooklyn, New York high school

If you signify, you qualify.

—Streetcorner philosopher

Generally speaking, black and white middle class youngsters play testing games on their parents as part of their maturational development and growth. For lower class streetcorner youngsters, however, testing their ability to run a game and to hustle or manipulate their teachers helps them develop what their environment has taught them are streetcorner social and economic coping and survival techniques.

Joseph White reinforced this and pointed out that many disadvantaged youngsters have developed survival skills and a mental toughness that he feels makes them "in many ways superior" to their white suburban counterparts. Indeed, black inner city youngsters know how to deal effectively with building superintendents, pimps, corner grocers, bill collectors—as well as with death and sickness. They also are psychologically original and clever in their ability to "jive" school personnel, juvenile authorities, and welfare workers. These youngsters realize early in life that they exist in an often hostile and complicated world. What they have mastered, although they probably cannot verbalize it, is the sense of the basic human condition that existential psychologists write about—"that in this life, pain and struggle are unavoidable and that a complete sense of one's identity can only be achieved by both recognizing and directly confronting an unkind and alien existence."[3]

Although these testing games used by inner city youngsters are sometimes modifications of black lower class male streetcorner survival and coping techniques, reporting suggests that almost all lower class urban male groups, not just blacks, play verbally and physically aggressive streetcorner games. Herbert Gans, for example, reported on the lifestyle of lower class Italian teenagers and young adults in the Roxbury section of Boston where there was lively competition for status, respect, and power. The residents' "action-seeking" behavior consisted of ongoing encounters intended to show skillfulness and superiority of one person over the other. Their encounters took the form of continuous verbal and physical duels and card games. The Italian West Enders expressed their verbal strength and skills by denigrating the achievements and characteristics of others by teasing, bragging, wisecracking, and insulting others.[4]

In another study of black and white, early, middle, and late adolescent males and females living in "slum districts," Walter Miller found that "in the syndrome of capacities related to 'smartness' is a dominant emphasis in lower class culture on ingenious aggressive repartee." He found this skill practiced and learned within the context of streetcorner group life. Often, the repartee took two forms: the semiritualized razzing, kidding, ranking, and teasing, and the more highly ritualized mutual insults interchange of the "dozens." Although he found the dozens practiced on its most advanced level by black adults, he found "less polished variants" played by male and female lower class whites.[5]

It must be reemphasized that for lower class black urban streetcorner men, rhetoric, repartee, and gamesmanship are survival and coping techniques in the aggressive, hustling, verbal world of the streetcorner. These almost ritualized games are, in a sense, attempts at coping with and surviving economic and social racism, and are to some extent a way of getting even, beating "the system," or "gettin ovuh."[6]

On the streetcorner, verbal ability is rated as highly as is physical strength. Most often, when men gather, a boasting or teasing encounter takes place.

Verbal contest participation is an important part of peer relationships. Starting a verbal attack is "mounting" or getting above an opponent. To lose a verbal battle is to become feminized. Strength and masculinity are shown by boasting or "putting down" an adversary or a group of adversaries. Roger Abrahams's reporting emphasized the manliness involved in verbal encounter. "Being bested in a verbal battle in front of a group of men has immense potential repercussions because of the terror of disapproval, of being proved ineffectual and therefore effeminate in the eyes of peers." Furthermore, the ritual battle of words is accepted and rated as a means of masculine release from anxiety.[7]

Abrahams also wrote that, "through the dozens or some other verbal context, one establishes his place, his reputation in male street society—especially during the swinging years."[8] The importance of the verbal repartee was also reinforced by a black high school student who told me, "Look, Dr. Foster, when I ease to Jefferson Avenue, it's the con and conversation that's *important—nothing else.*"[9]

Edith Folb, in her study of the language and culture of the black teenager, identified "three Recurring images in teenage vernacular vocabulary that seem to put in perspective much of the manipulative or coercive behavior that teenagers play out in their attempts to exert power over another's personal and psychological space."[10]

These three are, the:

1. "game"—a contest of wits, wills, physical force, or some combination of the three where the participants verbally and creatively battle with one another, often before an audience;
2. "front" or "front off"—in which you display what you have, what you are, your material possessions, that is, your clothes, car, home, box; and
3. "action"—this pervades the front and the game which is manipulative, ongoing, gamelike, performative, dynamic, and kinetic; the idea is to compete for recognition, money, status, prestige, men, and women.[11]

To help the reader differentiate between these verbal contests or ritualized coping and survival techniques as played out in the classroom, the three broad categories of "ribbin'," "jivin'," and "playin' the dozens" will be used.

The reader should be aware, however, *that the name given a contest in one city, or even a section of the same city may be different from designated names used elsewhere.* The age group or sex of those involved in the verbal encounter may determine the supposed sophistication or lack of sophistication of the repartee. There also may be some difference between the way the game is played on the streetcorner as compared with the classroom. What is important, though, is that: (1) we not get hung up in a purist argument over what the proper designation for the game is; (2) the reader begin to understand that these verbal games exist and should begin to recognize them; (3) educators begin to develop nonpunitive techniques for coping with the games; (4) urban educators learn how to use these games as indicators of a student's academic potential; and (5) urban educators study possible use of these games for their teaching and learning potential.[12]

RIBBIN'

The term "ribbin'" or "ribbing" is used in Buffalo, New York to describe the verbal game of taunting, denigrating, or making fun of someone, for example, their clothing or parts of their body—particularly their genitals or matters related to sexual intercourse. A black Buffalo junior high school student told me that her friends use the term "dippin'" to refer to "gettin' into personal things." A junior high school youngster once told me that "you laugh on someone when you rib on them." Other terms and places include: Yonkers, New York, "chopping"; Pottsville, Pennsylvania, "sounding"; Oklahoma, "medlin'"; Brooklyn, New York, "ranking" and "sounding"; Elmira, New York, "ragging," "busting," "dogin'," and "hasling"; Ypsilanti, Michigan, "cappin'," "crackin'," "burnin'"; St. Paul, Minnesota, "cappin'"; Fort Wayne, Indiana, "crackin'" "conin'"; and Manhattan, New York, "snappin'." A Buffalo, New York, junior high school student's response to what ribbing is sums up its meaning. "She is talkin' about you—but she is only playin'. Sometimes she is ribbin' good, and I can't take it. And, I'll fight her. But sometimes, I can take her ribbin'." In the primarily white northern suburbs of Buffalo, New York, and in many middle class areas, the game, played with less intensity and less often, is referred to as "mocking out."

The rules governing the number of participants in a ribbin' game are flexible. Ribbin' may be directed against any number of persons; for example:

1. One youngster ribbin' another youngster.
2. Two or more youngsters ribbin' one or more youngsters.
3. One or more youngsters ribbin' a teacher or teachers.
4. When an unknowing teacher or administrator tries to intercede and break up a student ribbin' session, the students may join and turn to rib the teacher or administrator.
5. A student who is being humiliated in a ribbin' game with another student or group of students may turn on a teacher or student he feels is verbally or physically weaker and start ribbin' that person. This is a diversionary tactic to take the pressure off of him while keeping the game going.
6. A student may be so humiliated by another in a ribbin' encounter that she may lose her temper and attack the other student physically.
7. Similarly, a teacher may try her ability in a ribbin' contest with a student only to be bested by the student, whereupon, she may report the youngster

for "insulting" her. This is a negative move for the teacher. What she is doing is asking others to help her solve a discipline problem that she created.

8. A teacher may be in a ribbin' contest with a student when other students join in ribbin' the student. The teacher must be careful to make sure that the encounter does not become too humiliating for the student.

A separate reality will not be used to describe each example of ribbing. Instead, Reality 50 will be used as an example for ribs related to clothing. Reality 51 will illustrate ribs related to sex. Reality 52 will demonstrate ribs related to parts of the body where there do not appear to be any sexual overtones or implications. Additional examples will be provided with each reality.

Most often, regardless of what is being used as a vehicle for the rib, the two important aspects of the encounter are: (1) the students are most likely vying for control of the class; and (2) they are playing to their fellow students to assist in disrupting the class. If these students are also dominating the class physically, the teacher may have additional problems that go beyond merely ribbing.

There are two additional side effects of the ribbing or any of the verbal repartee or events that provide ego satisfaction for the winner or winners, even if the winning is fantasy. The first is the ego support received when the ribbing or other event has thrown the teacher off balance. Tom Wolfe described the feelings experienced when blacks saw whites off balance, reeling, and fearful from woofing, or, as Wolfe refers to the event, as "mau-mauing":

> There was something sweet that happened right there on the spot. You made the white man quake. You brought *fear* into his face. . . . And now, when you got him up close and growled, this all-powerful superior animal turned out to be terrified. You could read it in his face. He had the same fear in his face as some good-doing boy who just moved onto the block and is hiding behind his mama . . . while the bad dudes on the block size him up. . . . It not only stood to bring you certain practical gains. . . . It also energized your batteries. It recharged your masculinity. You no longer had to play it cool. . . . Mau-mauing brought you respect in its cash forms: namely, fear and envy.[13]

The second side effect is the additional ego support gained when the students discuss, fantasize, and relive the teacher's humiliation, loss of control, or discomfort from the event. Wolfe described these feelings after the confrontation, again from mau-mauing.

> [T]he aces all leave, and they're thinking . . . We've done it again. We've mau-maued the goddamn white man, scared him until he's singing a duet with his sphincter, and the people sure do have power. Did you see the look on his face? Did you see the sucker trembling? Did you see the sucker trying to lick his lips? He was *scared*, man! That's the last time that sucker is gonna try. . . . He's gonna go home to his house in Diamond Heights and he's gonna say, "Honey, fix me a drink! Those mother-fuckers were ready to kill me!" . . .

And then later on you think about it and you say, "What really happened that day? Well, another flak catcher lost his manhood, that's what happened." . . . did you see the *look* on his face? [14]

REALITY 50

The class was seated waiting for the period-ending bell. Suddenly, there was yelling from the back of the room, and two boys started fighting.

The teacher broke up the fight and asked what had happened.

One of the boys, still whining, said, "He say I be clean 'cause it mother's day."

The teacher looked puzzled. "So what," he said, "is that a reason to start a fight?"

Later, one of the other youngsters explained that mother's day is the day the welfare check arrives—usually on the first or fifteenth of the month. The intent of this rib was to say that the youngster was on welfare and is dressed well only because his mother's welfare check arrived.

Sometimes the wording may be slightly different although the intent is the same. The wording may be changed to "You look clean, it must be the first of the month," "You look clean, it must be the fifteenth of the month," or just pointing or looking at a youngster's clothing and saying, "It must be mother's day." This can be done to any piece of clothing or possession. Taunting someone about clothing and welfare is common. Being on welfare can be touchy and can have all sorts of negative feelings for many schoolchildren. As I will discuss in Chapter 8, the importance of clothing for students and educators is little understood, discussed or written about by educators.

To some of those who have an abundance of material goods, clothing may mean little. To the youngster who does not have the money, the correct clothing becomes an important and visible status symbol. The pimp or hustler with his expensive clothing and big car is still a respected and envied role model for many ghetto adolescents.

When money came into ghetto youngsters' hands via the poverty and work study programs of the Johnson administration, most often, clothing was the first item purchased. And, as noted earlier, Mercer Sullivan's study found that "when asked what they [adolescents in trouble] wanted money for, the first answer given by almost all of them was clothing." [15]

Some of the specific ribbing about clothing includes such negative terms as "Pacific Oceans," "floods," and "high waters." The implication of these terms is that the pants are too short for the youngster's height. A similar taunt used when I was a kid was, "Why don't you have a party and bring your pants down to meet your feet."

Ribs related to welfare are GWs, SAs, or GRs. Referring to someone's clothing as GWs or SAs refers to the youngster as being poor on on welfare—GW referring to Good Will and SA referring to Salvation Army. Or, as a junior high school youngster stated, "They tryin' to say they got cheap clothes. He got them in a rummage sale." Or even saying, "I saw George down at Goodwill the other day." GR means you grabbed the clothing and ran.

In addition to the aforementioned ribbing, clothing in general is target for ribs. Someone saying, "You got your brother's shirt on," may start a fight. Someone's socks, shoes, jacket, or any article of clothing may be the target of ribbing.

The style of clothing being worn is particularly important. A youngster wearing low instead of high socks may inspire ribs such as: "Hey, you got your ankle breakers on" or "Where did you get the ankle breakers?"—the implication being that if the socks got wet they would shrink and break your ankles.

Another rib concerning clothing is related to the color of a youngster's socks. A youngster walks into the room wearing red socks, whereupon someone yells out, "Did somebody cut you?" The class bursts into laughter. "I know you burnin'" might be said to a youngster wearing heavy pants on a warm day. Heavy pants worn on a warm day are known as a burner.

A female student may have a run in her stocking and will be ribbed about it. Or, someone may rib on another student's shoes for not having high platform soles and heels. Female students are often ribbed for supposedly wearing their brother's clothes.

Teachers are also fair game for ribbing. Ghetto youngsters' delight in ribbing teachers, particularly about their clothing. If the teachers' clothing is out of style, student ribbing may be carried on in front of them or behind their backs. Youngsters usually know, for example, how many suits, sport coats, dresses, skirts, or shoes teachers own or wear to school. Sometimes, they even bet about what a teacher will wear. It is common to hear, "Shit, she wore that raggedy dress twice this week already."

As a part of a new-teacher program with the Buffalo schools, a coed panel made up of some of the tougher discipline problems in the Buffalo schools discussed the ribbing of a teacher.[16] The following was transcribed from the panel discussion:

"Like, we used to rib on one teacher . . . and he [the teacher] would turn red and everything, and we used to get on his clothes, and his hair, and everything, and I think one time he got on somebody in our room. He got on pretty strong.

"And, you know, we felt kind of bad. We didn't think he had it in him, and we kind of cooled off for then. Then, we started up again. And then he got on another one of us so we sort of cooled again.

"It didn't help him. He got mad, ran out of the room. We was talking about something he had on. He ran out of the room. got Mr. _____ , and everything.

I don't know, I like them better, rather like them better if they, if they, get us back—we sort of shut up a little while."

Sneakers are high-prestige wear and are probably the biggest targets for ribbing. The importance of wearing the "correct" sneakers has spread, and black and white parents are usually under tremendous pressure to purchase the more expensive and prestigious sneakers or running shoes for their children. A literature of articles (and even letters to the editor) has developed related to sneakers.[17]

A student may be walking the hall and say to another student, "I see you got your brogans on." This seemingly innocent remark may result in anything from laughter, to an argument, to a fight. The word "brogans" was used to ridicule someone's old, worn out, less expensive, or less popular brand of sneakers, tennis shoes, or running shoes.

With only one exception, everywhere I have ever spoken or run a workshop had a name for the cheap, inexpensive, or unpopular sneaker. Though the staff may not have known, and there may have been some student controversy over which sneaker had the highest prestige, every student knew what the cheap sneakers were called: "brogans," "cousins," "liberty specials," "buddies," "skippies," "cat heads," "K Marts," "blue light specials," "rejects," "jeepers," "Twin Fairs," "maypops," "dash," "slip & slides," "state issue," "statos," "space pacers," "skids," "runners," "tennies," "red ball jets," "sweat boxes," "roach stompers," "bo-bos," and "Pic-ways."

Once when I asked two students why two girls had fought when someone used the word buddies, one's response was, "Something about sneakers. Like, um, somebody got on some old raggedy sneakers, say Diana, for instance. And, you could talk about their sneakers and they might not like it. Because, you know, they spent their own hard earned money for it, and they get mad. You know, and they don't like you doin' it so they'll fight you about it."

You sometimes get the feeling that these youngsters cannot really explain why they respond to ribbing by fighting. Or even why the insults have such an effect on them. Sometimes it seems as though some unwritten code of honor says they must fight, and so they do.[18]

The prestigious sneaker and sneaker styles hold on in some schools; in others they change rapidly. In the past few years, high-top sneakers appear to have replaced the long run of low-cut sneakers. Sometimes, the youngster who cannot afford the prestigious sneaker will purchase less expensive imitations at discount stores. They might then draw the requisite number of stripes or stars on their less expensive sneakers, making them resemble the prestigious ones.

Another area for ribbing is related to aspects of sex. This includes the use of standard vocabulary words with a second meaning, usually a sexual meaning. Most often, as discussed in Chapter 5, these second meanings are unknown to the teacher. These ribbing techniques are used effectively against students and teachers.

In Realities 24 and 25, examples were provided of how female teachers are ribbed by students using the word "trim." Another word that is used often, and was also mentioned earlier, is the word "ho," which is short for whore. There are a number of clever derivations in the use of ho for ribbing on students and teachers. Reality 51 is one example.

REALITY 51

The 5th period was just ending. A new young female teacher was having a rough 5th period. Her students were lined up waiting for the bell when one of the girls walked up to her and asked loudly, "Mrs. Elderson, are you a garden tool?"

Mrs. Elderson, beaten and harried, asked, "What do you mean? What kind of a question is that?"

Her students began to laugh just as the bell rang. They kept laughing and jostling one another as they ran from the room.

The sixth period for Mrs. Elderson was unassigned. So, she pulled the curtains down, locked the door, sat down at the desk, and just cried.

So many new teachers in inner city schools take such an emotional beating that many do just sit down and cry. And many who don't wish they could—men included.

Although these youngsters did not tell Mrs. Elderson what a garden tool was, instinctively she knew that something was amiss—that she was being made the butt of another prank.

There are also occasions when a male or female student will ask a teacher, "Are you a virgin?" in a loud clear voice for all students to hear. This form of ribbing is done most often to young new teachers.

Another rib related to whore is where the students take a piece of paper at least 8½ × 11 and hand print ƎoԿ on it. The paper is then tacked or pasted somewhere near the teacher. This rib is one that teachers don't catch too easily. The idea is to turn over the paper so that ƎoԿ becomes hoe.

A favorite rib is for a number of youngsters to get together and plan to hum "Hi, ho, hi ho." The students will come into the room, sit down, and start humming. If the teacher walks close to someone who is humming, that student will stop and others farther away will pick it up. Sometimes the humming will go up and down the rows. When this has happened, I have observed teachers running up and down the rows trying to find a portable radio.

I was standing outside a classroom one afternoon when I heard a commotion coming from inside. When I saw the teacher later, I asked what had happened. She told me that she was yelling at her students because they were always asking to leave the room when one of her bigger students had come up to her and said, "Give me a pass for the third period. I want to go ho hunting."

Male and female students often play this next rib usually on female teachers. A student will approach the teacher and say, "What you need is a jones." Or, sometimes, "What you need is a johnson." Both words have the same meaning: a penis. Sometimes the connotation is a black penis. Those who saw *Putney Swope* may recall one of the actresses saying to one of the actors, "I'm gonna soften your johnson."[19]

A female graduate student who is teaching told me this story. She was in her junior high school class when one of her students approached her and said, "What you need is a jones." She shook the youngster up when she responded with, "I know, I got one and he is great." Of course, the youngster's objective of ribbing the teacher backfired as the class laughed at him.

Whereas it used to be that male students usually ribbed on female teachers, ribbing on both male and female teachers is about even now. Many male and female students have the ability to sense a teacher's insecurity with his or her sexuality.

Female students will walk up to a male teacher, look at his crouch, and ask, "You got a bonner?" Or, the student may ask how "big" he [his penis] is.

Another form of ribbing is to use graffiti to get at someone or to get a number of youngsters at one another. This is accomplished by leaving some graffiti somewhere in or around the school.

I came across a graffitied bulletin board in a guidance office that was a combination of ribbing and signifying.[20] Under the graffiti "Hoes of Buffalo sign here" were five names. This was a ploy to get the youngsters mad at each other. What usually happens in such an incident is for someone, probably the graffiti writer, to go to each of the girls and say, "Did you see what ____ wrote about you?"

In discussing this ribbing through graffiti with a number of female students, their response was, "No one would do that. It was done by someone who was agitatin'. It looks like somebody try to be smart. Like, it wouldn't be nobody who will sign their name up there. Who wrote that sign somebody's name up there as if to say they wrote it up there."

While discussing ribbing techniques with a coed group of junior high school students, someone mentioned the word "trim" and it set off the following very rapid verbal exchange.

Female student: "Somebody always askin for some trim and haven't even got anything."

Male student: "Your hole ain't no bigger than a pin hole."

Female student: "You a story."

The exchange ended as quickly as it started, and we went off to another subject. Such an exchange can perplex a teacher as to his role. Too often, the teacher will keep the discussion hot and going by interceding. Usually, if the teacher can get the students moving to another subject or get them to return to the subject they were discussing before the outbreak, he or she will be better off.

The last group of ribbing games to be described is related to parts of the body with no apparent sexual overtones or implications. Also, some of the ribbing that appears is related to nicknames. Reality 52 provides an example of name calling.

REALITY 52

The bell had sounded and the students were changing classes. Suddenly, there was yelling and fighting at the end of the second floor. About fifteen youngsters were involved.

After the teachers and administrators broke up the fighting and had control, they brought those fighting to the main office. Upon calming everyone down, they managed to find out what had happened. One of the boys had called a girl a "pumpkin head" as he passed her in the hall. This young lady was in a bad mood, was twice the size of the young man, and promptly started to pummel him, whereupon a number of their friends took sides and got involved.

Inner city youngsters are masters of the art of making up nicknames for one another. Sometimes, of course, the names demean. However, whether the nicknames demean or not they are usually accurate and descriptive. Sometimes, the nicknames are personalized: for example, "block head," "cabbage," "toad," and "big head." Sometimes, the names are generalized for a school. For example, in one school any youngster called a "piranha" is insulted in the highest order and is usually compelled to fight back physically. Of course, how students react to these ribs usually depends upon how they feel on that day or at that moment and on how many other students are around to witness the actions. And also, of course, which teacher or administrator happens to be nearby.

In a school I visited, a ribbing comment such as "your comb is all green and junk," could start a fight. In this school, the word "green" used in reference to clothing or some other possession appears to be an insult. Such expressions as "You look like some burnt pussy," and "Oh! you ain't shit," also usually elicit violent reactions.

Someone may have a permanent or temporary physical deformity that becomes fair game for ribbing. Youngsters may be ribbed about an operation, protruding or missing teeth, a face or body blemish, height, and weight. A girl with short hair may rib a girl with a "bush" by saying, I got more hair than you," and the like. Parts of the body are also the objects of ribbing. A young man may start by saying, "My arms are better than your legs." And, the other youngster may come back with "Those raggedy things arms?" Sometimes, even the way a youngster walks is a source for ribbing.

JIVIN'

A number of the verbal coping and survival techniques that black urban males have developed and refined in order to manipulate, persuade, and hustle others will be discussed under "jivin'." Those to be discussed are "shuckin' and jivin', " "woofin'," and "signifying," and "rappin'."

The versions of these verbal techniques used in school may be less sophisticated than adult streetcorner usage and may be used differently when with friends as compared with an authority figure such as a policeman or a teacher. Jivin' behavior may also differ when a male is confronting a male teacher as compared with a female teacher or with one of his "people" as compared with a girl whose "nose" he wants. Further differences in usage may also depend upon age and sex, section of the country, or even section of a particular city. What is important is how youngsters play out these games in school, not what the games are called.

The manipulative jivin' games usually work because of the fantasies and expectations blacks and whites have of one another. White fantasies alternate between blacks being hedonistic, aggressive, gorilla studs, or shufflin' children requiring help. The black streetcorner youngsters know the fantasies whites have about them and fulfill these role expectations to manipulate them. If all else fails, they can always switch from the cat role to the gorilla, bogarding role, because they may feel most whites are faggots and fear them.

Shuckin' and Jivin'

Some of the coping and survival techniques are defensive mechanisms blacks started developing during slavery days and have perfected in order to cope with overt and covert racism. One of the techniques is called shuckin' and jivin', or shuckin', or jivin', and possibly other names depending upon location.

John Dotson mentioned shuckin' and jivin' as part of the recent arguments over black exploitation films. Many middle class blacks and whites attacked movies such as *Shaft* and *Super Fly* for reasons from "creating a poor black image" to providing a "fantasy black stud image" that, to some extent, misses the essence of the movies.

> There is more to enjoy in the new black movies than just the superspade stuff. There is a special humor that some of the pictures impart. Harry Belafonte's shucking and jiving in "Buck and the Preacher" was a particularly telling portrayal. When in trouble with the white folks, he grinned and preached for that was his protective shield, but when he was with Buck he became a sly, crafty gunslinger.[21]

Schuckin' and jivin' is a verbal and physical technique some blacks use to avoid difficulty, to accommodate some authority figure, and in the extreme, to save a life or to save oneself from being beaten physically or psychologically. Gestures, facial expressions, speech pronunciation, and body poses are all used to provide the authority figure with the appearance deemed acceptable and subservient to placate him. Shuckin' and jivin' also often requires an ability to control and coneal one's true emotions.

Eldridge Cleaver provided an example of shuckin' and jivin' in *Soul on Ice*:

Then one day, we were out driving and I ran through a red light just a little too late and this motorcycle cop pulled me over.

"Say, Boy," he said to me, "are you color-blind?" I didn't want a ticket so I decided to talk him out of it. I went into my act, gave him a big smile and explained to him that I was awfully sorry, that I thought that I could make it but that my old car was too slow. He talked real bad to me, took me on a long trip about how important it was that I obeyed the laws and regulation and how else can a society be controlled and administered without obedience to the law. I said a bunch of Yes Sir's and he told me to run along and be a good boy."[22]

Reality 53 tells of a middle-aged, prim, proper, and very bigoted white female teacher I once witnessed drag a black female high school student to the assistant principal and demand that the assistant principal "Make her tell me her name."

REALITY 53

The teacher marched into the office with her hand holding the student's arm tightly.

"Make her tell me her name," she spat out at the black assistant principal as she released the girl's arm.

The student gave her name in a southern accent.

The teacher was not hearing her. "Make her tell me her name," she yelled.

Again, the student gave her name in a southern accent.

"_____ , tell her your name," said the assistant principal in a soft voice.

The student slouched, and in a trembling voice once again repeated her name. This time, however, in a hesitating voice minus the southern accent.

"Thank you," the teacher said curtly as she turned on her heel and walked away. The student burst into tears.

The teacher had continued her psychological brutality until the youngster had acquiesced to the teacher's concept of how a black female student should talk. When she gave her name for the first time in the office, I was easily able to understand her. The teacher was using the youngster's dialect as an additional way of venting her racist feelings.

Many streetcorner youngsters have developed an amazing sense for determining the shuckin' and jivin' behavior that school personnel want and expect from them. Thomas Kochman noted this ability in nonschool settings. "They [those who are shuckin' and jivin'] became competent actors. Many developed keen perception of what affected, motivated, appeased or satisfied the authority figures with whom they came into contact."[23]

Shuckin' and jivin' is a survival technique to avoid trouble. It is also used to escape suspension or punishment for misconduct when caught. In fact, it is also used to escape being caught. Reality 54 provides an example of a youngster shuckin' and jivin' his way out of a misconduct charge. Reality 55 depicts a youngster shuckin' and jivin' his way out of being caught.

REALITY 54

A sixth-grade female teacher was walking in the hall. One of her male students approached her and asked, "You wanna grind?" (The grind is a slow sensual dance in which the couple dancing barely move anything but their pelvises in a grinding motion.)

The teacher ignored the question and walked on. The question, however, bothered her. Instinctively, she knew there was something wrong about it, and she reported the young man and the question to her assistant principal.

The assistant principal called the youngster to his office. When questioned about the incident, the youngster went into his shuckin' act.

He explained that he guessed he had not spoken too clearly because what he said was, "Would you wanna grind a carrot with me?"

The assistant principal let the young man go with a warning to speak more clearly and wrote a note of explanation to the teacher. Of course, if we attach the double meaning of penis to carrot, the youngster had really jived them both.

REALITY 55

There were about ten minutes left in the last period of a ninth-grade history class. A youngster was playing around and had the class in stitches. He had managed to involve a number of his fellow students in his disruptive pranks. The teacher, in desperation, called for assistance on the intercom.

The disruptive youngster ran out of the classroom seconds before the assistant principal arrived; they almost collided. The youngster walked the assistant principal away from the door as he began to shuck and jive.

"Boy, am I glad you got here," he said in a hesitating almost whining voice. I was about to go and get you to help Mrs. Frank. There are some crazy cats in there who are trying to get me in trouble again. They won't let her teach," he added as the bell rang.

"OK, if I go?" he asked weakly but quickly, "I got to go and pick up my kid sister."

"Yes, I guess so," the assistant principal responded, getting out of the way of running students.

By the next morning, the assistant principal had forgotten that he had even been called to the room.

Reality 56 concerns a nonschool incident of shuckin' and jivin' that parallels Reality 55 but this time with a tragic result. As reported in the *New York Times* a man allegedly "tricked" police officers into shooting and killing a transit patrolman.[24]

REALITY 56

It started on the platform of the Hunts Point station of the IRT in New York City. An off-duty transit patrolman in civilian clothing allegedly saw a black man named Richardson carrying a gun in the waistband of his trousers. The patrolman, after identifying himself, ordered Mr. Richardson to lean against the wall. Mr. Richardson appearing to comply, supposedly pulled out a .32 caliber hand gun, shot the patrolman in the shoulder, and ran for an exit with the wounded patrolman pursuing and shooting at him.

As Richardson rushed from the subway, he was met by a number of police officers hurrying to investigate the commotion. Richardson called to them that there was "a crazy man with a gun" shooting at him. The police seeing the on-coming out-of-uniform patrolman brandishing his gun instantly reacted hitting him six times with gunfire. The patrolman died four hours later in the hospital.

This time, however, the shuckin' and jivin' helped no one. Mr. Richardson was indicted by a grand jury on seven counts: felony murder, manslaughter, attempted murder, escape, possession of weapon, reckless endangerment, and possession of stolen property—a correction officer's badge.

Malachi Andrews and Paul Owners defined "Shuck" as "Worthless, no good rappin. Usually followed by jive. 'Why don't you quit SHUCKIN and jivin',"[25] Their definition holds in particular for school youngsters shuckin' and jivin' one another. H. Rap Brown gave an example of shuckin' and jivin' a friend.

We went and got some "pluck" (wine) and I told him I was in college. He asked what I wanted to be. I told him rich. He looked up at the ceiling and paused for a minute before he said, "You know, I've never given any thought to what I want to become." I told him he should think about it, but I knew I was shuckin' and jivin'. Hell, hardly any of us ever thought about what we wanted to become. What was the future? That was something white folks had. We just lived from day to day, expecting whatever life put on us and dealing with it the best we knew how when it came. I had accepted the big lie of a Black man succeeding.[26]

John O. Killens mentions shucking and jiving in *The Cotillion: or One Good Bull is Half the Herd*.[27]

Woofin'

Another survival technique streetcorner youngsters often use to test a teacher's mettle is "woffin'." How a teacher reacts to a heavy "woof" may determine his tenure in a classroom. Andrews and Owens defined wolf (pronounced woof) as "a vicious verbal attack, similar to signifying except that it's not as intellectually cunning as signifying. Also, there are three people directly involved in signifying, two in woofing."[28] Their definition is reasonably accurate. However, it must be remembered that in most cases, school youngsters challenging a teacher or classmate are also usually playing to their audience. Therefore, although two are involved in the verbal aspects of woofing, the audience that may be affected by the outcome may also determine the outcome by their presence and reactions to the woofing encounter. Woofing is another jivin' or manipulative technique. Lou Shelly described "whoofin" as "to tell an improbable yarn," and classified as G.I. jive.[29] There are, of course, other definitions.[30]

Youngsters may woof on one another or they may woof on a teacher. And, as noted earlier, to accept a challenge to a fight is to accept a Woof Ticket. In one case, however, a Woof Ticket was used to stop a fight.

REALITY 57

While still teaching graphic arts in the "600" schools, I gave a friend who was an assistant principal in a Harlem junior high school a number of Wolf Tickets that my students had printed.

Some time later, he told me of an incident in which two male students had been fighting. No matter what he did verbally, they would not stop. Then, remembering the Wolf Tickets he handed one to each of the protagonists. The fight stopped immediately and soon the whole class was clamoring for a Wolf Ticket. Interest in the tickets superseded interest in the fight.

Just as with many of the other terms we are discussing, usage and definition differ in different regions and social groups. In some areas, signifying and playing the dozens may be called woofing by certain age groups. Or, as described by H. Rap Brown, the act of loud, threatening talk can be called woofing while what you are using as a tool for woofing may be the dozens. "He just stood there and woofed at the police, talking about their mamas and shit like that. You know a blood. Play the Dozens in a minute."[31]

Brown pointed out that to woof well you always have to be on the offensive. "I knew damned well they wasn't goin' let a nigger get the drop on the sheriff and then let him go, but you got to stay on the offensive all the time. 'What you mean I'm under arrest? for what, goddammit?' I was woofing like a champ."[32]

Sometimes, "loud mouthing," "loud talking," "sounding," "screaming on someone," "bogarding," "dogin'," or even "running a strong rap," may be considered woofing. Woofing can take such forms as: (1) standing in the hall and blocking a teacher; (2) standing in front of a teacher or walking down the hall with a belt opened; (3) yelling and moving ones body in a "menacing way" while arguing about a grade; (4) just standing and staring at a teacher; or (5) almost any nonverbal, verbal, or physical form of intimidation.

For the middle class teacher, woofin' can be a terrifying experience; or it can be a false perception of reality. For the woof to work, though, the person or persons being woofed on must become intimidated by the woof. According to H. Rap Brown, "the whole thing is that if you can woof and woof hard enough and long enough and be willing to back it up, few people will push you."[33]

Therefore, if someone's fantasies, expectations, or feelings about blacks indicate that blacks only want to beat on people, steal, and sexually molest white women, then that person is conditioned to be susceptible to a woof by someone who is black. As a rule, when that person is woofed on, all his or her negative feelings about blacks will generate tremendous fear of the person woofing.

Conversely, where there are few Mexican-Americans, a Mexican-American's woof probably would not work because the person being woofed on, most likely, envisions the Mexican-American sleeping under a tree with a big sombrero on his head.

The woofin' observed most often in public schools takes the form of a youngster making a face and yelling at a teacher. Woofers may also move their bodies in a menacing way to make their woof more threatening and intimidating.

He may woof for anything from a pass to leave school early to gaining control of the class by frightening the teacher. Or, he may woof on the teacher to get another sandwich at lunch or to get into class without a pass when late.

I observed a woofin' contest in a junior high school where students roamed the halls refusing to go to class during a minor uprising. In one room, however, most of the students were in class but giving their new teacher a rough time. An experienced teacher from another school happened to be there, and he entered the room to help when he saw the teacher having problems.

As he spoke with the students, one of the bigger boys jumped up from his seat and woofed the visiting teacher with "I'm gonna punch you," as he started walking toward him.

The teacher looked at the youngster, laughed loudly, and said, "You gonna punch me?"

The youngster stopped in his tracks, looked at his fellow students who were now laughing, and started laughing himself. As he returned to his seat, he said, "Naw, I was only kidding."

The teacher talked with the class for about twenty minutes about what was going on and then left.

Woofing appears to be used even more often in the halls. One of the reasons for this may be that in the halls students have more anonymity and the halls are where some of the tougher streetcorner youngsters hang out *Posin' to Be Chosen'*.[34] In Reality 58, a basic woof will be described and examples provided of how three teachers handled the same woof.

REALITY 58

A new teacher was walking in the hall when a few boys approached him from the opposite direction. One of the boys peeled off from the group, and as he and the teacher came face to face, he moved his hand out in front of the teacher, placed his palm against the wall, and looked at the teacher.

Think about it, what would you do?

In the first example, the teacher looked at the student apprehensively, looked around, and walked under his arm.

The second teacher also looked at the student apprehensively, looked around, and then said, "Why are you doing this to me? I am not prejudiced like the other teachers."

The student kept looking at him malevolently.

Next, the teacher said, "You know, if you would not act this way and you would behave, you could be a leader of your race."

The student did not move and kept looking at the teacher.

The teacher panicked and punched the student. Whereupon, the student punched the teacher.

In the third case, as the student moved his hand in front of the teacher, the teacher grabbed his arm at the pressure point, and moved him out of the way.

Which of the three would you opt for? You will recall the earlier discussion of the expectations that we have of one another.

In the first example, the teacher was fearful of the student and thought about whether he should walk under the student's arm or just around him. Whatever the reason, the teacher opted to walk under the student's arm.

Later that afternoon when the student and his friends were walking in the hall and saw the teacher again, the youngster who had woofed on the teacher called out, "Hey, Mr. Faggot." The teacher could not make it in the school and soon left for another job.

In the second example, the teacher was also fearful of the student. After he panicked and punched the student and was punched back, he reported the student for punching him. His report mentioned only the student punching him. As a result, the student was suspended and eventually sent to a program for emotionally disturbed and socially maladjusted adolescents.

The third teacher was aware of woofing, was not afraid, and moved the youngster out of the way. The student then made a couple of face-saving comments. His friends, seeing that the teacher was not afraid, gently taunted their friend with some innocent verbal comments—"What you tryin' to do, make the teacher walk around you?"

Unquestionably, in the third example, the teacher's moving the student out of the way could have caused the student to punch or push the teacher. That is the chance you take whenever you touch a student.

Recently, at a conference after I had presented, an administrator working in a day secondary school for problem youngsters told me this next reality.

REALITY 59

"I attented your presentation at last year's ANYSEED conference and took home a bunch of your Woof Tickets and put them in my office desk drawer.[35]

"I am a supervisor in a day treatment center and figured that I would be able to tell the staff about the woof tickets sometime, and I would be able to use them.

"Well, one day I was walking out in the hallway, and I saw one of the older kids [he was fourteen years of age] in the school walking down the hall and all of a sudden he is coming right at me with his head down. Now, after your presentation, I kinda knew the game he was playing. So, instead of moving out of his way, as I had probably done many times before, I just walked right up to him, stood there, and said, 'Wait a minute, I have something for you—stay right here, don't move, OK!'

"I ran back to my office, pulled the woof ticket out of my drawer, got back to him and said, 'Here, this is for you. Next time use this instead.'

"He just looked at me and a big smile came over his face. He walked around me and went back to class. We didn't have another problem with him.

"After that, since we knew it was a game, I would see him walking down the hall and get in his way and stand there.

"He would say, 'Git outa here, stop doin' that to me,' and kind of chuckle."

Reality 60 describes a teacher using a "soft" woof on five junior high school inner city youngsters and getting away with it.

REALITY 60

A teacher was walking down the hall when he noticed a commotion near an auditorium door. Walking to the door, he found five boys giving Mr. Rice, the guidance teacher, a hard time. Mr. Rice was not in trouble but was having a problem extricating himself from the conversation with the students.

"What's the matter, Mr. Rice? Can I help," he asked.

"These guys won't go away. I have to work with the kids inside on a play and these guys are trying to come in," responded Mr. Rice.

"Oh heck," said the teacher. There are only onnne-twoo-threee-fourrr-fivvve of them. Five, that's light stuff. You go inside, and I'll take care of them."

The students looked from Mr. Rice to the teacher.

Two of them said, "Shoot."

They all turned and walked away. Mr. Rice and the teacher laughed. The teacher left, Mr. Rice closed the door and started his rehearsal.

Sometimes, youngsters will work together to run a woofin' game. This can happen if youngsters want class disrupted because they did not do their homework, they don't want to take a test, they don't like the teacher, or for almost any other reason. Woofin' can also be planned when a youngster comes to a teacher's classroom door and woofs until the teacher loses his or her composure and chases the student while the class spills out into the hall to watch the action. In one case, I actually had to restrain physically the teacher and push him back into his classroom while telling him that I would get the youngster.

The knowledgeable person can observe woofing, in varying ways, being used daily in the world outside the school. My colleague, George, has used the woof, too. I recall a very specific instance in Indianapolis.

During the period when the city of Indianapolis was entering its initial move toward school desegregation and integration programs, George and I were often invited to speak and do staff development workshops. During one period, whenever we arrived at our hotel, it had been overbooked and our rooms, though reserved, were not available.

The first time, we went elsewhere. After the second time, we knew what was up. The next time, George looked at me and I eyed him back; we both shrugged our shoulders and George, who is a black man about six feet three inches tall, went into a woof routine. He leaned forward across the counter, glared into the clerk's eyes, and with a somewhat loud, gruffy voice said, "What do you mean you don't have a room for us?"

After more words and gestures, the clerk retreated and then returned to ask whether we would be willing to accept a room at the facility around the corner, which was an exclusive private club. With another intimidating stare, George and I asked, "What about our luggage?" The clerk briskly instructed his bellman to take our luggage and direct us to the club. George just might have been the first black ever to have slept there.

Although we had made prior reservations at our hotel, Axel Foley (Eddie Murphy), in the recent movie *Beverly Hills Cop*, doesn't. In a hotel scene parallel to our situation, Axel woofs on the hotel clerk and her supervisor to get a room.[36] Axel, dressed in a T-shirt, sweat shirt, and jeans, uses his voice, and the threat that the clerk was discriminating against him, in order to get a room at a posh Beverly Hills hotel. He ends the woof with:

No, I'm Axel Foley, as in Rolling Stone's Axel Foley, and I'm supposed to be doing a story on Michael Jackson gonna' be called Michael Jackson is sittin' on top of the world but I guess I better tell Michael he may be sittin' on top of the world but he better not do it at this hotel cuz' they don't allow NIGGERS![37]

Film critic Richard Schickel wrote that Murphy was "terrorizing a snooty hotel into giving him a room despite his lack of a reservation."[38] Another critic, John Curran suggested Murphy went off into a "brassy rage."[39] Each explanation of this scene is, in essence, describing a woof.

There was a very different kind of woof in the movie *Moscow on the Hudson.* In one scene, Vladimir Ivanoff (Robin Williams) is riding on the subway with his black security guard friend, Lionel Weatherspoon (Cleavant Derricks), when a rather tall black guy with a bandanna tied around his forehead tries to put a staring woof on Vladimir. To get the woofer to leave Vladimir alone, Lionel suggests Vladimir "look mean." When that doesn't work, he suggests Vladimir "look crazy." That apparently works, as the big black guy turns and walks away mumbling, "you crazy man."[40]

When the Reverend Jessie Jackson entered the Democratic primary, the campaign began to resemble a school that had its first black student. A close look at the Democratic primary television debates and the newspaper coverage highlighted the white candidates and press's lack of understanding and experience (1) in working with and covering blacks as equals, and (2) of black streetcorner behavior and the black church. A close look at the Reverend Jackson's campaign revealed a mastery of black church and black streetcorner behavior.

Gerald M. Boyd wrote about the shifts in Reverend Jackson's position, "whose tone and mood have alternated in recent weeks between hard line and conciliatory, actions that have created confusion and concern within the Democratic Party."[41] Similarly, James Reston, in a piece entitled "Jackson's Arrogant Pride," wrote:

"I am somebody," he proclaims, but he treats Mr. Mondale like a nobody and "supports" him on television with grudging and suspicious eyes.

The trouble is that this is no longer a personal but a party fight, and Mr. Jackson's tardy offers of support always seem to imply the vague suggestion that "it is in the power of my hand to do you hurt."

Nobody denies that he's a powerful force, but when he lets himself go before the television cameras, arms waving and eyes flashing, his tendency is to stun and frighten rather than to persuade.

He is, however, a loner, a proud and arrogant man who plays by his own rules.

With his rhymes and chants, he has come to the aid of the people in trouble.[42]

The above comments could all be descriptive of the streetcorner trickster who alternates between playing the cat and playing the mouse. Jonathan Friendly also wrote in the *New York Times* and described Jackson woofing on the reporters who knew they were being intimidated but didn't quite know what to do about it.

The Rev. Jesse Jackson, running for the Democratic Presidential nomination, often ends his speeches by asking young adults in the audience to register to vote. The call is conducted in the style of a revival meeting, and it ends with a host of black supporters around him.

Then he asks his audience to be silent while he tends to another task, answering questions from reporters who have also been standing in front of him and are by then surrounded by enthusiastic Jackson partisans. The questions are usually less pointed and insistent than when the same reporters confront the candidate alone or in a room crowded with other reporters.

Mr. Jackson, in an interview last week aboard his chartered plane, . . . said the tactic was not intended to intimidate reporters, but he acknowledged it had "a sobering effect on all people involved." It forces reporters "to take the people into account," he said, while teaching his young followers what the press is like.[43]

In Buffalo, New York, professional boxer Livingstone Bramble, a Rastafarian, pulled a Muhammad Ali in his prefight woofing and psyching of Ray Mancini, a white boxer. The prefight hype-woofing reporting had Bramble keeping a pet boa constrictor, having a snakeskin on the wall of his apartment, and importing Dr. Doo, his personal witch doctor.[44] Don Esmond, writing in the *Buffalo News* after Bramble's fourteenth-round technical knockout of Mancini was sharper than most reporters.

He seemed, at first, the largest of fools, a man to be taken as seriously as a red-eyed wino slumped against a tenement wall.

He looked the lightweight champion in the eye and declared the title vacant. He bought a boa constrictor and named it Dog. His dog, he named Snake. He wore funny hats and didn't own a tie. And when he imported a voodoo doctor from his native Virgin Islands, those who thought vaudeville was dead reconsidered.

Yet, in retrospect, what seemed a performance was merely a prelude. Livingstone Bramble was more a prophet than fool.

He was different, and his eccentricity smokescreened the truth.[45]

Most of the aforementioned woofing examples were of individuals or a few students attempting to intimidate some teachers for some brief individual, small, or short-term gain. The use of woofing by adults so far described was also on an individual basis.

However, since the civil rights movement of the 1960s, some black groups have used woofing as a political tactic. These streetcorner-based tactics became a new power wedge used by blacks in the confrontation and in-fighting to achieve stated or unstated demands. This behavior provided a new dimension for what whites call "gut politics."

Streetcorner behavior has been observed and reported in use by adults as well as students in testing devices in school confrontations and bargaining sessions with whites and sometimes middle class blacks on many college campuses, in public schools, in city halls, in government agencies, and in many of the encounters dealing with community control. Often, by using streetcorner behavior, the blacks have attempted to achieve their ends by intimidating the middle class blacks and whites with whom they are bargaining.

Tom Wolfe described these streetcorner behavior tactics beautifully. He wrote about San Francisco blacks "mau-mauing the flack catchers," for financial gain. Or, in other words, how some San Francisco blacks and their friends would turn their streetcorner behavior games and tactics into playing on the fears and fantasies of the white government functionaries to secure federal poverty funds. To some extent, this is the same way many inner city youngsters "run their game" or woof on teachers.

> Going downtown to mau-mau the bureaucrats got to be the routine practice in San Francisco. The poverty program *encouraged* you to go in for mau-mauing. They wouldn't have known what to do without it. The bureaucrats at City Hall and in the Office of Economic Opportunity talked "ghetto" all the time, but they didn't know any more about what was going on in the Western Addition, Hunters Point, Potrero Hill, the Mission, Chinatown, or south of Market Street than they did about Zanzibar. They didn't know where to look. They didn't even know who to ask. So what could they do? Well ... they used the Ethnic Catering Service ... right. ... They sat back and waited for you to come rolling in with your certified angry militants, your guaranteed frustrated ghetto youth, looking like a bunch of wild men. Then you had your test confrontation. If you were outrageous enough, if you could shake up the bureaucrats so bad that their eyes froze into iceballs and their mouths twisted up into smiles of sheer physical panic, into shit-eating grins, so to speak—then they knew you were the real goods. They knew you were the right studs to give the poverty grants and community organizing jobs to. Otherwise they wouldn't know.[46]

Blacks who play these confrontation games usually know exactly what they are doing. In many cases they have their tactics down to an art, even as to what to wear.

> "Now don't forget. When you go downtown, y'all wear your *ghetto rags* ... see. ... Don't go down there with your Italian silk jerseys on and your brown suede and green alligator shoes and your Harry Belafonte shirts looking like some supercool tooth-picking-noddin' fool ... you know. ... "
>
> "Don't nobody give a damn how pretty you can look. ... You wear your *combat* fatigues and your leather *pieces* and your shades ... your *ghetto rags* ... see. ... And don't go down there with your hair all done up nice in your curly Afro like you're messing around. You go down with your *hair*

stickin' out . . . and *sitting' up!* Lookin' wild! I want to see you down there looking like a bunch of *wild niggers!*[47]

Mau-mauing usually frightened the whites. And mau-mauing, or similar tactics, in the schools usually frighten school personnel. (This now also happens in schools of higher learning.) However, the whites upon whom the games are being played are usually not in any danger. The danger comes about when they begin to act irrationally—irrationally, that is, in the sense of ghetto expectations. To quote Wolfe again:

> Ninety-nine percent of the time whites were in no physical danger whatsoever during mau-mauing. The brothers understood through and through that it was a tactic, a procedure, a game. If you actually hurt or endangered somebody at one of these sessions, you were only cutting yourself off from whatever was being handed out, the jobs, the money, the influence. The idea was to terrify but don't touch. The term *mau-mauing* itself expressed this gamelike quality. It expressed the put on side of it. In public you used the same term the whites used, namely, "confrontation." The term mau-mauing said, "The white man had a voodoo fear of us, because deep down he still thinks we're savages. Right? So we're going to do that Savage number for him." It was like a practical joke at the expense of the white man's superstitiousness.[48]

Abrahams suggested that these tactical games have

> become a central aggressive technique used by black militants in confrontations with whites. Because this aggressive technique of interpersonal behavior has as its aim playful aggression and coercion, and because it is almost solely used by blacks and is aggressive, whites read it as hostility (which it may be in certain cases). . . . Whites carry certain expectations into these confrontations which blacks have learned to counteract immediately, and thus they disarm whites and make them play their own game (generally without whites even knowing it). . . . However, we deem such behavior inappropriate for high-tension encounter occasions. . . . Consequently, white arbitrators, who come from the sector of the establishment most insistent about its concepts of decorum, are embarrassed and threatened and they fall to their barest displays of power as they resort first to call for "reason" (really a white plea to permit power-play and coercion in their terms), then to silence and rumination, then to appeal to the rules of society (made for all to be accepted by all) and finally to the whole law-and-order dimension of the argument.[49]

These gamelike tactics continue to confound and frighten innumerable whites who have come to fear blacks. Many middle class blacks fear ghetto blacks, too. The tactics are to a large extent an enlargement and refinement of the tactics or games many schoolchildren have been using to test their teachers. Actually, Abrahams's description is also reminiscent of the middle class teachers' plea to black children to try to get them to cease and desist testing of them.

Realities 61 and 62 provide additional examples of black confrontation tactics. Reality 61 describes a black versus black confrontation; Reality 62 describes a black political confrontation with the white power structure.

REALITY 61

In 1968, as part of the stormy controversy in Ocean Hill-Brownsville between the United Federation of Teachers and the Ocean Hill Governing Board, the services of nineteen teachers were "terminated." This action precipitated a disruptive conflict between teachers and community, between teachers and teachers, and between communities. Martin Mayer described the meeting, at which street-corner behavior was used in a threatening way to sway a vote helping to terminate the services of the nineteen teachers.

> Over the weekend before, Assemblyman Wright had pleaded with the governing board not to take arbitrary action on personnel during the week the State Legislature was to begin its consideration of decentralization bills. Nevertheless, when the governing board met that Tuesday evening in executive session the report of the personnel committee was called up for approval. Professor Lockwood opposed the report, and urged that the board at least call the accused staff before it to talk over the charges before acting. Especially when complaints relate to behavior rather than to competence, he argued, people must be given a right to some kind of hearing. Moreover, if the teachers refused to appear at the meeting, they would be automatically guilty of insubordination. Several of the parent members stirred uneasily while Dr. Lockwood spoke.
>
> Presently, as though on signal, the door to the meeting room burst open and 15 to 20 militants rushed in and ranged themselves against the wall. This was a community board they said, and they were the community, and they were there to see that the board did what the community wanted. ("At this point," the minutes of the meeting say gallantly and rather glumly, "the community entered the room.") In this atmosphere, the report of the personnel committee was approved, and McCoy was ordered to write letters to the 19, "terminating their services" in the district [my emphasis] .[50]

REALITY 62

On September 11, 1968, the New York City teachers returned to work after summer vacation. To quote Mayer again:

> At J.H.S. 271, a group led by Sonny Carson of Brooklyn CORE, who is widely regarded as terrorist in his inclinations and does nothing to discourage that opinion, had blocked the front door against the returning teachers. Prin-

cipal William Harris had come out, and with the help of police had escorted the teachers into the building. There he told them, as the other principals were telling the other U.F.T. teachers through the district, to report to the I.S. 55 auditorium for an orientation session with McCoy. When the teachers arrived at the auditorium, they found about 50 Negro men, some wearing helmets, carrying sticks or with bandoleers of bullets, who shouted curses at them. The 83 teachers clustered in the center of the auditorium, terrified, and McCoy entered. As he started to speak, choruses of jeers from the men drowned him out, and after a few minutes he left. The lights in the auditorium were then flicked on and off, and the teachers were told from the crowd that if they came back to the district they would be carried out in pine boxes. Finally, McCoy returned. If the teachers still insisted on returning to the district, he said, they should report to their schools at 1 o'clock.

The teachers left the auditorium, caucused, and decided to go through with what they had come to do. When they reported to their schools again, they found they had been given no teaching assignments and there were no time cards for them to punch. J.H.S. 271 pupils were encouraged to leave the school by some nonunion teachers and members of the governing board. On their way out, they jeered at the union teachers, and, in some cases, maneuvered as though to assault them. Harris locked the teachers into a room for their own protection, and arranged a police escort for them out of the building at 2:15. That afternoon, the Ocean Hill teachers reported on their experiences to the executive board of the union, which exercised the option in the motion which had ended the preceding strike, and called for the city's teachers to walk out again on Friday.[51]

REALITY 63

In the city of Buffalo, New York, there is an all-black, Saul Alinsky-organized community action organization, BUILD, which stands for Build Unity, Independence, Liberty, Dignity.[52] In their early days, the organization employed streetcorner tactics and games at public hearings (some of which were televised) in an attempt to achieve their goals.

BUILD's appearance at most public hearings followed a similar pattern of behavior. Whenever one of their speakers rose to address the meeting, a number of "big guys," some in dashikis, Afros, goatees, and sunglasses would jump to their feet and stand big and tall with hands folded on their chest. Two or three other men or women would stand in similar manner and dress behind their speaker. Most often these tactics were successful in frightening the whites who watched.

While writing the above, I discussed the incident with someone who had worked for a poverty agency in a large northeastern city. When I gave her the exerpt to read, she began to chuckle and told me of her experiences. However, she used the word "rap" to describe what has been called woofing.

REALITY 64

"It seems that every time a new budget was coming up for approval—which was about every nine months—there would always be a problem because our program wasn't one of the priority programs. It was a tutorial program. It was always to be one of the program that would be cut.

"The State didn't realize that our program included about 150 community people. So when the people from the Office of Economic Opportunity and the State office would bring their budgets and let us know that we either had been cut out completely or cut down, we would get together as many people as we could—not only people employed in our program but everybody, their friends, and their relatives. We would go down to City Hall and rap. I would always stay in the background because I was one of the few whites there. Some of the black women who had had long experience in dealing with institutions because of welfare and the schools and so on would be in the front and be the speakers.

"We would always get the whole thing—the routine. The man in charge couldn't see us because he was in an important meeting. They would send some second grade flunky out to talk with us and the women would say, 'No, we're only talking with the boss,' and eventually the boss would leave his meeting and come out and talk. They would, in very plain down-to-earth, street people way, let the guy know that this was a program that they intended to have . . . and we always got funded."

Woofin' is also used at some institutions of higher education. Whereas in elementary and secondary schools woofin' is often used for disruptive purposes per se, in higher education, the woof is usually used for personal or group gain.

In a rare case, woofin' was used to procure an undergraduate degree in mostly independent study and has been used to procure an undeserved higher grade. Black streetcorner students sometimes woof on administrators, faculty, secretaries, white student government leaders, or adult advisors, frightening them into providing funds either improperly or by skirting established student government procedures. Assuredly, some of the woofin' was precipitated by whites trying to deny blacks goods or materials promised or rightfully theirs. Unfortunately, woofing may be the only skill some black streetcorner students have to use in these situations because they may lack the appropriate prosocial middle class facilitating skills. In my experience, it is a rare white higher education student, faculty member, or administrator who is capable of standing up to a woof.

Signifying

A good deal of signifying goes on in inner city schools. It usually starts when one youngster approaches another and says something like, "You know what Russell said about you?" The fellow signifying keeps at the other until he provokes him to go after Russell, who may not have said anything at all.

Sometimes, inner city youngsters will signify one teacher against another, student against teacher, teacher against student, and administrator against teacher or vice versa.

Although there does not appear to be consensus as to exactly what signifying is, there is agreement that it does exist as a technique that differs from shuckin' and jivin' and other forms of provocation or put down. Signifying has been defined by a number of writers. Andrews and Owens wrote that signifying is to tease someone, or to provoke someone into anger. "The signifier creates a myth about someone and tells him a third person started it." They suggest signifying is successful "when the signifier convinces the chump he is working on, that what he is saying is true and that it gets him angered to wrath."[53]

Signifying, according to H. Rap Brown, is one of the many forms of "what the white folks call verbal skills. We learned how to throw them words together." He wrote that the person signifying has an option of either making someone feel good or bad. If someone was down, signifying could also make him feel better.

Signifying was also a way of expressing your feelings:

"Man, I can't win for losing
If it wasn't for bad luck, I wouldn't
have no luck at all. . . .
I'm living on the welfare and things is
stormy
They borrowing their shit from the Salvation
Army. . . ."[54]

Signifying is also telling tales or stories or "throwing the bull" or what in Yiddish is called "fonfering."[55] Brown wrote that real signifying is best when, "brothers are exchanging tales. I used to hang out in the bars just to hear the old men 'talking shit.' By the time I was nine, I could talk Shine and the Titanic, Signifying Monkey, three different ways, and Piss-Pot-Peet, for two hours without stopping."[56]

Ed Bullins, who grew up on the streets of North Philadelphia, also has a concept of signifying. Jervis Anderson interviewed Bullins and discussed a press release that appeared to be motivated by the earlier black exploitation films. He then wrote that, "there is a lot of what Bullins would call 'signifying' in that release. It contains digs at real people but the names have been changed to protect the guilty."[57]

Abrahams, who has been prolific in his reporting of black verbal behavior, suggested that to signify is "to imply, goad, beg, boast by indirect verbal or gestural means."[58] Further, signifying is a device linking the dozens to childhood behavior, and it can have any number of meanings.[59] In the Signifying Monkey toast, it "refers to the trickster's ability to talk with great innuendo, to carp, cajole, needle, and lie."[60]

In still other cases it can mean the ability to talk around a topic without ever coming to the point. Signifying can also refer to talking with eyes and hands and innumerable gestures and expressions. It can also be used to refer to making fun of a situation or a person. Indeed, telling stories about neighbors to stir up a fight is also signifying, as is ridiculing a police officer by imitating his actions behind his back.[61]

According to Kochman, when signifying is used to shame, embarrass, frustrate, or to downgrade someone, a direct signifying taunt is used. Furthermore, when the object of signifying is direct action, the signifying is subtle, deceptive, and indirect and counts on the gullibility or naiveté of the recipient for its success. "[T]he signifier reports or repeats what someone else has said about the listener; the 'report' is couched in plausible language and hostility. There is also the implication that if the listener fails to do anything about it—what has to be 'done' is usually quite clear—his status will be seriously compromised."[62]

Claudia Mitchell-Kernan agreed that signifying is usually a verbal dueling tactic that is an end in itself and that the discussion most often reported relates to that concept of signifying. She pointed out that signifying "also refers to a way of encoding messages or meanings which involves, in most cases, an element of indirection."[63] Although Mitchell-Kernan could not obtain a consensus from blacks in defining signifying, she reported "most informants felt that some element of indirection was critical to signifying."[64]

Her reporting also suggested the black concept of signifying includes basically a "folk notion" and that dictionary reportings of vocabulary are not always adequate for interpreting messages or meanings. The real understanding of a word may go further than the reported interpretations. Left-handed methods may be used to make a complimentary remark. The context in which a word is used may determine its actual definition. What is assumed to be informative may actually be designed as persuasive. Tone of voice and facial expressions also are used to interpret true meaning. While meaning is narrowed by situational contexts, knowledge of the personal background of a speaker may show a different interpretation. "Expectations based on role or status criteria enter into the sorting process. In fact, we seem to process all manner of information against a background of assumptions and expectations."[65]

To this point, she held that indirection or metaphorical reference is one of the defining characteristics of signifying. Abrahams also mentioned indirection. "The name 'signifying' shows the monkey to be a trickster, signifying being the language of trickery, that set of words or gestures achieving Hamlet's 'direction through indirection' and used often, especially among the young, to humiliate an adversary." Though this indirection appears to be a function of style, it may also serve the function of being diplomatic or euphemistic.[66]

Indirection means here that the correct (referential) interpretation or signification of the utterance cannot be arrived at by a consideration of the dictionary meaning of the lexical items involved and the syntactic rules for their combination alone. The apparent significance of the message differs from its real significance. The apparent meaning of the sentence "signifies" its actual meaning.[67]

The real meaning of "indirection" grows from the decoding of the participants' shared cultural knowledge and operates on two levels. First, the participants must understand that signifying is taking place and "that the dictionary-syntactical meaning of the utterance is to be ignored."[68] Second, "this shared knowledge must be employed in the reinterpretation of the utternace."[69] Additionally, the artistry of the speaker is judged by his other cleverness in directing all involved in the shared cultural knowledge.

Geneva Smitherman suggested that signification, a mode of discourse, "refers to the verbal art of insult in which a speaker humorously puts down, talks about, needles [or signifies on] the listener. Sometimes signifying . . . is done to make a point, sometimes it's just to be more subtle and circumlocutory than the other verbal activities."[70]

Furthermore, according to Smitherman, signification can be either heavy or light. Being heavy is a way of driving home or teaching a cognitive message without lecturing or preaching. That is, to put someone in check by making them think about their behavior, and correcting it. Heavy signifying might contain aspects of sarcasm, but it is not personally debilitating or venomous.[71]

Verbal posturing via sounding or capping could be considered lightweight signifying.[72] Also, signification may contain the following characteristics:

Indirection, circumlocution; metaphorical-imagistic (but images rooted in the everyday, real world); humorous, ironic; rhythmic fluency and sound; teachy but not preachy; directed at a person or persons usually present in the situation context (siggers do not talk behind yo back); punning, play on words; introduction of semantically or logically unexpected. [It] can be witty one-liner, a series of loosely related statements, or a cohesive discourse on one point.[73]

Jack Kerouac, in his book *On The Road*, wrote about a bus ride with Henry Glass, who had just gotten out of Terre Haute federal pen and told him what it was to signify. "Anybody that's leaving jail soon and starts talking about his release date is 'signifying' to the other fellas that have to stay. We take him by the neck and say, 'Don't signify with *me!*' Bad thing, to signify—y'hear me?"[74]

Paul Cowan also reported, "My neighbors and Rachel and I used to bowl and 'signify' as they called their special, supple, and witty form of conversation."[75]

Mezz Mezzrow reported that to signify is to "hint, put on an act, make a gesture." He wrote about the Harlem scene when bootlegging and the numbers were flourishing.[76] The hip Harlem Negroes did not "take" to the rackets' leaders and their trigger and muscle men. Instead, just as on the streetcorner, they respected the man who could make out by his wits. Mezzrow described a signifying scene in Big John's bar in Harlem, when about five of Dutch Schultz's torpedoes swaggered in and ordered drinks for the house.

One of them ankled over to the juke box to play some records. As soon as the music started, one of the guys in our crowd yelled real loud, looking straight at this guy, "Man, that a *killer!*" He could have been talking about the music, but everybody in that room knew different. Right quick another cat spoke up real loud, saying, "That's *murder* man, really murder," and his eyes were signifying too. All these gunmen began to shift from foot to foot, fixing their ties and scratching their noses, faces red and Adam's apples jumping. Before we knew it they had gulped their drinks and beat it out the door, saying good-bye to the bartender with their hats way down over their eye brows and their eyes gunning the ground. That's what Harlem thought of the white underworld.[77]

As with the other verbal techniques, signifying may be played with more or less sophistication depending upon the age of the participants, their sex, the section of the country they are from, or even whether they are in a junior or a senior high school. Additionally, signifying may also be called woofin', sounding, screaming, or other names.

In school, it appears that signifying is often combined with the dozens or with ribbing. Since the dozens is still to be discussed, only a few examples will be provided here.

Typically, in signifying by using the dozens, one youngster may come up to another and say, "George, he say yo' mothar is a ho," or "Larry, he be saying some nasty things about your sister Dolores." Or someone may come up to a female student and say, "Harold telling everyone you pulled a train last night." Some may approach a male student and imply something about his manliness by saying, "Jim told me you punked out last night, he say you laid in the cut while your people went down on the Chaplains." (To lay in the cut could be to stay on the corner or in your house while the other members of the gang fought.)

Signifying in school can also revolve around athletics in general or a particular team. For example, if someone did something foolish in a game, he may be signified about it. Girls are also the objects of much signifying by male students. The signifying may relate to a girl's looks or whether she was having sexual relations or allegedly having them with her boyfriend or others.

Assuming that none of the story descriptions are true, the youngster signifying is attempting to goad into fighting the youngster to whom he or she is telling the story or perhaps trying to break up a friendship with the youngster he or she claims is spreading the story. Sometimes, a signifying story may get to someone third hand.

In the basic toast or story of the Signifying Monkey, the monkey uses childish devices to goad the lion into fighting the elephant. The ensuing dialogue is typical of the verbal art of signifying. Just as happens so often in school, without any obvious provocation, the monkey starts signifying to getting the lion and elephant into a fight.

"Deep down in the jungle where the coconuts grow
Lived the signifyingest motherfucker that the world ever know.
He said to the lion one bright sunny day
It's a big bad burly motherfucker coming your way.
I'm going on off in the jungle and stay out of sight.
Cause when you two meet its going to be a hell of a fight.
But if ya'll two fight, I know you can win."

Above, we see the monkey getting the lion upset and annoyed. He then starts his signifying, which is similar to the examples provided of school signifying.

"He said your mama was a slut like a dog in a pack
Running around the street with a mattress on her back."

The monkey plays the dozens with those two lines and then gets onto the other members of the lion's family.

"He talked about your daddy and put your sister on the shelf
He said your sister had the illness and your daddy got
  the claps. . . .
He said he fucked your baby sister and poked your baby niece
And when he sees your little brother he's going to ask him
  for a piece
He said your sister sold pussy and sucked dicks for cash . . .
He even talked about your grandma and I told him she was dead
Long cow-pussy bitch, that's all he said. . . . "

After the lion and the elephant fought, the lion "crawled off to the jungle more dead than alive. . . . And that's when the monkey started his signifying jive." The monkey then tells the lion how his strong rap got him to fight the elephant.

"I set it up and you fell into my trap
And I copped your dumb butt with my bad-ass rap."

The monkey's signifying gets him so excited he falls out of the tree, and

"Like a bolt of lightening and streak of white heat
The lion was on his ass with all four feet."

The monkey must now extricate himself. He does this by calling for sympathy by copping a plea and then challenging the lion's pride in manliness.

"The monkey looked up with tears in his eyes
And said please Mr. Lion I apologize.
The lion said ain't no use in apologizing
I'm going to put an end to your signifying.

The lion grabbed the monkey by his bullet shaped head.
And said I'm going to beat your little ass till you're damn
      near dead.
The monkey said if you jump back like a gentlemen should
I'll kick you big ass all over the woods.
If you just let get my dick out of the sand
I'll fight you like a natural man.
The lion jumped back and squared off for a fight
And the monkey hit the tree and jumped clean out of sight. . . .
He said you're so motherfucking dumb you make me sick.
But if you think you're bad and you want to bend
I'll turn you over to my elephant friend."[78]

In this story, the monkey lived to continue his signifying. In other versions, the monkey is killed.

Most interested inner city school personnel appear to have problems differentiating between ribbing and signifying, at least as far as school is concerned. Reality 65 describes what most teachers felt was signifying. Their reasoning was that an "inside" definition was used to make fun of someone. Everyone else knew about the "inside" definition except for the teacher involved or the person being taunted. This is somewhat akin to earlier explanations.

REALITY 65

Mr. Shaw was in his room preparing a test. Three boys walking the hall stopped in to chat. As they were leaving, after talking for a few minutes, one of them pointed to the teacher's socks and said,

"Hey, Mr. Shaw, those are nice ankle huggers you got on."

Mr. Shaw smiles, looked down at his socks, and said, "Yes, I like them. I just bought them."

Once outside his room, they gave one another five and ran down the hall, laughing.

At lunch, Mr. Shaw commented to some of the teachers, "I must finally be making it. Some of the kids complimented me on my socks. One of them called my socks 'ankle huggers.'"

Two of the teachers almost choked on their food as they tried holding back their laughter. A third teacher explained to Mr. Shaw that he was really being ridiculed because the expression "ankle huggers" refers to low socks, and low socks are out of style for men, only being worn by lames (a chump, a stupid person).

The guidance counselor who told me the story reasoned that signifying took place because the students knew what ankle huggers were and the teacher did not.

Rappin'

When I first heard the expression "rappin'" or "runnin' a rap," it had a sexual connotation. The object of the rap was to "get a girl's nose open," or "get into her pants." That is, to get her into bed.

The expression was used in other ways, too, as described in Reality 66.

REALITY 66

One morning I was working in my office, and one of our students came in and started moving up and down and said he had to go to the lavatory. I listened, kept working, sort of ignored him, but watched him out of the corner of one eye.

Finally, after a few minutes, I turned to him and said, "No, you can't go. Your rap is weak."[79]

He laughed and said, "Ok, see you later." And he tipped on back to class.

From his response, it was obvious that he did not have to go to the lavatory. Whether he just wanted to get out of class, test his rap on me, or practice his rap is speculation.

As indicated so often earlier, there is a blurring of the differences between, for example, rappin', woofin', signifyin', and jivin'. Generally, though, rapping can mean anything from casually speaking with someone, to trying to get a woman into your bed (manipulative), to boisterous talking.

Adolescent rapping can lead to school problems because of misunderstandings. In particular, problems can arise when the rappers are black adolescent streetcorner youngsters and others involved are unfamiliar with black adolescents in general and black streetcorner verbal behavior in particular. In the ghetto, verbal interactions are constantly being judged for the performance aspect, the strong words, the hyperbolic expressions, and the ability of those involved to get with it, to get into it, and to get everyone else involved. The better and stronger the rap, the greater the esteem.[80] Additionally, to rap consists of form and content and the rapper's personality and style.[81] One of the most important aspects of a rapping style is related to action. One does not just speak a rap, one "throws a rap" with a great deal of vitality by often using very active verbs.[82] The narratives and conversations are replete with action verbs that include slang terms, folk metaphor, and colloquial expressions.

Kochman reported that a rap was related to three common uses: (1) providing information to someone or running something down; (2) whupping the game—the verbal dimension of conning someone; and (3) rapping to a woman—"a colorful way of asking for some pussy—at the outset of a conversation that, hopefully, will lead to a sexual relationship."[83]

Abrahams put the rap session in a context that explains, in essence, why rapping can cause problems for unknowing blacks and whites. Referring to talking style, he said,

> One can observe the same aesthetic operating in woofing or rapping sessions, especially as they get heavier and involve attempts to *score* or *cap*. Here, too, we find the constant emphasis placed on a voice overlap that stands for individuality and peer-group community at the same time. Here, too, the instigating performer tries to heat up the scene while proclaiming his own cool. And the interaction is structured in a way that encourages anyone present to lend a voice individually and in encouragement.
>
> A number of features of Black talk contribute to an artful or stylized effect because they call attention to the conversation as a performance, rather than focusing on information-passing. Black talk more commonly emphasizes personal word power and verbal contests as entertainment.
>
> All forms of *rapping* are considered by the talkers to be artful, for stories illustrative of good *raps* of all three types are often told, and in such a way that one focuses on the style of the *rap* (its artifice) and the way in which it has put the talker into a position of control. It is this element of control, of the power of words and well used, and of the status one can achieve through good talking, that is perhaps the most difficult aspect of Black oral culture for Euro-Americans to fathom.[84]

Furthermore, according to Smitherman:

> Since it is a socially approved verbal strategy for black rappers to talk about how bad they is, such bragging is taken at face value. While the speakers may or may not act out the implications of their words, the point is that the listeners do not necessarily *expect* any action to follow. As a matter of fact, skillful rappers can often avoid having to prove themselves through deeds if their rap is strong enough. The Black Idiom expression 'selling woof [wolf] tickets' (also just plain 'woofin') refers to any kind of strong language which is purely idle boasting. However, the bad talk is nearly always taken for the real thing by an outsider from another culture. Such cultural-linguistic misperceptions can lead to tragic consequences. Witness, for instance, the physical attacks and social repression suffered by black spokesmen of the 1960s, such as the Black Panthers. . . . [T]he white folks thought the bloods was not playin and launched an all-out military campaign. These aggressive moves resulted partly from White America's sense of fear that the radical rhetoric (much of which was really defensive, rather than offensive) constituted more than idle threats. The whites were not hip to braggadocio and woof tickets; at any rate, they wasn't buyin none.[85]

The piece that Abrahams does not mention that is also part of this is the non-middle class loud talking and physicalness of rapping or talkin' shit sessions. When these are put together in a school hall situation of a few black adolescents walking together, gesturing, maybe pushing and shoving one another and talking boisterously, the educators, unused to this type of physical-verbal behavior, usually become very uncomfortable and, in the extreme, very fearful. Very often, this leads to teacher-student confrontation and suspension.

Such loud talking is inappropriate for school classrooms and hallways. However, if teachers are not fearful and understand what rapping or talkin' shit is all about, they usually can get the rappers to cool it with an appropriate request. Such a request should be considered a sound professional move. Incidently, I have observed middle-class blacks and whites very fearful of very loud talking, moving, and jostling rappers in public areas, not just in schools.

Another aspect of rapping that causes problems and was mentioned briefly above, is the male rap as it relates to woman and sex. This too has caused problems for women teachers, and now, interestingly, with sexually insecure male teachers.

In addition to what Kochman noted above, the rap is a facilitating device, a street culture mechanism, "which makes a woman approachable to every black man." Furthermore, even if the black male is not serious in pursuing the relationship, "He will 'rap' to sharpen his line, his wit, or as one informant remarked, to 'deposit his image.' "[86]

Edith Folb, a white woman, writing about her field work, described her encounters with black males:

> Not a verbally shy person myself, . . . I honed my own set of verbal strategies to counter the male rap—and to deposit my own image as someone who was interested in taking care of a different kind of business. Mutual verbal play and put-down marked a number of my conversations with young black males. Mostly I experienced it as a natural part of the male-female encounter and felt that it allowed for simultaneous observations and participation in a wide variety of cross-gender speech acts.[87]

According to Abrahams, a woman is in jeopardy of having to deal with or put up with men and their jive when she places herself in a public situation. What is serious communication in the church or home becomes "a playful one in the more open context of porch and road and country store. If a woman's sense of respectability is challenged in such a situation, she may fight fire with fire, becoming as verbally open and aggressive as her contenders, resorting to a very tendentious sort of *smart talking.*"[88]

Unquestionably, the school or classroom is really not to be considered on par with a porch, road, or country store. However, the school's hallway is a much more open and public area than the classroom, and streetcorner teenagers may see it as equivalent to a streetcorner, where any woman is fair game for a rap.[89]

Smitherman wrote that love rappin, as part of the oral tradition, allows for a strange black woman to be approached by a strange black man without any fear of strong condemnation.

> Black women are accustomed to—and many even expect—this kind of verbal aggressiveness from black men. Black culture thus provides a socially ap-

proved verbal mechanism with which the man can initiate conversation aimed at deepening the acquaintance. Rappin also accounts for what whites often label as "aggressive," "brash," "presumptive," or "disrespectful" behavior by black men toward black women.[90]

Many black rappers "specialize in the verbal art of romantic rappin" and use love raps for "getin ovauh with woman."[91]

Although a black male adolescent's putting a love rap on a teacher is really inappropriate behavior, because of a number of recent historical events, he may be more willing to take the chance. For example, (1) in movies and in real life, more older women are having affairs with or marrying younger men; (2) there is less stigma attached to white women being seen with, dating, having affairs with, and marrying black men; and (3) women in general are living much more open lifestyles.

However, many black male adolescents and middle class women teachers have paid a price for the clash between love rappin' and middle class sexual teasing. Each, inexperienced with the other's culture, reacts as their culture has taught them to react. The result of such a cultural clash is often a suspended student and frightened, disheartened, and disgusted woman teacher.

Accepting that heavy rapping or love rapping to a woman teacher is inappropriate, because the teacher is the professional, women teachers must figure out how to understand what is going on and how to deal positively with the behavior. Hence, if the educator understands what rapping is all about, it should not be such a conflict-producing and disruptive influence. However, if youngsters using this behavior continue to be suspended or placed in special education classes, it may be that educators are reacting inappropriately to rapping.

THE DOZENS

From personal observations, playing the dozens in schools probably causes more school fights and disruptions than does any other activity. David Cohen, reporting what appears to be lower class Negro behavior, described the dozens as a prolific source of stabbings and shootings.[92] Donald Clemmer wrote that in prison, playing the dozens "has caused more fights among prisoners than any other cause."[93] The dozens is also evident everywhere in black literature.

The dozens and playing the dozens has also been referred to as, among many other names, sounding, signifying, crackin' or gettin' on the kitchen folks, going in the kitchen, getting down on the crib, ribbin', playing, mamma talk, soundin' on the moms, getting on moms, joaning, putting a man on the wheel, and giving a man the spoke.[94] However, most school youngsters probably refer to the game as "talkin' about moms."

My first experience in being put in the dozens is described in Reality 67. The experience was educational and enlightening since neither my religious nor cul-

tural background had either exposed or prepared me for the game.[95] Consequently, my initial reaction to a student putting me in the dozens disgusted my
students. My response, or more accurately, my lack of response, went against
every concept they had of how a man should react when he is put in the dozens.

I had observed students playing the dozens with one another for a long time,
although I did not understand its ritualistic and cultural ramifications. One of
the first times I tried breaking up a bout of the dozens between two boys, it happened that they had the same mother but different fathers. No matter what they
said or how they tried to explain their actions to me, I could not understand
their talking about their mother the way they did.

William Grier and Price Cobbs similarly raised the question of what white
members of the armed forces must have experienced during World War II when
they were exposed to the dozens for the first time. "It is a pity that the reactions of the young white soldiers when first exposed to the dozens were not
recorded, for surely that must have been the purest example of 'cultural
shock.' "[96]

Again, this reinforces the point that what is important is how your students
feel you should react to an incident, and how you feel you should react. *Most
often, streetcorner youngsters respect the teacher who can best them at their
games without losing dignity and without coming down too hard on them.*

REALITY 67

I was in my room with about ten high school students when two of them began
verbally abusing one another. As they became louder, I told them to cut it out.
Instead of stopping, the fellow who was being bested began to direct his feelings
toward me.

"I fucked your mamma last night Mr. Foster," he said.

"Oh, cut the crap out," I said.

Since they left one another alone, I tried getting everyone back to work,
thinking everything was straightened out; but not in my students' opinions.
They seemed to be taken aback and could not quite understand my lack of concern and anger over what had been said about my mother. They came at me
verbally.

"You afraid of him?"

"Shit, hit him man!"

"Go upside his knot."

"Why you let him say that about you moms?—shit."

And so on.

Slowly, I realized that I was doing something wrong; I had better do something right and fast. I was not, somehow, following an unwritten code of action
and honor that they were privy to. Then, luckily, I began to catch on.

"Why should I be mad? I said, "He can't be talkin' about my mother 'cause I know my mother. At least I know who my mother is."

As I said these last words, I looked at the youngster who had put me in the dozens and started chuckling. The other students laughingly pointed at him.

"He ranked you out," one of them said laughingly.

Still another said, "Oh, sound."

While two others gave one another some skin.

He sulked off to his seat, and we got back to work. I knew I had done something right when one of the students put his hand out for some dap and returned it after I had given him some skin.

The dozens has been described as a ritualized game or survival technique used to: (1) express aggressive feelings, (2) develop verbal skills, (3) cut a boy free from matriarchal control or (4) teach youths how to control their feelings and tempers. There is also evidence of a clean and a dirty dozens.

Although there are usually two participants in the dozens, at times more play or participate. Often, the participants also play to the audience. Although the dozens is usually played by boys, girls also play. Actually, "some of the best Dozens players [are] girls."[97]

Sometimes, the dozens may be a game of amusement where two or more exchange obscene references and rhymes to see who can creatively best the other. They may be alone or have a large audience. At other times, the dozens may become vicious, with someone being beaten, stabbed, shot, or killed as a result of what is said.

The dozens sometimes takes the form of rhymed couplets; at other times, insults, taunts, and curses are circumventive or to the point. These usually consist of references to alleged adulterous or incestuous activities of the opponent's mother, grandmothers, daughters, sisters, wife, or other female relatives. At other times, statements are made concerning the cowardice, homosexuality, stupidity, or inferiority of the participants and their families. Sometimes, a bystander may be brought into the game by one of the participants; usually by the one who is being bested.

The three lengthiest investigations of the dozens are by John Dollard, R. Berdie, and Roger Abrahams.[98] In Dollard's study entitled "The Dozens: Dialect of Insult," he reported on the dozens in a number of southern and northern large and small cities where his informants included adolescent and adult groups which crossed social class lines. He reported that the dozens appears to be played very widely among Negro Americans and exists in all social classes within the "Negro caste."

The dozens follows a "pattern of interactive insult," and is guided by rules that are well recognized and which govern and permit emotional expression. He found the dozens played by boys and girls, adolescents, and adults. The forbidden notions of the dozens are often expressed by adolescents through rhymes. For some, the only purpose of the game appears to be to amuse onlookers and participants. While the game may be described as an aspect of aggressive play, at other times fighting displaces the game aspect. The group's response to the sallies and rhymes of the players is crucial; "with group response comes the possibility or reward for effective slanders and feelings of shame and humiliation if one is bested."[99]

The joking appears to take as its theme those aspects that our social order condemn the most in other contexts. Accusations are made about the opponent's committing incest with his sister or mother, passive homosexuality is inferred, cowardice is suggested, taboos related to cleanliness are said to have been broken, and personal defects such as inferiority, stupidity, or crossed eyes are played upon. The mentioning of dead relations, however, appears to be taboo.[100]

In his southern big-city study, Dollard found that lower class youngsters most commonly used sex themes. Very often, the dozens was used to exploit a youngster's weak point, such as a father in jail or a sister with an illegitimate child. Often, a fight was the only recourse to a noneffective comeback.

Dollard found southern big-city middle-class adolescents playing basically the same type of dozens as did big-city lower class boys. Though middle class boys had a "slight tendency" to supress vulgar expressions, class status dozens such as "Your mammy is a nigger" had a particularly stinging effect.[101] In some cases, it appeared as though the players would quiet down but for the ridicule of the observers. Additionally, when an out-group member pursued the dozens with an in-group person, a fight usually ensued. In some cases, he found that the dozens was played by middle class boys to break the monotony of a dull party.

Dollard noted that southern big-city lower class adults depended "on directly improvised insults and curses, and seem to be altogether more crude and direct in the expressions."[102] Their jives appeared to be related to homosexual practices and the promiscuity of a protagonist's mother or sister.

In a small southern city, he found the dozens characterized primarily by obscene references and rhymes. The upper and middle class adolescents appeared to play the dozens for amusement and considered fighting over them as foolish. However, lower class verbal dozens bouts usually ended in fights.

In a northern big-city, Dollard found the middle and upper class boys played by using items related to cowardice, stupidity, and various types of inferiority. Often, the offended person expressed a sense of loss of "personal honor," which was perceived as insult resulting in fist fights and broken friendships. The lower class boys more often used sexual themes for the dozens.

Berdie, while working with black and white prisoners in a Navy Disciplinary Barracks, asked over 100 whites and 100 Negroes whether they had ever heard of playing the dozens or knew its meaning. None of the whites expressed any knowledge of the dozens while more than 90 percent of the blacks had heard of the term and could give some inkling of its meaning. The only whites who had some knowledge of the term were mental health professionals working with blacks.[103]

Berdie described the dozens as a "formalized expression of aggression,"[104] where one or more persons attempts to arouse another to the point where he will initiate fighting. The dozens is played by combatants exchanging insults to the approval and encouragement of observers. The exchange becomes "progressively nastier and more pornographic, until they eventually include every member of the participants' families and every act of animal and man."[105]

One of the participants, most often the subject, usually reaches his saturation point and goes after this tormentor using fists, a knife, or an improvised weapon. When this happens, the tormentor, sometimes joined by the observers, often physically injures the subject.

In addition to the one-on-one dozens, Berdie reported the game being played as a sort of round robin with insults passed around from person to person, each trying to insult all the others. A small riot is the usual end to this game. He further reports the dozens played with "rhymes and limericks," that had almost "traditional respectability," while some were improvised during the encounter.

Sometimes the dozens was played as entertainment to relieve boredom. The group appeared to give social approval to the initiator of the game if he could manipulate the subject into losing his composure. "The individual who strikes the first physical blow carries the stigma, the first person struck has the glory of defending his honor. The tormentor, who bears the responsibility for the conflict, is thus saved the disgrace of starting the fight, and the subject is responsible in the eyes of his mates because of his inability to 'take it'."[106]

According to Abrahams, the substance and form of lore reflects the special problems and values of a group and those within it. Hence, studying the dozens provides insight into the "cultural imperatives" of the lower class black. Abrahams reported on his two years of research with blacks in a South Philadelphia neighborhood and additional observations in Texas. He suggested that the dozens is an institutionalized mechanism lower class black youngsters use in searching for masculine identity. The dozens represents the point in his life where "he casts off a woman's world for a man's and begins to develop the tools by which he is to implement his new found position, as a member of a gang existence."[107]

The dozens functions as a verbal game, training lower class black youths for their changing world and the verbal needs of adulthood. Indeed, the dozens is a verbal contest that plays a significant role in the psychological and linguistic development of the players. When boys play the dozens, according to Abrahams, the protagonist verbally insults someone from another's family, and those observing and waiting for the vilifications goad the combatants on. The insulted youngster must then reply in kind concerning a member of the protagonist's family. The reply must be clever enough to defend his honor and hence his family. Throughout this bantering, the onlookers continue goading the two. At this point in the dozens, Abrahams reported boredom or some other subject or interest usually takes over. He reported that fighting is "fairly rare."

When dozens players are just entering puberty, the emphasis is on reversing the roles of the mother and the father in the rhymes.

"I hear your mother plays third base for the Phillies."

"Your mother is a bricklayer, and stronger than your father."[108]

As youngsters grow and become more sexually aware, the puns, rhymes, and vilifications of the mother begin to take on sexual meanings; the contests become more heated. Abrahams provided an example of two fourteen- and fifteen-year-old boys playing the dozens:[109]

In a joking conversation, someone mentions the name of the boy's mother. Someone in the group replies with "Yeah, Constance was real good to me last Thursday."

Constance's son must then respond. " 'I hear Virginia (the other's mother) lost her titty in a poker game.' "

The other youngster may then respond with " 'Least my mother ain't no cake; everybody get a piece.' "

The other youngster has to do better and may come back with,

"I hate to talk about your mother,
She's a good old soul.
She's got a ten-ton p---y
And a rubber a--h--e.
She got hair on her p---y
That sweep the floor.
She got knobs on her titties
That open the door."[110]

The retorts continue as each tries to outdo the other. As boys grow, their verbal dexterity expands to where innuendo and subtlety replace the obvious rhymes and puns.

Abraham's research indicated that playing the dozens appears to wane as an institution between the ages of sixteen and twenty-six. However, the game lingers and is not forgotten. He also pointed out that when the dozens is played under "very tense and restrictive conditions of regimentation for which the young Negro is not completely suited," it usually leads to a fight.[111] Additionally, when the dozens is played by adult males in a poolroom or bar, "it usually ends in battle."[112]

He also reported that signals are provided in the dozens by pitch and stress of voice and sometimes syntax. The language used when "playing is different from the contestants' everyday language. Abrahams also reported that the insults used by young adolescents in particular are directed against or toward certain things and these are rather rigidly constructed. Adult male players, on the other hand, only fleetingly refer to the family and not usually against any specific aspect of life. However, most often all playing concerns sexual matters.

Abrahams also reported a "clean dozens" and a "dirty dozens." He found that in the clean dozens, the insults are mostly personal with only some directed at mothers. In the dirty dozens, the slur is almost always about the other's mother, and these usually take the form of "illicit sexual activity, usually with the speaker."[113]

David Schulz, over a three-and-one-half-year period, studied 108 persons from ten families who at one time lived in large public housing projects. He reported the "custom of 'playing the dozens,'" as part of the masculine struggle against female domination.[114] His subjects reported the dozens as a predominantly male game also played by some girls. Whereas boys usually begin to play at about age eleven, girls begin to play at about age eleven and one-half. The dozens also functions as a sexual "primer," acquainting children with details of sexuality before they are usually aware of them.

Grier and Cobbs pointed out the psychological aspects of the dozens as a puberty ritual leading to manhood and "a way traveled by all black boys." The ritual of the dozens requires black boys to put aside a mother's special sanctification. The natural inclination to defend a mother's honor must be suppressed as young black males move to their world of men where love of mother "is perverted in the medium of wit." Black males know that while freeing themselves through the dozens they also betray their mothers.[115]

According to Smitherman, today, as black living has become even more urbane, the dozens have become more sophisticated and played with fewer of the "original programmatic responses."[116] Smitherman also provides the neophyte players and unknowing educators some sound advice:

> Since the Dozens can be a potentially explosive game, it would be well to pay attention to its fundamental rule: "insult" hurled must not represent an accurate statement of reality, or a battle—a shonuff one—will ensue. (Since the speakers are "playing" the Dozens, even in the original sexually "insulting" versions, nobody has actually had intercourse with anybody else's mother.)[117]

In addition to the above, there is other reporting of the dozens.[118]

The Dozens in Literature

In 1969, a play *The Dozens* opened at the Booth Theater in New York City. The play did not last long, and Leonard Harris, WCBS-TV arts editor, signified the play on the Eleven O'clock Report by saying, "But *The Dozens*, as played at the Booth, turns out to be a dull and pointless game."[119] Richard Watts, Jr., in reviewing *The Dozens* for the *New York Post*, wrote that "the meaning of the play's title is rather unclear to me, although I gather it has something to do with a game of insults played in Harlem."[120]

When Clive Barnes reviewed J.E. Franklin's *Black Girl*, he wrote,

There is a game in the ghetto called "The Dozens" where people pile insult upon insult on one another, not only with good humor, but also with a purely esthetic appreciation for the insults thus piled. It seems to me that an understanding of this is essential to the white understanding of black dramatic writing. There is both an exaggeration and also a wryness that flavors the black playwright.[121]

To name but two movies, the dozens was acted-out in *M*A*S*H* during the football game. It was almost played in *Cotton Comes to Harlem*. In one scene, two New York City policemen are sitting in a car when one of them, Raymond St. Jacques, starts the dozens only to be stopped by Godfrey Cambridge's response "I don't play that game." At times the dozens in a mild form can also be observed being played on TV's "Sanford and Son."[122]

Gordon Parks and Claude Brown, in their autobiographies, wrote about the pressure of maintaining your manhood by having to fight when put in the dozens. Parks described his run-in with the dozens in a Civilian Conservation Corps (CCC) camp: "Tate became enraged and called me a dirty son-of-a-bitch when I beat him in a checkers game. I ignored him at first but then he 'put me in the dozens,' or, to put it simply, he cursed me in the name of my mother. For this, unless you were a coward, you fought."[123]

Brown recounted how he forced someone to fight him by putting him in the dozens: "We wouldn't have had that fight if I hadn't said something about his mother. He had to fight after that, because a guy who won't fight when somebody talks about his mother is the worst kind of punk."[124]

Hurston in early "Harlemese" jive, described two down cats playing the dozens in a style that is rarely used today. Additionally, the cats can be observed trying to outdo one another as they proceed from banter to almost fighting and then back to giving some skin.

"Sweet Back, you fixing to talk out of place."
Jelly stiffened.
"If you trying to jump salty, Jelly, that's your mammy."
"Don't play in de family, Sweet Back. I don't play de dozens. I don told you."
"Who playing de dozens? You trying to get you hips up on your shoulders 'cause I said you was with a beat broad. One of them lam blacks."
"Who? Me? Long as you been knowing me, Sweet Back, you ain't never seen me with nothing but pe-olas. I can get any frail eel I wants to. . . . I recon I'll have to make you hep. I had to leave from down south 'cause Miss Anne used to worry me so bad to go with me. . . . Man, I don't deal in no coal. . . . If they's white, they's right! If they's yellow, they's mellow! If they's brown, they can stick around. But if they come black, they better git way back!" . . .

"Aw, man, you trying to show your grandma how to milk ducks. Best you can do is to confidence some kitchen-mechanic out of a dime or two. Me, I knocks de pad with them cack-broads up on Sugar Hill, and fills 'em full of melody. Man, I'm, quick death and easy judgment. Youse just a home-byoy, Jelly, don't try to follow me."

"Me follow *you*! Man, I come on like the Gang Busters, and go off like the March of Time! If dat ain't so, God is gone to Jersey City and you know He wouldn't be messing 'round a place like that." . . .

"Jelly, de wind may blow and de door may slam; dat what you shooting ain't worth a damn!"

Jelly slammed his hand in his bosom as if to draw a gun. Sweet Back did the same.

"If you wants to fight, Sweet Back, the favor is in me."

"I was deep-thinking, then Jelly. It's a good thing I ain't short-tempered. 'T'aint nothing to you, no how. You ain't hit me yet."

Both burst into a laugh and changed from fighting to lounging poses.

"Don't get to yaller on me, Jelly, you liable to get hurt some day."

"You over-sports your hand your ownself. Too blamed astorperious. I just don't pay you no mind. Lay de skin on me!"[125]

Playing the dozens is almost a reflex action for blacks. In Nathan Heard's *Howard Street* a drunk reacts to what he has overheard as a challenge to him via the dozens.

The bum lying on the floor woke up again. "Whatcha say, kid?"

Jimmy realized that he'd spoken aloud, but he repeated it automatically to the wino. "I said, 'How the hell was we to know it was his mother?'" But he'd said it softly, almost to himself.

"Whatcha talkin' about, kid. You talkin' about my dead mother? I don't play the dozens, kid. Don't talk about my mother. I'll kill ya right now."[126]

The dozens has also appeared in books written by whites. Bernard Malamud in *The Tenants* wrote about the conflict between a Jewish and a black author. Lesser, the Jewish author, is sleeping with a black woman while Bill (the black author) is having an affair with Lesser's white girl friend. Lesser attends a party of mostly blacks and is put in the dozens. However, he does not appear to understand the game and only half-heartedly plays.

One of the blacks at the party taps his finger against Lesser's chest and tells him, "We have a game we got we call the dozens. Like the brothers play it no ofay has that gift or that wit, and since whitey ain't worth but half a black I'm gon play·you the half-dozens." Lesser is informed that the dozens is a game of "naked words, . . . and the one who bleeds, or flips, or cries mama, he's the loser." As the game gets underway, Lesser is told that if he is going to fuck black he has to face blacks. Bill informs Lesser that he is not going to be too hard on him to start with; he will not "work on your mama and sister, which is the way we do it, but come right to the tough-shit funk of it. . . . " Lesser is told to do better than Bill on that one but stands mute. Finally he comes back with a good one and the blacks laugh. They appreciated a good comeback, regardless of the author. The game ends as Bill comes down heavy on Lesser, and Lesser throws in the towel. The observers also get bored by Lesser's poor showing. The next day, Bill tries to explain to Lesser that his use of the dozens as a form of verbal aggression saved him from physical aggression. "Sam wanted the brothers to beat up on you and crack your nuts for putting the meat to his bitch, but I got you in the game so they could see you get your shame that way and not want your real red blood." [127]

A number of reports, books, and articles evolved from the Watts riot. Only one, Robert Conot's *River of Blood, Years of Darkness*, appears to report accurately on the verbal discourse of the combatants. Conot described some blacks coming down hard with the dozens on a white police officer.

> Few women ever go into the park, and it was strictly a masculine crowd that formed a semicircle around the car.
> "Hey man," a youth called to the white officer. "I saw your mother the other day!" The crowd laughed, knowing what was coming. "She come down here wanting to know what a real man could do, and I give her the best fuck she ever had."
> "That's right, man," another called out, grinning. "She even give me a blow job for six bits." [128]

Another white author, Joseph Wambaugh, also reported on the dozens in his book *The New Centurions*.

> "Shut your mouth," said Serge.
> "*Chinga tu madre!*" said the boy.
> "I should have killed you."
> "*Tu madre!*" . . .
> "*Tu madre*," the boy repeated, and the fury crept over Serge again. It wasn't the same in Spanish, he thought. It was so much filthier, almost unbearable, that this gutter animal would dare to mention her like that. . . .
> "You don't like that, do you, gringo?" said the boy, baring his white teeth in the darkness. "You understand some Spanish, huh? You don't like me talking about your moth. . . . " [129]

Tom Wicker, in his book *A Time To Die* about the Attica riots, reminisced about the summer of 1946, when, at age twenty, he was being discharged from the U.S. Navy. To receive his discharge, he had to travel for about ten days from Seattle, Washington to Little Creek, Virginia by troop train. Although, in those days, the armed forces were still segregated, in his car were twenty-seven blacks and two other white servicemen. As luck would have it, he was appointed to be master-at-arms for the car. The black servicemen soon challenged his ability to lead, which was not unlike a teacher-student power struggle.

"You're master-at-arms for this car. Anything goes wrong, your fuckin' ass belongs to me. Muster every morning, post details, and send up a fuckin' mess cook every third day. You got sense enough to understand that?"

"I got it," Wicker said unhappily.

. . . The door had hardly closed behind him when a tall black sailor leaned against a tier of bunks at the other end of the car called out.

"Hey you, Red!"

Silence fell on the car like soot from a steam engine.

"Yeah," Wicker said.

"Suck my black dick."

Half the blacks laughed, a little uncertainly. Most of the others and the two other whites pretended not to notice. One or two blacks eyed Wicker stonily. He could not tell if he was being teased or challenged by the tall black, but as he stood with the other whites by the tier of bunks, . . . he was astonished by the outburst—astonished in the perennial Southern manner that the tall black thought there was any reason to be hostile, even more astonished that a black man would dare to speak so to a white. He was not so liberated from his Southern background as he had thought, and he perceived that he would have to deal with this other youth as a Southern white man would deal with a colored person, whether nigger, nigruh, or Negro, and back it up; or else he would have to deal with him as one human with another, and live with the consequences. . . .

He did not *think* at all about his response. Out of something stronger than mind, some instinct deeper than the Southern experience, from the core of what D.D. and Esta Wicker had made of him—by their lives and decency as much as by their overt shaping of his character—he set the face of his life away from the South.

"Why, your buddy there told me you didn't even have one." A fragment of an old joke had flickered in his memory. "Said a hog bit it off."

"Shee-it." The tall black sailor grinned. The other blacks laughed, all of them this time, some obviously in relief, some in derision of the tall boy as he thought up his reply. "You git home, man, you ask your girl friend, see if I ain't broke it off in her pussy." The blacks howled with laughter.

"After mine." Wicker said, hoping for the best. "I reckon she wouldn't even *feel* that little old biddy toothpick of yours."

There was more laughter and backslapping, and even the other white boys grinned, rather painfully.

"Hey, Red," another black called, amiably. "You the head man, when we gone chow down?"

Just then the train lurched off; there was a rush to the windows and doors, breaking up the exchange. One of the white boys lingered with Wicker.

"Ought to have bust his black ass," he said.

"We got to live on this thing," Wicker nodded at the crowded car. "A week, two weeks. We don't need fights and hard feelings."

"All the same, you got to . . . "

Wicker knew what was about to be said and broke in:

"We got to live with 'em, that's what we got to do." He walked away, deciding he would give the white sailor the first latrine detail, just on general principles and to balance the ticket a little. Maybe that would keep him in *his* place. Boldly, he pushed the tall black sailor in the ribs. "Hey, Big Shot, where you from."[130]

What is important about the above exchange is that Wicker assumed his leadership through an approach that was related to that time and situation. However, one of the white sailors felt that the black sailor, who started the exchange, still ought to be taught a lesson. Similarly, too often there are some educators less interested in just getting order and teaching than they are in forcing their students to "show" them respect.

Robert A. Heinlein's *Glory Road* revealed an interesting form of the dirty dozens.

We walked over and joined Rufo. He was making donkey's ears at Igli and shouting, "Who's your father, Igli? Your mother was a garbage can but *who's your father?* Look at him! No belly button! Yaaa!"

Igli retorted, "*Your* mother barks! Your sister gives green stamps!"—but rather feebly, I thought. It was plain that that remark about belly buttons had cut him to the quick—he didn't have one. Only reasonable, I suppose.

The above is not quite what either of them said, except the remark about the belly button. I wish I could put it in the original because, in the Nevian language, the insult is a high art at least equal to poetry. In fact, the epitome of literary grace is to address your enemy (publically) in some difficult verse form, say the sestina, with every word dripping vitriol.[131]

Alston Anderson in *Lover Man*, Ed Bullins in *The Reluctant Rapist*, Ralph Ellison in *The Invisible Man*, LeRoi Jones in his play *The Toilet*, Louise Meriwether in *Daddy Was a Number Runner*, Richard Wright in *Lawd Today*, and John A. Williams in *The Man Who Cried I Am*, to name a few, all have some of their characters playing the dozens.[132]

Bullins wrote about Jess and Chuck walking to Jess's home. They walked together and Jess "lied and laughed with Chuck, finding out what he could about Chuck so he could use it later for some put-down or the dozens game."[133]

Ellison's use of the dozens would probably get by all but those who are familiar with its usage: "From your ma-" I started and caught myself in time. "From the committee," I said.[134] Earlier in his book, however, he actually mentions the dozens: "I looked at him, feeling a quick dislike and thinking, half in amusement, I don't play the dozens. And how's *your* old lady today."[135]

The Toilet by Jones vividly portrays the language and raw life of the street-corner played out in a high school boy's toilet. The dozens is played often in the play. Ora talks about "your momma's house," and Love responds with "At least I got one." Ora's retort to the accusation that he gets his kicks out of rubbing up against half dead white boys is, "I'd rub up against your momma too." To which Love responds with, "Ora, you mad cause you don't have a momma of you own to rub up against." Ora comes back with "Fuck you, you boney head sonofabitch. As long as I can rub against your momma . . . or your fatha' . . . I'm doin' alright."[136]

Meriwether wrote that "I had to curse some though to stay friends with Suki, but I didn't play the dozens, that mother stuff. . . . "[137] John Williams, in addition to using jive lexicon in his novels, has his characters play the dozens too.

> *"Your mamma's a nigger."*
> *"Oops! The dozens, is it? I made you salty, eh? Now you slip me in the dozens, just like that? I told you, you was a nigger."*
> *"Your mother's a nigger."*
> *"Hee, Hee, well, your mother don't wear no drawers. How could she, when she was giving birth to you—my son. Ha! So you know your mother don't wear no drawers. How's that? Youse a motherfuckin' mutherfucker, Oedipus Rex! Thas how come you knows so much."*
> *"I know so much because I'm you daddy."*[138]

Wright also used jive lexicon in his stories. In *Lawd Today*, for example, his characters went from ribbing to signifying and ended up playing the dozens—all for recreation. The bout is conceived when Jake noticed and became annoyed with Al's new shirt and smug composure. Jake wanted to shake Al's composure and take it for himself. He started his agitating by asking Al where he stole his shirt. Wright then goes beyond just putting words into his characters' mouths. He also keeps the reader informed as to what is transpiring. He writes that Bob and Slim, who were listening silently, hoped that Al and Jake would get into the dozens. Wright then had Jake explain what Al was doing by having Jake tell Al to cut out his signifying. Finally, Al and Jake get into the dozens. Jake escalates the signifying to the dozens by telling Al "Colonel James was sucking on your ma's tits."

> Al came back slowly, to make sure that none of his words would be missed. " . . . when . . . Colonel James was sucking at ma's tits . . . your . . . baby brother . . . [was] . . . watching with slobber in his mouth. . . . "
> As a comeback, Jake looked out of the window rather nonchalantly, crossed his legs, and responded with, " . . . grandma was . . . in the privy crying 'cause she couldn't find the corncob. . . . "
> Al, not to be outdone, narrowed his eyes and retaliated with, " 'When . . . grandma was crying for the corncob, your . . . aunt Lucy was . . . back of the barn with . . . Colonel James' old man, . . . she was saying . . . : Yyyyou kknow . . . Mmmister Cccolonel . . . I jjjust ddin't llike to sssell . . . my ssstuff . . . I jjjust lloves to gggive . . . iit away. . . . ' "[139]

The point made earlier about how the contestants are also playing to their audience, is also shown by Wright. Throughout the contest, Slim's and Bob's reactions as onlookers are reported. They held their stomachs while rolling on the sofa; stomped their feet as they groaned; howled and screamed holding one another; and they beat their fists on the floor.

Finally, Al gave Jake the crusher: "When my greatgreatgreatgreat grandma who was a Zulu queen got through eating . . . chitterlings, she wanted to build a sewer-ditch to take away her crap, so she went out and saw your . . . greatgreatgreatgreat*great* grandma sleeping . . . with her old mouth open. She didn't need to build no sewerditch. . . . "

Jake tried hard to think of a return. No matter how he bit his lips or screwed up his eyes, he could not think of a return. His mind was a complete blank. Al's latest image was too much for him. "Then they all laughed so that they felt weak in the joints of their bones."[140]

In Anderson's second chapter entitled "The Dozens," James's friend Mutton Head dies and James feels it's because Mutton Head played the dozens. "Since that day I don't play the dozens no more, and whenever I hear anybody playing them I leave the room."[141]

The dozens can also be found in poetry by blacks. Harrison's Hamm tried to hip Adam by putting him in the dozens.

Hamm: . . . In the jungle your only duty is to survive, man. Ask your mama bout that.
Adam: Don't be talkin 'bout my mama.
Hamm (derisively): I wouldn't talk 'bout your mama. Wouldn't let anybody else talk 'bout your mama. Your mama is all right with me Adam. In fact, she'll be my horse if she never wins a race.
Adam: I don't play that shit, Hamm."[142]

Another example of the dozens can be found in the works of John O. Killens.

"Go on Mother," Bad Mouth said, good-naturedly. "Go sell your papers on another corner." . . .
"I ain't your mother," the old lady repeated, shouting even louder this time. "If your mother hadda brung you up right, I wouldn't have to be putting your backside down this late in life." . . .
"Grandma putting old Bad Mouth in the natural dozens—damn!"
"Blow, grandma! Blow, baby!"
"Old Bad Mouth do not play the two-time sixes!"[143]

Oliver wrote about Speckled Red spending twenty years playing the southern levee camps and the sawmills "leaving everywhere the memory of his riotous, obscene barrel house version of the Dirty Dozens." Eventually, Speckled Red was one of a number who cut records of the dirty dozens.[144]

In the first act of Melvin Van Peebles's Broadway play, *Aint Supposed to Die a Natural Death*, there is a song entitled "The Dozens."[145] On George Carlin's record *Occupation: Foole* there is a cut "White Harlem" where he talks about playing the dozens.[146] Prelude Records released a rapping record *Ya Mama—Wuff Ticket*.[147]

The Dozens is also a fictional movie account of Sally, a young white woman's efforts to make a successful transition from prison to life on the "outside." In his review in the *Boston Globe*, Jeff McLaughlin found the dialogue superb throughout and capturing the poetic vernacular of the streets without any gratuitous vulgarity or condescension. He said that "Sally is expert at 'The dozens,' a traditional street game of improvised, rhyming insults that is 'won' by the player with the toughest hide and quickest wits, and when she does win parole, her language (some in voice-over commentary) remains a delight."[148]

When "Chico and the Man" was one of the highest rated TV situation comedies, an article described costar Freddie Prinze as follows: "With his impish little-boy eyes, infectious smile and street swagger, [Chico] is a character Prinze began creating years ago, when he would crack up the local kids with the old 'you-know-what-your-mother-is?' jokes."[149] After Prinze's death, a *New York Times* article reported that he excelled at a game called "snap."

> "You'd say something like, 'Your mother's so old she eats rust.' " Mr. Solar explained. "And he'd snap, 'Your mother's so old she wears Confederate underwear,' or 'Your house is so hot the roaches carry canteens.' Whoever got the most laughs won, and Freddie could snap anyone down. One time he snapped a kid so good the kid started crying and beat him up."[150]

A Bamboozled in Bend, Oregon wrote asking Dear Abby what to do when a customer calls on the phone and cusses you out using "four-letter-words," without giving you a chance to explain and refuses to give you his name? Dear Abby responded: "DEAR BAM: Say, 'Sir if you can't give me your father's name, please give me your mother's.' I'll bet he hangs up in a hurry."[151]

In Buffalo, New York, a stray bullet from a sniper's gun killed a seventy-five-year-old man as he watched television. According to Police Chief Donovan, the two youths involved in the killing, "were out to repay," another youth "for derogatory remarks they said he made against" one of their sisters.[152]

History of the Dozens

There does not appear to be any definitive work substantiating the origins of the dozens. There does, however, appear to be some evidence that similar forms, styles, or behaviors of the dozens have been developed independently in this country and around the world by many groups. Berdie suggested that the behavior involved in the dozens in the United States, or other versions, is characteristic of many groups. However, only one group appears to have labeled the game.[153]

Joking relationships and insult contests have been reported among the Manus and the Tikopia, in the songs of the Aleutians, in the "drum fights" of the Greenland Eskimos, and in many groups throughout Africa and Europe.[154]

The cultures of ancient Rome, Greece, Germany, as well as Colombian and Arabic tribes have reported similar outlets for frustration. The *munafra* was the Arabic version of the dozens. The Norse *jul feast* includes a "comparing of men." In the contest between Thor and Odin, celebrated as part of the Edda song, the *harbardslojad*, there are variations where a form of the dozens is played by two gods or royal kings.[155]

There is also reporting of African origins for the American dozens. William Schechter reported verbal contests common among Ashanti natives, who sang *opo* verses.[156] According to Thomas Johnson, the calypso has origins in the West African insult songs and to the *mamaguy* of Trinidad, which is a game "quite similar to the 'dozens' of black America."[157] Ram Desai, in reporting on the kinship system and tribal origins among the Gikuku, found that the worst a man can do to infuriate another man is to "mention his mother's name in an indecent way." Usually, this resulted in fighting to defend the mother's sacred name.[158] William Elton also tied the American dozens to the "joking relationship" particularly among the Dahomeans and the Ashanti of Africa.[159] Jones reported the dozens as a survival of the African songs of recrimination.[160]

Further support for the African origins of American Negro dozens is presented by Edward Hobel. He quoted a Dr. Manet Fowler as reporting that twenty-five years ago in Louisiana, "The taunt 'your mother!' was enough to start a good fight," among Negro boys. He also pointed out that Louisiana was one area where we know Ashanti slaves were brought.[161]

Both with the Ashanti and the Trobriands, insults to the chief or his court retinue were capital crimes. Whereas for ordinary men, "insults were private delicts," to insult a chief the same way meant you were deprecating his royal ancestors' character too. "To say, 'wo'ni' (your mother!), 'wo'se' (your father!), 'wo'nana' (your grandparent!) carried a freight of implications that was enough." Insults of a more explicit nature included "the origin of your mother's genitals." Though thumb-biting and nose-thumbing were unknown to the Ashanti, holding the thumbs upward with the fists close together could imply all of the above insults.[162]

Personal discussions with blacks around the country found many suggesting the dozens as a game that taught them to keep their tempers; many remembered just sitting around with other boys playing the dozens. Ossie Guffy was born in 1931 and grew up in the "world of lower middle class America." In *OSSIE: The Autobiography of a Black Woman*, she described an incident that reinforces the concept of the dozens as a form of game that teaches control. She and four other youngsters were playing when one of the boys gets hit and starts "doin' the dozens" instead of hitting back. Her grandfather overhears this and lectures and paddles them.

> "When I was coming up," Grandpa said, "I heard about that game, only I heard about it the way it used to be, and I heard how it started and why it started. It was a game slaves used to play, only they wasn't just playing for fun. They was playing to teach themselves and their sons how to stay alive.

The whole idea was to learn to take whatever the master said to you without answering back or hitting him, 'cause that was the way a slave had to be, so's he could go on living. It maybe was a bad game, but it was necessary. It ain't necessary now."[163]

Ossie's mother, however, does not find much wrong with the game: " 'doin' the dozen'—there's nothing wrong with that game. My brothers used to play it back in Cincinnati and they always said it taught them to hold their temper."[164] White also supported the historical explanation of the dozens being a game that has taught blacks "how to keep cool and think fast under pressure."[165]

As for the term "dozen," Schechter reported that the commonest theory for the origin of the term derived from a "recurring insult whereas the opponent's mother was supposed to be one of the dozens of women available to the sexual whims of her master."[166]

According to Dan Burley, research has revealed that the dozens originated with American "field slaves" who used it in place of physical assault on the "more favored 'house slaves' on Southern plantations."

> Knowing they would suffer the lash or be deprived of food if they harmed the often pampered house servants, the lowly cotton pickers, sugar-cane workers, and other laborers in the field vented their spleen on the hated uniformed black, brown, and yellow butlers, coachmen, lackeys, maids, and housekeepers by saying aloud all types of things about their parents and even their most remote ancestors. As this discomfort of the abused became known, the vilification steadily became more lewd, pointedly vulgar, and filthy.[167]

Furthermore, Burley wrote that the dozens, just before World War II, moved into Negro folklore on a level with the development of the Negro spiritual, the blues, and jazz. By 1917 the dozens were refined to "where one talked about another's parents in highly explosive rhythmic phrases."

The Dozens in School

If you discuss the dozens with secondary school youngsters, and in many cases adults too, they may not know the game as the dozens unless you describe it. Except for the more sophisticated and street-wise students, few know the game as the dozens. Furthermore, new inner city teachers may not realize that they are being put in the dozens unless they are aware of the game and local street connotations, as per Reality 68.

REALITY 68

As a new male teacher was walking into the students' lunchroom, he was approached by a youngster with a sad look on his face. This took place as he came abreast of a table around which sat a number of ninth-grade boys.

The youngster said, "Hey, your mother be on the corner of Franklin and Chipewa sometime?"

The teacher looked at the youngster and at his seated, leering friends, and got a queasy feeling in his stomach as he walked away quickly looking straight ahead at the other door without answering. The youngsters at the table started laughing.

Basically, the teacher was put in the dozens by the youngster calling his mother a prostitute. He added emphasis that was a low-class prostitute—a two-dollar hooker—by implying that she worked the corner of Franklin and Chipewa, a corner of disrepute in the city of Buffalo.

Reality 69 is an example combining ribbing and half the dozens. I do not remember how it all turned out. It happened to a new, white male teacher in a junior high school.

REALITY 69

Student: "You married?"
Teacher: "Yeah."
Student: "Do you have a naked picture of your wife?"
Teacher: "What! Are you kidding?"
Student: "No. Do you want to buy one?"

Sometimes, youngsters walking in the halls may start with ribbing and end up with the dozens. Sometimes this type of incident can escalate into a real brawl. However, in most cases, if teachers would not interfere, these incidents would sputter out. If the teacher interfering in what he perceives as a threatening situation is a weak teacher, the youngsters involved will join to take him on.

In such cases, one of two things usually happens. Either the teacher will lose because he cannot compete verbally with them in their games, or he may report and discipline them for what was not really an incident of consequence. Reality 70 is a typical situation.

REALITY 70

The first student is walking down the hall. He approaches another youngster.
Second student: "Skinny."
First student: "Owl eyes."
Second student: Say, you mamma what?"
First student: "She had to—to feed you."
First and second student both laugh and walk on.

Reality 70 is presented verbatum from the teacher's anecdotal report.

REALITY 71

"As I was walking into a fifth-grade room to sub once, there was a big fight between two boys in the doorway. I asked what the problem was, and this is the answer I got:

"Joe said, 'He say he saw my mother at the gas station yesterday.' The inference was that Joe's mother *pumped* (fornicated). I asked Joe what his mother did; did she work? He told me that she worked at the hospital. I turned to the other boy involved and said, 'You must have made a mistake. Joe's mother works at the hospital and she was there yesterday. Now, you may both take your seats.'

"Somehow I got out of that situation fairly easily!"

The teacher who wrote Reality 71 was in her mid-twenties, white, and attractive. My reason for mentioning this will be discussed further in the next chapter. However, the point should be made here that you do not have to be a muscular male to teach successfully in an inner city school.

I gave a talk in a Buffalo area suburban school district a few years ago and was uncertain whether what I would have to say about the games inner city youngsters played on their teachers or on one another would be appropriate for that district, since I did not think the particular school district had many black youngsters or poor whites attending their schools. However, when the presentation was over, a number of teachers approached me, and we talked about their experiences.

One male teacher was all smiles. He told me that he had only one black child in his class, and she happened to be very bright. However, she constantly disrupted his class and he was at a loss as to how to deal with her. Laughing, he said, "Now I know, she was playing the dozens on me. Every time she said something the entire class broke up laughing," he added. Interestingly, the white students in the class knew the game and the teacher did not.

Many of the books written about inner city and urban schools also contain descriptions of the dozens being played in school—for example, James Herndon's *The Way It Spozed to Be*, Herbert Kohl's *36 Children*, Robert Kendell's *White Teacher in a Black School*, and Mary F. Greene and Orletta Ryan's *The School Children Growing Up in the Slums*.[168]

Though the dozens behavior was described in the above books, many authors did not indicate any real understanding of the behavior. It seems possible, therefore, that the dozens is played a good deal more in all schools than is reported or understood. Indeed, it is possible that many discipline problems have the dozens as their root. However, because educators are generally unfamiliar with the behavior, they may not be dealing with the real cause of many problems.

Reality 72 reports on observers for a doctoral dissertation involving forty-eight ninth-grade black children having problems "detecting" the dozens in relation to classroom discipline, which they were observing and reporting. Of course, this raises a host of questions related to the validity of any research or reporting that involves black streetcorner children.

REALITY 72

Instances of aggression proved to be the most difficult category. Outside observers were not as skilled at detecting "playing the dozen." Students would "play the dozen" by singing a theme from a popular television show or commercial or song that encompassed the name of someone's mother or father in the class. For example, a student might sing "Mary Hartman, Mary Hartman," Mary being the first name of a student's mother. Or, he might sing "M-I-C-K-E-Y M-O-U-S-E," "Lilly Mouse," Lilly being the name of a classmate's mother. This type of "playing the dozen" was difficult for outside observers to determine. However, it was easy for an investigator/teacher to detect because of their familiarity with the technique as well as their knowledge of parents' names.[169]

SOME ADDITIONAL GAMES

Although many of the streetcorner coping or survival techniques or games were covered in this chapter, there are a few more that should be investigated, for they too affect classroom teaching and learning. Two additional ones that will be mentioned briefly are "working game" and "putting someone on." Most of these games are used to manipulate others. Streetcorner youngsters are masters of these games. Sometimes they will work in consort to run a game on a teacher.

To "put someone on" or "hype" them is to lead a person into believing you are going along with them or what they have to say while subverting (hence rejecting) what they are trying to get across. Of course, the put-on fails if the other person becomes aware of the game. David Wellman provided further insight in his article "Putting on the Youth Opportunity Center."[170]

I have observed innumerable youngsters "working game" on teachers, including me. Sometimes they will do this to get money from the teacher without any intention of ever paying it back. Schulz, providing some examples of this, said "they always had a ready reason for needing the money."[171]

Hip youngsters will run these games on one another as well as on their teachers. Sometimes, when one youngster realizes that another has run a game on him and will not return the money or a borrowed item, a violent confrontation results.

THE ROLE OF SCHOOL PERSONNEL
IN GAME PLAYING

The first suggestion for school personnel is that everyone in the school should become aware of the games and understand them. This is *not* "lowering yourself to their level." This is learning what is going on so that you can ameliorate rather than exacerbate a simple situation that could result in disorder and interfere with the teaching and learning.

Second, as I suggested earlier, teachers should develop a teaching style reflecting his or her personality. Similarly, if you can judiciously play the games and maintain order and teach, do so. Those who cannot, should not. I have observed some excellent and some poor teachers playing the games. I have also observed some outstanding teachers who will not have a thing to do with the games. I would question, though, whether these teachers really reached their students on an affective level.

One of the points that must still be remembered is that the streetcorner youngsters respect you if you can achieve in the area that they deem important. If you speak with school-age youngsters, you will find that they usually like the teachers who are "different" or sometimes a "little crazy" but not to the point of trying to be "one of the kids."

Herbert Gans wrote about Jews and Protestants moving out of Roxbury in Boston and poor Italians moving in. Today, however, the Italians are gone, and Roxbury is populated by blacks. Many of the problems experienced by the Italians are similar to those being experienced by blacks today. "The caretakers and West Enders related to each other across a system of cultural and emotional barriers that prevented the development of satisfactory interaction."[172] One of the problems that Gans reported was germane to this chapter and involves the unruly and destructive Italian adolescents and their settlement house workers: "[B]y their actions, they hoped to taunt the caretakers into giving up their middleclass standards, and into resorting to revenge."[173] However, one staff member was able to relate to the teenagers fairly well because he could play their games without giving up his values.

Only one staff member was able to deal with the teenagers. This he did essentially by adopting peer group competitiveness. Able to return wisecracks or hostile taunts, he even invited them, thus giving the teenagers an opportunity to measure their skill against his. At the same time, he never surrendered his allegiance to the settlement house and did not cross to their side. While the teenagers did not always obey him, they did respect him, and were attracted to the relationship he offered. He respected them in turn, partially by not being afraid, and by not retreating either from them or from his values. . . . he was able to insist on limits to their hostility and destructiveness.[174]

Claude Brown, who certainly was a streetcorner youngster, verbalized the reasons he and the other boys at Wiltwyck School for Boys liked a counselor named Nick. Relating Brown's appraisal, however, does not mean my acceptance of all his criteria for a good counselor.

> In a couple of months, Nick was running Carver House. We were all part of his gang. He would never help us rob the kitchen and stuff like that, but he used to take us on hikes around Farmer Greene's apple orchard and look the other way sometimes. He . . . liked a lot of the things we liked. He would play the dozens, have rock fights, and curse us out. But I think we liked Nick mostly because he was fair to everybody. Nick never liked to see anybody get bullied, but he was always ready to see a fair fight. I liked the way Nick was always lying to us. Everybody knew he was lying most of the time, but we didn't care, because he used to tell such good lies. Nick didn't get excited real quick. . . . Nick had sense. I was always getting into fights with Nick, since I knew I wouldn't lose too bad.[175]

I know many excellent teachers who used to and still do play the dozens with their students. One of them did an amazing thing one day. His students just would not stop getting on one another's mothers. No matter what the teacher did they kept at it. No real fights, just continuous digging at one another.

REALITY 73

When his students returned from lunch, he called the roll. However, he did it differently than they had ever heard it before.
"Bertha"
"Gwendalyn"
"Gussy"
"Rosemary" . . . etc.
His students did not say a word. He was calling the attendance by their mothers' first names. It was a low blow, but it worked. His students did not play the dozens in his class again.

I discussed with some students how they felt about teachers who ribbed on them. Generally, their feelings were that it was all right if the teacher did not get mad when ribbed back. They told me about a teacher who sometimes ribbed on the boys by saying "yes, ma'm," or "yes, dear." "There a teacher down the hall, he rib on you for nuthin'. You rib on him, he rib you right back. You don't mess with him." I also know of teachers who allowed themselves to get into ribbing contests with their students. Then, when they were put down hard, they reported the students for cursing or ridiculing them.

There appears to be a standard retort for stopping ribbing, jiving, or playing the dozens in your classroom: To say "I don't play the game" or, "Don't play that game in my room," usually works. Of course, your students have to sense that you can back up your demand.

NOTES TO CHAPTER 6

1. Langston Hughes, ed., *The Book of Negro Humor* (New York: Dood, Mead, 1966).
2. H. Rap Brown, *Die Nigger Die!* (New York: Dial, 1969).
3. Joseph White, "Toward a Black Psychology: White Theories Ignore Ghetto Life Styles," *Ebony*, September 1970, p. 45.
4. Herbert Gans, *The Urban Villagers: Group & Clans in the Life of Italian-Americans* (New York: Free Press of Glencoe, 1962), pp. 81–82.
5. Walter B. Miller, "Lower-Class Culture as a Generating Milieu of Gang Delinquency," *Journal of Social Issues* 14, no. 3 (1958): 10.
6. Geneva Smitherman, *Talkin and Testifyin: The Language of Black America* (Boston: Houghton Mifflin, 1977).
7. Roger D. Abrahams, *Deep Down in the Jungle: Negro Narrative Folklore from the Streets of Philadelphia* (Chicago: Aldine, 1970), p. 56.
8. Roger D. Abrahams, "Talking My Talk—Black English and Social Segmentation in Black Communities," *Florida FL Reporter* 10, no. 1 & 2 (1972): 36.
9. Jefferson Avenue is the main street of the black community in Buffalo, New York.
10. Edith A. Folb, *Runnin' Down Some Lines: The Language and Culture of Black Teenagers* (Camgridge, Mass.: Harvard University Press, 1980), p. 88.
11. Ibid., pp. 88–90.
12. In the "600" schools, I worked with supposed nonreaders who could recite stories about Shine in his Great Titanic adventures and also go on for hours with various versions of the Signifyin' Monkey. For two versions of Signifying Monkey, see Oscar Brown, Jr., "Signifyin Monkey," *Sin & Soul*, Columbia, CL 1577 and CS 8373, 1960 and Rudy Ray Moore, "Signifying Monkey," *The Second Rudy Ray Moore Album: "This Pussy Belongs To Me,"* Kent, KST-002, 1970. For the Titanic see Rudy Ray Moore, "The Great Titanic," *The Rudy Ray Moore Album: Eat Out More Often*, Comedian, COM S 1104, n.d. For additional information on The Great Titanic, The Signifying Monkey, and other toasts, see: Roger D. Abrahams, *Deep Down in The Jungle*; Bruce Jackson, *"Get Your Ass in the Water and Swim Like Me": Narrative Poetry from the Black Oral Tradition* (Cambridge, Mass.: Harvard University Press, 1974); Dennis Wepman, Ronald B. Newman, and Murray B. Binderman, *The Life: The Lore and Folk Poetry of the Black Hustler* (Philadelphia: University of Pennsylvania Press, 1976).
13. Tom Wolfe, *Radical Chic & Mau-Mauing the Flak Catchers* (New York: Farrar, Strauss & Giroux, 1970), pp. 119–20.
14. Ibid., pp. 118–19.

15. Mercer L. Sullivan, "Youth Crime: New York's Two Varieties," *New York Affairs* 8, no. 1 (1983): 38.

16. See Chapter 9 for a description of the New Teacher and Teacher Aide project.

17. Harlen C. Abbey, "Soul of the Foot: The Sneaker Has Come a Long Way From the Old Canvas-Top," *Buffalo Courier Express*, June 28, 1981, pp. 14–15; Dennis Albert, "'Sneakers' Hit the Canvas: Final Tribute," *New Times*, September 19, 1975, p. 68; "Army May Travel on Its Sneakers," *New York Times*, May 2, 1982, p. 24; Karen Brady, "Beaded Friendship Pins Skip onto Youth Scene," *Buffalo News*, April 6, 1983, p. C1; Scott Cohen, "Sneaking Toward Democracy," *Village Voice*, May 19, 1975, p. 134; Mei-Mei Chan, "Snazzy Sneakers Jump to Fashion's Forecourt," *USA Today*, April 24, 1984, p. 1D; David A. Fryxell, "Putting Your Best Foot Forward: A Confused Consumer's Guide to Athletic Shoes," *TWA Ambassador*, March 1978, pp. 39–41; Andrew D. Gilman, "Pity the Sneaker: Its Era Is Ended," *New York Times*, December 18, 1977, p. S2; Pamela G. Hollie, "Race Is On for Running Shoe Money," *New York Times*, October 24, 1977, p. 45; Parton Keese, "Two-Piece Tennis Shoe," *New York Times*, February 13, 1978, p. C13; "Loafers Who Wear Sneakers," *New York Times*, July 15, 1979, p. F15; Carey Adina Sassower, "The Rise and Fall and Future of Brooks Shoe," *New York Times*, January 24, 1982, p. F23; Samuel H. Schwalb, "Sneakers Still Survives on Nation's Playgrounds," *New York Times*, January 8, 1978, p. 2S; Tony Swan, "Shoe-Boom Shoe-Boom," *Apartment Life*, April 1977, pp. 4–6; Robert McG. Thomas, Jr., "Sneakers Scoop," *New York Times*, May 9, 1983, p. C2; Thora S. Van Horn, "Footwear Fashions, Yes; $15 Kids' Sneakers, No," *Courier Express*, September 17, 1976, p. 14; Michaele Weissman, "Footloose in Manhattan (in Sneakers)," *New York Times*, November 4, 1981, p. C14; Stephen Wigler, "An All-Star in the Fashion Game: Converse's Classic High Top Is the Hottest Thing on Feet," *Democrat and Chronicle*, March 29, 1983, p. 1C.

18. There appears to be some African traditions for the taunting behavior. See Lawrence W. Levine, *Black Culture and Black Consciousness: Afro-American Folk Thought from Slavery to Freedom* (New York: Oxford University Press, 1977), pp. 8–9. For example: "In the days of their kings, Dahomeans too had annual rites in which the subjects were encouraged to invent songs and parables mocking their rulers and reciting the injustices they had suffered."

19. Robert Downey, dir., *Putney Swope*, Cinema V, 1969; Vincent Canby, "Screen: 'Putney Swope,' A Soul Story," *New York Times*, July 11, 1969, p. 19.

20. H. Rap Brown, pp. 27–29, presented his version of signifying: "Signifying is more humane. Instead of coming down on somebody's mother, you can come down on them." Also, "Signifying allowed you a choice—you could either make a cat feel good or bad. If you had just destroyed someone or if they were just down already, signifying could help them over. Signifying was also a way of expressing your own feelings."

21. Sidney Poitier, dir., *Buck and the Preacher*, Columbia, 1972; Vincent Canby, "Buck and the Preacher," *New York Times*, April 29, 1972, p. 19; John I, Dotson, "I Want Freedom to See the Good and the Bad," *Newsweek*, October 23, 1972, p. 82; Gordon Parks, dir., *Shaft*, MGM, 1971; Vincent Canby, " 'Shaft'—At Last, A Good Saturday Night Movie," *New York Times*, July 11, 1971, B1; Gordon Parks, dir., *Super Fly*, Warner, 1972; Roger Greenspan, "The Screen: 'Super Fly,' " *New York Times*, August 5, 1972, p. 14.

22. Eldridge Cleaver, *Soul On Ice* (New York: Ramparts, 1968), p. 168.

23. Thomas Kochman, " 'Rapping' in the Black Ghetto," *Trans-Action*, March 1969, 29.

24. Alfonzo A. Narvaez, "Off-Duty Patrolman Slain in IRT Station Gun Battle," *New York Times*, June 29, 1972, p. 27; C. Gerald Fraser, "Man Accused of Tricking Police into Shooting Indicted in Slaying," *New York Times*, July 19, 1972, p. 24; Alfonzo A. Narvaez, "Jury Inquiry Due on Slaying in IRT," *New York Times*, June 30, 1972, p. 29.

25. Malachi Andrews and Paul T. Owens, *Black Language* (West Los Angeles: Seymour-Smith, 1973), p. 93.

26. H. Rap Brown, pp. 24–25.

27. John O. Killens, *The Cotillion; Or One Good Bull Is Half the Herd* (New York: Pocket Books, 1973), p. 193.

28. Andrews, and Owens, p. 106.

29. Lou Shelly, *Hepcats Jive Talk Dictionary* (Derby Conn.: T.W.O. Charles, 1945), p. 50.

30. For example: *Woofing*, n., aimless talk, as a dog barks on a moonlight night—Zora N. Hurston, "Story in Harlem Slang," *American Mercury*, July 1942, p. 96; *a woofer*, n., applied to one who talks constantly, loudly, and in a convincing manner, but who says very little—Hugh Sebastion, "Negro Slang in Lincoln University," *Speech* 9 (1934): 289; *Woof*, To talk much and loudly and yet say little of consequence—Sebastion, "Negro Slang in Lincoln University," p. 290; *Wolfing*, Bluffing—Howard C. Brooks, *Soul Dictionary* (Buffalo, New York: E. Marie Mays, 1971), p. 45; *woofing* v. to threaten in the manner of a bluff; You're just woofing, man.—David Claerbaut, *Black Jargon in White America* (Grand Rapids, Mich.: William B. Eerdmans, 1972), p. 86; *woof*, boast, bluff—Edith A. Folb, *Runnin' Down Some Lines*, p. 260; *wuffin'*, when some little boy picks on a big boy orally (Buffalo, New York, 1970); *wolf*, v., to make fun of someone—Herbert L. Foster, "A Pilot Study of the Cant of the Disadvantage, Socially Maladjusted, Secondary School Child," *Urban Education* 2 (1966): 99–114; *wolf*, a male who chases women—Dan Burley, *Dan Burley's Handbook of Jive* (New York: Jive Potentials, 1944); "The whole thing is that if you can woof and woof hard enough and long enough and be willing to back it up, few people will push you."—H. Rap Brown, p. 81; "I turned around and started wolfing at the guy, and he just strolled off."—Lew Alcindor, "UCLA Was a Mistake," *Sports Illustrated*, November 3, 1969, p. 36.

31. H. Rap Brown, p. 58.

32. Ibid.
33. Ibid., p. 81.
34. Richard A. Marotto, " 'Posin' to Be Chosen': An Ethnographic Study of Ten Lower Class Black Male Adolescents in an Urban High School," *DAI* 39 (1978): 123-A (State University of New York At Buffalo).
35. Personal interview.
36. Janet Maslin, "Film: Murphy in 'Beverly Hills Cop,' " *New York Times*, December 5, 1984, p. C25.
37. John Curran, " 'Beverly Hills Cop' is Pure Eddie Murphy at Hilarious Best," *Business First Magazine, Buffalo*, December 17, 1984, p. 18.
38. Richard Schickel, "Eddie Goes to Lotusland," *Time*, December 10, 1984, p. 92.
39. Curran, p. 18.
40. D.A., "Brave New World," *Newsweek*, April 16, 1984, p. 93.
41. Gerald M. Boyd, "Jackson Charges Mondale Ignored Him On No. 2 Spot," *New York Times*, July 11, 1984, pp. 1-A, 17.
42. James Reston, "Jackson's Arrogant Pride," *New York Times*, September 2, 1984, p. E15.
43. Jonathan Friendly, "Jackson Candidacy Raises New Questions of Press Performance," *New York Times*, March 8, 1984, p. B14.
44. Louise Continelli, "A Boxer's Image: Ali's Was Real; Leonard's Wasn't, Promoter Says," *Buffalo News*, May 31, 1984, p. B-11; Bob Curran, "Early Wouldn't Bean Mom," *Buffalo News*, June 7, 1984, p. C17; Donn Esmonde, "Boxing Is Back in Buffalo Tonight," *Buffalo News*, June 1, 1984, p. B-1, B-2; Donn Esmonde, "Bramble Holds Fire; Mancini Retreats," *Buffalo News*, June 3, 1984, p. B-1.
45. Donn Esmonde, "Bramble Struggles To The Top," *Buffalo News*, June 7, 1984, p. B-1.
46. Wolfe, pp. 97-98.
47. Wolfe, pp. 99-100.
48. Wolfe, p. 154.
49. Roger D. Abrahams, "Feedback From Our Readers: Rapping in the Black Ghetto," *Trans-Action*, May 1969, p. 53.
50. Martin Mayer, "The Full and Sometimes Very Surprising Story of Ocean Hill, The Teacher's Union and the Teacher Strikes of 1968," *New York Times Magazine*, February 2, 1969, p. 42.
51. Ibid., p. 58.
52. Just before organizing BUILD in Buffalo, Alinsky's organization had helped some Rochester blacks organize FIGHT. It was suggested that the fear of whites for the name FIGHT prompted those involved in Buffalo to reach a more positive and less fearful name, BUILD.
53. Andrews and Owens, p. 95.
54. H. Rap Brown, p. 29.
55. In Leo Rosten, *The Joys Of Yiddish* (New York: McGraw-Hill, 1968), p. 119—"Fonfering" and a "fonfer" is defined as "to nasalize . . . a double talker . . . , a shady, petty deceiver . . . , and a specialist in hot air, baloney—a trumpeter of hollow promise."

56. H. Rap Brown, p. 30; see also note 12 above.
57. Jervis Anderson, "Profiles," *New Yorker*, June 16, 1973, p. 76.
58. R. D. Abrahams, *Deep Down in the Jungle*, p. 264.
59. Ibid., p. 51.
60. Ibid., p. 52.
61. Ibid., p. 71.
62. Kochman, p. 32.
63. Claudia Mitchell-Kernan, "Signifying, Loud-Talking and Marking," in Thomas Kochman, ed., *Rappin' and Stylin' Out: Communication in Black America* (Chicago: University of Chicago Press, 1972), p. 315.
64. Ibid., p. 316.
65. Ibid., p. 317.
66. Roger D. Abrahams, *Positively Black* (Englewood Cliffs, N.J.: Prentice-Hall, 1970), p. 326.
67. Ibid., p. 326.
68. Ibid., p. 326.
69. Ibid., pp. 326–27.
70. Smitherman, pp. 118–19.
71. Ibid., p. 120.
72. Ibid.
73. Ibid., p. 121
74. Jack Kerouac, *On The Road* (New York: Signet, 1955), p. 209.
75. Paul Cowan, *An Orphan in History: Retrieving a Jewish Legacy* (Garden City, N.Y.: Doubleday, 1982), p. 117.
76. Milton "Mezz" Mezzrow was a white Jewish clarinetist who was very much a Titan on the jazz scene in the 1930s and 1940s. With Bernard Wolfe, he wrote *Really the Blues*, his autobiography. His obit was printed in the *New York Times*, August 9, 1972, p. 34. In *The New Cab Calloway's Cat-Ologue*, rev. 1939, ed. (n.p., Ned E. Williams, 1938), under M "Mezz' (N)—anything supreme, genuine. Ex.—'This is really the mezz'."
77. Milton Mezzrow and Bernard Wolfe, *Really The Blues* (New York: Signet, 1964), p. 197.
78. For additional information, see Jackson, 1974; Wepman, Newman, and Binderman, 1976.
79. Our school was not unlike so many inner city schools where the lavatory or lavatories were locked. Often, they were opened during class changes or at other specific times. Recently, I have found some suburban schools beginning to lock their lavatory doors.
80. Roger D. Abrahams, *Talking Black* (Rowley, Mass.: Newbury House, 1976), pp. 19–20.
81. Kochman, *Rappin' and Stylin' Out*.
82. Folb, p. 92.
83. Thomas Kochman, "Toward An Ethnography of Black American Speech Behavior," in Norman E. Whitten, Jr., and John F. Szwed, eds., *Afro-American Anthropology: Contemporary Perspectives* (New York: Free Press, 1970), p. 147.
84. Abrahams, p.

85. Smitherman, p. 83.

86. Abrahams, *Talking Black*, pp. 83–84.

87. Folb, p. 12.

88. Abrahams, *Talking Black*, p. 75.

89. Marotto.

90. Smitherman, p. 85.

91. Ibid., p. 83.

92. David L. Cohen, *God Shakes Creation* (New York: Harper & Brothers, 1935), p. 161.

93. Donald Clemmer, *The Prison Community* (Boston: Christopher Publication House, 1940), p. 9.

94. Roger D. Abrahams, "Playing the Dozens," *Journal of American Folklore* 75 (1962): 209.

95. I have since observed some black and white male teachers who grew up playing the dozens react almost violently to being put in the dozens by a student.

96. William H. Grier and Price M. Cobbs, *The Jesus Bag* (New York: McGraw-Hill), p. 9.

97. H. Rap Brown, p. 27.

98. John Dollard, "The Dozens: Dialect of Insult," *American Imago* 1, no. 1 (1939): 3–25; Ralfe F. Berdie, "Playing the Dozens," *Journal of Social Psychology* 42 (1947): 120–27; Abrahams, *Deep Down in the Jungle.*

99. Dollard, p. 4.

100. Ibid., p. 5.

101. Ibid., p. 10.

102. Ibid., p. 14.

103. Berdie; The men were divided between the north and the south.

104. Ibid., p. 120.

105. Ibid.

106. Ibid., p. 121; This concept and others of the dozens *must* be understood to provide school personnel with insight and understanding into some of their school discipline problems.

107. Abrahams, "Playing the Dozens," p. 215.

108. Ibid., p. 210.

109. Ibid., p. 20.

110. Ibid., p. 48.

111. Ibid., p. 211. An argument could be presented that this reporting holds for the school too. In this case, Abrahams was referring to the armed forces.

112. Ibid.

113. Ibid., p. 40.

114. David Schultz, *Coming Up Black: Patterns of Ghetto Socialization* (Englewood Cliffs, N.J.: Prentice-Hall, 1969), p. 67.

115. Grier and Cobbs, p. 5.

116. Smitherman, p. 133.

117. Smitherman, p. 133–34.

118. John Baugh, *Black Street Speech: Its History Structure and Survival* (Austin: University of Texas Press, 1983), p. 26; John M. Brewer, " 'Hidden Language'—Ghetto Children Know What They're Talking About,"

New York Times Magazine, December 26, 1966, p. 32; H. Rap Brown, p. 15–26; Folb, p. 32, 235; Clemmer, p. 9; Adrian Dove, "Soul Story," *New York Times Magazine*, December 8, 1968, p. 38; Greer and Cobbs, pp. 3, 4–5, 9–10; Ulf Hannnerz, "Another Look at Lower-class Black Culture," in Lee Rainwater, ed., *Black Experience: Soul* (Chicago: Aldine, 1970), p. 177; Langston Hughes and Arna Bontemps, *The Book of Negro Folklore* (New York: Dodd, Mead, 1966), p. 483; Hurston, pp. 95–96; Kenneth R. Johnson, "Teacher's Attitude Toward the Nonstandard Negro Dialect—Let's Change It," *Elementary English* 48 (1971): 180; Donald J. Merwin, *Reaching the Fighting Gang* (New York: New York City Youth Board, 1960), p. 295; Mezzrow and Wolfe, p. 304; Paul Oliver, *The Meaning of the Blues* (Toronto: Collier, 1960), pp. 152–52, 176; Sebastian, p. 284; William Schechter, *The History of Negro Humor in America* (New York: Fleet, 1970); Smitherman, pp. 131–34; White, p. 32.

119. Leonard Harris, "WCBS-TV arts editor Leonard Harris reviews 'The Dozens,'" a new play, *WCBS-TV News Release*, March 17, 1969. (Mimeo.)

120. Richard Watts, Jr., "American Blacks in New Africa," *New York Post*, March 14, 1969, p. 62.

121. Clive Barnes, "Stage: The Maturity of a 'Black Girl,'" *New York Times*, June 18, 1971, p. 27.

122. Ossie Davis, dir., *Cotton Comes to Harlem*, United Artists, 1970; Vincent Canby, "Ossie Davis,' 'Cotton Comes to Harlem,'" *New York Times*, June 11, 1970, p. 50; Robert Altman, dir., *M*A*S*H*, 20th Century Fox, 1970; Roger Greenspan, "'M*A*S*H' Film Blends Atheism, Gore, Humor," *New York Times*, January 26, 1970, p. 26; "Rising Complaints Shake Film Truce with Blacks," *New York Times*, September 27, 1972, p. 37; "Sanford & Son," *New York Times*, June 17, 1973, pp. 1, 3.

123. Gordon Parks, *A Choice of Weapons* (New York: Berkeley Medallion, 1967), p. 128. The Civilian Conservation Corps (CCC) was a federal agency organized as part of the New Deal in 1933 and formally organized by Congress in 1937. Its function was to provide training and employment for unemployed young men in such public conservation work as building dams, planting trees, and fighting fires. When the CCC was abolished in 1942, more than 2 million men had served.

124. Claude Brown, *Manchild in the Promised Land* (New York: Macmillan, 1965), p. 61.

125. Hurston, pp. 88–90.

126. Nathan Heard, *Howard Street* (New York: Dial, 1968), p. 78.

127. Bernard Malamud, *The Tenants* (New York: Farrar, Strauss & Giroux, 1971), pp. 132, 137.

128. Robert E. Conot, *Rivers of Blood, Years of Darkness* (New York: Bantom, 1967), p. 231.

129. Joseph J. Wambaugh, *The New Centurions* (Boston: Little, Brown, 1970), p. 121.

130. Tom Wicker, *A Time to Die* (New York: Ballantine, 1975), pp. 202–5.

131. Robert A. Heinlein, *Glory Road* (New York: Berkeley Medallion, 1963), p. 77.

132. Alston Anderson, *Lover Man: Stories of Blacks and Whites* (Garden City, N.Y.: Doubleday, 1959); Ed Bullins, *The Reluctant Rapist* (New York: Harper & Row, 1973); Ralph Ellison, *Invisible Man* (New York: Signet, 1947); LeRoi Jones, "The Toilet," *Kulchur III* 9 (1963): 25–29; Louise Meriwether, *Daddy Was a Number Runner* (Englewood Cliffs, N.J.: Prentice-Hall, 1970); Richard Wright, *Lawd Today* (New York: Walker, 1963); John A. Williams, *The Man Who Cried I Am* (Boston: Little, Brown, 1967).

133. Bullins, p. 131.

134. Ellison, p. 400.

135. Ibid., p. 211.

136. Jones, pp. 26, 33.

137. Meriwether, p. 28.

138. Williams, p. 188.

139. Wright, pp. 79–81.

140. Ibid.

141. Anderson, p. 18.

142. Paul C. Harrison and Ed Bullins, "Tabernacle," in William T. Couch, ed., *New Black Playwrights* (New York: Avon, 1971), pp. 71–152.

143. Killens, pp. 26–27.

144. Oliver, p. 80; Speckled Red, "The Dirty Dozens," *The Dirty Dozens*, Delmar, DL-601, n.d.

145. Melvin Van Peebles, "The Dozens," *Aint Supposed To Die a Natural Death*, A&M Records, SP 3510, n.d.

146. George Carlin, "White Harlem," *Occupation: Foole*, Little David, LD 1005, 1973.

147. J. Mason et al., *Ya Mama—Wuf Ticket*, Prelude, PRL D 644 AS, 1982.

148. Christine Dall and Randall Conrad, dirs., *The Dozens*, Calliope Film Resources, 1980; Janet Maslin, "Screen: 'Dozens,' a Woman in Prison," *New York Times*, March 29, 1981, p. 58; Jeff McLaughlin, "'Dozens' Deserves To Be a Winner," *Boston Globe*, October 23, 1981, p. 35; Personal correspondence with Randall Conrad, February 16, 1983: "Indeed we did name the film after the street game of rhymed insults, basically just because it seemed an apt symbol of the obstacle course encountered by the film's character following release from prison. The film opens with off-screen voices doing the dozens (instead of, say, opening with theme music). The main character is white, but her cell mates are mostly women of color, and she has picked up an extra bit of street talk during her time in the relatively cross-cultural life of the institution."

149. Jeannie Kasindorf, "'If I Was Bitter, I wouldn't Have Chosen Comedy'." *New York Times*, February 9, 1975, p. D27.

150. Joyce Maynard, "Friends Recall Freddie Prinze of 157th St.," *New York Times*, February 4, 1977, p. B2.

151. "Dear Abby . . . ," *Northliner Magazine*, Spring 1975, p. 20.

152. "Murder Charged to 2 in Misfiring of Sniper Shot," *Buffalo Evening News*, February 21, 1975, p. 1.

153. Berdi.

154. Margaret Mead, "Kinship in the Admiralty Islands," *Anthropological Paper of the American Museum of Natural History* 34 (1934): 181-358; Raymond W. Firth, *We, the Tikopia* (London: George Allen & Unwin, 1936); Edward M. Weyer, *The Eskimos* (New Haven: Yale University Press, 1932); William I. Thomas, *Primitive Behavior* (New York: McGraw-Hill, 1937); Johan Huizinga, *Homo Ludens, Study of the Play Element in Culture* (Boston: Beacon, 1950).

155. William Schechter, *The History of Negro Humor in America* (New York: Fleet, 1970).

156. Ibid.

157. Thomas A. Johnson, "Off to Trinidad," *Black Enterprise* 1, no. 10 (1962): 56.

158. Ram Desai, *African Society and Culture* (New York: M. W. Lads, 1968), p. 17.

159. William Elton, "Playing the Dozens," *American Speech* 25 (1950): 148-49, 230-33.

160. LeRoi Jones, *Blues People* (New York: Williams Morrow, 1963), p. 27.

161. Edward A. Hobel, *The Law of Primitive Man: A Study of Comparative Legal Dynamics* (Cambridge, Mass.: Harvard University Press, 1954), p. 240. If a teacher is attempting to stop the dozens playing, the teacher must realize that, sometimes, just saying, "she," "m," or holding your wrist, or even holding your elbow, could be considered putting another boy in the dozens.

162. Ibid.

163. Ossie Guffy, *Ossie: The Autobiography of a Black Woman* (New York: Norton, 1971), p. 48.

164. Ibid.

165. White.

166. Schecter, p. 13.

167. Dan Burley, "The 'Dirty Dozens,'" *Citizen Call*, July 30, 1960, reprinted in Langston Hughes, ed., *The Book of Negro Humor*, pp. 119-21.

168. James Herndon, *The Way It Spozed To Be* (New York: Simon & Schuster, 1965); Herbert Kohl, *36 Children* (New York: New American Library, 1967); Robert Kendell, *White Teacher in a Black School* (New York: Devin-Adair, 1964), Mary F. Green and Orletta Ryan, *The School Children Growing Up in the Slums* (New York: Pantheon, 1965).

169. George O. McCalep, Jr., "Contingency Management in the Junior High School," *Dissertation Abstracts* 38, (1977), 2693 (Ohio State University), p. 36.

170. David Wellman, "Putting On the Youth Opportunity Center," in Lee Rainwater.

171. Schultz, pp. 80-82.

172. Gans, p. 155.

173. Ibid., p. 156.

174. Ibid.

175. Claude Brown, p. 81.

7 DISCIPLINE

"Mrs. Oliver, my homeroom teacher, didn't even bawl me out for being late as I slide into my seat. I was disappointed. Maybe she didn't like me anymore."

—Louise Meriwether, *Daddy Was a Numbers Runner.*[1]

The kind tone of this answer, the sweet voice, the gentle manner, the absence of any accent of haughtiness or displeasure, took the girl completely by surprise, and she burst into tears.

"Oh, lady, lady!" she said, clasping her hands passionately before her face, "if there was more like you, there would be fewer like me,—there would— there would!"

—Charles Dickens, *The Adventures of Oliver Twist*[2]

Five points must be made. First, all the earlier chapters should be read before reading this one. Second, if I can generalize from the courses I have taught and the lectures and workshops I have given, teachers who have positive feelings, emotions, and attitudes about teaching in inner city and other schools and who have been frustrated by *teacher-room negativism* and by harried and frightened administrators, will gain strength from reading this book to go back and do battle again —with their fellow professionals, not with their students.

The third point is that there are innumerable lower class black youngsters who display middle class behavior and life style. However, I have not written about them, but rather about the tough, lower class, streetcorner youngster whose testing games have been causing the inner city school problems and now suburban and rural school problems, too. In addition to some streetcorner youngsters moving to suburban and rural schools, their misunderstood street-

245

corner testing and survival techniques and games have also been picked up by many white blue-collar youngsters who are using the games on their suburban and rural teachers. These testing games must be understood if these students' disruptive influence and self-destructive behavior is to be stopped.[3] In so doing, we can then educate the students exhibiting this behavior as well as educating more of the poor and blue-collar children who may have a middle class orientation.

The fourth point and possibly the most important is that all teachers must decide whether their role in classroom discipline is *passive* or *participatory*. Do teachers have a role in achieving discipline in their rooms, or are their students expected to enter their rooms quietly, be seated quietly, and quietly await their teacher's lessons? A teacher cannot teach unless there is a degree of discipline and order in the classroom. Since discipline and order are not always present in inner city classrooms, the teacher has two choices. The first is the passive role, insisting that the students must discipline themselves.[4] The second is the participatory role, where the teacher actively brings about the discipline and order required for teaching and learning.

Once this passive-participatory teacher role in discipline is resolved, we can proceed to solving inner city school discipline problems. Of course, the related proposition, as noted in Chapter 4, of the inner city secondary school students' perception of their teachers' role in disciplining them may make the teachers' feelings about their role superfluous. I believe that the teacher must play an active participatory role in classroom discipline, not only because he or she is an adult, but because inner city students *expect* their teachers to make them behave. The teacher who does not accept this philosophy will not succeed in an inner city school, and perhaps not in any school.

In the state of New York, and many other states, the State Education Department convened a number of committees to discuss the problems of disruptive students. Mr. Daniel Klepak, former director of the Office of Education Performance Review, reported that his letter survey of superintendents and school board members on the "crucial issues affecting the cost" of public education, revealed, among other things, "the high cost of attempting to teach unruly students."[5]

The fifth point is that this book has been written for, among others, professional educators. Therefore, I will not supply a blueprint for solving discipline problems. To supply such a blueprint for professional educators would be an insult. What I have provided and will continue to provide are some insights, some ideas, and some attitudes that will help you develop your personal techniques and teaching style based on your personality.

For the past years, the *Phi Delta Kappan* magazine and Gallup International have conducted national surveys of public attitudes toward education. Over the past years, discipline has been reported as the most important problem by laymen and professional educators. Innumerable articles, studies, books, and state and national committees and agencies have surveyed, studied, and reported on the issue.[6]

The ideas that will be presented in this chapter will be different from those traditionally presented in most articles, chapters, speeches, or books dealing with discipline, particularly discipline in inner city schools, and of course, discipline as now related to suburban and rural secondary schools. For some, the ideas may suggest a new outlook and approach to the teacher's role in school discipline. For others, the presentation will rekindle positive dormant feelings and attitudes that have been squashed by fears and pressures from traditional teacher education programs, graduate courses, in-service education, and peers and administrators.

THE NEW TEACHERS' FOUR-PHASE RITE OF PASSAGE

From a discipline point of view, most secondary school teachers appear to experience part or all of a four-phase rite of passage, just as I did. The four phases are (1) friends, (2) rejection and chaos, (3) discipline, and (4) humanization.

Although this four-phase experience is presented and discussed in relation to new teachers, many older and very experienced teachers in some urban, suburban, and rural districts used to middle class preppy students have begun to experience these four phases because of the new black, minority, immigrant, and blue-collar students they are now trying to discipline and teach. Also, because in most cases they are not receiving any real help from their administrators, despite all their years of hard work and loyal teaching, it is as though they are starting over.

The average new teacher enters the classroom with a positive, warm approach, and a middle class point of view that is somewhat naive. In his upbringing, discipline was probably verbal, reasonable, mild, and consistent. Relatively free and open verbal communication probably existed between him and his parents. He was reared in a relatively democratic atmosphere rather than through either laissez-faire or autocratic. His parents probably viewed themselves as reasonably competent adults, generally satisfied with themselves. His family life most often was warm and intimate, with a close relationship between himself, his brothers and sisters, and his parents.[7] If his parents were divorced, the reasons probably involved their psychological and emotional interaction.[8] He expresses himself symbolically and conceptually.

He has been in a dependency role all his life. His parents administered to all his needs from birth through public school and college. He did, though, work some summers and part time in school. The last time he was punched in the nose was in fifth or sixth grade or in junior high school.

Most undergraduate teacher education programs are too idealized and not pragmatic enough and are directed and staffed by many who never taught school, or if they did teach, did not have a very positive experience. So the chances are, the new teacher's only contact with students and the classroom was his student-teaching experience. He also probably lived in a white neighborhood and neither he nor his parents ever had any black friends.

He entered his new job with idealism, warm heartedly, and full of hope; he really wants to do a good job. He wants to like his students and he wants his students to like him. But something happens to him when his students do not react to him in an orderly fashion as friends.

Conversely, the typical streetcorner student has experienced a life that is characteristic of very poor families. Discipline has been inconsistent, harsh, and *physical.* Ridicule is used; punishment is based on whether his behavior bothered his parents. He was controlled largely physically and there was limited verbal communication within the family. There was little acceptance of him as an individual. He was most often reared through authoritarian methods. His mother usually ran the house, and when his father was home, he was primarily a punitive figure.

The streetcorner youngster's parents have a sense of defeat and low self-esteem. If his family is large, his parents' behavior may have been narcissistic and impulsive. He yielded his independence early and abruptly; he has and still has an "excitement" orientation. Sex is viewed as an exploitive relationship. His aggression is alternatingly restricted and encouraged.[9] If his parents are divorced, they probably viewed the "unstable physical actions of their partners" and financial problems as prime contributors to their discord.[10] He expresses himself physically. His social structure and poverty tends to foster a lifestyle that is characterized by poor impulse control, fundamental psychological depression, surrender to overwhelming odds, and hostility.[11] This is an overview of poverty lifestyles that studies suggest very poor people adopt and which research indicates are not associated with children judged to be mentally healthy in our society.[12]

On the streetcorner, the student's behavior is typically imitative of his elders, who "constantly work game, talk of sports and women, and get high."[13] There is a constant search for action, verbal taunting, and killing time. He must hustle or out-aggress the other guy all the time. Every day calls for another test of his machismo and toughness.

Because of the teacher's childhood, he does not have the need to be autocratic and to "boss" anyone around. He does not want to act the way the teachers he disliked acted. He enters the classroom with a passive (phase one) approach. He wants to be friends with his students, and he expects them to like him in return. He does not wish to be a disciplinarian.

Many of his streetcorner students, however, have a different expectation of their teacher, particularly if the teacher is a man. They want him to be tough enough to make them behave and to make them learn without being punitive or hurting them. And, if he has to, that is all right, too. They test him to see whether he possesses the machismo to control them. According to William Cvaraceus and Walter Miller, the student's norm-violating behavior "reflects a syndrome crystallized around a strong dependency craving" and is a further test of school personnel's ability to satisfy their need for being controlled.[14]

Strict control is highly valued among the lower classes. A close conceptual connection is made between nurturance and authority. The authority figure shows he cares when his control is firm. Therefore, according to Miller frequent attempts are made to test the authority to see whether he can remain firm. The firmer the control the more caring is perceived, despite protests to the contrary.

> Since "being controlled" is equated with "being cared for," attempts are frequently made to "test" the severity or strictness of superordinate authority to see if it remains firm. If intended or executed rebellion produces swift and firm punitive sanctions, the individual is reassured, at the same time that he is complaining bitterly at the injustice of being caught and punished. Some environmental milieux, having been tested in this fashion for the "firmness" of their coercive sanctions, are rejected, ostensibly for being too strict, actually for not being strict enough. This is frequently so in the case of "problematic" behavior by lower class youngsters in the public schools, which generally cannot command the coercive controls implicitly sought by the individual.[15]

Accordingly, the testing begins. In most cases, the new teacher does not know how to respond and he loses control. His class becomes chaotic and no one learns. When in desperation he asks a student what he should do, he is told he is too easy and he should "hit them—that's what they understand." This perplexes him because he feels his job is to teach, not to involve himself in discipline—and certainly not physically punitive discipline.

James Herndon describes his roll call with classes 9D and 7H. His description portrays how swiftly phase one can deteriorate into phase two.

> After roll call, I wasn't quite sure what to do. I had nothing in particular planned, but had counted on the class to give me a hint, to indicate in some way what it was they wanted or expected. . . .[16]
>
> 7H came charging and whooping up the stairs. . . . Later I came to recognize their particular cries coming up my way. . . . 7H dashed in, flung themselves out again. . . . They scattered from seat to seat, each trying to get as much free territory around him as possible, jumping up again as the area got overcrowded and ranging out to look for breathing space. . . . From these seats, wherever they were, they confronted me with urgent and shouted questions, each kid, from his claim of several empty desks, demanding my complete attention to him: Are you a strict teacher? You going to make us write? When do we get to go home? Where our books? Our pencils? Paper?[17]
>
> At that moment there came a tremendous outcry from over by the door. I looked over and three or four kids were standing there, looking up at the door and yelling their heads off. Naturally the rest of the class soon began

shouting insults at them, without any idea of what the trouble was. Everyone was standing up; calls of "water-melon-head!"[18] filled the room. The kids by the door wheeled and rushed up to me, furious and indignant. Vincent, who was one of them, was crying. What the hell? I began to yell in turn for everyone to shut up, which they soon did, not from the effect of my order but out of a desire to find out what was the matter; . . . Alexandra began to threaten me with her mama. Roy, tempted beyond his own indignation, began to make remarks about the color and hair quality of Alexandra's mama.[19] It shows how upset Alexandra was; it was fatal to ever mention your mother at GW, which Alexandra of all kids knew quite well.[20]

Phase two (rejection) begins as the teacher becomes fearful, humiliated, frustrated, and isolated, even though only a few of his students are testing him. Most are just looking on, hoping that he can be adult enough to get some order so that they can learn; sometimes, though, they too join in the taunting and fun.

The result is that the teacher begins to feel ineffective and, therefore, inadequate as a teacher and as a human being. He begins to have doubts about his future as a teacher and to question his attitudes about blacks because they will not return his invitation to be friends. He may break his engagement, or his marriage may become shaky. He may begin to lose or gain weight and go to his doctor for tranquilizers. In the morning when he gets up he gets a queasy feeling in his stomach. He may even break out in hives or suffer other physical symptoms as a psychosomatic nature.

For some, phase two does not mean introspection and growth but rather scapegoating. The principal and the curriculum are blamed for being unsupportive and irrelevant. Some new teachers actually go so far as to justify what they are doing or not doing in the name of self-expression, democracy, and relatedness. Some give up and leave teaching. Others go on to suburban or other supposedly "easier" schools. Some go on to graduate school to become psychologists or guidance counselors. Some leave the real profession to write about their experiences, condemning the "system," and becoming self-certified professional critics, educational lecturers, and writers. Others become professors of education.

Of those who remain, a number realize that something is wrong and begin to take an active participatory approach as they enter phase three: discipline. They become disciplinarians. They participate in gaining control of their classes. At this phase, some sensitive teachers begin to hate themselves for what they are doing in the name of discipline. (I tell new teachers that when they begin to hate themselves for their toughness, they are beginning to grow and make it as a teacher.)

During this phase, they start giving youngsters the grades they deserve instead of giving them a "break." They do not give so many second, third, or fourth chances. When speaking with parents, they become honest. They also begin to solve their own discipline problems without sending students to the "office."[21]

Unfortunately, out of every ten teachers who remain, I have found seven or eight remain fixated at the discipline phase. They remain at this level—constantly on guard, never trusting, never expressing any positive feelings, and never relaxed. Their students are controlled and supposedly educated with worksheets, notes for copying, and other fruitless forms of "busy-work." The teacher remains ensconced at his desk throughout most of the period.

Phase four is humanization. Few teachers, perhaps two or three percent, achieve this level. The phase-four classroom has a relaxed atmosphere where feelings are expressed. The students have run their testing games and have learned their teacher's limits. Learning takes place in this positive, structured, yet relaxed atmosphere. Students move about the room knowing that no one will steal from them, that no one will pick on them, that no one will steal their clothing from the closet, and that their teacher is fair and will answer their questions. He respects them and they respect him. Their teacher is in charge and in control; now they can relax.

New teachers may approach and achieve each of these phases differently and experience them for a different period of time.

THE NATURAL INNER CITY TEACHER

The first major comprehensive study of teacher relationships with students in the United States was reported by Fred W. Hart in 1934. Since then, numerous studies have been published, all reporting similar "good" teacher qualities of (1) fairness, (2) strictness, (3) ability to maintain discipline, (4) high standards, (5) knowledge of subject, (6) friendliness, (7) sense of humor, and (8) an ability to teach. During the past years, almost everyone who has written about teaching in inner city schools has also suggested lists of "good" qualities required for inner city teachers.[22]

The eight qualities listed above apply to the professional whom I refer to as the "natural" inner city teacher. However, I will discuss this teacher relative to personality, curriculum, and discipline; a few more attributes will be added to the eight listed above, although some of these may merely reflect an aspect of one or more of the above qualities. In this section I will discuss briefly those attributes that stand out as common among natural inner city teachers.

Personality

"Natural teachers are structured and organized and possess great inner strength. They have warmth and really like children and adults. They have a sense of humor and are secure and capable of applying their personal standards pragmatically in the classroom. They have great physical energy and understand and are happy with their physical being. Their physicalness come across through the way they walk, talk, relate to students and others, and the way they calmly straighten out disruptions without displaying panic or fear.

Because these teachers are at home with their physical being, they are capable of getting close to their students physically without provoking them sexually. This is also because they have dignity and demand to be treated in kind.

Many male teachers relate physically to male students through playful rough-housing. Where middle class children are fondled by their parents, particularly in early childhood, the lower class child is treated more harshly by his parents in early childhood. However, the lower class child still craves the fondling he missed. Therefore, he invites and enjoys his nonpunitive physicalness from many of the male teachers he likes. Often, the fearful teacher or administrator is horrified by this teacher-student physicality. Indeed, inner city principals and supervisors often express this fear with such edicts as "Never touch a child under any circumstances." Interestingly, when I discuss this topic with university students and teachers, many who are pacifists and many who are not secure with their sexuality and physicalness often accuse me of wanting to beat children. No matter how often I stress my opposition to corporal punishment, they are unable to separate the idea of hitting a child from warm physical fondling and occasional roughhousing.

The young natural female teacher also realizes that her female students may be more competitive with her because they see her as threat for their boyfriends. However, that does not prevent the natural female teacher from discussing clothing style and makeup ideas with her students.

The natural teacher is also introspective. To be introspective is to know that the medication you may be taking; your relationship with your parents, your spouse, your lover, your child or children, your boyfriend or girlfriend; your financial resources; or even the weather may determine your physical and emotional state and affect how you feel and relate to your students on any day. The natural teacher who is female realizes that birth control pills or PMS may affect her feelings. Aware of all of these very personal daily realities, the natural teacher also tries to understand these personal feelings in order to maintain positive relationships with students.

The natural teacher practices what he preaches. By respecting the school's rules, he gets his students to understand and respect his rules. He teaches by example and by providing a model for emulation.

The natural teacher dresses stylishly and tastefully, being careful not to dress as the students dress, and being careful not to dress seductively or provocatively.

The natural teacher knows that *all* students can learn when taught through their appropriate learning style. Also, the natural teacher is capable of accepting student negative aggression while: (1) looking through the negative aggression to find its cause, (2) helping students understand the reason for their negative aggression; and (3) helping students develop the prosocial skills they may have never learned which would then negate their need to express the negative aggression.[23]

Unquestionably, nonracist teachers are desired. However, they are not necessary. Many black students have been hurt educationally and emotionally by supposedly nonracist white teachers who did not demand that their students produce educationally. Similarly, middle class black teachers have also hurt many black youngsters because they could not relate to their students' lower class lifestyle. Some black teachers have also hurt black students because their students' "middle classness" clashed with the teacher's concept and feelings of black militancy. Therefore, what is needed are teachers who will insist their students learn rather than loving them to death or being more interested in the political concept of blackness.

Finally, my natural teacher is "down with the action" in the school and neighborhood—that is, he or she knows her students' peer styles.

When one of my doctoral students visited relatives in Brooklyn, New York, recently, I asked her to please bring back some information on student styles. The report, from a hispanic youngster, fifteen-year-old Brenda Lee from Fort Hamilton High School, follows:

> The hispanic teenagers wear just Lee jeans and in all different colors. They wear white Adidas sneakers with assorted colored laces; matching with the tops they are wearing. These laces are loose. They usually wear 'Le Tigre' shirts and windbreakers, and Lee jean jackets.[24]
> The words they are using now are:
> (1) "bad" or "deaf"—these words mean its nice. For example, "Those pants are bad."
> (2) "fresh"—means "new." For example, "That shirt is fresh, isn't it?"
> The way they walk is called "bee-bop walk," ups' and down.
> The anglos wear Wrangler or Levis jeans and jackets. Sneakers are the same as hispanics but not as clean, they don't take care of them. They wear only white laces and tight. They wear T-shirts displaying rock groups or band names. For example, Police, ZZ Top, etc.
> They don't pay attention to the way they dress. They don't care."

For black students, the natural, Afro, or bush is usually now cut shorter or closer to the head. A variation is called the "shag." The process or "do," is now making a comeback with adolescents and adults. The shower cap, because of activator spray, has in many cases replaced the woman's stocking doo-rag in holding down the Gerry Curl à la Michael Jackson.

In Buffalo, according to Dr. Richard A. Marotto, assistant principal at Kensington High School, black students also coordinate their shoelaces with their tops. However, in some case the coordination is between socks and tops.

Also, those wearing crew-neck sweaters use a variation of the military crease. Whereas the military crease has two creases on the shirt, one down the center of each pocket, the student's now iron one crease centered on the sweater from the neck all the way down, and one crease on each sleeve.

Instead of the pick or wide-tooth comb, which used to drive teachers crazy, many students now continually use a brush on their hair.[25]

Curriculum

Teachers and university professors sometimes claim that the irrelevant curriculum is at fault for deadening classrooms, when in fact the classroom is deadened by ineffective teaching. I recall one teacher who taught a different academic subject each term. Every time he had problems in his class he would walk into the hall and observe another teacher doing a great job teaching another subject. Instead of realizing that *he* was the problem and not the curriculum, he badgered the principal into allowing him to teach the other subject the following term. Needless to say, he had the same trouble. Or, should we say his students had the same trouble. The greatest curriculum taught by an uninterested teacher will still turn students off.

Because my good teachers love the subject they teach, their enthusiasm, excitement, and command of the subject ignite and motivate their students into enjoying the subject they do not complain about out-of-date materials. If the materials are inappropriate or inadequate, they spend a good deal of their own time making relevant ditto masters. They also teach reading regardless of their subject. Instead of complaining about where their students are, they individualize their instruction, wherever possible, and teach to their students' varied learning styles.

Discipline

Natural teachers have the ability to make their classroom safe and secure so that all students can relax and learn. Their class is disciplined because their students know they are in charge. It means that somehow, by the way they walk, talk, react to a crisis situation, and arrange the room, they let their students know that they respect them and do not fear them. They rarely raise their voices. They listen to their students. Their intuition and instinct are correct; therefore, they act instinctively.[26] They contact their students' parents early, not waiting for trouble. They also contact parents to compliment them on their children's positive accomplishments.[27]

There is something about them that made some of their students fear them at first. The fear, however, has grown to respect. They moved their class from being disciplined to being disciplined and humanized. Though students do not sit with their hands clasped on the desk, there is no question of who is in control.

PSYCHING, ACTING CRAZY, AND REPUTATION

This section related to three concepts that are not usually discussed in relation to discipline or even teaching. The first concept concerns the teacher psyching himself as well as his students. The second concept relates to students respecting the teacher who is slightly "crazy." The third concept refers to a teacher earning a reputation as a teacher who is tough and not fearful.

Psyching

Reality 74 provides an example of how, as a new teacher, I sometimes used to psych myself. Realities 75, 76, 77, and 78 provide additional examples of psyching. Reality 79 is a teacher's report of how he earned his reputation.

REALITY 74

As a new "600" schoolteacher, after taking a verbal and emotional beating from my students for about two weeks, I knew I had to do something if I was going to last as a teacher. When this would happen, I would fall back on my psyching routine.

On Monday, I put on my "manly" outfit consisting of a short-sleeved shirt, a bow tie, and a corduroy sport coat. Wearing this combination somehow psyched me to feel like a MAN. The second part of my psyching routine consisted of waiting in the hall until my class was in the room, and then facing into a little alcove near the door of my shop, clenching my fists, shutting my eyes, and saying to myself something like, "I am a man, I will not take this from a bunch of kids. Who the fuck do they think they are even to try to do this to me. I am a man—'I'm twenty-three years old—I'm a veteran—I will not take any more of their fuckin' crap. I'll show them."

Thus psyched, I adjusted my jacket and tie, and walked into the room. The psyching affected me so that when I walked into the room, somehow by the way I walked and carried myself, I created an atmosphere. My students sensed that there was something about me today that told them, "don't mess around with this guy today." I guess I psyched myself into overcoming my middle class "nice-guy approach, and they could feel it.

Reality 75 provides another example of psyching. This time, however, it was a student teacher who did the psyching.

REALITY 75

"I was speaking with one of our female student teachers and was teasing her about all the rings she was wearing on her fingers. My position was that her generation of students had attacked mine and earlier generations for being materialistic. However, she and her female peers seemed to be wearing a ring on almost every finger. By my standards, this is crass materialism, which makes her generation hypocrites.

"She finally interrupted me and said, No, that's not why I wear rings. I had difficulty separating my role of a student at the university from that of a teacher. So, by putting the rings on, psychologically I was putting myself into a different state of mind. Normally, I don't walk around with rings on. The rings were part of my past when I used to dress up a lot. I started wearing the rings when I started student teaching.'

"In her case, wearing the rings helped her establish a line of demarcation between her university role and her new role of student teacher. Even though the rings were associated with an earlier and younger period in her life, they also helped her convey an attitude of confidence. In her case, it may have been that her four years at the university were without constraint. Therefore, by her wearing the rings, she brought herself back to the earlier constraints of her high school days."

I have observed and participated in many forms of psyching. Psyching is particularly effective when the student you are trying to psych is big with a mile-long record of teacher and student assaults and continual disruption. Sometimes he can be psyched out to behave and listen to you without having to go to a physical confrontation.

At one of the high schools where I taught, we had a supposedly rough student who, at two hundred and thirty pounds, was no slouch. He played Sunday sandlot football and a number of teachers used to go and watch him play and then discuss the game with him. Some of us also showed him pictures of us playing football at an earlier time. We also participated in some schoolyard touch football games with him. Our interest in him also gave him some self-respect and helped in psyching him to where he was rarely in trouble in our school.

I know of some cases where some of the male teachers would go to the gym to play basketball with students they were trying to psych. Smilingly, they would go in for a layup and knock the youngster down. They would then go over to him still smiling and brush off his clothes while commenting something like, "Sorry, but once I get going I can't stop."

Other teachers have been observed just going to the gym to play so that their students would see them playing. Another teacher I knew used to "accidentally" bump or brush against the youngster he was trying to psych in the hall and almost knock him down. Another teacher I knew had a dramatic routine he worked out with some of the bigger students that he used occasionally when new students entered his room. Reality 76 describes this.

One point must be made here before going further. In this psyching, the teachers were conveying to these students, on terms *they* could understand, that physically they were not fearful. This approach is often effective with a particularly physical youngster. He has to "feel physically" that you are not fearful of him. Also, the teacher using this type of psyching has to be sure of the youngster's emotional stability on the day he is acting physical. If it is the wrong day, such actions could cause a fight. This approach should not in any way be considered corporal punishment or a punitive approach. Actually, this approach alleviates the desire to use corporal punishment while recognizing that the youngster respects physical prowess.

REALITY 76

A teacher had worked out this routine with four students prior to the class. Three of the students entered the class and sat around close to the new students. About ten minutes into the class, the fourth student came in late.

The teacher approached him at the door and wanted to know why he was late.

His response was, "Man, I had to go."

Thereupon, the teacher would grab him by the shirt front and begin to make believe that he was slamming him against the door. Each time he would push him against the door, he would kick the bottom of the door with his foot.

Throughout this routine the youngster being pushed against the door would be screaming for mercy while promising never to come to class late again.

Meanwhile, the three other accomplices would be helping with the psych job by suggesting to the new students.

"Man, that teacher is crazy. He don't take shit from no-one."

"That teacher is a black belt."

"Jiiiim, that mutha nearly killed me two weeks ago."

As the new students took all this in, the teacher removed his hands from the student, and the student slid down the door to the floor, settling in a heap.

The teacher would walk toward his desk saying, "Don't anybody help him." As he nears his desk, the student would get up and walk toward his seat calling out, "OK, my word, I'll never be in late again."

For further effect, the teacher would walk around the room and stop by the desks of the new students.

These physical techniques worked for the teachers involved. The teachers were not sadists. They taught their students well and developed techniques based upon their personalities and the lifestyles of their students. All were teaching in very tough schools. Before anyone condemns these psyching techniques, he or she should spend some time teaching in a tough inner city secondary school.

Although psyching is rarely, if ever, discussed educationally, it surrounds us in the real world. The classic example of a psych job was carried out by the old hustler Bobby Riggs on Margaret Court.

> He saved his best efforts for weakening his rival. Riggs reminded Court of the pressure of carrying the banner of liberated women everywhere; he also referred ominously to her alleged history of folding in tense situations. Margaret had no such history, but Riggs is such a consummate con man that he soon had many people—perhaps including Margaret—believing him. Then he climaxed his psych job by arriving for the Mother's Day match with a bouquet of a dozen red roses and presented them to his foe at center court. . . . Margaret never did regain her composure. . . . She succumbed with all the docility of Riggs' kind of woman.[28]

(Of course, Billy Jean King eventually outpsyched Riggs and beat him badly.)

Those who watched the 1968 Olympics in Mexico will remember how Richard Fosburg of the United States used his "Fosburg Flop" to win the high jump. When asked why he was rocking back and forth at the starting line, he responded that he was psyching himself.

Although psyching is spoken of most often in sports, Golda Meir, former prime minister of Israel, allegedly tried to psych out the Pope on her visit to the Vatican in 1973. She was reported to have said that she looked the Pope in the eyes and refused to take her eyes from his.

Boxers at weigh-ins usually attempt to psych one another.

> Kingston, Jamaica, Jan. 22—Joe Frazier and George Foreman met eyeball-to-eyeball today in the most momentous confrontation since Golda Meir's confrontation with Pope Paul VI. It was only the weigh-in for their fistfight for the heavyweight championship of the world . . . but they traded glares so freighted with menace that the temperature around them dropped 20 degrees.[29]

Muhammed Ali is well known for his physical and verbal psyching and woofing. The United States swimmers had a "Psych Room" at poolside during the 1972 Olympics at Munich.[30] Jay Meisler, a schoolboy high jumper, ate sandwiches and sodas between jumps that helped him get rid of butterflies and "also psych me up and give me strength. I usually offer some to the other guys, but they get mad. It probably psychs them out."[31] At a wrestling match in California, the Southern California College coach entered a female wrestler in the match. The coach did this in the hope that the other team would default. "She said she had hoped her opponent would back off. 'At first, she psyched me out,' Peryer admitted, 'I wondered if she knew karate or something',"[32] And more than chess buffs remember the way America's Bobby Fischer psyched out Russia's Boris Spassky.

A few years ago, I was speaking at Ohio State University and had just gone over my jive test when a young white student came up and started speaking excitedly and emotionally about his experiences playing high school basketball for his all-white school that played some urban all-black teams. Reality 97 is his description of how he and his teammates were psyched out.

REALITY 77

"I'm from North Columbus, and went to a white suburban high school that happens to be in the Columbus City League. We had games with teams from the inner city, and one of the teams was the perennial city champs.

"When we would go to play them, they would have us psyched out because we thought their players were better. The crowd and just the entire atmosphere of the gymnasium was such that it was intended to disrupt our concentration and just totally throw us off; and, it did.

"As a matter of fact, one cheer that comes to mind took me so much by surprise. I had to listen to it at other games to try to pick up the rhythm of this certain cheer that seemed to have no rhythm when I first heard it. But, after some time, I picked it up. And, it would go something like this. . . . (He clapped his hands indicating the rhythm) . . . , and then they would yell 'kill.'

"Except, I didn't know they were yelling kill until I kept listening for what they were cheering. When I found out it was kill, it just, sort of, furthered my thought of a cheer. . . . And their cheerleaders, the way they would cheer would be totally different from the way our schools cheered.

"You know, we would have pyramids and cheerleaders would build things, and we wouldn't yell very loud, and we wouldn't clap very loud.

"The black schools would clap very loud, stomp very loud, yell very loud, and just, over all, try and disrupt our concentration."

The first course in my graduate program is a course in which teachers discuss problems, questions, or ideas. The object is for teachers to help one another resolve teaching-related questions or problems they may have. As part of the course, students are required to keep a journal related to the course.[33]

Reality 78 is from the journal of a new woman physical education teacher working in a suburban high school.

REALITY 78

Monday

Started out to be a lousy day. First day the unit started and quite a few individuals have "forgotten" to bring their clothes.

There is a group of black girls in my first period class who seem to demand special attention. They do not feel compelled to participate with the rest of the class. They isolate themselves from other students.

I am very confused. I try to be patient but when 13-year-old girls get obstinate and sassy, I get angry. What do you do with students who refuse to do anything? Do they act that way to rebel, to cover up their inadequacies (skills), to get attention? I wish I knew.

Tuesday

Brought up the problem that I'be been having in school at class [the university class] tonight. I may have some ideas on how to handle those monsters! Looking forward to the challenge!

Monday

Knew today was going to be my "favorite" first-period class. I finished reading your chapters on discipline and classroom contests last night. I really felt better and even gained strength from knowing I was not dealing with unique situations. On the contrary, they appeared to fall on the mild end of a rather large continuum of potential discipline "problems."

My first step was to drop my usual patient, understanding manner with my "problem" girls. After talking to their teacher from the previous year, I decided a stern maybe even hostile approach was needed. "You will or else" ultimatum until they realized their responsibilities.

Because this is an unusual behavior for me, I took pains to psyche myself up for this act. I wore my favorite sweat suit (Because of the material, color and fit I feel very physical in this particular suit—ready for action!), and had myself all set for an encounter! I was willing to sacrifice the whole period to straighten these girls out.

One of the girls approached me during their dressing time to tell me she did not have her sneakers and couldn't take class. I told her due to her past record either she was prepared and ready to participate in four minutes, or she would have detention after school for the entire week. This message was delivered in calm and very assertive manner.

Low and behold, the entire group appeared completely prepared for the activity—A miracle.

The Class went fine and at the end, I reminded the class what I expected from them and what consequences would be if the rules were broken.

I felt and sounded in complete control. At this rate, I might wear out that suit before Christmas.

Acting Dramatic or Crazy

An area sometimes discussed in the educational literature is the importance of teachers acting dramatically as a strategy for motivating students, particularly the noninterested or had-to-motivate youngster. A form of this drama for teachers could be referred to as "acting crazy." Claude Brown wrote about acting crazy as part of streetcorner life.

The bad nigger thing really had me going. I remember Johnny saying that the only thing a bad nigger was scared of was living too long. This just meant that if you were going to be respected in Harlem, you had to be a bad nigger; and if you were going to be a bad nigger, you had to be ready to die. I wasn't ready to do any of that stuff. But I had to act crazy.[34]

I thought they were all jive. The way I saw it, those niggers weren't so crazy. They were just acting like they were crazy. And they'd only act like that with cats who didn't know any better. Now I knew that if I was to breeze and they came after me, one of us would get hurt—me or whoever it was. But I just couldn't get too scared of them. I'd seen cats like that just about all my life.[35]

There is reporting of how acting crazy affects athletic opponents, too. For example, during the first qualifying round of the 1972 Olympic soccer competition, the United States drew three games with El Salvador, and each team was given five penalty shots. The United States players made all five.

When El Salvador converted its first two penalty shots, [Skip] Messing took matters into his own hands to end what appeared an interminable match.
All he did was go slightly berserk. "Nothing was planned," he said, "it was really quite spontaneous."
"Just as the El Salvador player was to take the third kick, I ripped off my shirt and started screaming obscenities in English. I actually left the goal and went out and slapped the guy on on the back to encourage him not to miss." Messing said. "Well, the guy was so confused he made the worst penalty kick I have ever seen."[36]

Although the streetcorner youngster is not technically the teacher's "opponent," he often acts that way as he contests the teacher for control of the class. Actually, though the teacher may not consider the streetcorner youngster his opponent, the youngster does indeed consider the teacher his opponent, as he does all authority. Therefore, very often the teacher who acts in a dramatic, "crazy" way not only throws off the streetcorner youngster's game of attempting to manipulate the class to his own ends, but may also win over the other students to his side. *The teacher can only control the class when he controls the streetcorner youngster.* And remember, the teacher can only teach in a class where he has control and a degree of order.

Acting crazy as a teaching style is not for all. I would emphasize again that each teacher must develop a teaching style based upon his or her personality. In my observations of teachers concerning the crazy style, I have found that those who succeed at this style are usually outgoing, good humored, and extroverted. Crazy teachers may be male or female. They may jive or woof on their students and enjoy going a bout of ribbing with them. "She was a crazy teacher. She rib on you for nothing. You rib on her, she rib you right back" may be heard about this sort of teacher.

Though these teachers play these games, they control their classes. They separate play from work. Their students are taught that play must stop when work starts. This teacher might be told laughingly, "You ought to see the principal—you are crazy," or "The next time I see the counselor, I am going to tell her to give you an appointment because you are sick."

Some incidents for which my high school students called me crazy involved two of the reference points of the streetcorner—talking and physical prowess. I often played a verbal game.

My class would be seated around a large work table. After taking the attendance, I would pick up my *New York Times*, open it and read.

"Wow, did you guys see his?"

"John Frank was picked up by the police outside of the A&P on 125th Street for stealing a lolly pop from a baby in a baby carriage."

The class would laugh and howl, and I would note who was laughing the loudest.

"José Rodriquez," I would make believe I was reading, "was arrested for knocking over a Boy Scout who was helping an 80-year-old lady across the street. According to the arresting officers, José was running after having stolen twenty-five cents from the poor box at the church around the corner."

I would go on for awhile and then we would get to work, all laughed out and relaxed.

Another crazy act I pulled one day was to pick up one of the boys and hang him by his coat on the top of the classroom door. Seeing the surprised look on his face as he hung there had us all laughing and rolling on the floor. Even he began to laugh.[37] Sometimes I would jump up on my desk or the work table in the midst of an impassioned presentation. I would get a good feeling when one of the students would say, "Come on, stop playing, I want to work."

In discussing the "crazy" teacher with white suburban youngsters, I found they like the crazy teacher too.

Reputation

One of the signs that a teacher has completed his rite of passage is the reputation he earns with students. If the teacher has cleared his rite of passage positively, his reputation talks about his toughness and "don't mess with him." If the passage has met with disaster, his reputation may be "Oh, he's a faggot, he's afraid of everyone." Female teachers also gain reputations. Their positive reputation is very much like the male's: "You can't run no games on her." If her passage was a disaster, boys may report her reputation as, "Shit, you sit up front you always see up her dress."

An interesting aspect of reputation building has to do with whether the students feel positively toward a teacher. If they do, minor incidents can be drawn all out of proportion in the teacher's favor. For example, after the gang fight described in Reality 16, I gained an exaggerated reputation. Some of the stories reported me beating up at least eight of the attacking gang. When questioned, I denied the story of inflicting a beating to the other gang. However, my students attributed my denial to my being modest. Of course, there are also the teachers who exaggerate incidents in an attempt at building their reputations on false foundations.

Reality 79 is a new white teacher's description of an incident between a male student and female student where the teacher intervened and earned an outstanding reputation in a tough secondary school. The situation described is not as atypical as it may appear.

REALITY 79

"One morning . . . while separating two students who were fighting in the halls during the change of classes, I was hit from behind with a sneaker. As I was restraining someone at the time, I could do little but look at who did it. It was somebody I didn't know or even recognize, and he was trying to agitate more trouble with shouts about the 'mother-fucking honkies.'

"I *asked* him to let her go. I was totally ignored. Then I moved closer and *told* him to let her go. This was met by a surprised look and a half-dozen obscenities and threats. He didn't let go and the girl continued to scream in pain. I then intervened by grabbing a pressure point on his wrist and forcing him to release the girl.

"By now, a number of students had gathered, as well as three neighboring teachers. The young man was now in a rage. . . . He threatened to kill me and then launched into an incredible racist tirade.

"He turned to put his sneakers down in preparation for a physical confrontation. I stood there silently listening and thinking that this guy must be deranged. I remained calm and cool, totally unmoved and showing no emotional reaction to his threats. The fact that I expressed no fear seemed to enrage him even more. Remember, we were now before twenty students who were just waiting to see how each of us moved and what we said.

"We stood face to face for at least a minute. Each threat or curse was met by a very matter-of-fact verbal response from me as I stood nonchalantly, with folded arms (with a sense of boredom and overconfidence).

"This attitude enabled me to remain detached enough to control my actions consciously. I was ignorant of the fact that he had a 6-inch straight razor in the hand he held behind his back. The students *were* aware of this and were amazed by my "courage." I was expecting that I might have to defend myself, but had no idea he had a weapon.

"One of the other teachers approached cautiously and suggested I return to my classroom as I was the object of his rage. I felt it best to let the other faculty present handle the situation. My very presence was enough to escalate the situation further. . . .

"It was only later that I learned about the razor. Kids came up to me all day asking if I was scared, and what would I have done if . . . ?

"This incident was the beginning of my particular school reputation. It was based essentially on fantasy, exaggeration, overstatement, and an unintentional situation in which my ignorance of circumstances enabled me to continue surviving.[38]

DISCIPLINE AND SOME GUT ISSUES

We have not solved the problem of discipline in schools because we have not been willing to come to grips and discuss openly some gut issues. The remainder of this chapter will discuss these issues as they are related to discipline.

These issues include: (1) control of those streetcorner youngsters who use real negative aggression and violence to test their teachers; (2) the interventionist model for training personnel to be able to cope with this real violence and aggression; (3) the differentiation between corporal punishment and physical restraint; and (4) teacher–student sexuality and discipline.

A Statement Concerning School Discipline

There are two questions here. First, is the teacher's role in discipline participatory or is it passive? Second, considering the class origins of most teachers and the inadequacies of teacher education and in-service programs, how much can we expect from teachers in disciplining the really tough aggressive acting-out youngster?[39]

Every time teachers get together, if you allow them to talk openly and honestly, someone will say, "But I didn't become a teacher to be a cop." How should this statement be taken? Should it be considered as a cry of despair by someone who should not really be an inner city teacher? Was it made by someone who was trying but just could not deal with one or two really tough streetcorner youngsters in his classroom? Was it made by a successful teacher who was describing what he perceived as a big part of his role and was bothered morally and philosophically? Or was it a little of each?

Accepting that many children test their teachers and always will,[40] the teacher must be capable of controlling the class and providing a healthy, relaxed atmosphere where learning can take place. Therefore, the teacher's role in discipline must be participatory. The teacher who looks at his role in discipline as passive—"My job is to teach, not to get them seated, quiet, and motivated"—maybe needs to find another profession.

In one of my graduate classes, a number of inner city and suburban high school youngsters were invited to talk with my students. The high school students were all on varsity teams. The ghetto youngsters were in one room and the suburban youngsters in another room. Neither group heard the other. My students heard both.

The contrast between the groups' feelings about testing teachers was predictable. Each group spoke of their testing teachers in a style that was commensurate with their social class lifestyle. They were at opposite ends of the continuum. The suburban youngsters talked about the importance of good grades, getting into good colleges, and not getting into trouble in school. They also talked about nonphysical ways of "getting away with things" only up to a point. Their outlook was realistic and always came back to getting into college and then a good job. Some of their suggestions included:

1. How to "brown" the teacher. (To "brown" or "brown-nose," is to curry favor from a teacher.)
2. "You see how much you can get away with."
3. "You don't push the teacher—then you find out what you can get away with."
4. "Never threaten a teacher. You can get thrown out of school if you do."

The inner city youngsters, on the other hand, in a tone that was physically aggressive, always talked about "running something," and not letting "someone take your stuff. You have to fight for all you got." Their approach to life also reflected their social class and black frame of reference for fame and fortune via either a "super star" or political role. In referring to teachers, they pointed out that "some of them have a natural fear of you. You bluff them hard and you can do anything." Their tactics included:

1. "Don't take no shit from anyone."
2. "If any teacher gives off the impression that he's afraid, I'll put the pressure on him and I'll keep on putting the pressure on him 'till I get him."
3. "Me and him have a stare-down all day."
4. "You can tell how a teacher looks nervous. He will fiddle with his pencil; look down and say 'ah,' 'ah,' 'ah,'; he will have a nervous smile; he will say 'I'll have your respect'; a quick nervous look around the room; you keep looking at the teacher—you move when he moves."
5. "Loud talk the teacher. Murphy and psych him out with double talk. If it is a woman teacher, sweet talk her."
6. "Tell the teacher to meet you in the gym or the parking lot. You tell him he better be able to back up his talk."
7. "Keep after the teacher that you want this and you want that."
8. "Like a murphy, you psych him into doing what you want."
9. "Nod out in class. When the teacher comes up to you, come up mad."[41]

In spite of the physical and aggressive bravado with which they test their teachers, at the end of their talk the students added, "Some better teachers would be a whole lot better." Hence, we see the inner city student's real desire for teachers who are capable of overcoming their actions to control them and make them learn.

Accordingly, we see their dilemma and the dilemma they cause in attempts to discipline them. On one hand, there is the need for the endless testing and proving of machismo, the never-ending drive to prove superior manhood. And, where the teacher is white, there appears to be a racial feeling added to the machismo drive. This feeling of black over white is akin to the writings of many black authors proclaiming that all white males are fags and all black males fearless studs. Where the teacher is black, the faggot feelings appear to be applied to the black teacher being tested because he appears to be playing the white, "nonmasculine" role of a teacher.

These youngsters do not seem to understand how self-destructive their behavior is. They do not realize how their behavior is preventing them and their fellow students from receiving an education. They seem to be playing out a street-ordained role over which they have no control.

At the same time, however, they long to be controlled by the use of tactics and emotions that are important to them and which they understand. They yearn for someone who can stand up to them, physically and emotionally. And, as far as they are concerned, it does not have to be in a nonpunitive way. I will argue, though, that it should and can be in a nonpunitive way.

One reason that this streetcorner youngster's physically aggressive approach to testing teachers is so effective is the difference between his lifelong exposure to real physical aggression and violence as compared with his teacher's contact with violence, which is usually vicarious.

Hunter Thompson, writing about the Hell's Angels of California, pointed out the phychological and emotional edge the Angels held over most middle class men because of the difference in experiences that each has had. He described a relationship that is analogous to the streetcorner youngster's experience with aggression and violence as compared with his teacher's experiences.

> There is not a Hell's Angel riding who hasn't made the emergencyward scene, and one of the natural results is that their fear of accidents is well tempered by a cavalier kind of disdain for physical injury. Outsiders may call it madness or other, more esoteric names . . . but the Angels inhabit a world in which violence is as common as spilled beer, and they live with it as easily as ski bums live with the risk of broken legs. This casual acceptance of bloodletting is a key to the terror they inspire in the squares. Even a small, inept street-fighter has a tremendous advantage over the middle-class American, who hasn't had a fight since puberty. It is a simple matter of accumulated experience, of having been hit or stomped often enough to forget the ugly panic that nice people associate with a serious fight. A man who has had his nose smashed three times in brawls will risk it again with hardly a thought.[42]

It is pointless to continue to blame inner city streetcorner youngsters, their families, their environment, or educators for the continued lack of discipline and learning in so many inner city schools. Without wasting time, energy, and emotions looking to assign responsibility or guilt, we ought to invest our time in resolving the problem.

The first order of business is to recognize that there are a number of lower class, black, male, streetcorner youngsters who test their teachers with a great deal of aggressive and sometimes violent behavior. Furthermore, because many of the school staff can not cope with this social class behavior in general, they become preoccupied with "getting order" and there is not enough time spent on teaching and learning.

The second order of business is for teacher educators and line educators to stop being so squeamish about aggression and lower class behavior and start dealing with educator ethnocentric and racist behavior that prevents them from understanding and dealing with lower class behavior in general and black streetcorner behavior in particular.

The third order of business is for districts to hire more principals who have the guts and temperament to get the order required for teaching and learning and to provide the leadership to help the staff move beyond their preoccupation with getting order and into learning and curriculum.

School personnel vary in their ability to cope with this behavior, just as the amount and type of disruptive behavior varies from school to school and area to area. Some school administrators and teachers already have the ability to deal with this behavior; consequently, in some schools the negative effects of aggression and violence are minimized.

Educators appear to respond with either of three traditionally punitive alternatives to discipline problems. The first response is the increasing cry for the return to "corporal punishment," more school suspensions, in-school detentions, and expulsions. The second approach is to ignore all preliminary signs of impending disorder in the hope that the problem will dissipate. The third response, usually after the disruption and violence has erupted, is to call the police.

The police presence, however, often creates additional problems. Their presence may not only provoke further disorder, but also—and more important— regardless of how unsafe and unmanageable the school situation that required police, the students', and often the community's, esteem for the school staff deteriorates when the police arrive. It is analogous to the inept teacher who has to call for outside help to discipline and motivate his or her class. Any respect students had for this teacher dwindles every time the outside authority arrives.

In the present school setting, except in the case of the most calamitous emergencies, adoption of unimaginative and traditional control devices seems to produce perverse and contraproductive results. Tensions and violence tend to be increased rather than reduced; basic constitutional rights, involving both substantive and procedural "due process," tend to be violated, thereby increasing the feeling of all too many young people that they are victims of authoritarian whim, not subjects of the equitable law that in civics classes they are asked to reverence.[44]

As a consequence, and because we just do not have enough personnel who can cope with either aggression and violence or lower class physicalness, it is imperative that we develop new staff and techniques to prevent and cope with this negative aggression and violence that has been interfering with instruction.

Numerous urban schools have some form of security officers. In some cases, the security officers wear uniforms; in others they wear blazers. However, most of these positions appear to be based upon a police-oriented security guard model, and their supervision and direction appears to come from former police officers.

To offset this trend, educators should develop an educational professional—the interventionist and interventionist aid—based on an educational model. It is imperative that this personnel model be developed form an educational model rather than from a police-oriented model. However, the interventionist must be capable of intervening to prevent or contain school-centered acts of violence by students and sometimes by nonstudents.

We have the beginning of such an educational model in special education and in many inner city schools. The interventionist is a more contemporary educator and paraprofessional developed from Morse's Crisis Teacher's role.[45] Although there is sparse literature that deals with educators coping with and preventing real violence, there are many years of unreported expertise and experience developed by those working with aggressive acting-out youngsters.[46]

The meager reporting appears to have come about because too many in leadership positions in education have either been unaware of or have refused to face the reality of violence in our schools. Whether this results from political or psychological reasoning or for other reasons is an area ripe for speculation and research.

I developed the interventionist concept from sixteen years of almost daily personal experience with aggression and violence in the New York City "600" day and institutional schools, as well as a short period with the Junior Guidance Classes Program. During my last two years with the "600" schools, I acted in the role of an interventionist and helped eradicate corporal punishment. In that particular school, through the interventionist philosophy, the level of negative aggression and violence was lowered significantly, if not erased. Additionally, a course at the State University of New York at Buffalo was conducted to prepare professionals to work with aggressive and violent youngsters and helped develop further the interventionist concept.[47] (See Chapter 9 for a description of the course.)

The interventionist's responsibility would include:

1. getting to know staff and students;
2. becoming sensitive to the early warning signals of impending overt aggressive behavior;
3. calming and talking with children on the verge of losing control or who have lost control and are interfering with instruction or becoming a physical threat to themselves, a teacher, or a peer;

4. replacing police in the halls or making their presence unnecessary; and
5. developing reciprocal communication links with all community groups.

Emphasis would be on intervention and resolution of problems and returning the youngster to class and preventing any interruption of instruction.

The education of the interventionists involves expertise in the two broad areas of: (1) verbal, nonverbal, and psychological intervention, and management concepts, techniques, and philosophy; and (2) nonpunitive physical intervention techniques. The interventionist's education would emphasize amelioration and resolution through verbal and psychological intervention techniques rather than through physical intervention. Interventionists would carry neither sidearms nor clubs, and they should be in civilian dress.

The responsibilities and expectations of the interventionist would depend upon each school situation. Requirements for those working in the inner city public school will differ from those who are institutionally based, those working in a day school for the emotionally disturbed, or those working in a suburban or rural school. Inteventionists should be teachers or guidance counselors.

Verbal, Nonverbal, and Psychological Intervention, and Management Concepts, Techniques, and Philosophy. In working with others, the interventionist's feelings, emotions, and attitudes would play an important role in the way he relates to each situation. Therefore, the first step in educating the interventionist to work with others is to help him recognize and understand his own emotions, feelings, and attitudes.

The interventionist's education would include discussions and readings on student problems and incidents, worker introspection, and the emotional aspects of his role in working with normal, disruptive, and aggressive students. An overview of the professional literature related to counseling, emotionally disturbed and socially maladjusted students, and life space interviewing would also be included. Particular emphasis will be placed upon historical and contemporary examples of how one man's or woman's action either calmed or exacerbated a particularly volatile situation. Additionally, the history of American violence should be studied as related to ethnic, religious, political, economic, racial, radical and antiradical violence, as well as violence in the name of law, order, and morality. Role playing would be used to discuss and discover the many behaviors that can be used in preventing, managing, and mediating crisis situations. Also, emphasized would be the legal and civil rights and responsibilities of all concerned—perpetrators, victims, and mediators.

In addition, the interventionist would be educated to differentiate between ghetto rhetoric and a real threat, as well as becoming conversant in black dialect or any of the nonstandard dialects spoken by the ethnic, religious, or racial minorities found in his school.

The interventionist should be well versed in first aid techniques. He should also be educated to "sniff out" the pot smoker and to differentiate between the alcoholic high, drug high, and acid high. He should also be educated to counsel and refer students on any of numerous problems. Some interventionists should be certified teachers, for the need may arise for the interventionist to remain with the class while the teacher leaves to work with the disruptive child.

The history of the contributions to the United States of the religious, ethnic, and racial minorities also would be included in their education of the interventionist. Particular emphasis would be placed upon the lifestyle of the group in the assigned school.

Nonpunitive Physical Intervention Techniques. It must be realized that no matter how expertly the interventionist deals with an acting-out student, the youngster may continue to demonstrate behavior that will have to be contained physically. For example, the need may arise to remove a student physically to protect another child, to prevent "contagion," (the spreading of the negative behavior), or for his own safety. Therefore, the interventionist would have to be educated in nonpunitive physical intervention techniques and philosophy. It must be emphasized that the interventionist should use physical intervention techniques only as a last resort.

Much of what is perceived as threatening and illegitimate violence is nothing more than the testing of the teacher's or interventionist's ability to control and set limits. Therefore, the interventionist would also be educated to differentiate between actual out-of-control behavior and lower class, norm-violating behavior that is not really violent or threatening, though often perceived as such by the ill trained or insecure.

Another important objective in the use of nonpunitive physical intervention techniques is to lower the level of violence by reducing the youngster's anxiety and need to retaliate. When a youngster loses control of his surface behavior, he often seeks controls from an outside source. However, when the outside physical controls are punitive, most often the child's anxiety and aggression is escalated even though the surface behavior may be controlled momentarily because of the fear of further physically punitive retaliation.

When the interventionist nonpunitively holds the child, he demonstrates a number of concepts and feelings to the child. First, because of the willingness to "get physical" with the child, he demonstrates that he is not afraid of the child. Second, by getting physical, the interventionist demonstrates that he is stronger than the child; hence he is strong enough physically to help the child control his impulses. Third, the interventionist has also demonstrated that because he is stronger than the child physically. he could have hurt him but has chosen not to. Elliot Shapiro, in describing an incident with a youngster, gives an example of the feelings that are transmitted when a warm adult is willing to become "physical" with a youngster.

> A few weeks later, he challenged me to box him. He had to reassure himself that physically I *could* take care of him. That way, if I were going to help him, my help would be worthwhile by his criteria. In other words, was I

"soft" only because I was helpless? You know, the man who lived with the "mother" who took care of John before she died was very cruel, but John missed his beatings in a way because he felt a man as strong as that could give him some kind of security. So he came into my office, I closed the door, and we boxed for about three minutes. Mostly I outfeinted him, although occaally I'd hit him lightly on the face. He was really trying, but he was quite pleased that he lost, because now he felt I could take care of him.[48]

Another important point is that the disadvantaged youngster equates the worker's willingness to use nonpunitive physical force with caring and warmth and he perceives fear as prejudice. Also, the way the interventionist copes with the out-of-control student may be an important factor in helping the youngster himself to cope with his own anxieties.

The interventionist's willingness to become physical can also help the child who has been forced into a fight to save face. This youngster may be too fearful to stop because he is afraid of his peers who forced or manipulated him into the fight. Here the youngster can use the interventionist's superior physical strength as a legitimate excuse for stopping the fight until his own controls are sufficient for him to withstand the verbal and physical onslaughts and manipulations of his peers.

I have observed supposedly out-of-control youngsters go directly to the interventionist or worker they knew was not afraid to control them physically. Conversely, when the professional shows fear, he may provoke an already frightened youngster to act out further.

Interventionists must be educated in the following "last resort" nonpunitive physical intervention techniques:

1. Methods and techniques of separating students who have lost control and who may be fighting.
2. The use of minimal nonpunitive physical force for disarming students or unauthorized visitors who may be threatening or attacking others with weapons.
3. Physical nonpunitive restraint of students or unauthorized visitors who are physically attacking someone, "ripping off" school equipment, "trashing," attempting to burn or blow up a building, or otherwise interfering with instruction or threatening a student or worker with physical harm.

The interventionist's confidence in his physical capabilities, secured through the mastery of techniques, will provide him with the following psychological set which will help him to resolve potential crisis situations:

1. removal of the fear of physical injury;
2. the ability to retain composure in a confrontation or violently physical situation; and

3. the knowledge that if the situation gets out of hand, he can handle it physically.

The student who has underdeveloped control of his behavior gains strength to control his behavior from: (1) the inner strength of the worker; and (2) if necessary, the willingness of the worker to restrain him physically. In most cases of disruption, the disorderly student gives innumerable warning signals that can be read by the well-trained worker to ameliorate or prevent the impending situation.

Ongoing Staff Communication.   When the interventionist is introduced into the school, a certain amount of time must be expected to elapse while the professional staff tests to see whether the interventionist will really provide the assistance he has been billed to provide. The interventionist will probably have to work hard to substantiate his worth before he is accepted.

To increase the proficiency and acceptance of interventionists, it is imperative that ongoing communication be scheduled between the interventionists and the staff to resolve issues that may arise. This articulation would, hopefully, overcome the tendency of the professional staff and the interventionist to develop inaccurate expectancies of each other's roles. A deep trust and respect for one another's roles must be developed.

Mutual trust is particularly important in relation to the removal and returning of children to class or to school. For example, the teacher must have faith in the interventionist's decision that the child is calm enough to be returned to class. Similarly, the interventionist must trust that the teacher seeks his aid because he needs it.

Teachers and interventionists must also become used to the nuances of one another's professional styles so that they may use these verbal and nonverbal signals to resolve potentially volatile situations.

In-Service Education
Physical Aspects.   The interventionist should keep in a high state of physical condition. His mastery of nonpunitive physical intervention techniques should be ongoing.

Affective Aspects.   Educational programs should be developed to effect positive changes in the feelings, emotions, and attitudes of the interventionists. For example, much discussion in the literature has centered upon teacher understanding of student aggression. However, there appears to be little literature related to helping teachers cope with their aggressive feelings which may build up after hours of working with aggressive and violent children. Included in the continued in-service program, therefore, must be a system to help the interventionist understand and release his pent-up emotions and feelings of aggression in a positive way. One such system is the discussion groups described in Chapter 9 as part of the New Teacher Project.

Help-Seeking System. Many systems have been suggested for use in securing the assistance of the interventionist. These systems have run the gamut from sending a child for help to the use of a buzzer or light system activated by a key or push button.

The system I suggest would provide each teacher with a small transmitter with its own frequency. These transmitters would be small enough to be hooked onto a belt, hung around the neck or placed in a pocket. Because of the size of the transmitter, the teacher could carry it on his person and actuate the transmitter which could activate a buzzer and light on a monitor panel.[49]

Parent Understanding of the Interventionist's Role. Upon intake of students, the role of the interventionist must be explained to parents, *particularly the interventionist's last resort nonpunitive physical restraining role.*

The question is no longer whether we need such professionals in our schools. A distorted model of the interventionist is already in many schools. The question is whether those who are now there should be allowed to continue to follow a police security model.

It appears that the majority of administrators have opted for the passive and easy role in discipline and security and have turned the job over to police-oriented security programs. Hence, a security instead of an educational-interventionist approach is being followed.

CORPORAL PUNISHMENT, HITTING, AND PHYSICAL RESTRAINT

There are differences between corporal punishment, hitting, and physical restraint. Technically, corporal punishment takes place when the child accepts the punishment that is being meted out for violating a particular rule—for example, two swats for being late to class. However, the Board of Regents in New York State voted to ban corporal punishment in New York State by September 1985 and defined corporal punishment as " 'any act of physical force' used to 'punish' a student."[50]

Hitting a youngster could take place for any number of reasons. For example, a teacher could get mad at a youngster for cursing and slap or punch him.

Physical restraint would be using as much force as is necessary to restrain a youngster. For example, a youngster may be hitting a fellow student and refuse to stop. Whereupon, the teacher would actually hold and restrain him physically to stop him from hitting the other student.

The concept of corporal punishment probably has been argued since there have been schools. However, the arguments against corporal punishment have not been very successful, when compared with other humanitarian advances, because most of those arguing against its use appear to have done so in isolation from the reality of school conditions. Very often, corporal punishment or the idea of hitting children is a teacher's perceived last resort in response to a continuing and intensely frustrating condition.

There are also differences in viewpoint between the suburbs and the inner city in relation to the corporal punishment discussion. Inner city parents seem less concerned about corporal punishment than they are of illegal suspensions, improper labeling of students, covert and overt racist ploys that some educators use knowingly or unknowingly on black youngsters, and the assigning of acting-out or handicapped youngsters to home instruction because of a lack of alternative, but often legally mandated, facilities.[51]

Some of the school conditions that must be considered within the context of the anticorporal punishment position include the following:

1. There are students who lose control of their behavior and act out in a negatively aggressive and violent way against their fellow students and teachers and thereby interfere with instruction and endanger the health and safety of students, school personnel, and themselves.
2. Many lower class students court aggression and violence and have been conditioned to expect and accept physical and autocratic discipline.
3. There are some aggressive and violent students who lose control of their behavior and must sometimes be stopped and controlled physically.
4. Few alternatives to corporal punishment have been available to educators when a student has refused a reasonable request for compliance with school rules.
5. Very few temporary placement alternatives are available to help the child who is not emotionally or physically handicapped or learning disabled.
6. The teacher is usually completely on his or her own with little or no support from principals or supervisors.

Throughout this and earlier chapters, many of these six considerations have been discussed. Therefore, this discussion will deal with the difference between negative physical punishment and physically intervening by restraining children who have lost control of their behavior.

The National Commission on the Causes and Prevention of Violence suggested that there is "legitimate" as well as "illegitimate" violence within the "context of a particular human society or cultural tradition."[52]

All societies must draw moral and legal distinctions between legitimate and illegitimate violence. One traditional and vital function of social order, of the state and its laws, has been to determine in particular cases when violence is legitimate (as in self-defense, discipline of children, . . .) when it is illegitimate (as in violent crime, . . .) .

There is, therefore, no universal agreement of a definition of the term "violence" which makes it mean something that is always to be condemned. For purposes of commencing our study, we have defined "violence" simply as the threat or use of force that results, or is intended to result, in the injury or forcible restraint or intimidation of persons, or the destruction or forcible seizure of property.

There is no implicit value judgment in this definition. The maintenance of law and order falls within it, for a policeman may find it necessary in the course of duty to threaten or use force, even to injure or kill an individual. Wars are included within this definition, as is some punishment of children. It also includes police brutality, . . . and the physical abuse of a child.

This definition has important implications for our understanding of the causes and prevention of the illegitimate violence that our society condemns. For example, it helps us to recognize that illegitimate violence, like most deviant behavior, is on a continuum with and dynamically similar to legitimate violence. The parent who spanks a child may be engaging in legitimate violence, but for the parent to break the child's arm would be illegitimate violence.

A neutral definition of violence also helps us to recognize that some minimum level of illegitimate violence is to be expected in a free and rapidly changing industrial society. Maintaining a system of law enforcement capable of eliminating all illegitimate individual and group violence might so increase the level of legitimate violence that the harm to other values would be intolerable. . . .

The elimination of all violence in a free society is impossible. But the better control of illegitimate violence in our democratic society is an urgent imperative, and one within our means to accomplish.[53]

With that in mind, one of the important points that must be understood is that when students act in a violent way against others, some form of counter-violence may have to be used to contain or stop their actions. However, the amount and type of so-called violence or force that must be used is what is important. The concept of physically controlling a child has implicit in its approach that one use only as much force as is necessary to physically restrain the youngster. Meting out punishment is not the role of the professional, and, as noted earlier, the youngster being restrained physically does not, then, have the need to "get even."

To establish further the difference between physical restraint and corporal punishment, the following definitions are suggested.

1. Physical restraint is intended to be used solely to stop the action of the child.
2. Physical restraint does not intend the force exerted to restrain to be experienced as a punishment; corporal punishment intends pain to be experienced as a penalty or punishment.
3. Physical restraint is applied only during the performance of the negative act by the child; corporal punishment may be administered during the performance of the act or after it has been completed.
4. When corporal punishment is used during the negative act, its function is both physical restraint and punishment. When applied after the act, it serves only the function of punishment. The important point is that where corpo-

ral punishment is administered during the act, physical restraint could have been used instead to stop the child's negative action.[54]

The use of physical restraint on a child does not preclude punishment if indicated. However, the punishment should be reasonably nonphysical and should not be carried out in the heat of confrontation.

Finally, it seems illogical and hypocritical for educators to preach the need for nonviolent resolution to problems while in the same breath calling for the retention of corporal punishment. Educators must realize that when they practice corporal punishment, a value is attached to the use of physical force to achieve goals, and this action becomes a model of negative aggression and violent behavior which could and often does lead to imitation by schoolchildren. There is already a good deal of evidence that finds physically aggressive children coming from homes where they were disciplined physically and aggressively. If educators do not play a role in stopping the cyclic nature of negative aggressive behavior, who will?

Furthermore, when a teacher uses corporal punishment, he foolishly allows his board of education to place him in this position by their not providing him with a nonpunitive alternative to controlling a child's negative behavior. Teachers should remember this point as discipline increasingly becomes an element in negotiations between teachers and school boards.

TEACHER-STUDENT AND STUDENT-STUDENT SEXUALITY AND DISCIPLINE

The phenomenon of teacher-student sexuality exists in all schools. As Herbert Greenberg noted, "Adults of varying experience and children in varying stages of psychosexual development encounter each other within the school, and inevitably many feelings are aroused."[55] Additionally, as George Gilder pointed out, "sex is the life force and cohesive impulse of a people, and their very character will be deeply affected by how sexuality is sublimated and expressed, denied or attained."[56]

Generally, in school, the expression of sexuality between students and teachers and students and students is handled in a mature and nondisruptive way. However, when teacher and student sexuality, repressed or overt, is based on widely differing lifestyles and socioeconomic levels, conflicting expectations, and racial fantasies, strong conscious and unconscious sexual feelings can be aroused and can play a role in creating discipline problems.

In more schools than ever before these aroused or repressed sexual feelings have resulted in and continue to lead to: (1) the suspension of black male students, (2) the assignment of black male adolescents to special education programs, (3) volatile behavior from black female students, (4) black and white student problems, and (5) personal and professional problems for male and female teachers who have problems with their sexuality and physicalness.

This section will discuss the relationship between student–teacher and student–student sexuality and discipline problems in schools having diverse populations of students and teachers. The discussion will not be all-inclusive; rather, it will be a beginning that others, hopefully, will add to with further discussion, investigation, and suggestions for amelioration.

Reality 80 describes a physical attack on a young white female teacher by a black fifteen-year-old male student. After the incident, the student was suspended and then sent to a special school for maladjusted boys. The description will show that the incident was a frightening experience for the teacher and for the student as well. Additionally, the incident could have been avoided.

REALITY 80

The class was seated waiting for the period to start. The teacher was at the door supervising the changing of classes.

A male student about fifteen years of age grabbed the teacher's arms as he entered the room. He pushed her toward the desk, while turning the lights off. He then bent the teacher's back over the desk and placed himself between her legs.

"You my woman. Everyone knows it," he said as he leaned over her holding her arms down on the desk beside her head.

The teacher in a frightened voice cried out, "No, I'm not. You are too young."

After a few more words, the youngster released the teacher and ran from the room.

If a sexual attack was intended, it never took place, as the youngster neither opened his pants nor fondled the teacher. If a physical attack was the objective, he did not succeed in this either, as he only held the teacher's wrists tightly. Actually, the incident was the culmination of the white teacher's inappropriate, and possibly unknowing, sexually provocative behavior.

The teacher was in her early twenties, about five feet four inches tall, slightly built, and frail in appearance. Her classroom discipline and organization was poor. Her students did pretty much as they chose. According to her, her guiding philosophy was to play the role of the forlorn woman and have her students discipline themselves for her.—a completely passive role in discipline.

She wore short skirts, which were then the fashion, and often sat on her desk when talking to the class. Older boys were known to pinch her backside when walking in the hall. In the main, she did nothing to discourage this student behavior.

In her relations with the student who attacked her, she had permitted a certain degree of intimacy. She often remained after school alone with him in her room. On many occasions, he helped her on with her coat, and she allowed him to look through the pictures in her wallet when alone with him.

After the incident, the youth's mother reported that she knew her son was uncommonly interested in the teacher. For the past few weeks he was dressing specially for her and talked about her incessantly at home. The mother, although worried and uneasy about her son's behavior at home, did nothing. Had the teacher been more mature and aware of her own sexuality and the historical problems associated with black male and white female relations, the incident need not have taken place.

Unfortunately, the actions of the youngster and the teacher in Reality 80 may be more typical than we wish to admit. There are three reasons for these teacher–student problems: (1) the historical perspective of our sexual customs, (2) the differences in the way lower class and middle class life experience educates and conditions us to cope with sexuality, and (3) the male and female black and white relationships that are affected by the historical racist fantasies related to black and white male and female sexuality.

Johnson and Johnson report that our attitudes, laws, and moral standards are an outgrowth of the Jewish patterns of the Old Testament. In the Old Testament, sex, although regarded highly, was subjected to strict regulation and was considered to be primarily for propagation. An additional influence on our sexual standards resulted from the highly negative attitude toward women that the early Christian fathers added to Jewish sexual regulations, which they adopted almost totally into the body of Christian sexual morality. Today, our official legal structure and sexual morality is based upon the Judeo-Christian sexual tradition that was brought in intensified form to America by our seventeenth century Puritan fathers, who added a "highly regulatory and antisexual pattern."[57] Innumerable threads of these three factors affect the relationships of black and white teachers and students in our schools.

In light of the above, sexuality in the United States has taken a number of interesting turns. Women's more openly expressed sexuality has been accepted in many areas of American life; for example, an unmarried woman's loss of her virginity is not usually looked on with disdain; many women are as sexually active and open as are men; and some women admit to looking at men's crotches as some men look at women's breasts.[58]

Open gay sexuality is also more accepted in certain areas, and there are openly gay communities in many sections of the country. There is even television advertising directed toward gays.

Despite the more open acceptance of our sexual attitudes, behaviors, preference, and sexuality, we still have some very real sexuality problems. The woman's body is still more sensuous than is the man's body, and men are much more easily aroused sexually. For whatever reason, in most cases, men possess no such power to arouse equally the *average* woman by merely being in close proximity. Moreover, even when men and women are sexually aroused in public, it is the man's anatomy, his erect penis, that frightens and embarrasses him.[59]

Also, for various reasons, young men are often inadequate when making love with a woman. And, as Kate Millett has informed us, "all the best scientific evidence today unmistakably tends toward the conclusion that the female possesses, biologically and inherently, a far greater capacity for sexuality than the male, both as to frequency of coitus, and as to frequency of orgasm."[60]

To which we can add Gilder's point that,

> males are the more sexual outsiders and inferior. A far smaller portion of their lives is devoted to specifically sexual activity. Their own distinctively sexual experience is limited to erection and ejaculation; their primary sexual drive leads only toward copulation. Beside the socially indispensable and psychologically crucial experience of motherhood, men are irredeemably subordinate.[61]

In addition, the middle class woman begins to develop her female sexual patterns, practicing even more and various forms of sexual display, adding to her innate sexuality—particularly that artful display of her body.[62]

Whereas impotence reports used to be heard about men in their forties and fifties, today, there are reports of impotent young men in their early twenties. Additionally, according to Professor Joseph LoPiccolo, the women's movement has given women confidence in their sexuality to where sex is more acceptable to them. Hence, rather than feeling they are oversexed, they are questioning their husband's sexual behavior, exhibiting greater sex drives than their husbands, and "dragging their husbands into therapy in growing numbers."[63]

Nevertheless, our middle class sexual mores permit, and even expect, a certain amount of provocative sexual teasing and gaming from attractive girls and women. When this sexuality is used with middle class males, the middle class males are expected to withdraw, suppress or sublimate their sexual feelings, or continue to play the sexual teasing and gaming without becoming too sexually aggressive. This is the baggage middle class males and females bring with them into our classrooms. Furthermore, to the detriment of all, rarely is sexuality and its ramifications ever discussed as part of undergraduate teacher education, graduate education, or in-service education.

In poverty and ghetto lifestyles, sex and sexuality in language and actions are treated with greater openness and acceptance. Alvin Poussaint reported that blacks have, in particular, a unique cultural and social experience. "From Africa, blacks brought with them an unperverted attitude toward sex and procreation. Though erotic outlets were regulated by the customs and mores of many different sub-groups, chastity was not necessarily a virtue and appropriate premarital relations were not frowned upon. Sex was considered an important and pleasurable part of life."[64] Lower class males and females, particularly males, are not conditioned to sublimate or repress their sexuality; in fact, the lower class lifestyle conditions for a more open sexuality.

Although the sex studies performed in the United States have ignored blacks, a study dealing with "Sexuality, Contraception, and Pregnancy among Young Unwed Females in the United States" by Melvin Zelnik and John Kantner had a total population of 4,611 aged fifteen through nineteen, of whom 1,479 were black females. Although they dealt with "simple demographic controls, such as age and race," and refrained from using controls related to socioeconomic status, undoubtedly some of the differences they found in sexual behavior between blacks and whites can partially be accounted for "in terms of differences in socioeconomic factors."[65]

They found pronounced differences between blacks and whites. Blacks, for example, had intercourse at a significantly earlier age than whites, and proportionately more of them had intercourse. Their data reported that by age eighteen, 80.8 percent of the black females had intercourse while only 40.4 percent of the white females had intercourse. By age sixteen, 46.4 percent of the black females had intercourse as compared with only 17.5 percent of the white females. Interestingly, the study also found that although more black females have had intercourse, the white nonvirgins were more promiscuous and had sex more frequently. This suggests that black nonvirgins are more loyal to their lovers than are white female nonvirgins. Hence, the black female may attach more feeling to her sexual experiences.

This may suggest an explanation for the volatility of black female students, particularly in the junior high school. For example, even in all-white schools, we find female students jealous of attractive female teachers and female student teachers. It appears that the female students see young female teachers as rivals for their boyfriends.

The same feelings may be going on in integrated schools intensified by the racial fantasies and socioeconomic differences between students and teachers. In the white middle class school, the behavior of the white female teacher is familiar to both students and teachers. In the inner city and integrated school, the white female, as both the forbidden fruit and the white queen, may act in a middle class flirtatious-sexually provocative way toward black female students' boyfriends in a way that the latter sees as unfair competition. Sensing or assuming this interaction between the white female teacher and their boyfriends, the black female students may react by being in a constant state of sexual jealousy; thus the volatileness.

The experiences of black and white workers in the southern civil rights movement also reflected the black females' feelings of being threatened by the black male-white female relationships. "Black girls were sometimes frantically jealous of the white girls and in a state of panic because they feared that they would lose their boy friends to white girls. The black girls were usually the most insistent in demanding that whites be put out of the movement and were the strongest supporters of exclusive black consciousness programs."[66]

Negro women tend to have a generalized, deep-seated resentment toward white women because of society's superior valuation of 'white standards of beauty.' . . . They see white female civil rights workers as competitors for their Negro men; and since the Negro man has been brainwashed for centuries with 'sacred white womanhood,' many of the Negro girls see these white girls as unfair competition.[67]

My contention about the negative effects of some white female teachers' flirtatious actions is further supported by the evidence gathered by Dr. Alvin Poussaint in interviews and personal participation with black and white workers during the Mississippi voter registration drive of the summer of 1966. Many of the actions of white female middle class civil rights workers were parallel to the actions of some white middle class teachers in inner city schools. Poussaint reported that the black power philosophy which came to the forefront in the summer of 1966, "in part reflected the already-existing strong anti–white civil rights workers' sentiments among black participants in the movement." Much of this was precipitated by the actions of the white workers, particularly the females.[68]

This antagonism came about for a number of reasons. Many of the white volunteers possessed "certain psychological attitudes of racial superiority which were often subconscious, which blacks sarcastically referred to as the 'White African Queen Complex' in the female and the 'Tarzan Complex' in the male."[69] Many of the white workers exhibited deep psychological problems. Not only did they use the movement to try to work out their problems, but they used the black communities as a setting to express their rebellious and antisocial behavior. In an attempt to show how "free" they felt they were about working with blacks, many of the white workers flouted the social and moral standards of the black and white communities they were working in with "unorthodox behavior." An unkempt style of dress was one of the more common manifestations of this pathology. (This is discussed further in the next chapter.) The local inhabitants who could not go North after the summer looked on this behavior as "thinly veiled white racism" and disrespect toward the black community.

Many of the white workers exhibited a pathological guilt need that caused them to court dangerous and painful situations that often led to jail or the sought-after badge of the bruises from beatings. That this behavior involved not only their safety but that of their black co-workers and the black community, often seemed to be of secondary concern.

Very often, the crisis in black-white worker relationships centered around sociosexual conflicts, as well as the need to suffer.

For instance, a white girl, wishing to display her newfound sense of racial brotherhood, might reach out and affectionately take the hand of a black male worker in front of a Mississippi Highway Patrolman or local white toughs, or worse still, both. In Mississippi, this might well be considered a suicidal gesture on the part of the girl. However, it could also be a homicidal gesture subconsciously directed at the male, who, under the circumstances, might easily be lynched or beaten up. Similarly, a black fellow might get beaten up by local officials while the white girl escaped with an epithet, if they were apprehended riding in a car together.[70]

In addition to the aforementioned, the black male and white female relationships greatly preoccupied the black males' time. They were very much aware that their relationships with white women broke the most sacred of southern taboos. Because of this,

> in nearly all social situations with white women, they were plagued by ambivalence as well as by a mixture of feelings of fear, hate, suspicion, and adoration. In fact, so much energy was expended by both black men and women on discussing white girls that there were many days when no project work was accomplished. The problem was further exacerbated by the sometimes deliberately flirtatious behavior of white girls. Even some of the "black nationalist" types continued a vigorous pursuit of the white volunteers.[71]

In turn, some of the white girls appeared overly preoccupied with how frequently they were propositioned.

Many of these white female workers, as well as teachers in inner city schools, experienced situations that were often physically dangerous as well as nerve-wracking. Most often, the white workers found "themselves at the center of an emotionally shattering cross fire of racial tensions, fears, and hatreds that have been nurtured for centuries."[72]

Some of the white women were insightful and mature enough to handle the cross-currents and problems and were able to function productively. Most, however, despite their good intentions and strengths, were not able to cope with tensions of their frustrations and personal fantasies concerning their missionary role in civil rights. Often, they were blamed for problems that any of the projects were experiencing; they became scapegoats. At times they became the targets of vulgar and lewd accusations. Often, no matter what a white woman's personal relations were, she was "accused by both white and black Southerners of having perverse sexual interest in Negro men."[73]

Although white males appear not to have created the sociosexual problems that the white females and black males created during the voter registration programs, their historical role in perpetuating sexual myths about blacks set the tense atmosphere for the problems.

The English who settled in America brought with them set social attitudes, sexual mores, as well as "certain more or less definite ideas about African sexuality."[74] Englishmen associated lecherousness and sexuality with "heathen, savage, beast-like men," which they considered Negroes to be.[75] Their association of potent sexuality with Africans and warm climates predated any real English contact with Africa. Virtually all those living on the continent were convinced by the literature of Europe that Africans were wanton and lustful.[76] One report by a Spanish Moroccan Moor who converted to Christianity wrote in 1526 that Negroes, in addition to other beastial qualities, "have great swarms of Harlots among them; whereupon a man may easily conjecture their manner of living."[77] Additional reporting described Negro men with "large Propagators."[78]

Although there were regional styles in racial intermixture, miscegenation was extensive in all the English colonies. In the American colonies, and even now, typical sexual liaisons involved white men and black women. The combination of white women and black men was "far more common than is generally supposed."[79]

In some colonies—the West Indian colonies, for example, and to some extent, South Carolina—the miscegenation practices were more inflexible than in others. White women neither married nor slept with black men; white men customarily took black women as mistresses. As black slaves assumed a greater work role, the white female appeared to become more protected and more of an ornament. She could "withdraw from the world or to create an unreal one of her own."[80] A tense biracial atmosphere was created where "she was made to feel that sensual involvement with the opposite sex burned bright and hot with unquenchable passion and at the same time that any such involvement was utterly repulsive. Accordingly, . . . she approached her prospective legitimate sexual partners as if she were picking up a live coal in one hand and a dead rat in the other."[81]

Winthrop Jordan also pointed out that the colonial American and English cultures and experiences were male dominated. Hence, the specifically masculine modes of behavior and thought that shaped the psychological needs of men to a considerable extent set the sexually oriented beliefs of the black that still hold in the United States today.[82]

The colonial male considered the black woman especially passionate. Though the white woman's experience inhibited her sexual expression, the situation in which the Negro woman found herself encouraged it.

> For by calling the Negro woman passionate they were offering the best possible justification for their own passions. Not only did the Negro woman's warmth constitute a logical explanation for the white man's infidelity, but, much more important, it helped shift responsibility from himself to her. If she was *that* lascivious—well, a man could scarcely be blamed for succumbing against overwhelming odds.[83]

The concept that the black male was rather promiscuous, lusty, and virile gave the white man a more potentially explosive and complex problem to deal with. Consequently, the English colonists in America appeared to add a half-conscious and interesting corollary that is still a part of today's fantasies and fears. He believed that all blacks lusted for white women. Of course, there probably was some basis for this feeling, as a black male's sexual intercourse with a white woman would have some symbolic gesture of retribution against white men, as indicated by Eldridge Cleaver.[84] However,

> No matter how firmly based in fact, . . . the image of the sexually aggressive Negro was rooted even more firmly in deep strata of irrationality. For it is apparent that white men projected their own desires onto Negroes: their own passion for Negro women was not fully acceptable to society or the self and

hence not readily admissible. Sexual desires could be effectively denied and the accompanying anxiety and guilt in some measure assuaged, however, by imputing them to others. It is not we, but others, who are guilty. It is not we who lust, but they. Not only this, but white men anxious over their own sexual inadequacy were touched by a racking fear and jealousy. Perhaps the Negro better performed his nocturnal offices than the white man. Perhaps, indeed, the white man's woman really wanted the Negro more than she wanted him.[85]

The white man's fear of the black's supposed superior sexuality had led to early laws calling for the castration of Negroes for crimes.[86] Additionally, many black men have been "publicly castrated and lynched for supposedly raping white women."[87]

These fantasies and fears that grew from our racism have conditioned many black and white Americans to act in ways based on their unconscious feelings related to black and white sexuality. Many of these actions can be observed being played out in inner city and other classrooms by teachers and students.

A black youngster may attach to his white teacher the image of a clean and wholesome middle class America; she may become his feminine ideal. And, depending upon her maturity, he may be helped or hurt. On the other hand, she may become the object of a black student's pent-up aggression and hate. To do something negatively to her may serve as a source of revenge for his pent-up rage. To some black males, to seduce or rape as many white women as possible is to sexually and symbolically restore their manhood. To Cleaver, for example, rape was his "insurrectionary act."

> I became a rapist. To refine my technique and *modus operandi*, I started out by practicing on black girls in the ghetto—in the black ghetto where dark and vicious deeds appear not as abberations or deviations from the norm, but as part of the sufficiency of the Evil of a day—and when I considered myself smooth enough, I crossed the tracks and sought out white prey. I did this consciously, deliberately, willfully, methodically—though looking back I see that I was in a frantic, wild, and completely abandoned frame of mind. . . .
>
> Rape was an insurrectionary act. It delighted me that I was defying and trampling upon the white man's law, upon his system of values, and that I was defiling his women—and this point, I believe, was the most satisfying to me because I was very resentful over the historical fact of how the white man used the black woman. I felt I was getting revenge. From the site of an act of rape, consternation spreads outwardly in concentric circles. I wanted to send waves of consternation through the white race.[88]

Philip Roth also expressed a need to get even, to get revenge. However, because he had experienced a different lifestyle, his revenge was not violent. Nevertheless, his revenge was also through a sexual outlet. For him, to seduce (not rape) a WASP; to make love to an "aristocratic Yankee beauty whose forebears arrived on these shores in the seventeenth century: a phenomenon known as

Hating Your Goy and Eating One Too," was enough.[89] ' "What I'm saying, Doctor, is that I don't seem to stick my dick up these girls, as much as I stick it up their backgrounds—as though through fucking I will discover America. *Conquer America*—maybe that's more like it.' "[90]

James Baldwin also wrote of the relationships between sex and violence in the experience of black men. His words graphically described the depth of the black man's feelings.

> In most of the novels written by Negroes until today (with the exception of Chester Hime's *If He Hollers Let Him Go*) there is a great space where sex ought to be; and what usually fills this space is violence. . . .
> This violence, . . . is gratuitous and compulsive . . . because the root of the violence is never examined. The root is rage. It is the rage, almost literally the howl, of a man who is being castrated. . . . [T]here is probably no greater (or misleading) body of sexual myths in the world today than those which have proliferated around the figure of the American Negro. This means that he is penalized for the guilty imagination of the white people who invest him with their hates and longings, and is the principal target of their sexual paranoia.[91]

An awareness of this background should give us some insight into the nature of the discipline problems evolving from white and black relations. Too often, female teachers, knowingly or unknowingly, act in sexually provocative ways. Sometimes, also, youngsters behave negatively against female teachers without being sexually provoked. At times, black male students may say something to a white teacher that may be only a test of her ability to control him and set limits without sexual connotations. At other times, his actions may actually reflect a reaction to her overt sexuality, or they may grow out of his own fantasies, or racism, or a combination of both.

Some white female teachers, conscious or unconscious sexually provocative actions that have been observed run the gamut from acting in an excessively flirtatious way, to placing or pressing one's breasts on the desk or against a male student's arm or body while helping him with his work, and include wearing a sheer or see-through blouse or tight sweater, with or without a bra; wearing an overly tight skirt, dress, slacks, or pants suit; or sitting in front of the class with an excessively short skirt that exposes her underpants when she bends over or reaches up to write on the board.

Depending upon his experiences, a lower class black male student may react to sexual provocation in many ways. However, his reaction to sexual stimulation and provocation is usually more direct than that of the middle class male student. The lower class black male usually *acts*, while the middle class white or black male usually sublimates or represses his response. Reality 80 was but one example.

A reading of report slips by white female teachers concerning black male students showed incidents in which students grabbed the teacher, threatened the teacher, stood in the door blocking her way (woofing), cursed, punched, took the teacher's keys, or pinched her. Others reported "rubbing against me, touching my dress, or touching me." Additional reports included, "He ran his hand down my backside"; "He ran his hand down my arm"; and "He ran his hand through my hair."

Most of these reports described reasonably controlled black male student reactions to white female teachers. Part of the reason for the reaction of the youngster described in Reality 80 was that the provocation obviously was of greater duration. Although he had more control to start with, even he had reached his saturation point.

Often, the white middle class female teacher is unable to differentiate between a threat, a proposal, rapping, and teasing. Usually she can differentiate and handle this from someone who is white and middle class, and possibly from someone who is black and middle class. She has not, however, been educated to deal with aggressive sexual behavior from someone who is black, male, and lower class.

In the next few realities, the black male student's actions toward white female staff are described. Whether they acted in response to the female teacher's conscious or unconscious sexual provocation is uncertain. However, the students apparently interpreted the teacher's style or specific actions in a way that suggested to the student that he try his testing or rapping game. Or, he may have believed all the racist fantasies he has learned. Consequently, black male students most often test new female teachers in a sexual way while testing a male teacher physically.

REALITY 81

The new teacher was attempting to teach a history lesson when one of her black male students said,

"You look very pretty."

She blushed and said, "Thank you," as the class laughed.

Whereupon, he said "I would like to take you to bed. Don't worry; I will know what to do."

Her blushing turned to tears and she ran from the room.

REALITY 82

The class had just ended. One of the boys remained to talk with the teacher.

"Are you going to the prom?" he asked.

"I'm thinking about it," she responded.

"Good, leave your husband home. We can go over to my place after the prom is over," he said, as he put his hand on her hand.

REALITY 83

The young teacher was attempting to get order so that she could start her lesson. As she approached the back of the room where a number of boys stood together, one of them mumbled, "I'm gonna fuck you."

REALITY 84

The assistant principal was in his office on the second floor when he received a call from the secretary.

"Please, come quickly," she screamed.

He ran down the two flights to the office and found her alone and looking frightened.

"What happened?" he asked.

Hesitatingly, she reported. "You know that tall boy that was reported to you yesterday? He came in here, stood in front of my desk, and opened his pants. Then he tucked in his shirt. After he tucked in his shirt, he closed his pants, zippered them up, put his belt back, and then left. It took him a long time to do it. He did it to me twice. I saw him standing outside waiting for the office to be empty."

The assistant principal thought for a few minutes and said, "Take this telephone book and put it over here on this front table. Then, if he comes in again, ask him to please hand you the book after he finishes tucking in his shirt. Or, if you want, tell him in no uncertain terms to get out of the office if he has to fix his shirt."

"I can't. You talk to him."

The assistant principal agreed and left to look for the youngster. After hunting through the school, he found the youngster in his class. He asked him to please step outside to talk.

"Hey, what the heck are you trying to do to the secretary downstairs," he asked.

"Oh man, nothin'," the youth answered.

"Look, you have that woman so scared, the next time you pull that pants business on her, she is going to panic and go out of the window. Then I'll get you on homicide—so cut it out. You proved your point. She is afraid of you."

His face broke into a smile and chuckled. He put his hand out for some skin, and said, "Ok, no more."

He never did it again. Actually, his behavior improved after the incident and he was eventually graduated from the school.

Some additional examples include the following. A young, short female teacher in a tight dress had a habit of turning her back to the students and reaching up to write on the top of the board. When the class left the room, she would stand in the doorway with her back against the door jamb. Consequently, the students had to be careful not to brush against her as they left. Once, one of the male students looked into her eyes as he was passing and said, "You got some fine legs."

REALITY 85

A black male high school student terrified a new art teacher when she was alone in her classroom. He entered, took a tray of paper clips from her desk and sat down on a chair directly in front of her. He stared at her as he slowly sank into his chair moving his legs out straight in front and apart. He then took one clip at a time and started to make a clip chain. The teacher sat looking at him transfixed and frightened, and not saying a word. The mood was broken when an older experienced teacher entered the room and chased him out.

As soon as he was out of the room, the teacher burst into tears. Whether the teacher's sexual fantasies about black males, or males in general, frightened her, we do not know.

Unquestionably, some male teachers and aides also flaunt their sexuality. However, the flaunting of their sexuality does not appear to cause as many problems as does a female teacher's flaunting of her sexuality. Male teachers and aides can be extremely flirtatious and sexually arouse some female students by wearing tight pants, wearing an open shirt exposing their chests, or wearing a see-through shirt without an undershirt.

They can also arouse or annoy a female student by touching her more often than is necessary, by staring at her breasts or her legs, or by teasing. They can embarrass, arouse, or annoy her to the point where she may become disruptive. Additionally, a male teacher who is very repressed sexually may cause problems for a female student who expresses a good deal of openness and sexuality.

These past few years, female students have been increasingly more aggressive in their sexual taunting and propositioning of male teachers. Indeed, just about every incident described about male students intimidating female teachers has also occurred against male teachers by female students. Adolescent girls are as perceptive as are adolescent boys in determining those teachers who are insecure with their sexuality and physicalness, and hone in on them.

Some of the girls, in company with other girls, may walk up to a new male teacher, look at his crotch, and ask, "Hey, you got a bonner?" "How big are you?" Further questions may include, "Are you a virgin?" "Are you good in bed? and "How would you like to fuck with me?" They may even signify on the teacher by taunting him with, "Mary told me you only got a little pee pee."

Some girls will use their menstrual cycle to take advantage of or give an insecure male teacher a rough time. For example, five girls may come up to a male teacher and say, "We gots to go with her, its her time." Then, without waiting for a response, all the girls will leave the room, and the teacher does not know what to do.

What is important here, however, is that, most often, the male teacher who takes advantage of a female student's proposition, makes advances on his own, or provokes a female student will be suspended, brought up on charges, or fired. Indeed, when there is a sexually motivated problem between a white female student and a black male teacher, the black teacher is almost always "guilty." Some white female teachers know that they are both the forbidden fruit and prize, and will consciously or unconsciously tease young black male students. Most assuredly, however, this teacher will usually break out of her fantasizing of being threatened and dominated by a stronger being, and the male students will be disciplined in no uncertain terms. Because of her conditioning, she expected that he was supposed to look but not touch. Taking all this into consideration, the relations between black male students and white female teachers appear to be more precarious and dangerous to the black student than are the relationships between white male teachers and black female students.

When white male teachers flirt with black female students, however, they are not violating the dogmas of the dominant white society. It appears that some of the liaisons do end in bed, where, presumably, each works harder at satisfying the other sexually in fulfilling America's sexual mythology.[92] In reality, however, in most cases, the sexual achievements of both remain the expression of their racist fantasies about one another.

What is important is that the black female student (who may even be more experienced sexually than her white teacher) will not be disciplined for "attacking" or "attempting to rape" her teacher. She is not usually sent to a school for disruptive or delinquent girls as a result of the affair. Hopefully, the liaison was not brutal and no emotional scars were left. In addition, although data are not available, it appears as though more male teachers than female teachers marry their students.

It must also be noted that black female teachers are increasingly having the same problems with black male students as do the white female teachers. One reason for this phenomenon may be that larger numbers of blacks are moving into the middle classes. Consequently, more black middle class females are becoming teachers.

The problem related to black and white male and female sexuality between teachers and students also exists between teachers and between students.

In many suburban schools with black middle class and lower class students many of the staff spend a good deal of time discouraging middle class white girls who pursue the school's black male athletes. They would expect this kind of behavior from girls from the school's lower economic groups, but not from "good" middle class families. Additionally, the staff are sometimes annoyed, sometime disgusted, and sometimes perplexed about why: (1) so many middle class white girls allow the black male students to continually run their hands over all parts of their bodies; and (2) why some black male students, with impunity, are *always* touching and feeling all the black and white girls?

Also in suburban and other schools, a good deal of faculty time is spent discussing, chasing away, or reporting male and female students who neck, pet, and fondle one another in the halls and around the lockers. What is so interesting about this student expression of sexuality, whether between white students, black students, or black and white students, that upsets so many teachers and administrators is that it is very rarely discussed openly at an administrator- or union-sanctioned problemsolving meeting. Most often, the sexuality problem is discussed at coffee klatsch, "down on everything" sessions.

SUMMARY

Those who had hoped for a prescription for discipline have not found it here. Instead my impressions and feelings, sometimes broad and sometimes pinpointed, were presented. Although I am against corporal punishment, I have not completely resolved my concerns about the physical testing of teachers by the really tough, physical, aggressive, and acting-out streetcorner youngster. What sometimes frustrates me are the seemingly implacable laws of street machismo.

What makes me sometimes hedge on my nonpunitive physical punishment philosophy are the realities and rules of the world outside of the school that are often brought into the school. For example, I have witnessed some outstanding teacher–student relationships grow from violent encounters between tough male streetcorner students and tough male teachers; they *had* to test one another physically and, sometimes violently, before they could offer one another respect and friendship.

What we need in our schools are *secure and mature* men and women who have feelings for their students and who respect them as well as empathizing with their problems, who love the subject they teach, who are at home with their physicality, and who are both good talkers and good listeners. Not only must they believe in their students' ability to learn, but they must not let their feelings of empathy get in their way of demanding learning and standards from their students.

Once the successful teacher gets beyond the first testing period, physical size, sex, or color is unimportant. Of these secure and mature teachers, male and female, each has to develop a teaching style based on his or her personality that is also compatible with the students' life style and expectations.

NOTES TO CHAPTER 7

1. Louise Meriwether, *Daddy Was a Number Runner* (Englewood Cliff, N.J.: Prentice-Hall, 1970), p. 23.

2. Charles Dickens, *The Adventures of Oliver Twist* (Chicago: Oxford University Press, 1949), p. 301.

3. If we could better educate these youngsters to where they would become contributing members of our society rather than being institutionalized or on welfare, we would save, in addition to lives, billions of dollars per year. The cost of keeping an inmate in jail in New York City in 1984 was $40,000. William G. Blair, "Inmate Cost Is Put at $40,000 a Year," *New York Times*, December 27, 1984, p. 1.

4. Very often, this teacher will take the point of view that he or she "did not become a teacher to be a cop."

5. Francis X. Clines, "New York State Education Reviewer to Study 2 Slum-Area Schools," *New York Times*, July 19, 1973, p. 22.

6. "Boston Panel Finds Fear and Violence in Schools," *New York Times*, December 4, 1983, p. 86; George H. Gallup, "Fifth Annual Gallup Poll of Public Attitudes Toward Education," *Phi Delta Kappan* 55 (1973): 39; "Urban School Officials Say Strong Measures to Curb Violence Are Working," *New York Times*, March 12, 1984, p. A12.

7. The Joint Commission On Mental Health Of Children, *Crisis in Child Mental Health: Challenge for the 1970's* (New York: Harper & Row, 1970), pp. 264–65.

8. George Levinger, "Sources of Marital Dissatisfaction among Applicants for Divorce," *American Journal of Ortho-Psychiatry* 36 (1966): 803–7.

9. Joint Commission, pp. 264–65.

10. Levinger, p. 806.

11. Joint Commission, p. 266.

12. Ibid., p. 264–65.

13. David A. Schultz, *Coming Up Black* (Englewood Cliffs, N.J.: Prentice-Hall, 1969), p. 100.

14. William C. Cvaraceus and Walter B. Miller, *Delinquency Behavior: Culture and the Individual* (Washington, D.C.: National Education Association, 1964), pp. 68–69.

15. Walter B. Miller, "Lower Class Culture as a Generating Milieu of Gang Delinquency," *Journal of Social Issues* 14, no. 3 (1958): 13.

16. James Herndon, *The Way It Spozed To Be* (New York: Simon & Schuster, 1968), pp. 33–34.

17. Ibid., p. 36.

18. This is an example of ribbing.

19. Interestingly, all of my black students disliked this book because they felt Herndon was ineffective in achieving order in his classes and giving his students direction. Most of my white students, however, thought he was a great teacher who was hampered by the administration, the curriculum, and the "system."

20. Herndon, p. 37.

21. When I worked with undergraduates in teacher education, I would ask my students how many teachers there were in their high schools. Most often, we averaged around sixty-five or seventy teachers. I then asked, "What do you think would happen if each period every teacher sent one student to

the principal? The students usually got the idea that they, to a large extent, had to resolve their own discipline problems.

22. Frank W. Hart, *Teachers and Teaching* (New York: Macmillan, 1934).
23. Arnold P. Goldstein et al., *In Response to Aggression: Methods of Control and Prosocial Alternatives* (New York: Pergamon, 1981).
24. When my daughters went to Amherst Central High School, they had to have boy's blue "Barricuda" jackets.
25. Another common style is "cornrowing." The hair is neatly placed into braids, starting at the hairline and all interlocking to the nape of the neck. A girl also might braid her hair in a perfect spiral around her head. These styles are from Africa. (See "After the Afro," *Newsweek*, February 26, 1973, p. 44.
26. The importance of teachers acting instinctively should be emphasized as part of undergraduate, graduate, and in-service education. Too often, a teacher's positive instincts get turned into inactivity and mediocrity by peer and supervisory pressures. Kenneth P. O'Donnell, David, F. Powers with Joe McCarthy, *Johnny, We Hardly Knew Ye* (Boston Little, Brown, 1972), p. 210, pointed out how "once again, in deciding to accept the invitation from the Houston ministers, Kennedy had instinctively done the right thing against the advice of all of his advisors."
27. Herbert L. Foster, "Teaching the Disadvantaged Child: An Individualized Progress Chart and Student Personnel Plan," *Industrial Arts and Vocational Education* 55, no. 1 (1966): 47–49.
28. "The Hustler," *Newsweek*, May 28, 1973, p. 77.
29. Red Smith, "Frazier, Foreman See Eye-to-Eye on Scales," *New York Times*, January 23, 1973, p. 33.
30. Pete Axtheim, "The Olympics: New Faces of '72," *Newsweek*, September 11, 1972, p. 67.
31. "Meisler's Lunch Aids Jumping," *New York Times*, February 18, 1973, p. S4.
32. "Girl Loses Toehold on Breaking College Wrestling Sex Barrier," *New York Times*, February 17, 1973, p. 24.
33. See Chapter 9.
34. Claude Brown, *Manchild in the Promised Land* (New York: Macmillan, 1965), p. 122.
35. Ibid., p. 138.
36. Alex Yannis, "Golie Says It Helps To Be Crazy," *New York Times*, August 6, 1972, p. S10.
37. For an excellent example of humor easing a tense situation, see Jerry Schatzberg, dir., *Scarecrow*, with Gene Hackman and Al Pacino, Warner Brothers, 1973; Vincent Canby, "2 Drifters on a Photographic Landscape," *New York Times*, April 12, 1973, p. 56; Stephen Farber, "Just a Locker Room Fantasy," *New York Times*, May 13, 1973, p. B13.
38. At a recent conference of the New York State Educators of the Emotionally Disturbed (ANYSEED), after a presentation, a woman told me that reading this reality had saved her life. Apparently, she had been in a simi-

lar situation. However, having read *Ribbin'*, she recalled the reality and carried off the appropriate behavior.

39.   Interestingly, in the early days of Motown's history, Berry Gordy, Jr. ran the company with a very tight control. See Bill Barol and David Friendly, "Mowtown's 25 Years of Soul," *Newsweek*, May 23, 1983, pp. 75–76.

40.   Being able to control a class of students has always been a problem. In a history of Niagara County, New York in 1821, the following was reported:

> In those days the question was not, "Has the teacher a good education?" but "Is he stout? Has he good government?" It was frequent practice in some districts to smoke out the entire school or to "bar out" the teacher. Frequently there was a conspiracy among the large boys to whip the teacher and break up the school. Their attempts in this direction were successful for several years, and then, when the district had won a bad name and come to be shunned by the generality of pedagogues, a stranger with well-developed governing powers would happen along, open a school and speedily reduce the belligerent, "big boys" to a condition of subjection and prompt if not cheerful obedience, thus setting the ball of education rolling on.

> *1821 History of Niagara County, N.Y. with Illustrations Descriptive of Its Scenery, Private Residences, Public Buildings, Fine Blocks, and Important Manufactures, and Portraits of Old Pioneers and Prominent Residents* (New York: Sanford & Co., 1878), p. 97.

41.   To "nod out" in class is to feign sleep or tiredness. Nod comes from the drug term.

42.   Hunter S. Thompson, *Hell's Angels* (New York: Ballantine, 1967), p. 128.

43.   The interventionist concept was first presented at the 49th Annual International Convention of the Council for Exceptional Children, Miami Beach, Florida, April 1971. A version of the presentation was also published as "To Reduce Violence: The Interventionist and Aide," *Phi Delta Kappan* 53 (1971): 59–62.

44.   Steven K. Bailey, Foreword to Owen B. Kiernan, *Disruption in Urban Public Secondary Schools* (Washington, D.C.: National Association of Secondary School Principals, 1970), p. v.

45.   William C. Morse, "The Crisis Teacher, Public School Provision for the Disturbed Pupil," *University of Michigan School of Education Bulletin* (April 1962): 101–4; William C. Morse, "The Crisis Teacher," in Nicholas J. Long, William C. Morse, and Ruth G. Newman, eds., *Conflict in the Classroom: The Education of Emotionally Disturbed Children* (Belmont, Cal.: Wadsworth, 1965).

46.   Herbert L. Foster, "The Inner-City Teacher and Violence: Suggestions for Action Research," *Phi Delta Kappan* 50 (1968): 172–75; Herbert L. Foster, *The Inner-City Teacher and Violence: Suggestions for Action Research* (ERIC ED 024 631); Herbert Foster, "The Inner-City School: Violence, Fear, and Failure," in *Innovations in Educating Emotionally Disturbed Children and Youth: Proceedings of the Fourth Annual Conference of the Association of New York State Educators of the Emotionally Disturbed* (Hawthorne, New York: Association of New York Educators of the Emotionally Disturbed, 1969); Herbert L. Foster, "Some Suggestions for

Action Research," *New York State Journal of Health, Physical Education and Recreation* 21, no. 1 (1968): 21–32; Herbert L. Foster, "The Inner-City School: A Different Drumbeat," *University Review* 2, no. 2 (1969): 29–32; Herbert L. Foster, "To Reduce Violence: Interventionist Teacher and Aide," *Phi Delta Kappan* 53 (1971): 59–62.

47. Herbert L. Foster, "The Interventionist Teacher and Aide: Contemporary Educators for Resolving and Preventing School Disruption and Violence," *Exceptional Children Conference Papers: Diagnostic and Resource Teaching* (ERIC ED. 052 401).

48. Nat Hentoff, *Our Children Are Dying* (New York: Viking, 1967), p. 23.

49. A system named Silent Communication Alarm System Network (SCAN)— designed by NORCON Electronics Inc., 1237 Utica Avenue, Brooklyn, New York 11202 — is now operating in a number of schools.

50. "New Corporal Punishment Rule Requires Reporting Complaints: Ban on Corporal Punishment in Public Schools Considered," *Learning in New York*, January 1985, p. 1.

51. Citizens Commission to Investigate Corporal Punishment in Junior High School 22, *Corporal Punishment and School Suspensions: A Case Study* MARC Monograph No. 2 (New York: Metropolitan Applied Research Center, 1974). I should make the point that I am opposed to corporal punishment as well as to the covert racist or inhuman ploys. I am on the Board of Advisors of the National Center for the Study of Corporal Punishment and Alternatives in the Schools, which evolved from a meeting of the American Civil Liberties Union and the American Orthopsychiatric Association. See Gene I. Maeroff, "Drive Is on To Ban Corporal Punishment in U.S. Schools," *New York Times*, May 8, 1972, p. 37.

52. The National Commission on the Causes and Prevention of Violence, *Progress Report of the National Commission on the Causes and Prevention of Violence to President Lyndon B. Johnson* (Washington, D.C.: U.S. Government Printing Office, 1969), p. 3.

53. Ibid., pp. 2, 3.

54. These points were presented in a slightly different form in a paper entitled "Corporal Punishment and Physical Restraint: There Is a Difference," presented by Ms. Adrienne James, then executive director of Operation Friendship, Detroit, Michigan at the 48th Annual International Convention of the Council for Exceptional Children, Chicago, Illinois, April 23, 1970. Printed with the permission of Ms. James. Also, see David Bogacki, "Issues in Physical Restraint—A Procedural and Legal Perspective," *Discipline* 1, no. 2 (1980): 3, 8–9.

55. Herbert M. Greenberg, *Teaching with Feeling* (New York: Pegasus, 1969), p. 178.

56. George Gilder, "The Suicide of the Sexes," *Harpers*, July 1973, p. 42.

57. Warren R. Johnson and Julia A. Johnson, *Human Sexual Behavior and Sex Education: Perspectives and Problems*, 2nd ed. (Philadelphia: Lea & Febiger, 1968), p. 86.

58. Women tell me that when they see a man who interests them, they usually take a good look at his crotch, the curve of his ass, the flex of his thigh,

and so on. See Rosemary Daniell, *Sleeping with Soldiers: In Search of the Macho Man* (New York: Hold, Rinehart and Winston, 1984); Nancy Friday, *My Secret Garden: Women's Sexual Fantasies* (New York: Pocket Books, 1973), pp. 217–23; Erica Jong, *Fear of Flying: A Novel* (New York: Holt, Rinehart and Winston, 1973).

59.   It is common for middle class adolescent males and young men to wear a "jock" over their underwear or to wear a number of pairs of jockey type underwear to a dance or party so that his dancing partner will not feel his erection. Hence, his embarrassment reinforces his conditioning to withdraw, to repress, or sublimate his sexual feelings.

An additional male depressant derives from the anatomical and biological aspects of male and female sexuality. Accepting that both are entitled to sexual satisfaction, we again find an unevenness in early sexual experience and conditioning. The quick climax and resulting loss of erection by so many adolescent boys and men often leaves their partner frustrated and them with feelings of inferiority and self-loathing. Hence, these early experiences often lead the adolescent male to repress, to be ashamed of, and to sublimate his sexuality.

60.   Kate Millett, *Sexual Politics* (New York: Doubleday, 1970), p. 116.

61.   Gilder, p. 42.

62.   To walk on a liberal higher education campus, most high schools, and most cities during the warm months is to be continually stimulated by women's sexuality, particularly those who are braless. When this is discussed with women, many insist that this is only a male problem; it is not their fault that males are affected by their sexuality.

In my discussions with many men and young men, they are repressing or fantasizing their sexual feelings when viewing either of the above scenes; to look and not touch can be a frustrating emotional experience. To argue that it is society that has conditioned the male to become so easily excited and that he will just have to learn not to become excited is absurd.

63.   "Women Show Greater Sex Drive," *New York Times*, January 12, 1985, p. 8.

64.   Alvin F. Poussaint, *Why Blacks Kill Blacks* (New York: Emerson Hal, 1972), p. 91.

65.   Melvin Zelnick and John F. Kantner, *Sexuality, Contraception and Pregnancy among Young Unwed Females in the United States* (Washington, D.C.: National Institute of Child Mental Health and Human Development, Commission on Population Growth and the American Future, 1970).

66.   Alvin F. Poussaint, "Sex and the Black Male, *Ebony*, August 1972, p. 10.

67.   Alvin F. Poussaint, "The Stress of the White Female Worker in the Civil Rights Movement," *American Journal of Psychiatry* 123 (1966): 403.

68.   Poussaint, "Sex and the Black Male," p. 7.

69.   Ibid., p. 8.

70.   Ibid., p. 10.

71.   Ibid., p. 11.

72.   Poussaint, "The Stress of the White Female Worker in the Civil Rights Movement," p. 401.

73. Ibid., p. 406.
74. Winthrop D. Jordan, *White over Black: American Attitudes toward the Negro, 1550–1812* (Chapel Hill, N.C.: University of North Carolina Press, 1968), p. 136.
75. Ibid., p. 33.
76. Ibid.
77. Ibid., p. 34.
78. Ibid.
79. Ibid., p. 138.
80. Ibid., p. 148.
81. Ibid., p. 149.
82. Ibid., p. 150.
83. Ibid., p. 151.
84. Eldridge Cleaver, *Soul On Ice* (New York: McGraw-Hill, 1968), p. 14.
85. Jordan, pp. 151–52.
86. Ibid.
87. Poussaint, "Sex and the Black Male," p. 114.
88. Cleaver, p. 14.
89. Philip Roth, *Portnoy's Complaint* (New York: Random House, 1967), p. 233.
90. Ibid., p. 235.
91. James Baldwin, *Nobody Knows My Name* (New York: Dell, 1963), p. 151.
92. My personal feelings must be pointed out here: It is wrong for any teacher to have an affair with a student.

8 COMMUNICATING THROUGH DRESS AND PERSONAL GROOMING

There are some promotions in life, which, independent of the more substantial rewards they offer, acquire peculiar value and dignity from the coats and waistcoats connected with them. A field-marshal has his uniform; a bishop his silk apron; a counsellor his silk gown; a beadle his cocked-hat. Strip the bishop of his apron, or the beadle of his hat and lace; what are they? Men. Mere men. Dignity, and even holiness too, sometimes, are more questions of coat and waistcoat than some people imagine.[1]

—Charles Dickens, *The Adventures of Oliver Twist*

Contemporary teachers and Rodney Dangerfield have at least one complaint in common: "No one shows me no respect." Whereas Rodney Dangerfield has parlayed his "no respect" jokes into a successful standing-room-only comedy routine, for educators it means low professional status and salaries.[2]

One of the major reasons that teachers "get no respect" is the unprofessional way that so many dress. The unkempt dress of so many (mostly male secondary) teachers also suggests that many do not have much respect for themselves, their students, their colleagues, or their occupation.

According to Erving Goffman, nonverbal communication in relation to dress, bearing, facial decorations, and so forth is institutionalized by all societies.

These embodied expressive signs can function to qualify whatever an individual may mean by a statement he makes to others and thus play a role in the focused interaction of, say, a conversational gathering. . . . Further, while these signs seem ill suited for extended discoursive messages, in contrast to speech, they do seem well designed to convey information about the actor's social attributes and about his conception of himself, of the others present, and of the setting.[3]

While speaking and working in schools around the country, I have found secondary school women teachers dressing more stylishly, neatly, and cleanly than their male counterparts. Many more male secondary teachers dress out of style, are often bedraggled, are in some cases downright filthy, and often look worse than a *schlepper*.[4] Male secondary teachers' dress may be an indication of a number of forces affecting them.

First, it may substantiate the argument that men just are not as aware of or interested in style and dress as are women. Second, it may be a protest statement against teaching conditions,[5] Third, it may be a conscious or unconscious way of "expressing distance" from either the profession, the students, or fellow educators. This may be akin to Goffman's example of beatniks and college students who expressed distance "from the employed adult population by a full beard, or a two-day growth, and by bedraggled clothes." Additionally, Goffman's discussion of the relationship of "work and clothing to the problem of fitting into gatherings," in this case teaching, may also signal alienation from the job.[6] Fourth, teaching may still be perceived as a female occupation. That is, for many American men it may not be considered macho enough.

Fifth, teaching may not be considered a real profession. For example, because so many teachers belong to unions, male teachers may see themselves more as blue-collar workers than as professionals. The New York State Board of Regents, for example, does not list teaching as a profession. Also, it might be that many male secondary school teachers view their job as similar to that of, for example, a policeman, a fireman, or a civil servant rather than as a profession. Additionally, in a recent study of moonlighting teachers, the authors concluded that (1) for some teachers, moonlighting is an accepted part of their concept of themselves as teachers, and (2) "teaching will remain at best a semiprofession as long as so many of its members are taking nonprofessional work for nonprofessional wages and benefits."[7]

Sixth, it may be that salaries for a male head of household are just not high enough for men to have money for clothing. And seventh, wives may be purchasing the clothing for their husbands, and they may not be able to dress their husbands as stylishly as they dress themselves.

However, none of the above arguments is reason enough to explain why so many of the male teachers I see look as though they had slept in their clothing for a week. Some teachers are wearing shoes that have not been polished since they were purchased; running shoes, which should not be worn to school in the first place; floods;[8] outlandish clothing combinations; and the same clothing over an extended period without cleaning or pressing.

Also, many male teachers are overweight and obviously out of shape. Dressing well, not being overweight, and being in reasonable condition go together with a healthy personality.

Hence, the male teacher's dress may indicate how he feels about himself, his role as a man, his present occupation, and those with whom he works. Teachers, particularly male teachers, will begin to gain more respect when they show they respect themselves by starting to dress "up" and dress "better."

By "up" I mean more shirts, ties, sport coats, suits, shoes that are shined, high socks, proper fit, and natural fibers instead of polyester.[9] By "better" I mean clothing that is fresh, neat, and clean. Unquestionably, it can be argued that teachers will dress better when they are paid better. However, by dressing better now, teachers may command the respect that may get them better salaries.

According to most state laws, teachers and students may dress as they wish to dress as long as their dress does not interfere with instruction, health, or safety. I would not change the law; I am not arguing for either student or teacher dress codes.

Though there is little research around teacher dress, there is a good deal of empirical evidence that teacher dress directly affects teaching and learning as it applies to classroom management, school discipline, and student academic accomplishment.

One of the first things I learned from my "600" school students was the importance of how what I wore affected their feelings about me, first, as a man they could respect, and second, as a teacher whom *they would allow and be proud of to teach them.*

REALITY 86

In my "600" school days, I received a dividend from my World War II converted GI life insurance and bought two pairs of stylish shoes, which I wore on two consecutive days. Before I knew what had happened, the word had spread throughout the school that I had worn new pairs of "bad kicks" on two consecutive days. Because of the shoe incident, I received skin from just about everyone and was a celebrity for quite awhile. I could not have made it as a teacher on the basis of two pairs of shoes. However, the shoes did help because they were important to my students.

It is incredible to me that so often parents coming to school for meetings are dressed nicer than those working with their daughters or sons. Educator insensitivity to this issue is a disgrace. These parents are showing educators more respect than the educators are showing for either themselves or the children with whom they work.

REALITY 87

My first responsibility at the State University of New York at Buffalo was directing a teacher center at a junior high school populated entirely with black students in the city of Buffalo. After awhile, I began to hear comments from the predominantly white staff and black student body about, "the dirty hippies coming here to teach."

I called a meeting and told our university students that what they wore away from or while at the university was their business. However, to remain in our program, they would have to dress differently when they came to the public school as part of our program. I told them they had to be generally neat, clean, and dressed up.

Also, I explained the reason for the dress rule. I discussed the civil rights movements in the South and northern inner city areas where many whites often wore dirty chinos or dungarees, did not use deodorant, had dirty nails, and did not wash their hair very often.

When asked why they dressed this way, often they said, "This is the way I can get along with and relate to these people, and clothing really isn't that important." Such a response indicated an unconscious racism from supposedly nonracist white liberals. Indeed, their dress, their behavior, and their verbalization of such a statement indicated a racist belief that blacks were dirty, and therefore, if they dressed that way, they could get along with them.

To further support my point, I related a story told me by a black university faculty member who had been involved in a number of neighborhood community action antipoverty programs that had many volunteer white undergraduates.

A typical wealthy undergraduate student from Yale become active in their program. His usual attire when working at the agency was dirty jeans and T-shirt. Finally, one of the black workers, who each day would get more and more annoyed and disgusted, yelled at him, "How in the hell can you help us? You can't even help yourself. Look at yourself!"

Another typical example was reported to me by a black woman psychologist. She was working in a school in Harlem where there was a white psychologist intern who always wore dungarees to the school. Finally, a number of the parents complained to her that they did not want the intern in their school because, as they said, "He does not respect us. We don't want him to come here."

I then also stressed a number of other points. In the classroom: (1) you show your respect for yourself and your students when you dress well, dress neat, and dress clean; (2) students will keep records of how often a teacher wears a particular dress, a particular shirt, or any piece of clothing; and (3) in some cases, when a teacher dresses outlandishly, some students simply cannot concentrate on what the teacher is saying.

I presented other examples that indicated the importance of dress to those who never had the money for clothing and those who finally did have the money for clothing. In a study of adolescent street crime in Brooklyn, Mercer Sullivan found that most of the adolescents involved in street crime reported they spent their legal or illegal income on clothing. "After clothing came marijuana and recreational outings to movies, roller rinks, and Coney Island.[10]

In an article in the *New Yorker*, Ken Auletta described a meeting in Mayor Koch's office that was being addressed by Deputy Mayor Herman Badillo. "Sixteen men in the room have their suit jackets draped over their chairs or at least unbuttoned. Badillo's sharply tailored charcoal-gray pin-striped suit jacket remains buttoned, and he sits erect in his chair.[11]

A few years ago, I visited my brother Jack and his partner's dress-manufacturing loft in Manhattan. There were four cutters working; three were white and one was black; all were in their sixties. The three white cutters wore short-sleeved shirts with no ties and had their collars open. The black cutter wore a long-sleeved starched shirt with a tie and had his collar buttoned.

After discussing the above explanations for setting the dress rule, we had very few problems with dress. We also related much better to the school staff and the public school students. Also, the friction between the public school staff and our students disappeared as our students' dress improved.

The next three realities provide examples that suggest that teachers are not the only ones who have their dress signals mixed up.

REALITY 88

A member of our law faculty talked with me about a problem his students were having in trying to work with some convicts. After he described his problem, I asked what his students wore when they went to the jails or holding centers to meet and work with the convicts.

He responded that they wore either chinos or dungarees. In response, I asked, "How many people do you know who would hire an attorney who wore chinos or dungarees during business hours?"

I guess he understood my message.

REALITY 89

I received a call from a young man directing a program for reformed hookers and convicts who would go into schools to talk with students about the mistakes they had made and encourage the students not to make the same mistakes. He was having some problems with the program, and a friend suggested he call me for some advice. When he called, I suggested we talk at lunch.

At lunch, as he explained his program and what he perceived as his problem, there was something he said that made me note his open shirt and unbuttoned golf sweater. I asked what he usually wore to his office.

He responded that, lately, he wore what he had on now. However, when he started the project, he usually wore a business suit with a vest.

I then mentioned my feelings of the importance of a professional, particularly a person in his position, dressing a certain way and how, especially when working with lower income groups, it was a way of showing respect for himself and for them. Halfway through that point, he interrupted, saying "That's what that was all about."

Apparently, a few days earlier, three of the men in his program complained to him about the way he was dressing. They informed him that they wanted him to go back to his suits so that, "we can show people who our boss is."

This next reality took place when I was speaking to a local psychologist and counselor group and, as an aside, mentioned the role of dress and personal grooming in communication.

REALITY 90

In my presentations, I mentioned how students and their parents have a very specific concept of how a middle class person or teacher should dress and that it is important for the professional to fulfill that expectation as a nonverbal mode of communicating respect and professional competence to the client. After my presentation, a counselor related the following story to me, which now made sense to him.

He was leading a group that consisted of prisoners at Attica State Prison. On a number of occasions, the convicts in his group remonstrated him for dressing so slovenly. He had been wearing low socks, shoes not shined, and suits that he only now and then had cleaned and pressed; he liked the unkempt style.

The convicts told him they could not understand how he dressed that way when he had gone to college, had a good job, and made good money. Slowly, he was beginning to understand the conflict between his feelings, his beliefs, and his standards around dress as compared with those of the men in his group, and how what he wore affected his relationship with them.

A few years ago, I carried out a volunteer internship in a special school for problem adolescents where I interviewed parents, students, and professional and nonprofessional staff and also reviewed the literature in preparing a school improvement plan. Reality 91 describes what was probably the most uncomfortable professional experience I have ever had other than my first day of teaching.

REALITY 91

I prepared the report and had copies distributed at least one week prior to our meeting to foster an open discussion. The report included five suggestions for improving student attendance, one of which was that the "staff should dress better and up."

As we gathered for the meeting, I could sense the hostility in the room. One of the teachers was wearing a tuxedo. A number of the staff took out newspapers and started to read. Still others began to talk in groups. They had no positive feelings about the report. Neither did they want to discuss it. Finally, in desperation, I said, "As professionals, if we cannot discuss something with which we disagree, what can we expect from our students?" Slowly, we did get some discussion going.

The staff yelled at me, glowered at me, and attempted to discredit me professionally. For example, someone asked me when the last time was that I was in a classroom. Another person asked me when my book was written, suggesting that it may be out of date. One of the women accused me of trying to foist my standards on black students. I pointed out that she mentioned standards, and I wanted to teach middle class salable skills, without which students could not aspire to make it into the middle class. Some of those skills are to speak, to dress, and to behave in ways appropriate to the social situation. Soon after that, we had to stop because of the limited time allocated for discussion. We never did discuss any of the other four suggestions. (Interestingly, this staff was probably the worst dressed I have ever observed in a school. Many were outright dirty in their dress and grooming.)

However, I felt better when the next presenter supported my point of view regarding dress. She was a well-dressed black woman working at a psychiatric institution who reported that her staff found clients tended to keep appointments with staff who were dressed well.

Often, when I am discussing dress and the need to teach middle class salable skills, someone will accuse me of forcing my middle class standards down the throats of black children. What is interesting about these accusations is that those who are accusing me are, in reality, the ones who are imposing their beliefs down the throats of black students.

Too often, it is the student who has the higher standard around clothing. It is the teacher who is not doing what is expected of him or her. Therefore, when the teacher dresses slovenly and does not make high academic and behavioral demands on students, he or she is guilty of imposing his or her beliefs on students.

Reality 92 is an excellent example of imposing values that involved the use of a name rather than around dress. However, the person involved in this reality realized that he was attempting to impose his beliefs upon the person with whom he was working.

REALITY 92

Professor Bruce Jackson, a member of the SUNY at Buffalo English Department, was doing interviewing field work in Texas prisons for a book on black convict work songs. A good deal of his recording time was spent at Ellis Prison Farm because the inmates there had been around for a long time as multiple recidivists.

His best song informant was a prisoner called "Chinaman," who had been in the penitentiary for most of the past thirty years. Chinaman and most of the men in his group addressed Professor Jackson as "Mister Bruce," which made him feel uncomfortable. He told Chinaman and the other prisoners to call him "Bruce," just as his students did. They assured him they would but kept calling him Mr. Bruce. He became insistent, saying that he could not call them by their first names and nicknames and have them call him "Mr." In response, Chinaman told him that there was nothing wrong with doing it that way, that was the way things were done.

What Professor Jackson later realized was that when he told them that was not the way things were done where he came from and that they should call him Bruce, his actions were "arrogant and self-righteous. And I realized that I was practicing a kind of colonialism of my own. I knew how things were supposed to be done and my insistence on doing things that way—however well intentioned I might have been—took no cognizance whatsover of the discomfort my patterns of speech and the relationships those patterns implied might have imposed on Chinaman and the other men."[12]

STUDENT AND PARENT OBSERVATIONS
ON TEACHER DRESS

There may be some differences in the way students react to teacher dress. In inner city and urban schools, students are much more outspoken about how they expect teachers to dress. For example, this statement by Theo, an inner city black student:

> Teachers always be walkin' around wearin' these high ole pants and everything [giggle] ... 'cause they wear anything [giggle], stripes on plaids and what not. . . . It ain't all that hip and everything you havin' a tie and all them situations. Like wow, they makin' so much money here and there, you know, they can afford to do this. . . . And, then come to school raggedy, and we sittin' up in the classroom, and we ain't raggedy. They shouldn't be raggedy in front of us.[13]

Whereas suburban and rural school students might be more accepting of variations in teacher dress, most have a minimum expectancy of how their teachers should dress. Indeed, whether or not a student admits to this, he or she, as well as everyone else is in our society, has been conditioned to respect the well-dressed and groomed person.

Students have a tendency to laugh at and put down the poorly dressed teacher as well as the teacher who exhibits poor personal hygiene. Sometimes, even the good teacher who is a poor dresser is made fun of or put down in student discussions.

The following realities were told to me by male and female students from inner city, urban, rural, and suburban schools; undergraduate and graduate students; and teachers and administrators who were also parents. The high school students relating these stories ranged from students in a resource room to honor students.

REALITY 93

This student went to school in the Bronx in New York City during the mid–1970s. She remembered a male English teacher about twenty-three years old who wore a pair of solid brown slacks on Monday, Wednesday, and Thursday. On Tuesday and Friday, he wore his red checked slacks. At the end of the semester, his students bought him a pair of pants.

REALITY 94

Two female students who were graduated from a suburban high school in 1983 indicated that teachers were divided into two groups. The first group was the "with it" crowd. The second group was the "polyester" crowd. Once a teacher was considered part of the polyester crowd, it was hard for that teacher to break his or her negative reputation.

In one of their classes, they had a pool going as to when a male teacher would change his pants. One of the boys in the class won the five-dollar pool for guessing the thirty-one consecutive days the teacher wore his pants.

These same students also felt sorry for the teachers because everything they do is scrutinized so carefully by students.

Two days later when I was discussing this incident with two undergraduate students, one of them said, "I can tell you who that teacher was." Since I knew what high school she had gone to, I told her that the teacher was not from her school. Therefore, there must be at least two male teachers who wear the same pants for more than thirty days in a row.

REALITY 95

This reality was told to me by a teacher who was also a parent:

"My seventh grade daughter had a social studies teacher, Mr. M —— , who my daughter said was not a good teacher.

"When I asked her why, my daughter replied that all he gave were dittos, that there were questions on tests which were not covered in class, and that he left the answer key on the desk for every test. But, above all, Mr. M —— wore the same suit every day with the same stain on the pants, that his nails were dirty, and that he smelled.

"Since I too am a teacher, and know how children exaggerate, I figured some of this was 'manufactured.' At open house however, I observed Mr. M —— . He was 'mousey,' noncommittal about curriculum questions and *above all*, he *was* dressed in a suit with stained pants, had dirty nails, and was very poorly—groomed.

"My daughter also claimed that the kids in his room passed notes and talked all the time and that she learned very little in his classroom."

In reading this reality and others, it appears as though poor dress might also be an indication of other problems a teacher or administrator may have. How a teacher dresses may be the tip of the iceberg in relation to his teaching ability and personality.

REALITY 96

"I received a call from my son's English teacher for a parent–teacher conference. When I asked my son, who was fifteen at the time, what the problem was, he said, 'You should see how she dresses, Mom.'

"I then asked him what that could possibly have to do with what she was teaching? All he could say was, 'Wait until you see her. She wears stripes and plaids together and all sorts of dumb things.'

"When I got home from the conference with the teacher, my son's first question was, 'What did she have on—do you see what I mean?'

"I had to agree with our son about the way his teacher was dressed. For some reason, our son would not behave or cooperate in this English class because he felt the teacher did not dress properly."

In a national study in 1983 by the Roper Organization, 2,000 respondents were asked, "When you meet someone of the same sex, which one or two . . . things about physical appearance do you tend to notice first?" In noticing the physical appearance of the same sex, 41 percent of the women and 39 percent of the men indicated they looked at how they're dressed/clothing first.

In noticing the physical appearance of the opposite sex, 35 percent of the women indicated how they're dressed/clothing as number one. The first aspect of physical appearance noted by 45 percent of the men was figure, shape, and build. The second item was: 29 percent of the women noted figure, shape, and build, and 34 percent of the men noted face. The third item noted was: 27 percent of the women noted face and smile; 29 percent of the men indicated how they're dressed/clothing.[14]

Intellectually, we can argue that schoolchildren, particularly on the high school level, should be able to move beyond the teacher's appearance and learn, because that is why they are in school. However, when I raised that question with a group of high school students, they said, "You gotta look at him while he is talking, and you can't help noticing the way he is dressed. You are just attracted to his dress, and it distracts from what he has to say."

Whether conditioning comes from mass media, lessons learned at home, or personal experiences with the adult world, to be realistic, teaching and learning must take into consideration not only the way the teacher is dressed but the teacher's personal hygiene and health habits as well.

Most often, when I discuss the importance of appropriate and proper dress and personal hygiene, I mention an incident that happened to me in my third year of teaching.

REALITY 97

I had been breaking my back trying to get through to one of my students. Finally, I felt I was getting him to learn. He was setting type when I walked over to him, put my arm around his shoulder, and told him he was really doing well.

He turned to me, pushed my arm off of his shoulder, looked right into my eyes and said, "Get your fuckin bad breath out of my face."

I moved away from him fast and didn't know what to do. It took me a long time before I could overcome my personal feelings of defeat and hurt from what he had said to me. Since then, I have observed other youngster and adults using that expression, even when untrue and uncalled for, as an excellent ploy, tactic, or weapon to upset a teacher or policeman.

The next reality was told to me by an always well dressed and excellent black woman high school teacher. She described how she handled her students when they questioned the way she had done her hair. This reality is presented to show that when you have yourself together and are aware of the importance of dress and personal grooming, you need not worry or overreact when students question or kid you about your dress or grooming.

REALITY 98

"I went to class with my hair style changed. It had gone wild. I looked awful. When I had gotten up that morning, there was nothing else I could do. I did little braids down the side here. . . . I managed to push that up in the back and pin the braids at the back of my head.

"When my freshman arrived that day, they didn't have the nerve to say a word, 'cause they weren't sure of what I was goin' to do. They would say mild little things like, 'Ah, Miss Bowles, you changed your hair style.' But in a non-committal way.

"The seniors came in and one kid says from the back of the room, 'Harriet,' (and I thought I'm not even gonna acknowledge him), and he said again 'Harriet.' When he said it three times, and I was not gonna acknowledge it, he said, "Ya know you look like Harriet Tubman with your hair like that.'

"And then from the other side of the room, another kid said something like, 'Ah, ya missed your hair appointment or something.' So, I said, 'Listen, I had a bad time with my hair this morning and you are not gonna make me feel bad, so you just go right ahead and say whatever you like and I will just continue with class.'

"It worked. They stopped talking about my hair."

IMPORTANCE OF DRESS IN THE WORLD OUTSIDE OF SCHOOLS

In reading newspapers and magazines, watching television, and observing the outside-of-school world, the importance of dress is continually evident. The following reporting provides many examples of the importance of dress in the world outside of school. In the main, this is the world our students will live in and, hopefully, succeed in.

Dan Rather, in his book *The Camera Never Blinks*, wrote about the importance of dress in cutting through race problems and gaining professional respect for his television camera crew while covering the civil rights clashes of the 1960s. The importance of dress as an indicator of professionalism was something he realized soon after arriving in the South.

> We also settled on a rule—for me, for all of us—to dress well. That decision may sound frivolous. But the rule proved important, as a symbol, because this was the first indication to these people that we meant business. I could walk in wearing blue jeans and a plaid shirt—and some did—and fade into the crowd and work around the edges. But that way was not as effective as showing up with my shoes shined, pants pressed, coat on and tie straight. That said: I'm a professional. Here to do a job. I want to get along. But don't try to con or intimidate me.
>
> That approach worked best with everyone but the fanatics. And nothing worked with them. It worked with the police chief, the sheriff, the mayor, the Chamber of Commerce and, yes, the station managers who so often had their foot on our oxygen line. I walked into many a station knowing that the manager felt, in his heart, we were at the least unfair and, at worst, Commies. Our goal was to establish a level of respect. Once we did, we could do business with them.[15]

To prepare themselves better for the continuing big business requirements of mass marketing their computers, California's Silicon Valley companies are moving from Levis to pinstripe-suited business executives.[16] Prime Minister Zoah Ziyang of China, in his much heralded U.S. tour, offered a piece of commentary on China's cultural mores. He said he was wearing a Western suit—the first Chinese leader to do so—as a political signal and because they were more comfortable. He added further that when the prime minister of China wears a Western suit, "nobody will fear to wear fashionable dress."[17]

Politicians and, in some cases, businessmen, have dressed in certain ways as either their power increased or their political aspirations changed. For example, Reverend Jessie Jackson changed from his dashikis and jumpsuits to conservative pinstripes as he moved into the Democratic presidential primary. It is interesting to note, however, that he moved back to jumpsuits when he made trips to Cuba and South America during the primary campaign. As noted by one journalist:

> Shortly before arriving at the luncheon, Jackson ducked into a room and changed from a pale blue gray checkered suit into a conservative, three-piece navy blue one, more like bankers wear.
> Checkered suit, blue suit, Khadafy-like khaki suit, ski sweater, blue jeans, longshoremen's coat, Jackson likes to let his costume fit the audience. . . . [18]

Mel King, a former dashiki and jumpsuit-clad Massachusetts state legislator, wore suits and a bow tie while standing for the mayoralty in Boston.[19] When the Reverend Ike was interviewed concerning his philosophy of life, he indicated that his philosophy concerning money had not changed, but his style had. Conservative pinstriped suits now replace his silk jumpsuits. "I look at some of the clothes I used to wear," he laughs, "and I say, 'Gee, that's strange. I wouldn't be caught dead in that now!'"[20] Speaker of the California Assembly, Willie L. Brown, Jr., likes to wear $1,000 to $1,800 Brioni suits, of which he has "less than 50 and more than 30."[21] The somewhat flamboyant Roone Arledge has also moved from his celebrated safari jackets to "sedate pinstripes handmade by the same tailor who dresses Walter Cronkite."[22]

MORE ON DRESS FROM THE WORK WORLD AND TELEVISION

My students tell me that when they are serious about purchasing an item worth more than a few dollars, they dress up or the sales clerk will not pay attention to them. A study by Hartmarx, the new corporate name for Hart, Schafner & Marx, found that "men felt it was important to dress properly" while shopping to get proper attention from a salesclerk. Of those interviewed who wore sport coats and suits, "41.9 percent said they believed that they would be treated worse if they wore blue jeans instead of a suit or sport coat while shopping."[23]

Kevin Flemming was able to photograph the assassination of Anwar Sadat because *National Geographic* has a dress policy that its photographers wear coat and tie when covering official state functions. He was on a routine assignment about the Sinai Desert for *National Geographic* and attending the parade where Sadat was assassinated. Flemming, carrying two cameras but dressed much like any official guest, was able to gain access and document the assassination. Meanwhile, other photographers who were dressed less formally were forced to leave the area at gunpoint, and some had their film confiscated by the Egyptian police.[24]

During the Nixon administration, photographer Harry Benson was able to get further into the White House and more often than any other photographer. When asked why he was always able to get to the second-floor private quarters, he responded that he always wore a suit and tie.

I told them [the other photographers] that if they stopped dressing like maintenance men their luck might change. Most often I wear a navy blue blazer, either a shirt and tie or turtleneck sweater, and either grey slacks or blue jeans, depending on whom I'm photographing, but I do try to fit in. From a president to a rock star, dress properly and there is no question you will get further.[25]

SUMMING UP

There must be something important about dress and personal grooming for personal and corporate economic gain or advancement in the United States, if not the world. Politicians, corporations, and individuals spend millions for personal dress and grooming advice, and sometimes for a corporate look or uniform.[26] Lawyers dress their clients in certain ways at a trial in an attempt to affect the jury in their favor.[27] College graduates often switch from their usual dungarees to business suits when job hunting.[28]

In the United States, the importance of dress may go back to our first commander-in-chief and president. George Washington was meticulous about his dress and selected the cloth for his shirts and suits, his shoes, and their buckles with great care.[29] We had almost the opposite in President Jimmy Carter. Clifton Daniels wrote in the *New York Times* that President Carter

did not seem to know what was expected of him as a national leader.
    Jimmy Carter ran against Washington, but in the end Washington won: The American people happily elected a peanut farmer from Plains, Georgia, but they didn't want him to behave like one in the White House.[30]

In other words, dungarees were all right on the farm, but not in the White House.

Just the opposite was President Harry Truman, also a farmer. Hugh Sidey wrote that, "Truman, the dirt farmer, looked his very best in white tie and tails. He always dressed well: neat and tailored. The famed bow tie was a signal of a sporty mood."[31]

Unquestionably, there are some teachers who are great teachers regardless of their dress. However, they are, at least, usually neat and clean. (There are, after all, not many Einsteins around.) Teacher respect and professionalism will grow as teachers dress closer to how their students and their parents expect educational professionals to dress. Not only will teachers begin to gain more respect, but more students will learn, there will be fewer discipline problems, and more budgets will pass in suburban and rural areas.

NOTES TO CHAPTER 8

1. Charles Dickens, *The Adventures of Oliver Twist* (London: Oxford University Press, 1949), p. 267.
2. John Curran, "Dangerfield Got No Respect on Kleinhans Stage," *Buffalo News*, March 24, 1984, p. B-11; "Low Teacher Pay and Status Faulted," *New York Times*, August 24, 1983, p. A12.
3. Erving Goffman, *Behavior in Public Places: Notes on the Social Organization of Gatherings* (New York: Free Press, 1963), p. 34.
4. See Leo Rosten, *The Joys of Yiddish* (New York: McGraw-Hill, 1968), p. 346; *Shlepper*, "2. Someone unkempt, untidy, run-down-at-the-heels."
5. George Leonard, "Car-Pool: A Story of Public Education in the Eighties," *Esquire*, May 1983, p. 60.
6. Goffman, pp. 222, 205.
7. Richard Wisniewski and Paul Kleine, "Teacher Moonlighting: An Unstudied Phenomenon," *Phi Delta Kappan* 65 (1984): 553-55.
8. "Floods" are pants that are inches too short.
9. Unquestionably, many pants and suits are made with polyester blends. In addition, there are some who are allergic to wool and who therefore must wear polyester blends. However, there are also those who are being chided here who wear polyester pants and suits with outlandish designs.
10. Mercer L. Sullivan, "Youth Crime: New York's Two Varieties," *New York Affairs* 8, no. 1 (1983): p. 38.
11. Ken Auletta, "Profiles: The Mayor-II," *New Yorker*, September 17, 1979, p. 121.
12. Personal discussions with Professor Bruce Jackson, December 15, 1983 and July 14, 1984.
13. Richard A. Marotta, " 'Posin' to Be Chosen': An Ethnographic Study of Ten Lower Class Black Male Adolsecents in an Urban High School," *Dissertation Abstracts International* 39 (1978), 123-A (State University of New York at Buffalo), pp. 35-36.
14. "Clothes Make the Person," *Psychology Today*, January 1984, p. 17; The Roper Center, Roper Report 83-5 (April 1983).
15. Dan Rather with Mickey Herskowitz, *The Camera Never Blinks: Adventures of a TV Journalist* (New York: William Morrow, 1977), p. 71.
16. "The New Valley Boys," *Time*, April 15, 1983, p. 100.
17. Maureen Dowd, "A Reporter's Notebook: Zhao's Lipstick Opinion," *New York Times*, January 19, 1984, p. A16.
18. Nancy Skelton, " '... I held My Own ... With the Big Boys....'," *Buffalo News*, July 1, 1984, p. F-5.
19. Kurt Andersen and Joelle Attinger, "Boston Wins by a Landslide," *Time*, October 25, 1983, p. 30; Alessandra Stanley, Joelle Attinger, and William McWhirter, "Two Kinds of Racial Politics," *Time*, November 28, 1983, p. 24.
20. "Rev. Ike Preaches About the Profits," *Newsweek*, December 20, 1982, p. 16.

21. Wallace Turner, "For a Politician, Power and Riches Go Together," *New York Times*, June 16, 1984, p. 6.

22. Harry F. Waters, Neal Karlen, and Lucy Howard, "The Wide World of Roone Arledge," *Newsweek*, February 6, 1984, p. 76.

23. "Men's Buying Habits Studied," *New York Times*, July 5, 1983, p. B6.

24. Kathryn Livingston and Amy M. Schiffman, "Oct. 6, 1981 . . . Assignment: Cover Parade. The Selling of Sadat," *American Photographer*, December 1981, p. 83.

25. Ronald H. Bailey, "Profile: Harry Benson: A Sporting Life," *American Photographer*, May 1982, p. 54.

26. Ron Alexander, "Finding the Right Color: Are You Spring or Fall?" *New York Times*, May 19, 1984, p. A20; Jay Cocks, Leonora Dodsworth, and Elizabeth Rudulph, "Designers Get Down to Work," *Time*, January 16, 1984, pp. 64–65; "Lesson for Executives Put Emphasis on Style," *New York Times*, July 9, 1984, pp. D1, D5; Enid Nemy, "At $1,500 a Suit, His Clothes Make the Man," *New York Times*, July 9, 1982, p. B6; Eloise Salholz, Pamela Abramson, and Sonja Steptoe, "Smart Shoppers For Hire," *Newsweek*, June 25, 1984, p. 64; Anne–Marie Schiro, "2 Stylish Looks for Women in Business," *New York Times*, November 23, 1982, p. C8.

27. Stephanie Mansfield, "Dressing for Acquittal," *Buffalo News*, January 1, 1983, pp. E1, E6.

28. Jay Boyer, "Neat Dresser Scores Extra Points in Job Interview," *Buffalo Courier Express*, September 10, 1982, p. B–1; "Eager Elis Suit Up for the Big Interview," *New York Times*, February 12, 1984, p. 64.

29. Hugh Sidey, "Above All, the Man Had Character," *Time*, February 21, 1983, p. 24; Neil Hickey, "Barry Bostwick Cannot Tell a Lie," *TV Guide*, April 7, 1984, p. 14.

30. Clifton Daniels, "Presidents I have Known," *New York Times Magazine*, June 3, 1984, p. 120.

31. Hugh Sidey, "Unadorned, but Proud," *Time*, May 14, 1984, p. 28.

9 SUMMING UP

Go back to Mississippi, go back to Alabama, go back to South Carolina, go back to Georgia, go back to Louisiana, go back to the slums and ghettos of our northern cities, knowing that somehow this situation can and will be changed. Let us not wallow in the valley of despair. . . .

This is our hope . . . with this faith we will be able to transform the jangling discords of our nation into a beautiful symphony of brotherhood. . . . And if America is to be a great nation, this must become true. So let freedom ring . . . from every village and every hamlet, from every state and every city . . . to speed up that day when all God's children, black . . . and white . . . , Jews and Gentiles, Protestants and Catholics, will be able to join hands and sing in the words of the old Negro spiritual, 'Free at last! Free at last' Thank God Almighty, we are free at last!'

—Reverend Martin Luther King, Jr. at the Lincoln Memorial, the March on Washington for Jobs and Freedom, August 28, 1963

The last chapter of most books about inner city schools usually deals with either of two concerns. One group of books, written by self-styled inner city teaching experts who taught for one or two years, ends by discussing why the author was fired or "could not take it" any more. Usually, the system, the curriculum, or the administration and teachers are blamed for their leaving. Never, no never, do they find fault with themselves for being poor inner city teachers. Always, someone else caused their problems.

The other group of books about teaching in inner city schools consists of collections of papers and articles collated by professors of higher education who usually conclude these books with something like "we are getting closer to a solution but we still have a long way to go." Or, "we have to do a better job of communicating with black disadvantaged children." Or, "we have to improve the preparation of teachers." The suggestions are usually philosophical rather than concrete, without any suggestions of "how to."

This last chapter discusses some of the ideas and successful programs with which I have been involved. This chapter will, hopefully, provide public school and university professionals with additional ideas to solve their problems.

LOOKING AT EDUCATOR PERSONALITY

As our public schools continue to have fewer middle class students and more students who are handicapped, some of whom may be middle class, minority, poor, or immigrants, the teacher's ability to work with them becomes more important. Therefore, we ought to begin to take a more careful look at educator personality, which certainly affects the ability to relate to a diverse student population. There are three studies, one of which was carried out with teachers, that should be looked at.

The first study was by Dr. Alfred M. Bloch and was carried out in the Los Angeles Unified School District in California between 1972 and 1975. Dr. Bloch performed psychiatric evaluation and treatment on 207 inner city "battered teachers," of whom 137 were female and 7 were male; all suffered the equivalent of combat neurosis or combat fatigue.[1] These teachers had been subjected to violence, bombing of classrooms, destruction and theft of school equipment, student and gang fights, weapons, murder, rape, drugs, dynamite, and so on.

Some of the psychological and somatic complaints expressed by these teachers included fatigue and weakness, blurred vision, irritability, sensitivity to weather, difficulty in coping, dizziness, malaise, and depression. Cardiovascular symptoms included palpitations, hypertension, arteriosclerosis, and coronary artery disease. Musculoskeletal symptoms included repeated upper respiratory infections and bronchial asthma.

Fear was the most potent source of arousal and subsequent stress response. These teachers presented many symptoms similar to those observed in studies of "combat neurosis" and disaster survivors.

Where there was no offer of administrative support, many teachers experienced physical and psychological depletion and ultimate collapse. Interestingly, all the "battered teachers" completed the Minnesota Multiphasic Personality Inventory, which indicated obsessional, passive, idealistic, dedicated persons who were unable to understand or cope with the violence directed toward them.

The second study, "Physical Assaults on Psychiatrists by Patients," was carried out by Denis J. Madden, John R. Lion, and Mandel W. Penna from the University of Maryland.[2] Their work with violent patients led them to question whether psychiatrists might overtly or covertly provoke their patients' violent behavior.

They surveyed, by questionnaire, 115 psychiatrists who held full- or part-time clinical and administrative positions. The psychiatrists were asked whether or not they had ever been assaulted and the nature of the assault. Those who reported they were assaulted were then interviewed personally or by telephone. Of the 115 psychiatrists who responded to the questionnaire, 48 indicated they had been assaulted with 68 assaults in all.

The psychiatrists who reported being assaulted varied in age and level of experience but most were assaulted in the early phase of their training by patients in active treatment. The assaults mostly consisted of slapping in the face, hitting on the head, or throwing objects. One patient, however, tried to set the therapist's clothes on fire, and one therapist was shot in the chest.

Upon being questioned about their retrospective anticipation of the assault, fifty-five indicated they could have anticipated the assault. Fifty-three felt they had acted in a provocative manner, and the majority reported they could have anticipated the assault because they made comments or interpretations that were unfavorably received by the patient.

Most of the clinicians thought they may have provoked assaults because of: (1) their refusing to meet a patient's request; (2) their forcing a patient to take medication; (3) their setting too many limits or not setting enough limits; (4) transference reactions; (5) homosexual panic; (6) material being dealt with in therapy—for example, forcing a patient to confront upsetting material or; (7) their inexperience and fear which may have been translated into an omnipotent facade; and (8) their acting in a seductive manner.

The authors found it surprising that 42 percent of the clinicians who reported being assaulted were attracted to the field because of its contemplative nature where verbal skills rather than physical management was required. Psychiatrists may be more in tune with the internalizations of aggressive urges. Hence, they may reward patients who show depressive symptoms because they are easier to treat than the aggressive patients. Indeed, the violent patients tended to be shunned.

The third study, "Attracting Assault: Victims' Nonverbal Cues," by Betty Grayson and Morris I. Stein, studied whether there were behaviors or specific movements that could identify a potential victim of an assault and signaled, or was perceived as signaling, their vulnerability to a criminal.[3] Furthermore, if there were such movements, could they be identified? They sought answers to those questions by having criminals rate the movement of people they indicated as likely to be assaulted.

Videotapes were made of persons selected at random walking in a assault area between 10:00 A.M. and 12:00 P.M. over a three-day period. Those taped were divided into four groups of fifteen each, according to their sex and age. There were two groups of men, young and old, and two groups of women, young and old. Those classified as old appeared to be over forty; those classified as young appeared to be under thirty-five.

A group of twelve intelligent and verbal prisoners who had been convicted of assault established a scale for rating an individual's assault potential. These inmates viewed the videotaped sequences and discussed the people in the video-tapes in relation to their being targets of assault. Descriptive evaluations of each of the videotaped individuals were culled from the discussions. These evaluations were used to establish an assault potential rating scale from one to ten, which was used later by a second set of prisoners.

Fifty-three inmates (different than the original twelve) convicted of crimes ranging from murder to simple assault on victims unknown to them were asked to rate the videotaped persons in terms of their assault potential. Of the fifty-three inmates, who ranged from age seventeen to fifty-six, 87 percent were black, 8 percent were white, and 6 percent were hispanic.

The videotapes were viewed by groups of the above inmates. They rated each of those videotaped using the "Scale for Rating Assault Potential." Labanalysis was then used to analyze the movement categories that differentiated between victims and nonvictims.[4] The Labanalysis code included twenty-one movement categories such as stride length, tempo, type of weight shift, body movement, and gaze.

Statistically significant differences were found for five of the twenty-one Labanalysis movements that differentiated the victims from the nonvictims. These categories were: (1) type of weight shift, (2) stride length, (3) feet, (4) body movement, and (5) type of walk. The difference between gestural and postural movement appeared to be the major difference between victim and non-victim.

It may be that some of the potential victims' behaviors involved what Erving Goffman named "gestural hinting," whereby they unconsciously indicate their vulnerability, and the criminal, also probably on an unconscious level, "reads" that signal.[5]

Additional support for this position was indicated by the respondents during their taped discussions that "any dude who looked different' would probably be a target of assault. . . . 'looking different' meant a different physical appearance in clothing and accessories."[6]

Although only one of the above three studies involved teachers, the areas studied certainly are related to teacher personality. Perhaps the possession of certain teacher personality traits should be looked at closer as a requirement in teacher education and teaching certification. First, however, comes the job of changing the personalities of those who guard the turnstiles.

UNDERGRADUATE TEACHER EDUCATION

The pendulum is currently swinging back once again to where a big shortage of teachers is expected. In addition to an upsurge of new children coming into schools, there appears to be a large number of experienced teachers about to retire. Hence, the teacher shortage may be even worse than anticipated. With this shortage in mind, there is universal agreement that teacher education programs must be improved.

Our former Office of Teacher Education had some outstanding teacher education centers located in public schools that could be replicated in part or whole by teacher educators. With meager budgets, we had a number of undergraduate programs running in a number of secondary schools. It was in these public schools that almost all of our students' classroom and practicum experiences were performed. The Woodlawn Teacher Education Center, one of those I directed, was designed to prepare undergraduates for teaching positions in inner city schools and will be described, briefly.

The Woodlawn Center program was housed at the formerly Woodlawn Junior High School in the city of Buffalo. The school had an all-black student population and was located in the so-called inner city area of Buffalo. I assumed the directorship of the Teacher Education Center at Woodlawn in September 1967.[7]

One of the outstanding aspects of the program was the involvement of the Woodlawn professional staff. Three of the then Woodlawn staff, Domenic Mettica, Judson Price, and Michael Romance, were given instructor's rank at the university and assisted in planning and teaching the course work and organized our students' practicum experiences. Many additional Woodlawn personnel helped in working with our students and student teachers in their practicum and student teaching experiences by coming into our classes to talk with our students whenever they were at Woodlawn.

After assuming responsibility for the program and organizing two additional centers in the Buffalo Schools, I began a series of meetings with the principals (or their representatives) of the schools housing our centers to discuss the center programs. After a number of meetings, we agreed to a "Statement of Understanding."

Basically, the statement set forth our feelings of the role and responsibility of the school and the university. One of the important points agreed to was that if a university student became involved, in any way, in a problem with a Woodlawn student or teacher, our student would leave the program, regardless of his or her involvement in the problem, if the school authorities so requested. This agreement provided a solid foundation and safety valve preventing problems. (None of our students was asked to leave.)

Next I integrated our staff of Woodlawn personnel and set a dress code for our university students when at the center. Many of our students had been arriving at Woodlawn in a dirty and unkempt state of dress and exhibiting poor personal hygiene. Interestingly, the Woodlawn students and many of the Woodlawn staff wanted to know who these "filthy hippies" were who were coming to Woodlawn to work with them.

Consequently, we set a dress code for the Woodlawn Center students. However, when a few of the students began to ignore the rule, we put it into writing as a prerequisite for the course. This one move paid tremendous dividends by gaining respect for our students and acceptance by the Woodlawn staff and students.

Of course, we explained to our students the reason for the rule. Usually, after discussion, our students were satisfied and accepted the rule. First, we explained that by dressing well you show respect for your students and what they respect. During the days of campus riots, many students felt they could relate better to black youngsters by wearing jeans and being quite unkempt and, in many cases, downright dirty. They were really taken aback when we explained that such a feeling was racist because it suggested that all blacks dressed poorly and are dirty.

They had no idea that the general feeling within the black community was rather conservative. Indeed, they could never imagine black parents being annoyed with their children's Afro as white parents might be annoyed by their children's long hair. They had no idea that black parents and children had feelings of how a teacher should dress and behave.

Interestingly, a number of our students who had long hair that they considered "au naturel" were really rocked back on their feet when black students called them faggots. They could not understand why the black students treated them so disrespectfully because they (the university students) felt they had compassion for "the plight of their people." All these students eventually left the program; they were confusing their middle class rebelliousness and insecurities with the racist problems faced by blacks.

It is interesting to note that Alvin Poussaint reported behavior similar to the above among many of the white workers who went South to work in the voter registration drives.

> There were some whites who, anxious to show off how "free" they felt around blacks, flouted the moral and social standards of the black community with their unorthodox behavior. One of the more common manifestations of this pathology was the attempt by many whites to get "soulful" and "earthy" affecting an unkempt style of dressing. Such individuals wore filthy clothes, refused to use deodorant, and rarely combed their hair because their warped conceptions of black people were that blacks were this way. None would have been willing to admit that such practices were racist because they conformed to the white-held stereotype of black people. It was as if these whites believed "anything goes in the black community."
>
> . . . Soon, local people viewed this behavior as a manifestation of disrespect for the black community and of thinly veiled white racism.[8]

Intake Into the Program

We did not use any unique intake procedure. All our university center programs were advertised to all sophomore students through mailings and a required meeting. Those who choose centers were interviewed by the various directors. In the case of the Woodlawn Center, we suggested students visit Woodlawn for a day or two to help make the decision to sign up or not.

We did, however, try to keep out those with obvious emotional problems and those who wanted to work in inner city schools to "love poor black kids." We looked for students who were emotionally secure, reasonably happy, good talkers, physical, and not burdened with white guilt. The program was integrated.

The Program

Almost without exception, our black and white university students reported they were frightened when they first entered Woodlawn. They were frightened by the students running in the halls or just by the students as they were. However, because of their involvement in the school, they soon lost their fear. They also soon become totally immersed in every aspect of the school.

Ideally, students entered the program in the lower half or fall semester of their junior year, starting a one- to one-and-a-half-year, four-course-and-practicum sequence.[9] The four courses were:

1. TED 321—Educational Sociology—fall of the Junior Year—4 credit hours.
2. TED 418—Teaching in Inner City Schools—spring of the Junior Year—4 credit hours.
3. TED 425-426—Student Teaching—fall of the Senior Year—6 credit hours.
4. TED 419—Practicum in Mental Health, Methods & Techniques of Teaching—concurrent with student teaching during the educational semester (student teaching semester) of the Senior Year—2 credit hours.

TED 321 and TED 418 met at Woodlawn Junior High School. The practicum experiences were either in the school or within its community. The first class meeting was held on the university campus to arrange for car pools, to explain the program to new students, and to provide maps and information about Woodlawn. The TED 419 class met everywhere—on the university campus, at Woodlawn, or at someone's home.

At the first meeting of the course, students were asked to list five of the areas they wanted covered. These lists were combined and divided up for perusal by faculty and student committees. These committees quickly reported back to the class, and the semester's objectives were set.

However, even with these objectives in mind, we were still flexible. For example, our students (the majority of whom were females), wanted to get more information from female teachers concerning such questions as how they would be tested, how to carry themselves, how to dress, how to handle sexuality, and so on. Because our program was housed in a school and we had excellent relations with the staff, at our next meeting we had four female teachers, black and white, carry on a dialog with our students.

The flexibility within our structure provided students with a reality model to emulate when they become teachers. Also on our first day at Woodlawn, we made sure everyone got to know one another. As students entered the room, they were given a three-by-five card and asked to write their name and three adjectives about themselves. The staff did this too. Next, we formed an inner ring and an outer ring. Each ring walked around and we read one another's cards and communicated nonverbally. Students and faculty then paired off with someone they did not know and spent about fifteen minutes getting to know one another verbally. The pairs then formed fours, and so on, until we got everyone to know everyone. A dittoed sheet was then made up with everyone's (faculty's and students') name, address, and telephone number. These were distributed to class members.

Students were then divided among the faculty. They worked with this faculty person throughout the program, sharing their feelings and observations, which were recorded in a log. Additionally, students were notified that staff were available around the clock in an emergency.

A sample contract was discussed and made final. As part of the contract, students were asked to list their expectations of the faculty. Arrangements were made for students to begin their practicum observations. All of this was accomplished by the second class meeting.

The overall objectives of the Woodlawn Teacher Education Center program were:

1. To help students develop a teaching style and techniques that would be relevant to urban disadvantaged children, their families, and the community.
2. To help students develop generalized techniques for preparing, structuring, and organizing the classroom and themselves to meet the needs of the children so that discipline becomes secondary and teaching the primary function.
3. To prepare teachers so that they may be able to bridge the difference between their culture and lifestyle and those of the children without the deleterious consequences of the "cultural shock."
4. To provide each student with a frame of reference that would infuse him or her with an awareness of the teacher's responsibility, as an agent of change, to relax, motivate, and educate.

Our students met for two hours of class work and two hours or more of practicum experiences per week. Practicum experiences involved various aspects of the community life, tutoring students, working with teachers and students, and participating in school activities. Students had one year of practicum experience at Woodlawn prior to their student teaching.

An overnight outdoor experiential adventure was required of all students. No tobacco, drugs, or alcoholic beverages were allowed on the outdoor education experience.

Contracts

As noted, we used a contract system with our center students. We were aware that our university students would teach the way they were taught. Some requirements applied to all students, while those students who chose to work for an A or B grade had to complete work beyond that required for an S or U. Students were presented with an open contract. After discussion, the contract was formalized and signed.

Another point that should be stressed is that our faculty would disagree, at times, in front of our students. Sometimes we did it purposely. Despite our overall agreement on philosophy and objectives, we had retained individual approaches and teaching styles. We agreed that what works for one teacher may not work for another. And, we let our students know about this.

Such an approach made at least two points for our students: Educators can have professional disagreements very openly and still respect and work with one another, and if the teacher is secure, he or she need not worry about differences of opinion or viewpoints opposing those of the teacher being expressed in the classroom. If our students experienced a classroom atmosphere that was open, where all sides were presented and argued (even against our faculty), and saw that respect for one another could continue despite the disagreements, then, hopefully, our students would be able to teach in this accepting way when they become teachers.

Another point stressed was that the teacher's control of the classroom is not an end in itself but rather a means toward an end, that end being the students' learning concepts and skills and developing their ability to reason. The teacher must be more than a disciplinarian. He must be prepared and know what he is going to teach, how he is going to teach it, and how he is going to measure his success. We also philosophized that structure, organization, and discipline were compatible with freedom and democracy. Indeed, students were looking to their teachers for realistic limits.

The evening group meetings referred to earlier were held at homes of our staff or students. These were the small-group meetings on the contract and attendance was optional. At these meetings the topics discussed sometimes were open and varied while at other times we had a single, prepared topic.

One incident that occurred during a small-group meeting stands out in my mind. We were meeting at the home of a black teacher. One white female student kept going upstairs to use the lavatory. Somehow, she and I got into a discussion later, and she explained why she kept going upstairs.

She had never been in a black person's home before, and she just did not know that blacks could own a home like hers. The reason for her going upstairs so much was really to look over the house and furnishings. Interestingly, this young lady grew up in a middle class home in a completely white community. Academically, she was no slouch; however, her experiential background had not included any relationship with blacks—other than the women who cleaned her home.

Another affective approach that we used was to remember our students' birthdays with a cake and candles. It was interesting to observe the feelings of some of our supposedly sophisticated college students when they were confronted with a birthday cake of their own. Birthday cakes are also provided in my graduate courses, where one day even I was surprised by a student's reaction to a cake. When the class was over that evening, the young male teacher for whom we had the cake stayed after class to speak with me. He thanked me for the cake and informed me that it was the first birthday cake he had ever had in his life!

THE NEW TEACHER AND TEACHER AIDE PROJECT[10]

Although the New Teacher and Teacher Aide Project helped new secondary teachers of disadvantaged students through their first-year teaching problems, the model could be replicated to help educators cope with and prevent problems related to stress and burnout and working with unfamiliar students.

The project was a cooperative venture between the Office of Teacher Education, Faculty of Educational Studies, the State University of New York At Buffalo, and the Buffalo Public Schools with funds provided by New York State Urban Teacher Corps Office, the State Education Department. The project was designed to help first-year secondary school teachers over their teaching hurdles. Built into the project was a program for teacher aides from the inner city areas of Buffalo, and in the second and final year of the project, we had a second-year teacher program.

University faculty, Buffalo Board of Education teachers, and advanced graduate students, many with teaching experience, were involved as staff. Additionally, the staff was integrated as so sex and racial background; members from minority backgrounds were in all positions.

An announcement concerning our project was mailed to all first-year secondary teachers in the Buffalo schools. Participation in the project was optional. The qualifications consisted of being a first-year teacher, and teaching disadvantaged secondary school students. All who met these qualifications were accepted. The criteria for the teacher aides included: (1) years of service as an aide, (2) other work experience, (3) whether they had taken prior college courses, and (4) a desire to become secondary school teachers.

Teacher participants received three hours of graduate credit per semester. A teacher who participated for both years of the project could have received twelve hours of graduate credit. The aides received twelve hours of undergraduate credit per semester as part of the project.

Our orientation ran in conjunction with the Buffalo schools' orientation and consisted of five afternoon sessions from 1:00 until 4:30 P.M. The Buffalo school people ran the morning part of the orientation.

The first afternoon consisted of a registration and introduction session, and a student panel. For the panel we picked some of the "toughest" black and white boys and girls in the schools. They discussed how they tested their teachers. Needless to say, most of the new teachers refused to believe them. The students also expressed their feelings about good versus bad teachers and then joined the rest of the orientation week as staff members.

The second day consisted of two panels, one of parents and the other of principals. Both parents and principals *told* the teachers what they expected of them. An interesting verbal scuffle broke out between the parents and the students who had been on the earlier panel. The parents turned out to be much more conservative concerning dress and behavior than were the students.

The panel for the third day consisted of a number of male and female second-year teachers who described their first year trials and tribulations. This was a particularly good panel and we had a good deal of questioning and discussion.

Teachers and aides visited their schools on the fourth day. Additionally, our staff was available for any private meetings with teachers of aides who had questions.

The last day of the orientation was spent at three activities. First, new teachers worked with our staff to plan their first week of school. The rest of the afternoon was spent in language desensitization and understanding.

My jive test, mentioned earlier, was given and we discussed communication in general and black dialect in particular. We next gave everyone a desensitization test.

Desensitization and Awareness

As noted in earlier chapters, some youngsters very effectively use many techniques to test their teachers. One of the more effective techniques is the use of "dirty" words or actions that upset their teachers and thereby interfere with the teaching and learning. This testing can take many forms. Sometimes the testing is subtle, sometimes it is carried out very aggressively, and often there are psychosocial, psychosexual, or psycho-racial-sexual overtones. In Reality 99, Claude Brown described the way many of his friends attempted rather unsuccessfully, to test a new female counselor at Wiltwick.

REALITY 99

Mrs. Meitner was not out of place in Affrey House. The first week she was there, she showed us a lot of judo and won a whole lot of friends. Guys tried to make her leave by walking past the stairs naked when they heard her coming down, but that didn't work. Mrs. Meitner would just stop whoever it was and make him stand there and talk to her. The cat who was naked would get embarrassed long before she did. After a while, people just stopped messing with Mrs. Meitner and faced the fact that she was there to stay.[11]

If all teachers could handle situations as Mrs. Meitner did, there would be fewer problems in the schools. However, most new teachers do not possess her ability.

In an attempt to deal realistically with this problem, we designed a desensitization and awareness exercise to help the participants develop immediate and ongoing strategies for coping with these problems. We felt it was imperative that our participants: (1) not be upset by so-called "dirty" words; (2) know the "other" meaning, particularly the sexual meaning, of the jive, slang, or dirty words in their students' vocabulary; and (3) learn the words specially designed to hide their true meaning—for example, "forget you" for "fuck you."

The usual college teacher preparation programs rarely discuss students' use of foul language. Where they do, most often only the environmental reasons behind the use of the language are considered. Sad experience, though, has taught that this is not enough.

With the help of experienced inner city teachers and inner city students, foul words were collected. From these words, a master list of thirty words was promulgated. These words were categorized, five each, under: (1) penis, (2) vagina, (3) sexual intercourse, (4) oral sexual stimulation or satisfaction, and (5) other parts of the body. Five signs were painted noting these categories and hung in front of the room.

Despite our belief in what we were doing, and out of respect for the moral beliefs of our participants, we notified everyone that on the next day we would carry out an exercise that would involve the use of so-called dirty words. We suggested that those who felt they would be offended would be excused for the afternoon. As it turned out, everyone attended.

As the participants entered the room the next afternoon, they were seated five or six at a table in coed groups. Participants were given an IBM scoring sheet and pencil.

We thought of putting the words on the overhead. However, after discussion, we decided that it was imperative that the participants actually hear the words.[12] Therefore, the words were called off and participants had to classify each word on his IBM sheet according to its category. Upon collecting the marked sheets, participants at each table discussed: the answers, what each word described, and possible antonyms and synonyms for the five categories of words. After a suitable time span, groups appointed one representative to stand and verbally assign one word to its category until all table representatives had turns and all the words were assigned categories.

Next, group members joined in a general discussion of such questions as: Why do students use these words? What is the students' and teachers' expectation of the other when the words are used in the classroom? Should the teacher differentiate between a child cursing him, cursing a fellow student, or cursing during the heat of a good but emotional discussion or in a ball game? What do you say to a student who asks a question such as "Can masturbation hurt you?"

Additionally, actual examples of incidents were read for discussion. The feelings of all groups were then shared with everyone. Folders were provided holding articles related to teacher and student use of sexually related words. We also provided copies of a number of newspapers such as *Screw*. With the exception of possibly three of those assembled, most of the new teachers and teachers aides appeared relieved and more relaxed that we had publicly discussed this subject.

After the orientation week, the project's assistance to new teachers and teacher aides was provided through: (1) small-group meetings, (2) topical presentations, (3) Saturday workshops, and (4) a crisis service.

Small-Group Discussions

The teachers and aides were divided into eight groups. Four groups met on a Tuesday after school and four groups met on Wednesdays after school in two centrally located inner city schools. Groups were assigned to each school on individual preference, but small-group assignments were made homogeneously as to sex and racial background. Teacher aides were assigned as evenly as possible to all groups.

The discussion groups were designed to meet several problems that arise with new teachers. First, school organization promotes the loneliness of the teaching profession. Teachers isolated from each other rarely have the opportunity to discuss their problems in teaching openly and frankly with each other. Consequently, many young teachers have difficulty distinguishing between problems related to difficult situations and those related to personal attitudes and emotions. Moreover, because most supervisors are also involved in evaluating them, most teachers are reluctant to go to their supervisor with problems. The game for the young teacher frequently is one of concealing and covering up mistakes rather than examining them in order to learn.

Second, help is usually made available only when the teacher is unable to handle a problem. In consequence, seeking help is an implicit admission of failure. The discussion groups built in the concept that problems are to be expected and permitted consideration of alternatives at an early stage in the teacher's awareness of a problem.

Third, young teachers frequently have problems in knowing (1) how much responsibility to take for difficult emotional and social problems among children in their class; (2) how closely they can permit themselves to relate; (3) how to deal with discipline, especially as it relates to the teacher's attitudes toward accepting and integrating the authority mold; (4) how to maintain an idealistic attitude when practical considerations force change; (5) how to relate to older teachers, principals, and supervisors; and (6) how to develop confidence in their own judgment. Discussion groups permitted the airing of these very personal, very important issues in a way that usually is not provided in schools.

Fourth, teachers in inner city areas frequently suffer from "culture shock," and it is important to explore the feelings and attitudes teachers develop as they work in situations that are difficult and different. Discussion groups permitted an airing of such issues and often a clarification for the young teacher.

The first goal of discussion groups was to reduce the personal anxiety, tension, and strain which is inevitable in young teachers. A second goal was to help young teacher deal with personal feelings and attitudes that may influence or interfere with problemsolving in the classroom. The range of alternative solutions available to the teacher may be greater as a consequence of the discussions.

A third goal was to help children through working with the teacher. It was our feeling that many problems (though certainly not all) can best be helped in the natural setting, by teachers. In any event, even if outside help is available, the teacher is still faced with handling the child's problem daily. Intervention at the level of the classroom is critically important in dealing with the 10 to 30 percent of children *defined by teachers* as having adjustment or learning problems.

The discussions in each group were coled by one faculty member who had experience in Group therapy or sensitivity groups and an educator from the project staff of part-time instructors. The discussions were problem centered, dealt with the teachers' concerns, and focused on here-and-now group processes only when such processes interfered with the ongoing consideration of problems (e.g., silence related to unvoiced disagreements; monopolization of "air time"; critical or nonaccepting attitudes of group members toward each other that promote defensiveness).

The groups were not for sensitivity training, nor did they assume psychopathology. They did assume that in any interaction with children, parents, or administration, teachers' feelings and attitudes play an important role. The group did assume that the first year of teaching is in the nature of a normal developmental crisis and that the resolution of that crisis shapes the teacher's professional self.

Sessions were taperecorded, with participant permission. Individual leaders often played back tape recordings for self-evaluation of their roles and to discover points in the discussion that needed more emphasis or clarification at later sessions.

All coleaders met weekly as a group with an outside leader, who acted as a consultant and facilitator in group process. We profited from this experience, which aided us in our relationship role with our own groups. Any problems confronting the leaders were brought out at these meetings and attempts were made to resolve them. Project administrative business was also a part of these meetings.

An analysis of the tapes revealed that because of the open format of the small discussion groups, a large variety of issues were discussed, including: (1) problems with discipline; (2) dependency, anxiety, and sexuality in children; (3) problems in teachers' handling of their own feelings of hostility; (4) the sense of discouragement over working in a difficult situation; (5) racial feelings; (6) problems with the administrative hierarchy of the school; (7) problems in obtaining help of school psychologists and social workers; and (8) problems in relating to parents and older teachers.

From the tapes, we felt that, for most of the participants, the sense of loneliness and isolation had been overcome. The most important index was the reluctance of the groups to disband as the program drew to a formal conclusion. In addition to the teachers, the group leaders reported feeling a sense of loss. Three groups decided to continue meeting a number of times past the original thirty sessions.

The discussion sessions provided a forum for the catharsis of feeling, for consideration of issues important in the schools but rarely explicitly considered or confronted in any other forum, and for replenishment of psychic resources used up during the teacher's professional activities. Teachers used the term "feeling refreshed" after a session. Several spoke of the relief from feelings of guilt and personal inadequacy they derived from learning that others were experiencing similar problems and perceptions. Virtually any time that these issues were broached during a discussion, an aura of "me too' comraderie emerged quickly and pervasively.

Topical Presentations

In the first year of this project, a second course was taught along with the small-group discussions. The course consisted of didactic instruction, with lectures, outside speakers, consultants, and small workshops in teaching methods for various subjects taught in the secondary school curriculum. In spite of the fact that the didactic instruction was felt to be meaningful, practical, and specific to classroom problems, the project as well as the participants' evaluations suggested it to be somewhat limited in reaching the participants. It appeared that not all the participants were benefiting from the presentations of any one meeting.

To reach a greater number of new teachers, yet retain the two-course content of the previous year; to help the clinical psychologists deal with public education problems unfamiliar to them; and as an outcome of faculty and student evaluations, a new format was developed. As noted, the weekly small-group discussion vehicle was retained throughout the year, led by the clinical and educator coleaders. Thus, personality problems as well as specific classroom problems were dealt with within the group as each leader lent the expertise of his or her professional specialty in helping to resolve arising problems. The sessions remained for the most part as group counseling sessions without either leader dominating discussions with lectures or passing judgments. Attempts were made to maintain a "group theory" concept as much as possible.

As a consequence of this new format, with the loss of a second weekly meeting for didactic instruction, teaching method suggestions and formal presentation of curriculum topic areas were drastically reduced. To compensate for this loss, two workshops were held. One dealt with aggression and how to deal with it in school; a second focused on the drug problem and its consequences upon public school youth. In addition, experienced helping teachers and second-year teachers were employed or asked to act as advisors to those of our teachers who appeared to be experiencing some difficulties; also, meetings concerning teaching methods were held when needed.

To further compensate for the loss of a second weekly meeting, a series of topics were scheduled for presentation. Attendance was optional except for the ones concerning behavioral objectives. Thus it was hoped that those truly interested and concerned would benefit more from the material discussed. The topics were as follows:

1. behavioral objectives;
2. report card grading;
3. questioning techniques;
4. pupil–teacher planning;
5. motivational techniques; and
6. individualization of instruction.

The above list constituted didactic instruction given during the early months of teaching, September through November. The experience of the first year of the program aided our decision in formulating the list containing the most important general problems faced by new teachers during these months. For the remainder of the year, we focused upon individual problems brought out in the group sessions where many of the above topics reoccurred.

Workshops

Two all-day workshops were organized for the teachers and aides in two pressing areas: aggression and violence in school and the drug problem. The workshops were also open to those not in our project. To address the issue of aggression and violence in the classroom, we were able to bring in Dr. Nicholas J. Long, then director of Hillcrest Children's Mental Health Center, Washington, D.C. and professor of Education at American University. He presented a provocative lecture, providing insights into the behavior of violent and aggressive youth. Suggested ways of dealing with these problem students were offered to the participants using individual human resources. The lecture was followed up by twelve small-group discussions led by staff members. The issue of drug abuse among school youth was addressed by a panel of experts in the mental health field, who presented factual information concerning the availability, dissemination, and behavioral aspects of drug abusers. Panel presentations were followed by ten small-group meetings with panelists, former addicts, and parents of addicts leading discussions. Follow-up questionnaires indicated much satisfaction with the informal gains made by the teachers. most felt the workshop to be helpful in future discussion of the drug problem with their students.

Crisis Service

Teachers and aides participating in the project had the opportunity to call upon any staff member with any personal or professional concerns at any time of day or night. A total of eleven persons participated in individual conferences with staff members. Five of them felt compelled and comfortable enough to discuss personal problems that indirectly affected their teaching competence. At the discretion of the caller, the conversations were held either over the phone or in person. A mimeographed list of all staff and participants' school and home addresses and telephone numbers was provided for everyone.

Evaluation

We felt that the general objective—to help new teachers to face the problems encountered in their first year—was achieved with a great deal of success. Only two teachers in our program left the Buffalo School System during the program's operation in the 1970–71 school year for nonprofessional reasons.

Weekly attendance was high, and discussion was lively in all groups. We were encouraged by the number of comments made by individual teachers who felt they were profiting from the openness of problems brought to the groups.

Pre- and posttesting indicated that the participants made positive changes in their attitudes and feelings during the program.

A questionnaire evaluation of the orientation was conducted. The data indicated that 90 percent of the participants felt they had gained helpful information and were encouraged in facing their new teaching positions. Because we profited from the first year's orientation program and participant comments, the orientation was felt to be a profitable one. There was a great deal more enthusiasm displayed by the participants and more discussion following panel presentations.

Two areas related to models for emulation that were neither part of the objectives nor formally evaluated but certainly had a positive effect on the participants were related to the fact that our staff was racially integrated and functioned together well; and its members disagreed with one another in class in a nonthreatening manner. This came about often in particular discussions of techniques of teaching, and it helped get across the idea of individual teaching styles and techniques and the possibility of not being threatened when someone disagrees with you in a classroom.

Many of the teachers informed us verbally that they would have left teaching were it not for our program. Some achieved greater acceptance of their feelings toward children, and some were able to feel more comfortable having obtained realistic expectations about what they might manage to accomplish with their students. In the main, our assessment was that most teachers received help in the form of support, but that significant gains beyond that remain problematic.

The first year of the New Teacher Program had a total of sixty-six teachers enrolled. Of these, fifty-nine teachers completed at least one semester of the program; fifty-two completed the entire program. The second year of the program included seventy teachers. Of these, sixty-six completed all or one semester of the program, and fifty-five completed the entire program. None of the teachers who left the program left for classroom reasons.

When the state no longer funded the project, and neither the university nor the Board of Education could find the funds to continue, many teachers did leave their inner city schools. Interestingly, a number of female teachers left because their husbands did not want them teaching in inner city schools.

By any method of evaluation, the project was a success. One word of caution, however; *the project was a success mainly because of the staff involved.* The same organizational structure could fail easily if the wrong staff is involved.

SCHOOLS AS REINFORCERS OF POSITIVE BEHAVIOR

While still teaching graphic arts in the New York City "600" schools, I designed a system for rewarding my students' positive behavior.[13] Basically, the system consisted of my sending a congratulatory letter to the parents of elected shop officers if they performed satisfactorily at monthly elected jobs.

Interestingly, a number of my students complained that their mothers were hitting them when they received my letter. Strange. Can you figure out why? When you were going to school, did any teacher ever contact your parents when you did something good? Probably not. We educators have conditioned parents to understand that the only time we get in touch with them is when their offspring have broken a school rule or in some way have done something wrong. Thus, my students' mothers thought that the receipt of a letter from school meant their child had done something wrong and was in trouble again. Even those parents who could not read were able to recognize the school's return address. It took some time but we eventually straightened out this misunderstanding.

Later, when I became an administrator, I moved my letter reward system to a schoolwide program. Youngsters earned letters for anything from attendance to citizenship. Sometimes, I would call parents just to say "hello," or to ask about a sick child. Even here, I trained myself to say quickly, "Hello, this is Mr. Foster from P.S. 624. Please don't worry; your son is not in trouble."

It is sad that so many educators are fearful of their students' parents. The parents of inner city youngsters take so much abuse from the "system" that if teachers and administrators would only allow parents to get their feelings off their chests without feeling threatened, we could turn around a good many of our inner city school problems.

EDUCATING STAFF TO COPE WITH AGGRESSIVE AND VIOLENT YOUNGSTERS

Empirical evidence has shown that teacher and administrator physical fear of inner city students, whether based upon racism of lifestyle differences, contributes to school negative aggression and violence. Stated differently, when someone shows fear of his or her students, the students are often provoked to act out even more.[14]

This hypothesis stems from two realities of school problems that are related to social class physicalness, aggression, and violence. The first is the middle class educator's fear of physicalness and aggressive streetcorner behavior. The second is that there are some severely disturbed and socially maladjusted youngsters who act out their pathology in an aggressive, physical, violent syndrome. Hence, one may be, to some extent, imagined or perceived violence while the other may be exceedingly real. Unquestionably, these two considerations lead directly to school problems that, to date, we have not been able to cope with—the reason being that we have refused to admit that they exist until the aggression has exploded into overt violence. Or, where we have admitted it exists, we have refused to assume any responsibility for amelioration of the problem other than in a punitive way.

Unquestionably, the school is just one of many agencies affecting this child's behavior and really cannot be assigned all the blame for causing him to behave the way he does. However, schools can do more to cope with these realities. If we would admit openly that the problems exist, we would find many teachers and administrators who possess the ability to cope with them. Some educators can cope more easily with negative aggression and violence than can others. For the real violence, though, we can educate interventionists who will be able to cope (see Chapter 7). We can also educate other staff to be able to cope with either imagined or real violence. I have been reasonably successful in accomplishing these objectives in a number of ways.

The first way to expose my undergraduate students, through the Woodlawn program described earlier, to the streetcorner behavior this book has reported. The second was through my graduate courses and workshops where we discussed not the fantasy but the reality of streetcorner behavior and how it is played out in schools. The third way was through a course designed specifically to help professionals cope with aggression and violence. The fourth was to participate with twenty-four University of Buffalo students through a winter Outward Bound experience.[15]

The course specially designed to help professionals cope with violence will be discussed here; the Outward Bound experience will be discussed in the next section.

An article in *Today's Education* concerning assaults on teachers reported Dr. Patterson from the New York City schools suggesting that school staff be educated in security and self-defense so that they will be able to deal intelligently with hostile pupils and emergencies. The article then went on to report that

> At least one course in this area has already been presented. In 1969–70, Millard Fillmore College of the State University of New York at Buffalo offered a controversial, no credit workshop, Methods and Techniques of Working with Children in Conflict. Taught by Herbert L. Foster, associate professor of education, the course met for 12 weeks—six weeks of lecture and discussion and six of gym instruction in physical intervention techniques. The purpose of the workshop was to instruct participants in how to help youngsters control aggressive and out-of-control behavior and how to become sensitive to a child's early warning signals of impending overt aggressive behavior.[16]

The course was organized through our Millard Fillmore School to enable a greater latitude of entry into the course. Participants included teachers, psychiatric nurses, social workers, a bus driver, case workers, and youth board workers.

The course was announced as "Methods and Techniques of Handling Children in Conflict." However, some discussion concerning the word "handling" ensued. To some, the word implied becoming physically punitive with a child. Consequently, the title of the course was changed to "Methods and Techniques of Working with Children in Conflict."

Because of all that has been written earlier in this book, and because some of our schoolchildren must be helped to control their aggressive and out-of-control behavior in order to work toward a positve prognosis, some workers have to be educated to cope with their students' aggressive, acting-out, and out-of-control surface behavior. They must also become sensitive to and work with the child's early warning signals of impending overt aggressive behavior.

We hypothesized that when workers showed fear, they could provoke an already frightened youngster to act out further. Additionally, the children who have underdeveloped controls or lack controls of their behavior gain strength to control their behavior from the inner strength of the worker and, if necessary, the willingness of the worker to restrain the child nonpunitively but physically.

In many classroom incidents of aggressive and violent acting-out behavior by the student either against peers, teachers, school property, or that which interferes with instruction, the student often gives warning signals or clues that, depending upon their reading by the worker, can either exacerbate or ameliorate the impending situation. Furthermore, most workers have strong feelings against intervening physically with a child's out-of-control behavior. Many feel they should never touch a child under any circumstances. It is also perfectly normal for an adult to fear an aggressive child.

It was felt that the way the teacher organizes the classroom—for example, seats or desks, bulletin boards, displays—affects the child behavior. The way the teacher structures the classroom procedures also affects the way the child relates in the classroom.

Finally, in interacting with children, parents, and administrators, the teacher's feelings, emotions, and attitudes play an important role in the way he or she relates to each situation. Therefore, the first step to educating workers to deal with their students' classroom aggression was to recognize that the problem existed and to help workers recognize their emotions, feelings, and attitudes.

Classroom Workshop Meetings

The workshop included discussions and readings on the management of classroom problems, teacher introspection, and the emotional aspects of the teacher's role in working with disruptive and aggressive children. Local, state, and national professional organizations and an overview of the professional literature were presented briefly. Teacher behaviors in preventing and mediating crisis situations and curriculum methods and techniques were included. Incidence, identification, and diagnosis of emotionally disturbed and socially maladjusted children were also discussed.

Probably the most helpful technique was the playing of tapes in which a worker described a behavior incident. Workshop participants then discussed the incident from all points of view. Helpful to these discussions were the strategies for mediating a child's surface behavior, as suggested in Fritz Redl and David Wineman's *The Aggressive Child* and listed separately in Nick Long and Ruth Newman's *The Teacher Handling of Children in Conflict.*[17] We also discussed incidents that were brought in by workshop participants. The most instructive evening evolved around a presentation by a woman schoolbus driver.

The emphasis was on the worker's not panicking and the positive educational and psychological management that prevents and ameliorates crisis situations. More pointedly, the emphasis was to intervene educationally and psychologically, thereby preventing the situation from deteriorating into a crisis. However, it was also discussed realistically that in some cases, no matter how hard and expertly the worker tries, a youngster may still demonstrate aggressive out-of-control behavior that would have to be contained or controlled physically by the worker. Or the need might arise to remove a child physically to prevent contagion or for his own safety. We strove to get the participants to understand their own attitudes, feelings, and emotions; to develop their own style; and to be themselves.

Physical Intervention Techniques

The learning and practice of techniques of nonpunitively intervening physically with a youngster's out-of-control aggressive surface behavior took place in various gyms. The objective was not necessarily to master techniques of physical intervention; rather, the objective was to reduce the worker's fear of aggressive children by demonstrating the most that an out-of-control child could do to the worker physically. This, to some extent, was demonstrated by showing the workshop participants that they could fall, be knocked down, have a dress or suit torn, get punched, have a watch or glasses broken, and still live to tell the story.

Participants practiced techniques such as:

1. how to break up fights;
2. how to fall;
3. how to disarm a child who may be attacking with a knife, scissors, or lead pipe;
4. how to use a "come along" to remove a child; and
5. how to restrain a child.

Throughout these sessions, the point was demonstrated and emphasized that the secure worker need not overuse force. As in the classroom meetings, it was argued that there is a difference between corporal punishment and nonpunitive physical intervention. Similarly, there is a difference between punitively and illegally overusing force as compared with the nonpunitive and legal use of physical intervention.

Another area emphasized was educating the worker to differentiate between out-of-control behavior and lower socioeconomic norm-violating behavior that is too often perceived by the worker as threatening or illegitimate violence or behavior. Much of what is perceived as threatening and illegitimate violence is nothing more than lower class testing of the worker's ability to control and set limits. If nothing else, the course demonstrated to the participants that someone was concerned and willing to discuss the very real everyday problems they were facing.

Additionally, as the course progressed and the participants became more aware of the reasons for negative student behavior, they became more understanding and accepting of this behavior. Hence, they became less threatened and were better able to cope with classroom behavior situations by intervening and defusing potentially explosive situations as well as learning when to ignore behavior.

The positive results and feelings from our course were further reinforced in a conversation with David A. Pratt, coordinator of Drug and Alcoholism Services,

Erie, Pennsylvania. Years ago, he was the only male worker in a residential psychiatric treatment center between the hours of 9:00 and 4:00 P.M. The youngsters in the facility were approximately six to fourteen years of age. Some fourteen years of age. Some of the twelve, thirteen, and fourteen-year-olds were aggressive "acting-outers" and sometimes bigger in stature than some of the nursing staff.

Frequently, he was called to "come to the rescue" of various female staff who were being challenged by one of the youngsters. Although this was usually a problem with the boys, occasionally one of the older girls would act out physically too.

According to Mr. Pratt,

> This created a problem for the acting-out child, who, having no internal controls to rely on, saw the external controls as being unable to hold his hostile angry behavior once his feelings would break loose. This caused him to panic and act out even more. Secondly, it caused the entire group to feel insecure in that they could not rely on the adults to protect them. Thirdly, my constant intervening made it impossible for me to carry out various group activities in which I was engaged when I received the S.O.S. My departure would anger the children in my group.

Although this problem was discussed frequently at staff meetings, no useful means of intervening in the problem was suggested until another area agency hired someone who happened to possess "fantastic methods of breaking up fights, of moving children from place to place without hurting them, etc."

A six-session course was set up with this worker at which he discussed his philosophy, and various physical intervention techniques were demonstrated.

> He suggested that the staff practice on one another but to say nothing to the children, feeling that this would merely challenge them further. As the lessons progressed, you could see the nursing staff developing attitudinal change as they began to think they *could* handle the children by themselves. After the lessons were concluded, we did nothing different in terms of group structure, composition, program policies or anything else. It was "business" as usual. To the best of my recollection, following these lessons, I was not called again to intervene in a one-on-one confrontation of child with female staff. More males were added to the staff but they were not called upon either.[18]

In a second situation, when he directed a residential children's center, a similar problem arose with a male and female staff member. He set up a similar course and observed similar results. Additional discussions with others around the country suggests similar results, too.

Controversy Concerning the Course

Our course became controversial for at least two reasons. The first was the anxiety of so many concerning the physical handling of youngsters. The second was an unfortunate incident concerning publicity about the course in a local newspaper.

The real controversy started when a letter was sent from our University Information Services to a local paper inquiring as to whether they would be interested in a reporter's doing a feature story on the course. Supposedly, the person to whom the letter was sent was away at the time. Someone from the newspaper thereupon turned the letter of inquiry into an article and injected the words "Core-Area Pupils."[19]

The headline read "UB Will Prepare Teachers to Handle Core-Area Pupils." The article also stated: "For five of the twelve class periods, students will meet with a Buffalo Police Academy judo expert, who will teach them to handle children with weapons and to control a class without causing the child or teacher to lose face."[20]

Things then began to happen. A black U.B. student presented a motion before our Student Polity that the course be discontinued. Complaints were made to our University Institutionalized Racism Committee and the Buffalo Human Relations Commission, and someone from the Black Teachers Association of Buffalo called us.[21]

On our part, we tried unsuccessfully to get the newspaper to print a retraction or correction. However, Professor Murray Levine, director of the Graduate Program Community-Clinical Psychology, who was helping with the classroom aspects of the course, and I wrote a letter to the editor of the paper and it was published.

We wish to correct an error in the article, "UB Will Prepare Teachers to Handle Core-Area Pupils," .... The course ... is designed to help teachers, nurses, social workers, child care workers and others to be more effective in their work with socially maladjusted children. The course is not, as reported, designed to prepare teachers "to handle core-area pupils."

One of the manifestations of emotional disturbance is aggressive and out-of-control behavior, which sometimes requires the adult to restrain the child and prevent him from hurting himself or others.

The teacher or other child care worker who is faced with the problem of controlling a disturbed child's outbursts routinely reports feelings of fear, guilt, and distress. The portion of the course which deals with physical intervention techniques is designed to help the worker to deal with the situation effectively and without hurting the child.

The teacher's ability to mediate a child's crisis situation often is the key to whether or not the child progresses.

The course also focuses on the emotional aspects of the teacher's role in managing the classroom and suggests psychological techniques to help children with problems. Much of the discussion centers on the teacher's ability to understand his own emotional state in his relationship with children in conflict.

Although the course is focused on teachers working with emotionally disturbed and maladjusted children in the classroom, it is open to anyone working with children.

The group taking the course includes teachers from suburban areas, Canada, Buffalo, social workers, and psychiatric nurses.[22]

We proceeded with the course while responding in a number of ways to our critics. In addition to the above letter, we prepared a packet of photo copies of the newspaper clippings, the course description, course announcement, and bibliography. This package was sent to various people around the city of Buffalo whom we knew had expressed an interest or were involved in education. We also met with the University Committee on Institutionalized Racism and calmed their fears.

The young man who raised the issue in our Student Polity came to see me. He was from Queens in New York City and other than his being black and my being white, we had much in common. His reintroduced motion in the Student Polity called for the course to be expanded to two semesters — one semester of emotional restraint and one semester of physical restraint.

The entire controversy eventually dissipated and we gave the course a second time. It should be pointed out that all of this transpired while our students were acting out against the university. Actually, had some of our university faculty and administration taken our course, maybe we could have escaped many of the problems we had.

Two last points that should be mentioned. Many of the older women who took the course had problems with the physical aspects of the gym sessions. Many of them dropped out. If the course were given again, we would try to build in a more gradual approach to the physical aspects of the course.

EXPERIENTIAL LEARNING

In the first edition of *Ribbin'* this section was entitled "Outdoor Education." However, because most educators and higher education faculty feel outdoor education is playing ball or some other recreational sport, I now use the expression "Experiential Learning," which is a bona fide curriculum area.

There were often objections to what I wanted to do in outdoor education; however, I was persistent and always managed to overcome the objections. That is an important point because too many teachers either give up after being told, "no" once by a supervisor, or told, "write it up for me." Instead of giving up or scapegoating, teachers should just do it, write it up for their supervisor, or start by giving a homework assignment that involves experiential learning.

In this section, I will describe some of the experiential learning programs I have had with my students as: (1) a scout leader in the "600" schools; (2) camping coordinator and curriculum consultant in the New York City Junior Guidance Classes Program; (3) an administrator in the "600" schools; and (4) a university professor. In addition, I have had a number of personal learning experiences that further impressed me with the need to provide for socially acceptable risk taking, challenge, and adventure for all our students, and even more importantly, for educators.[23]

For a number of years, I was on the Board of Directors of Camp Fire of Erie County and Chair of the Camp Board. One morning, I received a call that a child had been lost at camp, and the volunteer firemen and State Police had been searching all night for the youngster. So, I dressed quickly and drove to camp.

As I was nearing camp, a helicopter was flying away. The youngster had been found in good health and returned to his group. Since I was at camp, I had breakfast with the volunteers. As we ate and talked, I sensed an excitement and electricity in the air; the volunteers' adrenalin had been flowing all night and was still in their veins.

Suddenly it hit me that many of these volunteers needed the excitement and adventure of that night. Without this occasional adventure, for many, their lives would be stagnant and without much meaning. Therefore, I thought, if they have these needs for adventure now, how were these needs met when they were in school?

Unquestionably, the need for adventure can be met through jobs as policemen, firemen, telephone linemen, and members of the armed forces. Because we now see women in what were traditionally male jobs, my approach applies equally to men and women. Very often, when you speak to veterans of WW II, Korea, and even Vietnam, they talk of the adventure and the comradery, rather than the violence and the killing. Meanwhile, some in nonphysical and non-adventuresome jobs satisfy their adventure needs through being volunteer firemen, fishermen, and hunters. Some vicariously find adventure through specta-toritis by attending football, basketball, and other major sporting contests, and by the hour and half hour from watching television.

Interestingly, there are times when we find ourselves participating in socially acceptable risk taking, challenge and adventure experiences without any decisionmaking on our part. This may take place when we are caught up in natural or man-made catastrophies such as floods, blizzards, and blackouts when we are participants by circumstance rather than by choice.

In schools, sadly, most of the experiences we provide our students are homogenized as on television. The average school experience is of a secondary nature, mediated through a text book, a film, a film strip, a television presentation, or didactically. Of course, some children do learn and develop despite boring teaching, but some children even have problems with the four walls and colors of a classroom. Many of the children in special education come from minority or lower socioeconomic backgrounds who have learning styles different from stereotype middle class children. We should provide these children, as well as all children, with an optional or alternative curriculum experience that may better fit their learning style—a style that is experiential, more physical, and more emotional.

When young people are not provided with socially acceptable adventure at home, in school, or in their neighborhood, there are often dire results. Kurt Hahn, the founder of Outward Bound, wrote that our western world's advancing material prosperity has "brought evils" that bring about "insufficient satisfaction of the youthful interest for adventure and the decline of compassion which is reflected in the plain business of individual unhelpfulness one to another."[24]

Muriel Gardner wrote about young offenders who had committed violent crimes of murder and found they had, in common, never experienced socially acceptable adventure.

Need for adventure itself may play a part in many youthful crimes. A child or adolescent in our society has little opportunity for adventure, . . . a normal appetite, satisfied often in former days through the dangers of exploration or the vicissitudes of a frontier life. Where is the teen-age boy or girl to find adventure now outside of crime? The present great popularity of survival camps among young people is evidence of a need for challenge and adventure—an attempt to find it in a healthy way. . . . [O]ther competitive activities fulfill some of this natural need, but they are usually available only to those with money.

It is natural for a child . . . to prove himself. He wants to convince himself and others that he "has the guts." Those boys who doubt the strength of their own masculinity attempt by one means or another, to reassure themselves. In some unfortunate cases this takes the form of unacceptable aggression. Aggression is a normal, necessary drive, necessary for a realistic mastery of life, something every child is endowed with in varying degrees. The problem is not one of aggression itself, but of direction and control.[25]

James S. Coleman, speaking at the 6th Annual Conference on Experiential Education, pointed out the possible consequences of a lack of experiential nourishment.

We have intentionally cut off the child's nourishment by experience, for experience always contains difficulties and dangers that parents, looking back on their experiences, want to protect their children from. This deprivation of experience is accomplished largely by the school, aided by the increasingly sterile home which houses the child between school days.

It is at least partly in this context that one can see the various aspect of the youth movement that burst forth in the mid-sixties: that is, as a demand for experience—first in the pilgrimage from the cities of the North to the sit-ins and demonstrations and marches in small towns of the South, and then in the demonstrations and violence on college campuses. The subsequent accounts of these experiences by those who took part in them describe far less the goals of the actions and the larger aims of the movement than they do the texture of the experience itself, the feeling of oneness with one's fellows, the sense of collective euphoria, the emotions upon witnessing a demonstrator being beaten, how it felt to spend a night in jail, the excitement of confronting authorities to whom one once paid deference.[26]

So, how do we change?

First we should move toward an experiential curriculum that has minimally processed experiences. Curriculum experiences should be direct and primary and should be used to bridge the gap between the didactic and academically oriented school and the real world outside of the school. Remember, prior to the mass education of children, children learned about life skills from an apprenticeship in the world of work.

We need to work with an experiential curriculum model that is personalistic, learning centered, and activity orientated. It should emphasize teachers and learners working cooperatively to make curriculum decisions. Self-directed, self-paced, and sometimes unstructured and personalized instructional programs should be utilized. Personal feelings, attitudes, values, and experiences are critical to experiential curriculum content. The active involvement of students in planning learning activities is essential to maximizing learning outcomes.[27] Additional ingredients include trust, group processes and activity, integration of various academic areas, self-motivation, serving of different learning styles, and the building of all sorts of links, the thrust being prosocial.

The last link of these curriculum changes is to guide the student toward an experiential curriculum that includes socially acceptable risk taking, challenge, and adventure. This would, I believe, satisfy Kurt Hahn's conceptualization of education as "experience therapy."

Adventure has many meanings based on prior experiences or fantasies. What is adventure for one may be "child's play" for another; neither should be denegrated. For example, Jean Malaurie, in his book *The Last Kings of Thule*, described adventure for some Eskimos.

When adventure does not come to him, the Eskimo goes in search of it. In 1906, a group of eight families whom Peary had taken aboard his ship left it one day because they found the monotony of life on board oppressive and its comforts upsetting. . . . The families spent eight months travelling on foot over the hundreds of miles that the ship covered in twenty-two days. Their trip was in many ways dramatic. The families suffered cruelly and often came close to death. When they reached Etah, they had only a few half-starved dogs. But all of them were ready to start out again. How can life be worth living if it offers no surprises, no adventures.[28]

For many of our students, an experiential adventure activity may include community studies such as an urban exploration, a *Foxfire* cultural journalism project, a service project, or an oral history project involving students or senior citizens.[29] I have observed behavioral and academic gains after a backpacking trip, an urban adventure, or a one-day adventure at a local park. I have observed student-teacher and student-student relationships undergo positive change after a one-day or weekend adventure.

There is one danger, though. If through an experiential adventure curriculum your students become better adjusted, they may have problems with an overly rigid classroom and school and a pap-filled curriculum.

Because so many of our children are overprotected at home and in school, very often their reaching out to take risks, a normal growth pattern, takes on an antisocial direction. We need to encourage them to take risks through an adventure curriculum in a socially acceptable direction. As Professor Higgins stated in *Pygmalion*, "Would the world ever have been made if its maker had been afraid of making trouble. Making life means making trouble."[30]

An alternative and literally adventerous curriculum can provide students with an opportunity to experience the world in ways that will enlarge their sense of possibility and accomplishment. But the instructor's commitment must be genuine and knowledgeable. (Time and again I find myself drawing fresh inspiration from my ongoing experiences in Scout leadership and the Outward Bound program.) Only then will you be able to share your feelings of an excitement for life with your students through an optional or alternative curriculum built around socially acceptable risk taking, challenge, and adventure.

The "600" Schools—Boy Scout Troop 888

While teaching in an after school project, "Operation More," I organized Boy Scout Troop 888. As part of the troop activities, we did quite a bit of day hiking on Staten Island. As I recall, it was raining and snowing the day of our first trip. We went anyway because as Scouts we were "prepared." Some of the school personnel laughed at us; they referred to our trip as "Foster's Folly." Little did they know that the idea of going on a hike regardless of the weather was a challenge for some of the tough gang youngsters in our school. Harrison Salisbury wrote about our troop in his book *The Shook-Up Generation*.

> There is a Boy Scout troop at Public School 613. At first Boy Scouts were regarded as sissies by the street boys who make up the school population. Only a few boys joined, just one with a uniform. They went on Saturday hikes and cookouts. No matter what the weather, no matter how cold, how snowy, how rainy, the Scouts went out. They began to build a "rep" as tough guys. Bopping youngsters, tough members of the Chaplains, the Bishops, the

Stonekillers, admitted that Scouts were not "chicken" after all. A year later the troop had sixteen members. Most of them had uniforms. Some of the Bishops and Stonekillers had joined up.[31]

We related much of scouting's outdoor experiences to our school curriculum. Many of the academic teachers worked with us in arranging for Scouts to use their academic areas to relate pre- and posttrip experiences. Often, a good deal of juggling of classroom assignments had to be arranged for us to leave for the day. Sometimes, extra youngsters had to be taken if we wanted to go because of sudden teacher absence.

After innumerable day trips, we wanted to go on an overnight. However, we had a problem in securing permission for an overnight on school days. When informed that because of "insurance" considerations, we could not go, I asked, "Who said so?" Each pointing of the finger was tracked down until permission was obtained. Too often, new teachers give up too quickly when told "no" by an administrator. Instead, they should figure out a way of pragmatically manipulate the system to the benefit of their students. However, where the administrator's philosophy is diametrically opposed to that of the teacher, my advice is for the teacher to transfer out of that school.

In addition to the Scouts, I organized a hiking club that hiked to historical spots throughout the city. From what I hear, some of my Scouts have done well. One is now a teacher of special education, four own thriving businesses in New York City, and one is a radiologist.

The Junior Guidance Classes Program and Outdoor Education[32]

The Junior Guidance Classes Program received a $700 grant from the Johanna M. Lindlof Camp Committee to experiment with an outdoor education program.[33] This grant continued the New York City Board of Education's tradition of relating outdoor education to the curriculum. The Lindlof Committee and the New York City Board of Education conducted two earlier school-camping experiments. The first was a three-week sleep-in camp experience for sixty-two children and their teachers in June, 1947, at Life Camps. The second was a three-day sleep-over school camping experience conducted by the All-Day Neighborhood Schools at Hudson Guild Farm, Netcong, New Jersey.[34]

I was in the "600" schools and my transfer to the Junior Guidance Program to direct the experiment was finally approved three weeks before the first trip was set to go.

Seven Junior Guidance Classes from three schools in Manhattan were involved in the experiment. Four second- through fifth-grade closed-register classes were from P.S. 68. Second-, third-, and fourth-grade open-register classes from P.S. 199 were also included.[35] Two of the classes had five school camping experiences, the other two had one experience each.

We used the Flora Haas Site of the Henry Kaufmann campgrounds on Staten Island for all of our school camping experiences, thanks to Monte Melamed, then executive director of the Henry Kaufmann Campgrounds.[36] The Flora Haas Site was selected because of its proximity to Manhattan, the experience of the executive director, and the availability of the campgrounds on a year-round basis. Additionally, the Henry Kaufmann Campgrounds had pioneered in day camping programs for large numbers of city children.

The resource assistant, Judith Schmidt, and I worked with the teachers in developing curriculum goals and in providing materials and methods to achieve these goals. We met at least biweekly in school time and sometimes in the evenings. Three of the most significant objectives related to curriculum included: (1) increased socialization of our students; (2) increased academic learnings; and (3) sharpened sensory perception and increased appreciation.

According to the staff's observations and some of our pre- and posttesting, the students appeared to have increased their abilities in all objective areas. Additionally, the staff gained an understanding of how meaningful a unified curriculum could be.

Outdoor Education While an Administrator in the "600" Schools

A big plus at the Francis Parkman High School (P.S. 624, Manhattan) was our principal, Jud Axelbank's, favoring and supporting our experiential learning ideas. Despite his support, though, we still had to work out problems.

The food problem was worked out by getting the district lunch supervisors to provide us with a sandwich or cookout lunch as needed. At first, the lunch people opposed our proposals. However, they accepted our suggestions when we agreed to give them at least two or three weeks' notice of the date and type of lunch we wanted. This also included their providing ice for the milk or juice.

Once we set the date and type of lunch we wanted, however, we had to take the lunch even if a sudden rain washed out the trip. We shared these rules with our students so that they would be aware of all ramifications. When working with disturbed youngsters, even a lunch change could cause a youngster to become unduly upset.

We went just about everywhere in New York City. We visited the Staten Island Zoo, which is reputed to have one of the best reptile collections in the country. We went to Staten Island very often because of the ferry ride and Staten Island's parks. This ride provided an interesting, leisurely, and educational trip through New York Harbor.

We visited most of the parks and beach fronts on Staten Island. We did everything from planning meals and cooking out, doing art, nature study, to various sports activities or just lying in the sun.

We also started a schoolwide field day at McCombs Dam Park, which is across the street from the Yankee Stadium. The field day included morning track and field events and a student versus faculty softball game in the afternoon.

Curriculum was involved on all trips. The amount of curriculum planned for any trip depended upon where we were going and our objectives.

For example, even on a trip where we played touch football, we also had staff and students doing art work, creative writing, or exploring on a nature walk. Also, some teachers always did prior to and follow-up curriculum work in their classes. We also started a school newspaper that carried articles about our trips.

Another aspect related to curriculum that was very important was what we wore. We were always encouraging our students to dress appropriately for the social situation they were in. On our trips, students observed staff in dungarees and chinoes while seeing them in tie and suit in school. Seeing their teachers as ordinary people in an out-of-school environment helped the youngsters relate to them on another level.

Attendance was low on our first trip. Investigation revealed that our students had anxieties about going places other than the school and their neighborhoods. This was interesting when considering the supposed toughness of some of our students who held leadership positions in fighting gangs. However, under their tough exterior were many anxieties.

Our staff discussed this problem and we resolved it. The first thing we did was to prepare our students better for the trips in a number of ways. Some of us went to visit the site of the trip, taking pictures and slides which were shown to our students in classes and in the auditorium programs. Maps also were provided to show exactly where we were going; some teachers began bringing our trips into their class discussions. Some of us also began to stop at our students' homes the morning of a trip to pick them up and bring them to school. Our efforts worked out well, and attendance on all trips soared.

The trips had a number of positive effects upon the school. They brought both teachers and students together informally, creating additional positive relationships. Rarely do teachers get the opportunity to relate to one another on an informal basis. Therefore, the relationships induced by the trips created stronger staff and student relationships on all levels. Obviously, therefore, the trips had a good deal to do with the lessening of problems in the school.

Two more points: Where teachers related the trip experiences to their classroom curriculum, there was added interest and the youngsters worked more willingly. The second point is that in many cases, students disciplined one another on the trips. In one case, one of the youngsters started smoking pot while we were seated around a campfire. The staff had not been aware of the boy's having this with him. Before we noticed, another student took the "joint" out of the other youngster's mouth and threw it into the fire, berating him with, "Hey man, don't mess up! We want to go on these trips."

My SUNY-Buffalo Program

In this section, experiential learning will be discussed in relation to the areas of (1) Outward Bound, (2) my courses, and (3) my students taking their students on experiential learning adventures.

Outward Bound. For a while, after I arrived at the University of Buffalo, I did more talking than doing about experiential learning. Then I participated in an experience that changed me back into a doer: three other faculty members and I participated with twenty-four University of Buffalo undergraduates on an Outward Bound experience.

The Outward Bound experience had a profound effect on me. It somehow provided me with the set and emotional frame of mind to do what I dreamed of doing, and as a result of Outward Bound, I began to implement instead of just dreaming and fantasizing.

As noted earlier in the book, for a long time I had held the belief that many inner city teachers feared their students' physical lifestyle. Therefore, if I could somehow expose teachers to challenging physical experiences, possibly they would become more secure physically and emotionally, and thus less fearful of their students. Along with this idea, I had been reading about the program called Outward Bound.[37]

Outward Bound was started in 1941 in Aberdovey, Wales, to "instill a spiritual tenacity and the will to survive in young British seamen torpedoed during World War II."[38] The aims, as promulgated by Outward Bound founder and educator, Dr. Kurt Hahn, stand today to serve as a model to emulate for teachers (and others) anywhere, most specifically those working in difficult situations. "The aim of education is to impel young people into value-forming experiences . . . to insure the survival of these qualities: an enterprising curiosity; and undefeatable spirit; tenacity in pursuit; readiness for sensible self-denial; and above all, compassion."[39]

After World War II, an Outward Bound school was organized in Colorado. Today there are six Outward Bound schools throughout the United States. My belief was that Outward Bound could provide the vehicle to help educate and prepare teachers for inner city school positions by increasing their self-awareness and self-confidence and thus helping them overcome their fears.

After preliminary correspondence and phone calls with National Outward Bound, and some soliciting of faculty support, a number of us met with Robert Lentz, then educational director of Outward Bound.[40] From this meeting came a cooperative venture between Outward Bound and the University of Buffalo. We wanted to investigate whether or not Outward Bound would be relevant to the curricular goals of two ongoing teacher preparation programs—specifically, the inner city program and the Professional Health, Physical Education, and Recreation program.

In February 1971, students and instructors gathered at the Outward Bound Center at Dartmouth College in Hanover, New Hampshire, to pick up gear and receive their gang (group) assignments. The temperature on that morning was five degrees above zero, a foot of snow had fallen, and blizzard conditions prevailed. Once gear was packed, gangs were driven four miles to the Appalachian trail for the three-mile hike to Harris Cabin. Snowshoes had to be used almost immediately as the snow, although packed in places, was about three feet deep.

Upon arriving at Harris Cabin, gangs picked a spot in the surrounding wooded area and set up their two- and three-person tents. Gangs were assigned to such duties as loading the sledge at the road, pulling it to the cabin, and then unloading the food or wood pulled, digging latrines, and cooking.

For the next few days, meals were served in Harris Cabin and gang members became acquainted through various group techniques. Gangs planned their first expedition as to food, route to be taken, and the distance to be traveled. The first gang left Harris Cabin on its expedition on the second day. Within a few days, all gangs had pulled out, thus launched on a most challenging and demanding experience.

For the remainder of the Outward Bound experience, gangs participated in rappelling (rope descent on a rock cliff), three-day individual solos, a final expedition, and returned to Harris Cabin for the final marathon run and the awarding of Outward Bound certificates. The sequence of the above experiences varied with each gang. On the last day of the experience, all gangs hiked from Harris Cabin to Dartmouth, turned in their gear, showered, ate, and boarded a bus for Buffalo.

The final marathon run of four and one-half miles on showshoes was the crowning event for me. I took pictures at the start of the run and then started running. I came in thirty-fourth out of sixty. The last three-quarters of a mile or so almost did me in; I was really dead. What saved me and helped me to finish was my reverting to my old Boy Scout pace—I ran fifty steps and walked fifty steps until I finished. Upon finishing, one of my students took my picture which I enlarged. When I feel down or low, I look at the picture and get up and keep going (shown opposite).

The data and personal comments indicated that the University of Buffalo-Dartmouth Outward Bound experience was successful in many areas. Many student and faculty participants experienced some emotional or personal involvement that has been reflected in his or her personal or professional life. For many of the students and faculty, Outward Bound provided the cognitive and effective arena for looking and reflecting on oneself and moving to some form of action, change, or even reinforcement.

One of the pre- and posttests we gave our students was the Thurston Temperament Schedule. The results of this test found that the stability trait im-

Dr. H. Foster

proved significantly. Stability is characterized by being calm in a crisis and difficult to disturb or distract. This data supported the rationale for this study and suggested that the Outward Bound experience provided an excellent growth and learning experience for undergraduates preparing for teaching positions in inner city schools or, possibly, for teachers already teaching in inner city schools. One of the reported needs for inner city schools is for teachers who can retain their equilibrium amidst typical unsettling inner city school conditions. Experience has shown that the teacher's ability to remain calm and in charge often prevents a minor incident from deteriorating into disorder or a negative learning experience.

Some of the student participants commented that for the first time since they had arrived at the university, as a direct result of this experience they had found some direction and feeling about their life's aspirations.

These student reactions served to reinforce my original contention that this type of experience had a definite place in teacher education. Outward Bound provided me with the impetus to do all of the experiential education activities I had thought about but had not done.

Experiential Learning and My University Courses. After Outward Bound, I began to implement the idea of an experiential adventure as a requirement in all my courses. The process was slow, and, at first, the experience was a requirement as part of all my undergraduate courses.

Now, I have only a graduate program that has two experiential learning strands. The first strand is a built-in adventure as an option in almost all my courses. The second strand involves courses designed around experiential learning.

A course adventure option may include: (1) a backpacking trip, (2) setting up a base camp and day triping, or (3) going to a cabin. Of course, aspects of the kindergarten through twelfth-grade school curriculum are built into all adventures. The idea is for my students to experience the adventure and then design curriculum adventures for their students.

The second strand consists of courses designed around experiential learning per se. For example, two of the courses I teach are Experiential Learning for the Special Education Student and Experiential Approaches to Urban Education.

In the latter course, for example, adventures may include: (1) completing an urban shopping center adventure where curriculum investigations are made; (2) organizing a weekend adventure in, for example, Toronto.

Additionally, in the urban course, students must complete an urban adventure that includes riding alone on public transportation in the city of Buffalo. Apparently, this can be a very fearful adventure for suburban and rural teachers who have never ridden public transportation and have qualms about doing so. Based on my discussions with teachers, eight out of ten suburbanites are "terrified" of going into the city of Buffalo alone. The suburbanites might drive in to see a play or hockey game. However, as soon as the program is over, most go straight to their cars and leave for home. I have also tried to get urban teachers, who travel to work by car to take the buses their students use to get to school. I do not get too many takers for that one. The idea of the urban course is for teachers to design curriculum materials for using the city of Buffalo by their suburban, rural, or urban students. However, they should experience the urban adventure first.

There are innumerable learning interplays in these classes when we have students from diverse economic, racial, and ethnic backgrounds. White students are amazed to find black middle class teachers who live in the suburbs as frightened as they are about riding public transportation and going into certain neighborhoods. Also, a black master's degree student who grew up in New York City and was an active street gang member there had very real qualms about going on a backpacking trip.

Additionally, many black students are surprised to find white students willing to lend them sleeping bags and sleep alongside them. Also, black and white students sometimes have interesting concepts of one another's eating habits, even to the point of expressing some anxieties as to whether they will be able to eat what the other person of a different color eats.

The feelings of most participants are summed up in this excerpt from a student's paper.

> Many obstacles almost prevented me from making the weekend camping trip to Allegany State Park. It is mid-October, the weather has been rainy all week, and the FBI and other local and State law officers were trying to capture an extortionist who had been sighted in the park. As these events began to unfold during the week, I became more discouraged about making the trip. Friday finally arrived; a classmate came to school prepared to make the trip, and his only means of getting there depended on my overcoming my fears. His presence at school—his depending on me—I just couldn't disappoint him; I realized the distance that he had traveled to meet with me. . . .
>
> The group consisted of people with various ethnic backgrounds, from different parts of the world. This gave the group a nice mix of personalities. . . .
>
> The serenity one captures from being with nature gives a person a sort of reverence; color at this point means nothing here. An individual's inward hostilities towards others seem to disappear. I suppose this can be from the dependence each one has for the other in order to survive with the barest necessities. . . .
>
> I became frightened of a porcupine that had gotten trapped in the bathroom. When I saw it, I screamed and ran, and since it had rained all week, I slipped in the mud trying to get away from it. Although I was muddy and embarrassed it was really a conversation piece for the group. I will always remember it. It cannot be expressed as to the importance of such a trip; for it teaches an individual so many useful things, especially potential teachers who plan to teach in inner city schools. If the potential teacher can capture what living with the other side can project to them they will have defeated one of the biggest obstacles encountered in dealing daily with people of different social-economic backgrounds.[41]

A committee I have been working with from the Exceptional Children Education Department at the State University College at Buffalo has just completed a proposal for a new Ph.D. program in Special Education. In the SUNY system, the new Ph.D. will be: 1) the first special education doctorate; and 2) the first cooperative program joining two branches of the SUNY. I intend to make sure that the new Ph.D. in Special Education will emphasize experiential education for the handicapped and gifted.

My Students Developing Experiential Learning Adventures for Their Students.
Many of my students have developed experiential adventure programs with their students. The program I am closest to was organized by Kathryn F. Markochick and Joyce V. Wheeler with their special education students at Sweet Home High

School. Though Kathryn is now teaching special education at the University of Maine at Farmington, Joyce has carried on with Betty Schriver and Bill Monohan. In addition to ongoing curriculum-related experiential adventures, they do a four-day/three-night experience in Allegany State Park with thirty to forty of their students.

These past four years, as part of their program, another adult volunteer (last year it was Dr. Stephen Thomas) and I took seven to ten of their students on an overnight backpacking trip into Allgheny National Forest in Pennsylvania. Prior to the trip, I usually put in many volunteer teaching hours working with and getting to know the special education students at Sweet Home High School. My experiences with these students, and others, keep me in touch with the real world of the public schools.

CONCLUDING COMMENTS

I have presented my point of view about teaching and learning in all schools, not just inner city schools. I have also made some suggestions for ameliorating some of our school problems. However, from a very broad look at U.S. schools, very little has changed since the Dutch organized their first school in Fort Amsterdam on March 28, 1638. With some editorial license, the three similarities that existed then are still with us today.

Adam Roelansten, the first schoolmaster in New Amsterdam, was sentenced to be flogged or "scourged with rods."[42] And today the schools and their professionals are still the whipping boys of our society. They are still being blamed and "flogged" for society's ills.

Second, Roelansten was probably "the worst and, shall we say, therefore the most discussed of all the Dutch masters; the one who has most unjustly been taken as typical of all."[43] Similarly, still today, the poor teacher is most often discussed while the majority of dedicated teachers, who work a ten- to twelve-hour day, are for the most part ignored.

Third, the Dutch schoolmasters were expected not only to teach but also to make nets, to compose love letters, cut hair, collect taxes, make coffins, cure wounds, mend shoes, ring the church bell, keep the church clean, provide water for baptism and wine for the Holy Supper, lead the singing, give funeral invitations, dig graves, and toll the bell.[44] Today, though the role has changed with time, teachers are still expected, in addition to educating their students, to minister to all of their students' emotional and physical needs.

In this second edition, a number of broad points were made. First, U.S. educators have historically had problems educating minority and poor children while usually doing the best job in the world educating middle-class children.

Second, lower-class black male streetcorner behavior has spread beyond the streetcorner and inner-city school to almost all of U.S. life. Indeed, black streetcorner behavior is now being used by white students in most suburban and rural schools.

Third, lower-class black male streetcorner behavior was described and explained historically and through Reality examples.

Fourth, educator racist and ethnocentric behavior was described as also preventing more poor and minority children from being educated. Furthermore, racism and ethnocentrism were described as a problem for every nation in the world.

Fifth, the responsibility for overcoming streetcorner, racist, and ethnocentric behavior and educating more minority and poor children was placed on the shoulders of educators because they are the professionals. It is in the teaching-learning interaction between the educator and the poor or minority child where more educators must demonstrate more professional understanding to work through the cultural and class differences.

And sixth, we must continue to make the academic and behavioral demands on poor and minority children just as we have made on middle-class children. We must succeed at this responsibility so that more poor, minority, and new immigrant children will learn the middle-class saleable or marketable skills required for socially acceptable upward social and economic mobility. After all, that is what our free enterprise system is all about.

NOTES TO CHAPTER 9

1. Alfred M. Bloch, "Combat Neurosis in Inner-City Schools," *American Journal of Psychiatry* 135 (1978): 1189-92.
2. Denis J. Madden, John R. Lion, and Mandel W. Penna, "Assaults on Psychiatrists by Patients," *American Journal of Psychiatry* 133 (1976): 422-25.
3. Betty Grayson and Morris I. Stein, "Attracting Assault: Victims' Nonverbal Cues," *Journal of Communication* 31, no. 1 (1981): 68-71.
4. Rudolph Labon, *The Mastery of Movement* (Boston: Plays, 1972).
5. Erving Goffman, *The Presentation of Self in Everyday Life* (Garden City, N.Y.: Anchor, 1959).
6. Grayson and Stein, p. 74.
7. The Woodlawn Center was organized by Professor H. Warren Button in September 1965 as the Woodlawn Cooperative Teacher Education Center, an outgrowth of the Teacher Education Project of the Research Council of the Greater Cities School Improvement Program 1964-65.
8. Alvin F. Poussaint, *Why Blacks Kill Blacks* (New York: Emerson Hal, 1972), pp. 9-10.
9. SUNY/Buffalo does not have an undergraduate education degree. Our students take an undergraduate liberal arts degree of which at least twenty-two hours are education courses.

10. The official title of the project was the Cooperative Program for Pre- and Post-Service Teacher Education Aide Project for Auxiliary Personnel Indigenous to the Inner-City Area, under contract C-37075 and C-45609.

11. Claude Brown, *Manchild in the Promised Land* (New York: Macmillan, 1965), p. 86.

12. According to Nancy G. Faber, "Sex for Credit," *Look*, April 1969, pp. 39-40, 45.

13. Herbert L. Foster, "Teaching the Disadvantaged Child," *Industrial Arts & Vocational Education* 55, no. 1 (1966): 47-49.

14. If the reaction of SUNY faculty was anything like the reactions of faculties around the country to the campus upheavals of the late 1960s and early 1970s, faculty with national and international academic reputations were frightened of aggressive acting-out adolescents. The fearful behavior of so many faculty and administrators reminded me of inner city schools. Wherever faculty or administrators stood up to students in a mature and adult way, the students backed down.

15. Herbert L. Foster et al., *An Analysis of an Outward Bound Experience and Its Relationship to Teacher Education*, July 1972 (ERIC ED 161 160).

16. "Assault on Teachers," *Today's Education* 61, no. 2 (1972): 71.

17. Fritz Redl and David Wineman, *The Aggressive Child* (New York: The Free Press, 1957); Nick Long, William C. Morse, and Ruth G. Newman, *Conflict in the Classroom: The Education of Emotionally Disturbed Children* (Belmont, Cal.: Wadsworth, 1965).

18. Personal correspondence and discussion with David A. Pratt, ACSW, then coordinator of Drug and Alcoholism Services, Mental Health and Retardation Office, Erie, Pennsylvania.

19. "UB Will Prepare Teachers To Handle Core-Area Pupils," *Buffalo Evening News*, November 13, 1968, p. 17.

20. "UB Will Prepare Teachers," p. 17.

21. Rod Gere, "Polity Guidelines: Open Campus Advocated," *Spectrum*, November 22, 1968, p. 8; "Student-Faculty Legislature: Polity To Hear Government Plan," *Spectrum*, December 17, 1968, p. 5.

22. "UB Course Open To All Working with Children," *Buffalo Evening News*, November 20, 1968, p. 48.

23. This material was originally presented, in a slightly different form, at the 1982 Convention of the New York State Federation of Chapters of the Council for Exceptional Children. See Herbert L. Foster, "A Personal and Professional Challenge: Socially Acceptable Risk Taking, Challenge, and Adventure, *Forum* 8, no. 4 (1982): 22, 24-28.

24. *Kurt Hahn and the Development of Outward Bound: A Compilation of Essays* (Denver: The Colorado Outward Bound School), p. 343.

25. Muriel Gardner, *The Deadly Innocents: Portraits of Children Who Kill* (New York: Basic Books, 1976), pp. xx, xxi.

26. James S. Coleman, "Experiential Learning and Information Assimilation: Toward an Appropriate Mix," *Journal of Experiential Education* 2, no. 1 (1979): 7.

27. Arthur W. Foshey, *Considered Action for Curriculum Improvement* (Alexandria, Va.: Association for Supervision and Curriculum Development, 1980).

28. Jean Malaurie, *The Last Kings of Thule: With the Polar Eskimos, as They Face Their Destiny* (New York: E.P. Dutton, 1982); R.Z. Sheppard, "A Sahara of Ice," *Time*, October 25, 1982, p. 80.

29. See Eliot Wigginton, *Moments: The Foxfire Experience* (Kennebunk, Maine: Foxfire Fund and Institutional Development and Economic Affairs Service (IDEAS), 1975); Pamela Wood, *You and Aunt Arie: A Guide to Cultural Journalism Based on Foxfire and Its Descendants* (Nederland, Colo.: Institutional Development and Economic Affairs Service (IDEAS), 1975).

30. Bernard Shaw, *Pygmalion: A Romance in Five Acts* (Baltimore: Penguin, 1951), p. 31.

31. Harrison E. Salisbury, *The Shook-Up Generation* (New York: Harper & Row, 1958), p. 163. The inaccuracy of one point in Salisbury's comments pointed up a common fear. We never went on Saturday hikes. We always went on school time. Someone apparently told Salisbury that the trips were on Saturday in fear of revealing that we were going on school time. I wrote about my troop in "Scouting in the Blackboard Jungle," *Scouting*, October 1961, pp. 6-7, 26; also, "Scouting," *Congressional Record*, January 23, 1962, p. 108:A444.

32. The Junior Guidance Classes Program was a New York City Board of Education elementary school program for socially maladjusted and emotionally disturbed children.

33. In 1938 the Honorable Johanna M. Lindlof was presented with a $400 surplus from a dinner given in her honor by several professional and civic groups. Mrs. Lindlof donated this money to a camp fund for public school children, from which grew the Johanna M. Lindlof Camp Committee for Public School Children; Junior Guidance Classes Program, *The Junior Guidance Camp Experience: Outcome of a Grant from the Johanna M. Lindlof Camp Committee* (New York: Junior Guidance Classes Program, December 11, 1964). (Mimeo.)

34. The Board of Education of the City of New York and Life Camps, Inc., *Extending Education through Camping* (New York: Life Camps, 1948).

35. The open-register class consisted of fifteen youngsters in need of emergency therapeutic help. These youngsters were extremely disruptive and could not be maintained in a regular class. Each class covered overlapping grades and served the entire district. Closed-register class served poorly functioning children showing a wide range of behavior and personality symptoms. A track consisted of two class units, usually a second- and third-grade class. Ten to fifteen students were assigned to each starting class. Classes were single graded and divided equally between girls and boys and balanced between aggressive and withdrawn children of at least average intelligence. Efforts were usually made to limit the hyperactive and disruptive children to two or three. Though most of the students were from the host school, some came from schools within walking distance.

36. ı had directed the Mildred Goetz Day Camp of the Henry Kaufmann Campgrounds for many years and was also familiar with the Flora Haas site. The Flora Haas site was also used for many of the Scout trips described earlier. The Henry Kaufmann Campgrounds is an agency of the Federation of Jewish Philanthropies of New York City.

37. National Outward Bound, Inc. is located at 384 Field Point Road, Greenwich, Conn. 06830. Their toll free telephone number is 800 243-8520. The present Outward Bound Schools include: Colorado, Hurricane Island, Voyageur (was Minnesota), North Carolina, and Pacific Crest (was Northwest).

38. *Outward Bound* (Greenwich, Conn.: National Outward Bound).

39. Ibid.

40. Bob Lentz left Outward Bound, Inc. and organized Project Adventure in Hamilton, Massachusetts. He is now a high school principal in Birmingham, Michigan.

41. From "A Learning Experience," by Miss Juanita Brown for class TED 418—Teaching in Inner City Schools, Fall 1972.

42. William H. Kilpatrick, *The Dutch Schools of New York and Colonial New York* (Washington, D.C.: U.S. Government Printing Office, 1912), p. 56; Frank Moss, *The American Metropolis: From Knickerbocker Days to the Present Time: New York City Life in All Its Various Phases*, vol. 1. (New York: Peter Penelon Collier, 1897).

43. Kilpatrick, p. 51.

44. William M. French, "How We Began To Train Teachers in New York," *New York History* 17 (1936): 180-91; Kilpatrick.

INDEX

ABOUT THE AUTHOR

Herbert L. Foster is a teacher, researcher, writer, and educational consultant. Born in the Bronx, he grew up in Brooklyn, New York, and graduated from the New York School of Printing—a New York City vocational high school. After serving with the U.S. Army in the occupation of Japan, he received his B.S. and M.A. from New York University, School of Education, and his Ed. D. from Columbia University, Teachers College.

He was a teacher and administrator in the New York City Public Schools for 17 years, sixteen of which were in the "600" Schools and Junior Guidance Classes Program for the socially maladjusted and emotionally disturbed.

Dr. Foster presently teaches in the Department of Learning and Instruction, Faculty of Educational Studies, State University of New York at Buffalo, in a special education doctoral program with emphasis on experiential learning. He still finds time to do volunteer teaching with handicapped secondary school students.

Some of the journals his articles have appeared in include *Phi Delta Kappan, Exceptional Children, The Forum, Industrial Arts and Vocational Education, New York State Journal of Physical Education and Recreation, The Outdoor Communicator, Peace and Change Journal, Recreation, Scouting Magazine, Today's Education*, and *Urban Education*.